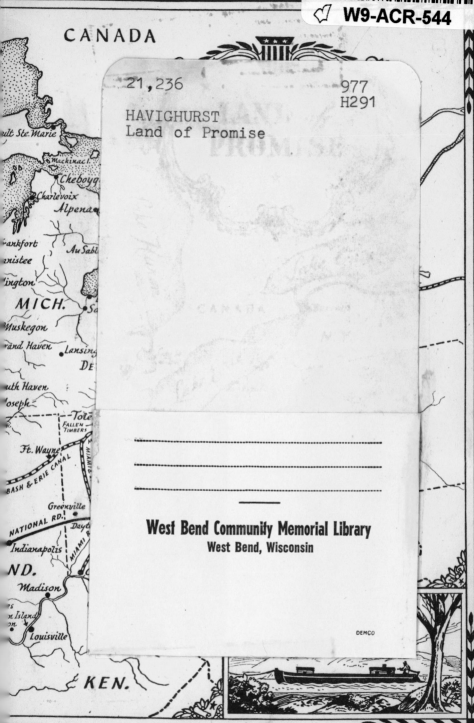

CANADA

ult Ste. Marie

Mackinac I.
Cheboyg
Charlevoix
Alpena

rankfort   Au Sabl
nistee
ington

MICH.
Muskegon
and Haven   Lansing
              DE

uth Haven
oseph

Tole
FALLEN
TIMBERS

Ft. Wayne
MIAMI

BASH & ERIE CANAL

Greenville
NATIONAL RD.   Dayt
Indianapolis   MIAMI R

ND.
Madison
s
n Island
on
Louisville

KEN.

Books *by* Walter Havighurst

The Long Ships Passing
Pier 17
The Quiet Shore
The Winds of Spring
(*The Macmillan Company*)

No Homeward Course
(*Doubleday, Doran & Co.*)

Upper Mississippi: A Wilderness Saga
(*Farrar and Rinehart*)

LAND OF PROMISE

The Story of the Northwest Territory

LAND OF PROMISE

The Story of the Northwest Territory

by

WALTER HAVIGHURST

*"The Promised Land always lies
on the other side of a wilderness."*
—HAVELOCK ELLIS

THE MACMILLAN COMPANY · NEW YORK
1946

PRINTED IN THE UNITED STATES OF AMERICA
BY J. J. LITTLE & IVES COMPANY, NEW YORK

FOR MARION—

CONTENTS

Part I

THE OLDEST SOUNDS IN THE WORLD

I

The Land Beyond the Mountains

IN A HARDY Virginia family two hundred years ago there was a tradition that children born with the red hair of a certain spirited grandmother would be remembered beyond their time. Six sons in that family grew up with long legs and broad shoulders. Two of them wore their coonskin caps on a thatch of fiery hair. Before their life was out their names belonged to history. George Rogers Clark won the Old Northwest from the British, and within twenty-five years his brother William found the Columbia River route to the Pacific. That quickly the first Northwest was supplanted by another, two thousand miles across the continent. But in the years of the nation's first westward growth the Mississippi seemed as remote as the shores of Oregon.

Two centuries ago, before the red-haired brothers had ever gazed west from a Virginia hillside, the territory between the Ohio River and the Great Lakes was the Northwest, the outlying land. It was an area, vague almost as water, blankly entered on the maps of the cartographers. It was land, merely, without time and without memories. Over it lay a great silence, broken only by the rushing wind and the running water—the oldest sounds in the world. The rivers flowed forever toward the sea, the wind rocked the naked forests of November and, in June, the prairies rippled like water to the sky.

Then there was no memory of Abe Lincoln, the gaunt, sad man with distance in his eyes; there were no white orchards blooming where the barefoot Johnny Appleseed had passed. No boatmen's voices echoed on the rivers, no highways laced the land. Tippecanoe and Fallen Timbers were not names for the thud of tomahawks and the rattle of musketry in the thin light of dawn. At that

3

time "Chi-ca-go" meant only the wild onions that grew in the marshes beside Lake Michigan, and "De-troit" was the French boatman's word for the strait that joins Lake Erie to Lake Huron.

A favorite book in the early years of the western country, when books were scarcer than records carved on a slate-smooth beech trunk, was *Gulliver's Travels*. "The Indians," Simon Kenton, border scout, recalled years after the West was won, "never made but two settlements in Kentucky—one at Slate Creek, and one at a place called Lul-be-grud." And Daniel Boone himself explained in a garbled way where that garbled name came from. "I encamped on the Red River with five other men," he said, "and we had with us for our amusement the History of Samuel (*sic*) Gulliver's Travels, whence he gave an account of his young master, Glumdelick, careing (*sic*) him on a market day for a show to a town called Lulbegrad. A young man of our camp called Alexander Neely told us that he had been that day to Lulbegrad and had killed two Broddigings in their capital." So there were two dead Indians in the canebrake, and from Gulliver was named Lulbegrud Creek, which remains on the map to this day.

The western country was as strange as the fantastic lands of Gulliver's four voyages. It was a domain of darkness and mystery, lying beyond the known America. All its dimensions were impressive, and the giant land of the Brobdingnags was a likely comparison. Its rivers ran broad and deep. Its northern lake spread vast as a sea. From Pennsylvania the land rolled over rough hills to unmeasured tracts of level country. For three hundred miles the Great Forest covered it like a rug, threaded by the rivers that the Indians had named the Muskingum, the Hockhocking, the Scioto, the Great and the Little Miami, the crooked Cuyahoga, the Sandusky, the Wabash.

The forest showed many shades of green in summer and a carnival of reds and yellows in the fall. Its great trees were maple, oak, walnut, sycamore, chestnut and beech, with a blossoming undergrowth of dogwood, redbud, wild plum, pawpaw and crab apple. That deep rug was worn occasionally with the delicate trail of deer or the trampled trace of buffalo. Traveled ways led from one river to another, to springs of cold sweet water, to salt licks where the ground was rimed like frost. Sometimes they converged on spacious clearings, where the gloom of the forest ended in a glare of light.

Ohio had a few of these clearings—the Pickaway, Sandusky and Darby plains and the Black Swamp that bordered Lake Erie at its western end. Indiana had more extensive prairie, though seven eighths of the state was timbered. Knobs and ridges ran up from the Ohio River, wooded with oak that later went into millions of barrels for the flatboat trade. That hardwood forest, with its seventeen species of oak and many maples, darkened the steep hills and sudden valleys of southern Indiana, and a varied forest of tulip, sycamore, beech and hickory covered the flat land of the central area. But beyond the upper Wabash River, the Grand Prairie began its long sweep westward. The woods ended and abruptly there was a flood of light. For two hundred and fifty miles that wavelike plain, broken only by thickets of bottom timber along the Kaskaskia, the Sangamon and the Illinois, rolled on to the Mississippi. In Indiana the prairie was a vast pasture of bluestem, tall as a mounted horseman, with occasional swamps of bull grass. Westward, in Illinois, were whole counties of tall beardgrass mingled with waving stems of cup plant, compass plant, vari-colored ox-eyes, blazing star, dragonhead, and large purple patches of ironweed. In the shorter grasses grew profuse cone flowers, bluebells and bright bur marigolds. For all its sameness this was a varied landscape. Over its long swales and swells the prairie wore a coat of many colors.

In the prairie country occasional stands of trees rose like islands from the grassland. Here the word "grove" came into use, and "clearing" had no meaning. Illinois has groves—Little Grove, Clary's Grove, Funk's Grove, Downer's Grove—as Ohio had plains —in each case the exceptional feature became distinguished. Groves of oak and maple dotted the central prairie, but in the north the forest began again. There the open places were excep-

tional, so the "oak openings" of Illinois and Wisconsin are
meadows framed in timber.

Wisconsin became a warring ground of Indians because its lakes,
meadows and forests were rich in fish and game. North of Lake
Winnebago and La Crosse the great dark pinery began. There
were no trails and traces in that country. Rivers were the paths
of trade and exploration, and the sounds of traffic were the swish
of canoe paddles and the voyageur's rhythmic song. The rivers
gathered, then as now, in the shadows of primeval pine and
hemlock and flowed in twilight toward the Mississippi. In that
north woods country of swamp and forest rose the old humped
hills of the iron ranges, containing metal riches of which the
Indians never dreamed. They knew places where a mysterious
purple stone thrust through the pine roots. It was stone too heavy
to be lifted, in a country of rough hills and sudden valleys loud
with falling water. Parts of the country they called bad medicine,
and kept their distance from it. For them the iron age had not yet
dawned.

Across the bright solitude of Lake Michigan lay another domain
of darkness. When the white man found it, the mitten-shaped
lower peninsula of Michigan was virtually covered with heavy
timber. A third of the way up the state the hardwood dwindled
and the pine began. North of the 43rd parallel lay unbroken pine
country, all the way to the straits of Mackinac. With few rivers
and virtually no lakes, the interior proved difficult even for Indians
to travel. The more populous Michigan tribes lived in the decid-
uous forest of the lower part of the state, and a few villages of
Chippewas and Ottawas made camps on the northern shores.
Great areas of the interior remained unknown until the timber
cruisers came in to map the pineries. And when the lumberjacks
raised their clamor in the woods, the silence of ages ended.

All this country was girdled by water—bound by four shining
and mysterious seas and by two lordly rivers which, at the tip of
the Illinois arrowhead, became one. It was a big domain, larger
than all of France. It drained in two directions—into the cold Gulf

of the St. Lawrence and the tropic Gulf of Mexico—yet its watershed did not actually divide the region. In Ohio at the future Akron, in Indiana at Fort Wayne, in Illinois at Joliet, in Wisconsin at Portage were located the "carries" of the Indians and the fur traders. Here, later, men built the canals which linked the Great Lakes with the Ohio and the Mississippi. At no place, from the source of the Muskingum in Ohio's hills to the source of the St. Croix in the dark woods of Wisconsin, was there a range of hills, or even a visible divide, to mark the height of land. Its topography made it a unified country, as in economic and social life it was destined to become a single region in the heart of the continent.

Time came quickly to this region. For two thousand or twenty thousand years it had been the same. Except for the burial mounds that a vanished race had heaped beside the rivers, the land remained as the receding glacier had left it—scarred rocks, casual, heaped moraines, hill-cupped lakes and many-colored prairies.

Two hundred years ago it was still that lonely, timeless land, its only landmarks the council-fires of Indians and the scattered trading posts, dark and rude as the forest itself, of the French fur merchants.

Into that silent land time came like the northern spring, with a rush of life and a pent-up urgency. Gurdon Hubbard, whom the Indians named "Swift Walker," roved the prairies of Illinois when there was no dwelling for a hundred miles. He took a string of pack ponies to the Wabash and drove back the first herd of hogs to be butchered in the straggling village of Chicago. When he died, the village had spread for a dozen miles along the sandy lakeshore and every day long trains brought thousands of cattle, hogs and sheep to the vast packing plants of Chicago. Then the lake lanes were white with the sails of commerce and the prairies were ribbed with railroads. Chicago had become the greatest transportation center in the world.

History, starting late in the Northwest, gathered momentum like the grain and the cattle trains on the level prairie roadbed.

From the Ohio to Lake Superior towns sprang up and cities spread out and counties doubled their population every decade. In 1837, when Queen Victoria's coronation procession moved through the massed, gray streets of London, Chicago was incorporated as a city with 4,117 persons—a place of mud streets and bare board buildings around an Indian fort. In 1901, when the good Queen's funeral cortege passed down the same gray London streets, Chicago with its two million population and an area of two hundred square miles, had become the center of an area more productive than all of England. No other region on earth has been so transformed in one life span.

With this urgent destiny there has been little inclination to recall the past. In all the Northwest the past is rarely felt. Detroit was founded as a fur trading post three generations before the United States existed, but the industrial Detroit of the twentieth century has no memory of those simple days when the French habitants tilled their gardens beside the river and the heavy-oared bateaux came down from Huron laden with baled beaver skins. In all the Midwest cities the newest building is more important than the oldest, the future has more pull than the past.

And yet the past lurks just beneath the hurrying life of the present. Detroit's teeming Michigan Avenue, with its laned traffic and spaced signal lights, was once the Great Sauk Trail that ran to Chicago and the Mississippi. A century ago wagon caravans of settlers rocked over the rutted road toward the unsettled country. At Sault Sainte Marie a golf course now occupies the site of a vanished Indian village at the great bend of the St. Marys River and off the fairway a player is as likely to turn up an arrowhead as a lost golf ball. The clubhouse, facing the St. Marys, contain a French canoe that, a hundred and twenty years ago, carried baled peltry down from Lake Superior, where now the long freighters steam past with 17,000 tons of iron ore in their caverned holds.

On the banks of the Mississippi, at St. Paul, once ende famous Red River trail, and the Sioux half-breeds drove their two wheeled carts through five hundred miles of woods and prairie to bring buffalo robes to the river landing. Now wheat trains stream in where the flour mills make a palisade above St. Anthony's Falls. But in a St. Paul museum stands one of the Red River carts still showing in the weathered wood the ax marks of its maker. At Marietta, the Plymouth of the Northwest Territory, where the first settlement in the western country was planted between the Ohio and Muskingum rivers, the original Land Office remains on Washington Street—the moss-colored little building where for the first time since the creation men filed claims to land beyond the Alleghenies. A hundred towns and cities have their landmarks of first settlement or oldest dwellings. Yet Johnny Appleseed seems as remote as St. Francis, and the vanished stockade of Fort Dearborn seems as legendary as the towers of Camelot. The way back leads through many changes and so the way seems long. Once palm trees grew in Illinois and a coral reef thrust out from the Chicago shore. That remote geologic past appears hardly more distant than Jean Nicolet's discovery of Lake Michigan, in a Georgian Bay canoe, three centuries ago.

Now the wilderness is gone. More completely than any other portion of America, the old Northwest is a tamed land. It is possessed and tilled and occupied, so that you know what lies over the horizon for a hundred, or five hundred miles. The Great Forest is gone and in its place is a region of farms and villages, of trading towns and industrial cities, linked by a network of roads and railroads and abandoned canal lines. The north bank of the Ohio was called the "Indian shore," until after Wayne's victory in 1794. Here in the tumbled hills of southeastern Ohio are the mines that yield the coal which the Indians never learned to use. It lies close to the surface and in places it has burned for years—a slow, sub-surface smoldering, so that a haze hangs on the hillsides and in some fields the winter's snow never whitens the ground. Central Ohio, along the historic National Road, has better earth. It is an area of level farms and shaded villages and county-seat towns that gather a network of cement roads from the outlying country. Northern Ohio has miles of vineyards and orchards along the tempered shores of Lake Erie.

The Ohio River valley is wooded and hilly, all the way from Pittsburgh to Cairo. Here changes have come slowly. Southern Ohio, Indiana and Illinois are regions of small hillside farms worked by a lean and sallow people who retain a Kentucky softness in their speech. Two or three generations ago they came from across the river, like Abe Lincoln's people. Here are old towns, the oldest in the West, built beside the rivers when trade and military power and settlement moved by water. The quiet town of Vincennes, on the Wabash, was once the seat of government for the entire territory from the Alleghenies to the Rockies, from the Gulf to the Great Lakes. All the original state capitals were in the south—Chillicothe, Corydon, and Kaskaskia flourished when Columbus, Indianapolis and Springfield were yet unborn.

Toward the fortieth parallel the country opens into the characteristic Middle-Western landscape. Generally the land is level; for great distances it is as flat as water. In winter, when wind and frost have stripped the scattered maple groves, you can look far off on all sides till the ringed horizon touches the up-curving sky. This is glaciated country, ironed out ages ago by vast ice sheets creeping down from the north. In their leveling process the glaciers left a deposit of black loam ten feet deep over the whole Mid-Western plain. Now white farmhouses and roomy red barns are repeated landmarks from the Muskingum to the Mississippi. Hardly a rod of land lies idle. Even the ten-acre prairie groves are pastures for sheep and cattle. And over the entire area, almost within sight of each other, the little farming towns gather about the grain elevators hunched above the railroad tracks.

But this is a region of cities too. Where the concrete highways converge and the railroads draw together, a skyline of twenty-story buildings appears on the horizon and the chimneys of industrial plants stain the prairie sky.

Toward the forty-fourth parallel, in Wisconsin and Michigan, the land changes again. A line drawn west from the mouth of

Saginaw Bay will cross central Michigan and enter Lake Michigan at Big Sable Point. It will cross Lake Michigan exactly halfway up the long lake's extent and will enter Wisconsin near the port of Manitowac. Its continuation bisects Lake Winnebago and reaches the Mississippi just north of La Crosse. At that line the North begins. There a hundred years ago, began the great pine forests. Now the woods are gone but the north country remains austere and elemental. There are great areas of cut-over land, with scattered farms amid the stumpland. Other areas of second-growth timber support small sawmill operations. It is an outlying country, best known to fishermen and hunters, where Indians live on reservations and where it is easy to remember that trunk highways and railway terminals and a stream of motor traffic were not always a part of America. The upper peninsula of Michigan is a big, rough, lonesome country with a few red-dusted iron ore towns and great tracts of brooding timberland. At last, on a border that seems final and ultimate, as though it were the shore of a continent, one finds the lonely beaches and dark headlands of Lake Superior.

In the north country, from Mackinac to the remote and rugged tip of Keweenaw Peninsula, are a people quite different from the Mid-Westerners of the Ohio Valley. They are miners, fishermen, lakemen, lumbermen, following the trades that, half a century ago, brought them to American from Finland, Sweden, and the old mining towns of Cornwall. Their speech retains the Cornish idioms or the singsong inflections of Scandinavia, even after a generation of American life and language. There are other racial groups in the Northwest—the Germans of central Wisconsin, the Hollanders of western Michigan, the New Englanders of the Western Reserve on Lake Erie's pleasant shore, the Hungarians and Czechs of Cleveland, the Poles and Italians of Detroit, and the great throng of mingled nations from Norway to Greece, in Chicago. To the future-bright middle states came peoples from all of Europe, and the great cities of the Old World were planted again in new soil. In the five states of the Northwest Territory there are two Lisbons, three Moscows, two Dublins, four Londons, four Parises, five Athenses, five Viennas, five Berlins, five Romes. A hundred years ago Herman Melville saw the emigrant ships in Liverpool crowded with people of twenty different nationalities bound for the midlands of America, and he said, "You cannot spill a drop of American blood without spilling the blood of the whole world."

This is a region, then, comprising many regions and it cannot be summarized. It is the wide green countryside of corn and wheat and clover. It is the warm summer night in an Illinois town with the Prairie Flyer racing through. It is the pounding life of Halsted Street and a dirt road through the hills of Brown County, Indiana. It is a hundred county-seat towns with the business gathered about Court House Square and a bandstand under the maple trees. It is the skyline of Chicago lifting above the Loop's blue haze, and Cincinnati spreading on her seven hills above the curving Ohio. It is the stately George Rogers Clark Memorial at Vincennes, the drab little house where "Cap" Grant lived in Galena before the world knew him, and the big bronze Lincoln on the lake shore at Chicago. It is the square farms that line U. S. 40 for five hundred miles and the long straight crossroads laid off at one-mile intervals.

The level landscape encourages monotony. One road is like another, one village is like the rest, the next town is like the last. Cities spread without barriers and so without distinction. Yet there has been room for many contrasts. You think of the old river town of Marietta with its elm-shaded streets named for Revolutionary heroes, and then you think of the noisy young city of Flint with its miles of motor plants and its annual Polish, Serbian, Scottish and Syrian festivals.

The iron-ore freighters coming down from the Soo pass the clustered village of Mackinac, white against the green hills of the island, serene after three centuries of troubled history. They dock, thirty hours later, at the smoky young steel town of Gary, built in a single season in 1907 on the dunes of Lake Michigan. You remember Gallipolis drowsing beside the Ohio River and Cheboygan drowsing beside Lake Huron—one with romantic memories of French artists and aristocrats and the other with its mountain of sawdust still yellow in the sun fifty years after the last pine logs went through the screaming mills. You think of New Harmony on the Wabash, which dreamed of greatness a century ago, and of the Great Lake cities which had no dreams at all but grew to prodigious wealth and power.

No one ever came to this part of America for its climate. Early travelers were astounded by the fierce heat of summer, when a man idle in the shade would find sweat pouring from him furiously. For two generations a frontier people ridden with ague accepted the "shakes" as a part of Western life. Even after that complaint was gone there remained the hot, humid summer, wilting to everything but hogs and corn, and the bleak, bitter winter so slow to pass that people invented "ground-hog day" in their vain wish for an early spring.

The one grateful season was the golden, slowly fading fall— the Indian summer with its haze on the horizon and a yearning, cloudless sky. No one ever hoped for a short autumn. Against that serene season loomed the violence of the other months—driving blizzards of mid-winter, menacing thunderheads massing in the June sky, sudden windstorms that swept the country like wrath. That willful weather was the rule. Inevitably it entered the character of the western people.

Buckeyes, Hoosiers, Suckers, Badgers and Wolverines, they called themselves when their states were young. Now they have outgrown that ebullience, but they still live in a young and yeasty land, with the future all before it. That has given them the restless energy, the inventiveness, the readiness for change that the Mid West signifies. Chicago is not only the hog-butcher and the freight-handler, but also the impatient young visionary who dreams with his hands. So Chicago has given the world the reaping machine, the Pullman car, the steel skyscraper, the streamliner.

At other places the same dreaming has gone on. In an Ohio

field the Wright brothers built their crude and flimsy kite that first carried a man into the clouds. On the dusty Pumpkin Vine Pike in Indiana, in 1894, Elwood Haynes cranked up his horseless carriage and drove three miles without a stop. At DeKalb, Illinois, Joseph Glidden made a strand of barbed wire to keep cattle within a fence. Three counties away, a Moline blacksmith, John Deere, turned an old buzzsaw into the world's first steel plowshare.

If these are not symbols of the good life, they are still the signs of the urgent new world, with its love of things and its passion for material mastery. So the territory that two hundred years ago was an outlying land has become the most essential region. The United States could remain the same nation without any other of her seven great regions, but not without the broad and varied basin between the Ohio and the lakes.

In 1789, the Ordinance of Congress designated this area as the Northwest Territory. Such terms have a fluid meaning in America. The Old West was Ohio, a state only a sixth of the way across the continent. Geographically the old Northwest has always been a central area. The topography of North America is unlike that of any other continent, having straighter and simpler lines and dominated by a broad central basin between coastal mountain systems. That makes a heartland in the country. Seventy-five years ago the proposal was made to move the national capital to the banks of the Mississippi. For fifty years the center of the nation's population has been moving slowly westward across central Indiana. So the geographic heartland becomes the social heartland also. Inevitably the main currents of political, economic and cultural life pass through it and, as is natural with a heartland, many of the currents are generated there.

A strong sense of the future fired the mind of Thomas Jefferson, who first designed the commonwealths of the unpeopled West. With a continent to grow in, the thirteen federated states, in 1784, had need of a plan for colonization and government of their newly won territory beyond the Alleghenies. So Jefferson, never hesitant

to make designs upon the future, studied the maps of the Northwest Territory and drew the boundaries of fourteen states—at one
prophetic stroke he overshadowed the thirteen original colonies
by the potent future of the West. In retrospect this seems an
obvious prediction. But the future of the unpeopled country was
far from obvious when he sketched his fourteen states. A year
later, in 1785, James Monroe made a journey of inspection to the
Northwest. Indian troubles compelled him to curtail his tour, but
he gained impressions which left him in little doubt about the
prospects of the country.

"A great part of the territory," he wrote, "is miserably poor,
especially that near Lakes Michigan and Erie, and that upon the
Mississippi and the Illinois consists of extensive plains which have
not had, from appearances, and will not have a single bush on
them, for ages." He doubted that those districts would ever be
sufficiently peopled to win membership in the Confederation.

Jefferson, however, was so confident of his projected states that
he named them, choosing a curious mixture of native Indian terms
and bookish designations from classical Greek. His most northern
and western state, embracing upper Wisconsin and Minnesota,
was called Sylvania. Michigania and Chersonesus lay respectively
west and east of Lake Michigan. Immediately south of these, comprising northern Illinois and Indiana, were Assenisipia and Metro-
potamia. Below these were Illinois and Saratoga, with Polypotamia
extending to the confluence of the Ohio and Mississippi rivers.
East of Polypotamia lay Pelisipia, and east of Pelisipia, comprising
what is now eastern Ohio, was the state of Washington. The four
remaining states in Jefferson's design lay south of the Ohio River.

This blueprint was not to be fulfilled. Jefferson's synthetic names
were discarded and the state boundaries were reconsidered. But
there remained his design of colonizing the new territory, not as
outlying possessions of the original colonies but as free commonwealths which would take their places among the sovereign states
of the Union. So when the historic Ordinance of 1787 was passed,
the destiny of the Northwest began to unfold.

With its birth in this broad and far-sighted Ordinance, the old Northwest began its political existence as a unified region. It was quickly won, with a few troops of uncouth riflemen and some paltry consignments of trade goods. There were no dramatic obstacles in its landscape and only the backward tribes to dispute possession. Most of its settlers had no part in the winning of the West—they came to a waiting welcome country. So the region has evolved, with that common background, a common outlook. It had great areas to occupy and rich resources to develop. It has become practical, productive, vastly prosperous. Sometimes its life seems thin, its towns monotonous, its cities duplicates of each other, its rich soil painfully barren to the spirit. Its struggles have been physical, with weather and wilderness, with hardship and isolation. Its dreams have been crude dreams of gregariousness and comfort. It has no lost causes, no vague aspirations, few deeply cherished traditions. Its memories are of toil and opportunity— of axes thudding in the forest, of breaking-plow turning the prairie sod, of hectic, fervid settlement when men of twenty races came to shape a new society where there were no restricting fences and no restraining past.

Yet these memories have a certain richness, accessible to all, and sometimes the sense of future illuminates the country like sunrise. Perhaps that is why it still can seem, as it seemed to Whitman and Lincoln three generations ago, the landscape of democracy. To its people it has been sufficient. The Hoosier thinks no river in the world is as beautiful as the Wabash murmuring in the moonlight between its fields of corn. Mark Twain through all his far-ranging life was haunted by the memory of a village drowsing beside the Mississippi. And Abraham Lincoln lies buried on a gentle Illinois hillside above the prairies that he tramped when the land was young.

THE WESTERN country had its *Mayflower* and its founding fathers. On a rainy April day in 1788 a rough-hewn flatboat drifted down the Ohio to the hill-framed mouth of the Muskingum River.

This *Mayflower* brought forty-eight New England men to the Ohio wilderness, and with them began the civilization of interior America. They named their town Marietta—in years to come people spoke of it as the Plymouth of the West.

At the old English channel port of Plymouth, where the Massachusetts Pilgrims embarked for the New World, many Americans have had their first look at the green hills of England. Above the broad harbor rises a long ridge known as Torpenhow Hill. That name encompasses fifteen hundred years of English language and history. Originally the Plymouth height was called the Tor. The word remains current in Devonshire where the high moorsides culminate in upthrust tors of rock. But in time that Anglo-Saxon syllable lost its meaning and the hill became Tor Pen—*pen,* or *ben,* is a Celtic word still familiar in the Scottish highlands where Ben Lomond and Ben Nevis rise above the lochs.

After a few centuries the meaning faded from that term, and the hill was called Torpen How—*how* is a Welsh word which remains in the designation of upthrust features in the mountainous tracts of Wales. But with time the Welsh syllable lost its meaning on the channel coast, and so the long green ridge became known as Torpenhow Hill. Now the name repeats, in four layers of English usage, one geographical designation—it is Hillhillhill Hill.

This is a kind of memory, layer upon layer of the past, which America is thought not to possess. But in recent years there has been a re-discovery of America, particularly in the Middle West, uncovering successive traditions in our past. For unmeasured time the land beyond the mountains was a domain of wandering tribes. For a century it was included in the province of Quebec, a part of the empire of New France. For a generation the British ruled it, though the life of the tribes was unchanged in the forest. Then George Rogers Clark and his file of men in buckskin won it for Virginia and the new American nation. By the Ordinance of 1787 the Federal Congress made it a national territory, and forty-eight men set out from Ipswich, Massachusetts, to plant a colony in the empty West.

Marietta was a settlement in a silent country, but when General Rufus Putnam led his men ashore they found a mysterious system of earthworks on the green Muskingum meadow. A vanished race had been there before them, leaving the outlines of their city and the mounded graves of their dead.

II

The Grass of Graves

IN THE SPRING of 1832, William Cullen Bryant, editor of the
New York *Evening Post,* made his first journey to the West,
visiting his brother who had settled on the spacious prairies of
Illinois. In the sweeping landscape of Bureau County, near the
great bend of the Illinois River, the author of "Thanatopsis" forgot the gloom of the Tadoussac Forest and the looming Berkshire
Hills. The new country was vast and airy, washed with light. It
was motionless yet full of motion, as cloud shadows shifted on the
plain and wind ripples ran across the grass. Unlike the stern New
England hills that had impressed his youthful mind with thoughts
of death and moral duty, it was multi-colored with its masses of
orange lilies, blue and pink fields of phlox, golden acres of coreop-
sis, purple cone flowers and bright bur marigolds. It was a new,
unshadowed, exhilarating land—"for which the speech of England
had no name"—the Prairies.

Yet, like every traveler from the first tentative explorers and
traders who groped into the unknown West, Bryant found that
the new country was an old country also. It held ghosts of the past.
From the Ohio River to Lake Superior the land was marked with
monuments of a mysterious race. Especially along the rivers rose
curious mounds, terraced earthworks, cones, truncated pyramids,
effigies of bird and beast laid out in gigantic size upon the vacant
land. On the prairies, in the forest, along the river banks, the
mounds appeared—thousands and thousands of them, speaking
mutely of the toil and superstition of a race that had vanished like
the snows of unrecorded winters. The prairie mounds, like those
that Bryant saw beside the creeks of Illinois, were carpeted with
grass and starred with little wind-flowers. The forest mounds bore

a growth of tall beech and maple groves—centuries had passed since the builders had heaped up their baskets of earth over their dead. So, in the long June days, in the new, unshadowed country, Bryant recovered the somber mood of his boyhood. He saw again the earth, even its wild and radiant gardens under the prairie sky, as the great tomb of man. He thought of the solitudes once astir with life and of the multitudinous dead who had raised the mounds to make "high places" in a level country.

From the first, the mounds prompted legend and fantasy. The solitude of time-softened earthworks gave a kind of solemnity to the vanished people who had lived in the great valley before history began. Like travelers before him, Bryant pictured a superior and powerful race who built their monuments of earth before the Greeks had hewed the marble of Pentelicus or reared on its high rock the Parthenon. He saw them tilling spacious fields with the shaggy buffalo drawing their burdens. (Actually the buffalo did not range the country east of the Mississippi until after the Mound Builders had vanished.) Looking over the vacant prairie he imagined their swarming cities and, unlike the poet of "Thanatopsis," he saw young lovers at twilight walking through the fields, speaking a lost language yet making love in a tongue that does not change. In fancy he heard them strumming forgotten instruments as they gathered on their flat pyramids to worship forgotten gods.

Then, as the picture went on in his mind, savage tribes swept out of the mountainous West. With quavering war cries they stormed the earthworks that the Mound Builders had erected for defense. They climbed the walls and shattered the gates and fell upon the peaceful cities. So the Mound Builders were exterminated by Indian warriors. And as he speculated on their passing, Bryant remembered that in his turn the Indian had been dispossessed by the musket and long rifle of the white man. So, he thought solemnly, the slow wheel turns.

Bryant's speculations were more romantic but no more fanciful than those of many a traveler and early settler in the Mound Builders' country. Pioneer periodicals were full of descriptions of the formations and conjectures about the vanished race. The general belief arose that the Mound Builders were a powerful race with temples and cities scattered over an empire from Hudson Bay to the Gulf of Mexico. The fact that a hundred thousand mounds dot the old Northwest, with a dense concentration along the rivers of Ohio, Indiana, Illinois and southern Wisconsin, encouraged fantastic ideas about their population. Surmises grew into a belief that the extensive earthworks on the Mississippi at Cahokia, Illinois, marked the site of their capital. Under a wise hierarchy of kings and priests they were pictured as carrying on an advanced civilization. There were various speculations about their origin—they were descendants of the Lost Tribes of Israel; they were Japanese carried across the Pacific by adverse wind and current; they were descendants of crews marooned from the ships of Solomon; their progenitors were a tribe expelled from Assyria.

Thomas Jefferson thought the American aborigines might have descended from a crew of Carthaginians separated from Hanno's fleet during his long voyage, and he believed that a study of Indian languages would provide a clue to their ancient history. He made a large collection of Indian vocabularies and thought he could relate them to the ancient languages of the Mediterranean. When he left Washington and the presidency, the linguistic documents were packed into a heavy trunk—so heavy that it tempted two Negro boatmen beyond endurance. The trunk was broken open, the papers were lost, and the classic origin of Indian languages was never demonstrated.

But Jefferson continued to be fascinated by the Mound Builders' remains and he had a small collection of artifacts at Monticello. After digging into a modest mound on the Rivanna River in Virginia, he guessed that it might contain a thousand skeletons. This was a great error—more likely it contained ten—but it was characteristic of the impression the mounds made on early observers. The geometric formation of certain Ohio and Indiana earthworks led to discussion of the engineering skill and mathematical method employed by the vanished people—though later archaeologists found that the geometry of the formations did not indicate any more mathematics than a counting of paces and a circle drawn with a stake and a thong. But the wonder remained. Even the hard-bitten Indian fighter William Henry Harrison speculated in terms almost as romantic as Bryant's about the Ohio earthworks at Marietta, Cincinnati, and at the mouth of the Great Miami River. When he used a flat-topped mound at Cincinnati for a military lookout, old Tippecanoe was pleased to think of the vanished people who had watched from that same height for the approach of their savage foes.

When archaeologists took up the study of the Mound Builders, the fantasy was dispelled and in its place came a systematic description of the life and activity of the tribes to whom the North-west first belonged. Maps of the remains showed that the Mound Builders had flourished chiefly along the river valleys tributary to the Ohio and the Mississippi. More than five thousand mounds were located in Ohio alone. The most common type are conical mounds, used solely for burial purposes. They range in size from a farmer's haystack to the pyramids of Egypt. The great Miamisburg Mound, in southwestern Ohio, covers three acres and supports a full-grown forest on its slopes. Another type is the flat-topped "house mound," or "temple mound," used for ceremonial purposes. The greatest is at Cahokia, Illinois, on the Mississippi, where in the midst of extensive earthworks the huge Monk's Mound spreads over sixteen acres and rises a hundred feet above the prairie. Most striking are the effigy mounds, appearing frequently in southern Wisconsin, where the raised formations show a gigantic shape of deer, fox, wolf, buffalo, turtle, eagle, swallow or goose. Less bizarre are the earthworks which commonly consist of embankments for miliary defense and geometric enclosures for social and sacred ceremonies.

After many excavations the archaeologists brought together their evidence—in the form of skeletons, bones, vessels, weapons, and objects of primitive art—and concluded that the Mound Builders were not a single federated race but many scattered tribes. Three large classifications emerged—some tribes, belonging to what the archaeologists called the Adena culture, were primitive; others, of the Fort Ancient culture, were moderately advanced; and still others, comprising the Hopewell culture, carried on an orderly and efficient civilization. All were identified as Indians—not an alien or separate race but the ancestors of the tribes to whom the white man brought trade, evangelism and war. The archaeologists dispelled a popular theory that the Mound Builders had followed the buffalo west to the plains and there lost their identity, by demonstrating that there were no buffalo east of the Mississippi during the period of mound building. Certain of the Mound Builder tribes did, however, become extinct—perhaps through epidemic, perhaps from the warring forays of the Iroquois who swept across the Ohio valley to the Mississippi in the century before Columbus sailed the western sea.

Though they had no unified empire, these people traveled transcontinental trails and carried on a trade in precious wares from remote regions. In mounds along the Mississippi, archaeologists have found shells from California beaches, fragments of obsidian from the naked ridges of the Rockies, copper from Lake Superior's headlands, pipestone from Canada, silica from the famed "flint ridge" of Ohio and wampum beads from the shells found only on the Atlantic shore. So the ends of a wilderness continent are represented in those quiet mounds. Far from the copper outcrop on Keweenaw Point and Isle Royale, the fastidious Hopewell people of Ohio used lumps of Lake Superior copper to form noses for the skeletons they buried in the timbered crypts of their mounds beside the Scioto River. In Mound City, Ohio, was found a battered chunk of obsidian, heavier than a bale of peltry, which must have been carried on some weary human back all the way from the valley of the Yellowstone. From Illinois mounds beside the Sangamon have come bracelets of the teeth of Rocky Mountain grizzly bears. The more advanced Mound Builders sent trading expeditions across the entire country.

Scores of modern cities have grown up on the sites of the vanished towns of the Mound Builders. Sometimes as at Marietta, the first American settlement west of the Alleghenies, their earthworks served the purposes of a later people. When Rufus Putnam and his boatload of colonists came ashore on the Muskingum, they found the outlines of a once populous village—conical mounds, platform mounds and rectangular enclosures—on that riverbank before them. So they built their fort at the corner of the earthworks and pastured their cattle in the enclosures. Marietta was the first capital of the Northwest Territory. When Cincinnati succeeded it as the seat of government, the capital city was again bordered by the grass-grown walls of a prehistoric town. Other Ohio cities—Portsmouth, Newark, Chillicothe, Circleville—were erected on the site of extensive remains.

Circleville took its name from great circular earthworks on the level land of Pickaway County and the original town was built in concentric circles in the pattern of the Mound Builders' own village. So Circleville had no corner anywhere. Circle Street conformed to the old enclosure, Circle Alley was the street within that and, in the center, an eight-sided courthouse looked in eight directions on a circular green. In the 1830s, when gravel was dug to build the Ohio canal, hundreds of skeletons were found in the Circleville gravel pits and a good many Mound Builders' bones went into the canal banks in Pickaway County. When the National Pike was built across the new western states it led straight to the great Cahokia Mounds at East St. Louis. Cahokia was the chief city of the Mound Builders and its site became populous again, as the National Road and the Mississippi River brought streams of settlers to the rich lands of the "American Bottom" along the Mississippi.

With modern settlement the mounds were put to various uses. Frequently extensive mound sites became parks, as they are to this day in Marietta and St. Paul and in hundreds of towns and cities between them. In Newark, Ohio, a series of earthworks is incorporated into a golf course—the greens guarded not by common bunkers but by the great Octagon and Circle Mounds. On June 21, when the sun reaches its northernmost point, the rays at sunrise fall precisely on the axis of these two mounds—a fact which led some archaeologists to believe that the Mound Builders made celestial observations.

Many farmers have complained of the mounds on their land when they wanted unbroken cornfields or a fence line straight and level. But farmers also have put the toil of a thousand years ago to a convenient use. In the Wabash River bottoms, in early spring, many farmhouses stand high and dry on a wooded burial mound while all the fields are under water. In Fulton County, Illinois, where the Spoon River joins the Illinois, hundreds of mounds are humped along the bluffs that overlook the two streams. The largest of these, the Dickson Mound, was originally crescent-shaped with points directed toward the east. It measured 550 feet along the curve and rose to the height of a sassafras tree. When a farmer needed a site for his house and buildings, he graded the high ground, leveling the ridge and filling in the crescent basin. In that process wagon-loads of skeletons were unearthed and hauled to another part of the farm for reburial. Thousands of flint, stone and bone implements were taken out, and other thousands still remained. When the grading was done, the mound had become an enviable raised farmyard, looking over level wheat lands and criss-crossed fields of corn.

Archaeology is still a new science in the Mound areas. Many thousands of formations have never been opened. Skeletons, stone axes, pipes, arrowheads, the little votive offerings of bears' teeth, eagle claws and twists of tobacco still lie in the darkness to which they were entrusted perhaps a thousand years ago. So, despite the classifications of their culture, the Mound Builders remain a shadowy race and some sense of wonder still clings to the great mounds that were landmarks in the western country when the first white men groped through.

Here, out of many thousands, are four of them, each in its own way meaningful to the imagination.

In Marietta, above the leafy terrace of the Muskingum shore, beyond the spacious Sacra Via and near the site of the Mound Builders' fortifications, lies the Mound Cemetery, where twenty-four Revolutionary army officers are buried. Its dominant feature is a lofty conical mound, now overgrown with tall-standing elm and maple trees. The mound, called Conus by the classics-loving Marietta settlers, is thirty feet high and one hundred and fifteen feet in diameter at the base. Its height is emphasized by an encircling moat fifteen feet wide, at the outer edge of which is a five-foot embankment. So Conus stands in its own frame, and even the modern stairway to its summit does not mar its impressiveness. Though known to be a burial mound, it has never been opened. To the white man's cemetery its quiet proportions and shady slopes give a solemnity beyond that of granite headstones. Around it nestle the graves of Americans who joined the vanished people in the long sleep of the earth. Now they lie together in a burial place as old as any on the continent.

Cahokia, Illinois, now a village on the edge of East St. Louis, was once the largest city in America. The city is gone but its outlines remain in a system of nearly a hundred mounds dominated by a flat-topped pyramid covering sixteen acres. This is the largest earthwork in the world. On its four lower terraces is room for hundreds of lodges and wigwams, while some vast ceremonial structure must have occupied the upper platform. It is named not for its builders but for a colony of Trappist monks, part of the French culture of the region a century and a half ago, who built their rude monastery on the mound's commanding summit. Though they lived there but a few years, from 1808 to 1813, and their buildings have disappeared, it has been known ever since their brief residence as the Monks Mound.

Whatever ceremony the Mound Builders observed on that broad height, it could not have been more rigorous and austere than the routine of the Trappists. Under Father Urbain some eighty monks lived there in log huts, sleeping on the floor, eating two meager vegetarian meals a day, communicating with each other by signs, never using their voices except in chant and prayer at their five daily masses. In their years on the mound, no females were allowed in the vicinity. The monks tilled a hundred acres, working in the fields in their dark habits, with cowl and crucifix and shaven head tending hogs and cattle. Summer fever took the lives of many, but not before they had dug their own graves in the mound. With shaking hands they hollowed out their burial places—that was a requirement of their order. Each season their number lessened and the row of unmarked graves lengthened across the mound. At last, decimated by fever, the diminished colony returned to France.

After the departure of the monks the mound supported a farmhouse and buildings, a garden, orchard and a deep well, out of which came scores of bones and hundreds of fragments of pottery. In time a St. Louis businessman bought it with the idea of erecting an entertainment pavilion on the summit. But the whole mounds area became the property of the state of Illinois and now it is a state park with an archaeological museum and a parking lot at the base of the great Monks Mound and log steps leading to a picnic ground on its summit.

Above the wooded gorge of the Little Miami River on its way to the Ohio is Fort Ancient, the greatest military stronghold in prehistoric America. Its grass and tree-grown walls extend four miles and enclose a hundred acres in two rudely triangular areas connected by a serpentine passageway. Thousands of travelers have wondered at its irregular shape and some have seen clearly marked the outlines of North and South America, joined by the sinuous Isthmus of Panama. So they credit the Mound Builders of a thousand years ago with a knowledge of geography that no European possessed until centuries later.

The purpose of the formation is plain enough. On a precipitous height three hundred feet above the river, enclosed on three sides by deep ravines, it is a natural location for military defense. Several burial mounds lie within the enclosures, but the fortifications dwarf them. There are miles of moats, now grassy but perhaps once filled with water, surrounding sets of parallel walls, terraces, platforms and solid-rock gateways. Here an industrious people built a strong place. But some fatality of warfare, pestilence or famine overcame them, and now only the time-softened walls of their citadel remain. Those walls have attracted hundreds of American and European archaeologists. In recent years, scale models of Fort Ancient have been set up in museums in England, France and Germany.

The most famous of the effigy mounds is still as mysterious as when the first startled explorers found it writhing through the Ohio woods two hundred years ago. The Great Serpent Mound, 1,330 feet from head to tail, stretches sinuously along the high shore of Brush Creek a few miles west of the Scioto River. Its folded body ends in a yawning mouth in front of which is an egg-shaped figure which the serpent is about to swallow.

The Great Serpent Mound was first accurately surveyed by Squier and Davis, pioneer archaeologists. Since then it has attracted archaeologists from distant parts of the world. They have paced its writhing folds, studied the curious figure at its head and dug into it at various places in its gigantic length. They have called it a shrine, a cemetery, a place of worship and of sacrificial rites, with the fruit in its jaws an altar for the sacrifice. And there was no way of determining the validity of any of their speculations. In 1887, Professor Frederick W. Putnam effected its purchase for the Peabody Museum of Harvard University. Later, Harvard presented it to the state of Ohio and it is now a state park.

The archaeologists developed various theories about the Great Serpent, but in 1902 a Baptist clergyman of Pleasant Hills, Ohio, came to a conclusion of his own. He had grown up in the woods and hills of Adams County and had known the mound all his life. As a boy he had played Indian along the three small streams that enter Brush Creek and had made cooking fires in the Serpent's open jaws. But when, years later, as a Baptist minister he read Job 15:13 "By His spirit He hath garnished the Heavens; His hand hath formed the crooked serpent," he suddenly saw the vast coiling quiet shape as older than any Ohio memory. So he declared that the Great Serpent beside Brush Creek marked the undiscovered Garden of Eden. He asserted that the effigy was created by the hand of God to commemorate the original paradise and to symbolize the fall of man. For the details of the effigy he had a ready explanation—the jaws of the serpent are open to swallow the fruit which tempted Eve, the serpent's writhing represents the pangs of sin and death. The three small streams that the clergyman remembered from his boyhood rambles now became a part of sacred allegory. He said they symbolized the Father, Son and Holy Spirit.

Officials of the Bureau of Ethnology demonstrated that the mound is no more than a thousand years old. Here, they said, a tribe of red men danced, feasted and worshiped. But the clergyman had the verse from Job on his side and he insisted that the creeks and woods of Adams County were the original Garden of Eden.

To more casual observers wherever the mounds hump out of woodland or meadow or riverside, the old, time-defying formations excite a quiet wonder. Many a farm boy has climbed a grassy cone to scan the pasture for the cattle, and in the slanting afternoon he has wondered for a minute about the people who buried their dead in this country long ago. Sometimes, as he tramped his American acres, a German or Swedish farmer has stopped to ponder over the mysterious earthworks where his cattle have been grazing. Standing there he has thought of the ancient groves of Saxony or Värmland, where old burial places are softened with the moss of ages and forgotten graves have grown vague with the centuries-old mantle of pine needles. So in fancy he has returned to the Old World where the forest was dark on the hills and on the highest summit a broken castle stood.

There are no castles on the Ohio or the Mississippi, but dimly comes the feeling that the New World, too, is older than all memory and its earth is enriched by the forgotten dead.

III

Travelers' Tales

TWO HUNDRED YEARS ago the West began at the crest of the Alleghenies. All the American settlements were on the Atlantic watershed. Beyond that height of land lay a little-known country. So where the West began, there also began wonder. A hundred miles of tumbled mountains separated the familiar seaboard from the strange inland country. That distance kept the East and West apart and beyond the Allegheny ridges the continent was covered with a marvelous haze.

The first shadowy impressions of the West were sketched from the tentative theories of geographers and the tales of Indians. It began as a country of myth. It took vague and impressive proportions in men's beliefs when there were only a few rivers on the explorers' maps and a few faint tracks in the forest. It was *terra incognita*, with its uncertain landmarks bearing uncouth Indian names. Vague as it was, the Western country ended in total mystery. Beyond the forests and the plains rose dark and shining mountains—more of legend than geography—and somewhere finally the western sea broke on unknown beaches.

For a long time American people refused to believe the vastness of their continent and each new evidence of its vastness disturbed and embarrassed them. It was an unlooked-for land, an obstacle in the path to India. Columbus made the first error, mistaking the natives of the newly discovered hemisphere for inhabitants of the oldest continent and calling them Indians. His error persisted, in many forms, for nearly two centuries. For a host of restless men China lay, luring with her riches, at no great distance from Quebec, and the Pacific washed an undiscovered shore at the western foot of the Alleghenies. La Salle's estate on the St. Lawrence was named, ironically, La Chine (China) because he had once dreamed of a canoe trade from that base with Oriental merchants. In 1634, while the Plymouth colony was still struggling to maintain itself on the Massachusetts shore, the bold Jean Nicolet thought he saw the shores of China rising from the waters of Lake Michigan. With seven Huron paddlers he had passed in his canoe through the Straits of Mackinac. Beyond these narrows the sea widened out to vastness—it was like the end of the new world, with the shores of Asia ahead. So when the forests of Green Bay took shape above the water, Nicolet pulled a robe of Chinese damask over his buckskin clothing, to be fitly dressed to meet the Mandarins. Instead, he was met by half-naked Winnebago Indians. The passage to China dissolved like the mists on the Wisconsin shore.

As the dream of the Northwest Passage faded, there remained the belief that some undiscovered water route connected the St. Lawrence basin with the western sea. From his estate at La Chine, La Salle looked westward over the broad reach of the St. Lawrence. His gaze ended with the dim forest of Beauharnois, but his imagination went on to the unknown land. At La Chine he was visited by Indian parties. When a troop of Senecas told him of the river "O-hy-o" which, rising in their country, flowed for a distance of nine months' journey to the sea, La Salle was sure that their river was the way to the western ocean. Restless, ambitious, full of imperial dreams, La Salle set out to travel that route for himself. In 1670, he crossed Lake Ontario and, though racked with fever and suspicious of his Seneca guides, made the long portage to a branch of the Allegheny, which led him to the Ohio. He descended that river to the falls which, generations later, became the site of Louisville. He could not know that he was still two thousand miles from the Pacific, but he did give up his hope of a canoe trade with the Chinese ports.

What the French found out about the inland country they did not share with the English. So, a year after La Salle's voyage on the Ohio, John Lederer, a German traveler, made a tour of exploration for Governor Berkeley of Virginia. In 1672, he published in London an account of his travels in the Virginia hinterland, "to the top of the Apalataean Mountains." At his camp in a Blue Ridge valley some Indians told him of a western country marked by waves. This was probably a reference to mountain ranges, but from it Lederer quickly concluded "the Indian Ocean does stretch an arm or bay from California as far as the Apalataean Mountains."

He was convinced that "they are in great error who imagine that the continent of North America is but eight or ten days' journey over the Atlantick to the Indian Ocean." Yet he was equally sure that a western gulf opened into the continent as far as the site of modern Pittsburgh. This was the map-makers' "Sea of Verrazano," and even as they were drawing its outlines the French explorers found the Mississippi Valley, the pine forests and the prairies and the plains rising toward an undiscovered range of mountains on what was supposed to be the bed of that sea.

While the "Sea of Verrazano" soon dissolved into an interior wilderness, the great problem of the map-makers remained. That was the question of the St. Lawrence and the Mississippi basins and their relation to each other. In his great *mapmonde* Mercator had supposed the interior country all one drainage area, dominated by the St. Lawrence system of waterways. He turned the Appalachians, at their southern end, into the West, placing the springs of the St. Lawrence in the present state of Arizona. Thus he portrayed the central valley of the continent as running nearly east and west for a full three thousand miles. That was in the late sixteenth century. Succeeding geographers, knowing the character of the Great Lakes, correctly limited the St. Lawrence basin to the northern country. But they conceived the St. Lawrence waters as somewhere uniting with the southward-flowing Mississippi, thus opening an unbroken water route from the Gulf of St. Lawrence to the Gulf of Mexico.

This conception was first presented by the Dutch geographer Cluverius, in his *Introduction to Universal Geography,* in 1624, and it persisted in various editions of that great work for a hundred years. European map-makers, knowing that French traders passed with their canoe caravans from the Mississippi to the Great Lakes, and drawing their maps four thousand miles away from the rough portages where files of men staggered under their loads to reach new-flowing water, simply drew the fine lines of rivers by which the Mississippi was united with the St. Lawrence. As late as 1747, Emanuel Bowen, English geographer, made the Wisconsin River an unbroken line between the Mississippi and Lake Michigan.

Actually there was nowhere a marked barrier between the two great basins. No mountain range, no hills, no discernible ridge separates the watersheds in the Northwest country. At the many "carrying places" the height of land was not something for the eye to see. But after a mile, or ten miles, of trudging over land the weary carriers found water running in a new direction, and men who had toiled upstream could guide their craft in a favorable current. In a later century, canals would actually link the river systems at five different places. But when the trade was an exchange of knives, blankets and picture cards of the saints for the Indians' robes of beaver, the portages were places where men carried their canoes with no hand left to fight the angry mosquitoes and the furious little stabs of the black fly. To explorers, traders and missionaries those carrying places were the first gruelling roads in the new country. They were the way into new regions, they were bitterly and triumphantly remembered.

All were alike in the toil and exhaustion of portaging, yet each was different. The Chautauqua Lake portage into Conewango Creek and the Allegheny River, the carry from Presque Isle—now Erie, Pennsylvania—to La Boeuf on French Creek that joined the Allegheny, the land bridge between the Cuyahoga River and the Tuscarawas, which led to the Muskingum, the passage from the Sandusky River to the Scioto, the twin routes from the Maumee River—one finding the Auglaize River and the Great Miami and the other the headwaters of the Wabash—all these were routes connecting Lake Erie with the Ohio River. The portages to the Mississippi were four—the prairie path between the St. Joseph River and the Kankakee, which in time joined the Illinois; the ambiguous swamp route between the Chicago River and the Des Plaines, which also joined the Illinois; the short haul between thickets of alder and deer-brush that linked the Fox River to the Wisconsin, and the pine-dark passage that led from the St. Louis River, beyond the tip of Lake Superior, to the stripling Mississippi.

The Mississippi was for a hundred years a river of solemnity and mystery. Long after the Spaniards had mapped its mouth, the French found it a mile wide beneath the bluffs of Wisconsin. But they had no knowledge of where its headwaters sprang or where it joined the sea. At St. Anthony's Falls a party of Sioux told Du Charleville, raising their voices above the roaring Mississippi, that he was standing midway between the source of the river and its mouth. So the maps of the early eighteenth century showed the Mississippi rising directly west of Hudson's Bay.

The persistent myth of a westward-leading river, such a river as Mercator had represented and La Salle had searched for, found its way onto later maps of the interior country. Traders among the Sioux got repeated impressions of such a river, and Baron La Hontan claimed to have found a great stream entering the Mississippi from the west near the broadening of the Mississippi which is called Lake Pepin. In the early 1700s, this "riviere longue" appeared on the maps, broader than the Mississippi itself, running straight west along what is now the southern boundary of Minnesota. According to the maps, the "Long River" ended under an abrupt range of mountains, over the crest of which another river set out directly west, toward the Pacific. La Hontan, who had seen much of interior America and recorded it faithfully, fell prey to the temptation to claim a voyage on this mythical river. He soberly recounted a journey up its sluggish currents and even described the populous nations that he found on its shores—the Eokoras, the Esanapes, the Gnacsitares, the Mozeemleks and Tahuglauks.

But his imaginary discoveries are pale beside the adventures claimed by Mathieu Sagean. This unrestrained Frenchman reported a voyage on the non-existent river in the course of which he encountered lions, tigers and leopards. Far up the river he came to the fortified towns of the Acanibas nation, whose King Hagaren was a descendant of Montezuma and was clothed in the skins of men. In the vestibule of the king's palace four bands played a never-ending concert, and the royal apartment was walled and floored with gold. According to Sagean these people carried on a rich trade with the Japanese. There were many exotic details in Sagean's account, which for a time was believed by the French minister Pontchartrain. But as the fur traders pushed beyond the Mississippi, the fabulous kingdom of the Acanibas faded with the "riviere longue" against the empty sweep of the western plains. Gradually even the adventurers forgot the Indian tales which described a western sea where lived bearded men "who pick up gold dust on the shore."

The desire to find a westward-leading river giving easy access to the Pacific still colored the conceptions of geography beyond the Mississippi. Fifty years after Sagean had been dismissed as a romancer, Jonathan Carver, wintering among the Minnesota Sioux, fell victim to the belief of a river into the west. He made an accurate surmise about the Mississippi's source, locating a height of land in the swamps and forests of northern Minnesota. From that point he traced rivers flowing in each of the cardinal directions. To the west, from what was later to become Beltrami County, Minnesota, he traced the "Origan" River, following it through unbounded plains "which probably terminate on the coast of the Pacific." To support that surmise he reduced the rumored Rockies to an isolated "mountain of bright stones." Carver, a quiet, reflective man approaching sixty years of age, who had spent most of his life as a New England shoemaker, carried beneath his melancholy manner a brightly burning dream. He hoped to end the long and ardent search for a Northwest Passage. A generation later the red-haired Virginian, William Clark, found the

Columbia River in wild mountain gorges a thousand miles west of Carver's river "Origan."

For a hundred years the Great Lakes with their vast distances and their shorelines cleft with bays and bold with promontories, were remote and impressive and only vaguely known. The upper lakes, being in line with the French approach through Lake Nipissing, French River and Georgian Bay, became the first known. The wilderness-girdled Lake Superior was mapped long before Lake Erie had been discovered, and its cold, deep waters carried canoe caravans before there was a beginning of trade on the lower lakes. Yet the vast northern lake remained for many years vague, marvelous and haunted by legends. It was then, as now, a sea of lonely shores, of radiant water, of mists that moved like white cliffs on the horizon. The Indians had tales of floating islands, and even the French voyageurs had seen islands inverted above the lake, with their base along the sky and the pine trees pointing to the water. Before the surveys and soundings of the nineteenth century, the map-makers had difficulty outlining its bays and headlands, and on the broad face of the lake they drew myth and mirage along with geography.

Evans and Pownall's great map shows the long rock-terraced island, "shaped like a battleship," that rides off Thunder Bay. On that map Isle Royale appears along with five other islands that never broke the sweep of that wide water—Elbow Island, Maurepais Island, Pontchartrain Island, St. Ann's Island and Minarig Island. They are spaced in an oval between Keweenaw Point and Thunder Bay, directly in the up- and down-bound courses where now the ore fleets pass. Isle Royale—the one indisputable island midway in Lake Superior—the Chippewas called Minong, for its wealth of out-cropping copper. It was reported to contain boulders, big as an ox, of solid copper, and it was said to abound with rabbits as large as wolves. According to Chippewa belief the island was not rooted to the lake's deep bottom but floated with the wind —one season it might be found off Keweenaw and the next off Shesheeb Point or Jackfish Bay. And there were strange currents along those shores. In the sober Jesuit "Relations" appear speculations about a subterranean outlet to Lake Superior—some deep, underground channel full of hurrying water.

At one time Lakes Michigan and Huron were conceived as a single sheet of water. On Jaillot's map, dedicated to the King of France in 1719, Lake Michigan is obliterated, and Green Bay (Bay of the Puants) is shown as a pocket of Lake Huron. When the lower peninsula of Michigan became apparent, its interior remained unknown, no explorer having crossed the twilit swamps and tangled forests between the two long southward-looping lakes. Mapmakers, drawing upon rumor and imagination, represented that country as an elevated terrace, treeless and level, with a path along its summit running for two hundred miles directly south from the Mackinac Straits. As late as 1776, the interior of Michigan from Mackinaw City to Ann Arbor was marked "Long Elevated Plains." Not until the nineteenth-century timber cruisers found their way into the great gloom of the pineries did this mythical "Michigan plain" disappear.

Lake Erie, or the Lake of the Cat, as Hennepin called it, from the meaning of the name of the Erie nation, remained the last of the lakes to be explored. The Senecas and Iroquois had so blocked penetration in the south that Lake Ontario was only partly charted and the Ohio shore of Lake Erie was not mapped for many years. The rude map attached to Father Hennepin's narrative of exploration—a map no more inaccurate than some of the imaginative priest's accounts of his travels—represents Lake Erie as three times the size of Ontario and shows it extending as far south as Nashville.

The British had the vaguest ideas of the westward extent of the continent, yet the charters of the British colonies claimed territories extending from sea to sea. According to those charters, Massachusetts and Connecticut crossed the Mississippi, climbed the Rockies and ended in Puget Sound and the coast of Oregon. With the Spanish possession of the trans-Mississippi West, the Pacific could not realistically be regarded as a colonial border, but it was generally agreed, as Captain de Pogés of the French Navy said in 1767, that New England was bounded by the Mississippi. Virginia and New York also had vast uncertain claims reaching into the hinterland, and Georgia and the Carolinas recognized no western boundary. The claim of New York was based on the ground that she was heir of the Iroquois tribes and so was legal possessor of all regions overrun by their warring bands. The other states based their claims on their charters. Only the claims of Virginia and North Carolina were supported by exploration and military activity. By the end of the War for Independence, their people had taken armed possession of extensive regions along the western rivers—the Ohio, Wabash, Mississippi, Cumberland and Tennessee. They could not wait.

So before it had any political life of its own the Northwest Territory was the object of claim and counter-claim. Disregarding the British charters, the French considered it theirs by right of discovery and exploration—in repeated ceremonies all the land drained by the Great Lakes and their tributary rivers and all the land drained by the Mississippi and its tributaries were proclaimed the dominions of the King of France—and they regarded the Northwest Territory as a part of the province of Quebec. It became unquestionably a British dominion after the French and Indian War, and then was wrested in turn from the British by George Rogers Clark and his Virginians. With the passing of the Territory into the control of the newly founded Union, the states took up the dispute over its ownership.

Virginia's original charter described the southern line of the colony as running due west, while the northern line ran northwest, toward Alaska, both lines ending by vague implication at the shores of the Pacific. When, as a result of deliberations by the new Federal Congress, Virginia relinquished her claim to western lands, Massachusetts was left to claim western New York and the southern areas of Michigan and Wisconsin, her claim ending at the Mississippi where began the vast domain of Spanish America. Connecticut claimed a strip of land extending west from her latitude, containing the future cities of Cleveland, Toledo and Chicago.

When Connecticut yielded her claim, it was not without a literal reservation. She acquired the title to the section along Lake Erie still known as the Western Reserve. In addition, she claimed an area west of the Reserve, designated as the Firelands, which she proposed to parcel out to her citizens in recompense for property which had been burned and pillaged during the War for Independence. She undertook to settle this entire region bordering Lake Erie, and for a generation it was known as "New Connecticut." Virginia likewise ceded her claim with reservations—the pre-empted "Virginia Military District" in central Ohio and "Clark's Grant" in southern Indiana became bounty lands for Virginia veterans of the western expeditions and campaigns. Thus, with qualifications, Congress won from the seaboard states a cession of western lands to the Federal domain, and the vast interior territory became the property of the people of the new nation.

THOMAS JEFFERSON was a man of many moods. He foresaw the inland country filling up with hardy, independent, enterprising citizens from the seaboard settlements. Seventy years before Walt Whitman, he heard America singing in the unpeopled woods and by the rivers, on the prairies and beside the wide lake shores. But in another mood, feeling the vastness and darkness of the wilderness—where the only roads were buffalo traces and the lost little stockades were ringed with the whoops of Indians—he was not so sure. At one of those times, brooding on the destiny of a wilderness six times the size of England, he conjectured that it would take a thousand years to settle the land east of the Mississippi.

But settlement came with a rush. Like a spring flood the wagon companies creaked down the Allegheny valleys and on the shores of the Ohio they built their arks and flatboats and embarked for the unpeopled lands. They had heard tales that lured them to that country. The traders, Cist and Croghan, the woodsmen, Boone and Kenton, and George Rogers Clark's lean men in buckskin had told what the West was like. So the wonders of the geographers' speculations were now replaced by the wonders that shrewd-eyed men had seen, and by the fantasies that their exuberance created. It was difficult to tell which was fact and which was fantasy. In 1790, the West was still a fabled land.

It was a country not quickly or easily surveyed. The Seven Ranges in Ohio had carried the government survey just forty-two miles west of Pittsburgh. Beyond that the land was as unrecorded as when La Salle paddled past on his imagined way to the Pacific. Though it had repeatedly changed hands in treaties across the Atlantic, it was still an Indian country. The warriors stalked their hunting grounds and the Indian women hoed their fields of maize in the river bottoms, regardless of papers signed and sealed in London or Paris. It was a land of many rivers, where the sun shafted though the leaning sycamores, of wide prairies where the buffalo ranged the sites of unborn cities. As the wagon trains creaked west through Pennsylvania, the dark life of the wilderness still possessed the land.

Simon Kenton once counted a thousand buffalo pacing in a single file to the salt licks along the Ohio River. In summer they lay on the sandbars of the river, humping the shallows into shaggy black islands around which the sluggish current passed. Traders and travelers in Indiana saw Wabash prairies dark with herds of buffalo—to this day the seal of the state shows bison grazing in a wide green valley. But abruptly, about the year 1800, as the flatboats darkened the Ohio, the buffalo disappeared from the country. According to tradition a cold winter following a heavy November sleet sealed the ground with ice for three unbroken months. Before that bitter season was over the buffalo herds had starved. That was a good year for the wolves and the hide-hunters. But few buffalo were seen east of the Mississippi after 1800. The shaggy beasts went out as the men with ax and plow and grubbing-hoe came in.

But there were other creatures. Naturalists have said that a billion squirrels inhabited the Ohio Valley and their numbers in-

creased with the first cultivated fields. Every spring and fall squirrels swam the Ohio River in thousands and the boys of pioneer
Cincinnati took wagon-loads of their carcasses. Red squirrels,
striped squirrels, black squirrels, fox squirrels, gray squirrels, chest-
nut-backed squirrels—they made the forest branches tremble. For
miles they filled the woods with chattering. Often a farmer's clearing was menaced more by these quick creatures than by Indian
marauders. A dozen times a day children went into the cornfields
to drive the squirrels out. The little animals raced in hundreds
through grain rows, took shelter in the trees that ringed the field
and then returned to the attack. At the approach of winter the
squirrels migrated southward toward the Ohio River and across
it, and at that season farmers banded together to destroy them.
Such an enterprise was a feast as well as a seasonal chore. The
naturalist F. A. Michaux took part in a squirrel hunt in which
a small hunting party had sixty roasted squirrels for lunch. Thousands of squirrels were killed in a single assault. According to the
Columbus *Gazette* a squirrel hunt in Franklin County, Ohio, in the
autumn of 1822, yielded 19,660 squirrel scalps, not counting those
unrecovered. And still, the next summer, the children chased the
squirrels out of the cornfields.

The Ohio Valley was a rich country, prodigal of its pests and
of its prizes. In 1826, the bounty on wolves paid by the state of
Ohio in Williams County was larger than the sum of all taxes
paid in the county. In those years crayfish destroyed pioneer dams,
and freshly seeded fields were eaten bare by flocks of wild turkeys.
The French habitants along the Mississippi told Father Gravier
that in August the mosquitoes came in such swarms that a man
could not be distinguished at ten paces' distance. George Croghan
said that a good hunter along the Ohio could easily keep a hundred
men in meat. Noah Major, one of the first settlers of Morgan
County, Indiana, said there were twenty thousand deer in that
county when he arrived in 1820. Fish could be caught in any
western river by throwing a spear into the flashing shallows or by
dipping a net in the shade of a leaning willow. Out of the Ohio

came pike which measured six feet long and black catfish weighing a hundred pounds.

Below Prairie du Chien, on the upper Mississippi, a fur trader, Peter Pond, reported catching three catfish which totaled 275 pounds. Twelve men ate a 100-pound fish at one sitting, "nor did I perseave that Eney of them ware Sick or Complaind." An Ohio settler boasted that his corn grew twenty-seven inches in the space of three days, after a soaking rain. On Sangamon prairies in Illinois an Irish immigrant, used to the thin, fenced fields of Donegal, farmed 640 acres which produced "forty bushels of wheat to the second crop without sowing."

These wonders gave the new country a Biblical fatness, an Old Testament expectancy of the Promised Land. The Shenandoah River was first named the Euphrates, and the early Ohio names of Gnadenhutten—the Tents of Grace—and Schoenbrunn—Beautiful Spring—expressed the assurance of felicity. Familiar proportions were left behind when a traveler crossed the Appalachians. One man reported a sycamore tree in the Scioto valley that measured sixty feet around; during a pelting rainstorm, he said, a cavity in its side sheltered thirty persons on horseback with room left for two on foot. Francis Andre Michaux, a scrupulous and careful scientist, said he had nowhere seen such trees as grew on the banks of the Ohio. A few miles above Marietta he measured a sycamore four feet above the ground and found it forty-seven feet in girth. The Ohio Company of Associates spoke so extravagantly of the western land that more sober Yankees referred ironically to the Ohio Purchase as "Putnam's Paradise" and "Cutler's Indian Haven." General Rufus Putnam had made sufficiently sanguine description of the region, but the Rev. Manasseh Cutler outdid him. On a visit to Marietta he reported finding a hollow tree that would hold eighty-four men and permit the passage of six horsemen abreast.

These were impressive facts that helped to stimulate fancy. John Cleves Symmes of New Jersey, who purchased a million acres of wilderness between the Miami rivers, lured prospective colonists by advertising that cotton and indigo would flourish in the Ohio bottoms. For centuries wild bees had hived in hollow trees and the report went out that on the Great Miami were trees that dripped a perpetual sap of pure honey. Watermelons were said to grow as large as barrels, the flax plant bore woven cloth on its branches and springs of rum and brandy gushed from the hills.

Since legend grows with distance, it is natural that in Europe the Ohio country became a land of marvels. A writer in the *Gentlemen's Magazine* of London described wild turkeys in Ohio weighing fifty pounds. The French purchasers of land at Gallipolis, on the Ohio, were told by agents of the Scioto Land Company that candles grew in the swamps of their land and French custard, ready for serving, hung from the trees. (The candles were cattails which, when properly dried, burned with a fitful, smoky light, and the custard was the fruit of the paw-paw tree which even an Indian could not stomach for long.) The French colonists were informed that cotton, tobacco and wheat would be their chief crops and that hogs could fatten on the uncultivated land. Starting with 3,000 sows the colony could count on exporting 30,000 barrels of pork the first season.

John Law's Company in Illinois, which burst loudly as the "Mississippi Bubble," advertised gold and silk as products of the prairies. At one time lead was mined, meagerly, at Peoria, but the only gold ever produced in Illinois was the wagon-loads of yellow corn that creaked to the river landings under the windy skies of October.

Many settlers toiling in the fever-ridden bottoms, lonely in their clearings, where there was not gold or indigo or miraculous plenty of any kind ("We live the same as the Injuns, 'ceptin we take an interest in politics and religion") were disillusioned by a country that did not make good the spoken tales or even the printed promises in the *Emigrant's Guide*. They had to hack the forest and drain the marsh and wait on the future to make it the promised land. But not one following of men—not the thin company of naturalists who entered virgin country where new species grew on every brushy hillside, along every creek bed and in every silent, teeming swamp. Their paradise was waiting. Alert and curious they tramped the country, seeking its wildest groves and thickets, resenting the settlements, wanting to hold back the future in an unspoiled land where the wheel of trade had never turned and the ax had not yet fallen. Their field grew thinner each season, as they watched the buffalo, the wild turkey, the little lacquered parakeets and the clouds of passenger pigeons disappear. But while the wilderness held on, they found their way to its hidden swamps and silent valleys.

Ardent and alone, filling their minds and their specimen sacks with new knowledge, they took their harvest before the first furrows cleaved the new earth. Picture one of them—the homeless Alexander Wilson, floating down the Ohio in his skiff the "Ornithologist," with his tamed parakeet on his shoulder, playing melancholy Scotch airs on his flute but keeping his eyes wary and his fowling-piece at hand to add a new heron to his collection or to bring down a strange hawk from the western sky. When the weather was bad he hunched his bony shoulders in the rain and let the wet winds chill him—his mackintosh covered his specimens and his drawings.

The bleak Scotsman had come a long way from his native Paisley moors, but even longer had been the journey of another homeless scientist—Constantine Rafinesque. The color of Constantinople was in his earliest memory. But that bizarre world faded in the strong fresh colors of the American wilderness. He arrived in the new world half naked and entirely penniless, having been shipwrecked in Long Island Sound. In America he lived like a gypsy, tramping the western country, restless, impulsive, followed by misfortune. He tramped not only on the edge of settlement but also on the borders of knowledge. To his encyclopedic interest the new country was inexhaustible. He gathered fossils from Ohio streambeds, he stuffed the skins of vireos and blackbirds, he dug into Indian mounds, he gathered plants and ferns and mosses unknown in the museums of Europe.

Far to the north, amid the twilit pineries and the birch-barred hills, Henry Rowe Schoolcraft traveled the canoe routes and the portage trails. Around the shores of Lake Superior, through the deep woods of the Chippewa country, he made his journeys, prying into the geology of the gaunt, worn, iron-bearing hills, taking specimens of forest growth and everlastingly jotting down Indian vocabularies for his great dictionary of the Algonquin tongues.

In the same years William H. Keating carried a heavy pack along the riverbeds of Ohio and Indiana. At the edges of the glacial moraine he found prodigal fossils, trilobites, brachiopods. He staggered triumphantly with that growing burden on his shoulders. And with him went Thomas Say, avid for insects, into woods and swamps that were an entomologist's paradise. Happy and insatiable, he tramped the woods and prairies, bottling beetles, wasps and dragonflies. Say and Keating, like good scientists, were curious about many things, even about phrenology, "the new and as yet uncertain science." When they came, on the upper Wabash, to the place where Little Turtle was buried, they grasped at a chance to measure a notable Indian skull. But the Miamis would not let them dig up the great chief's bones. They tramped on to the Wabash marshes.

While the settlements grew, the frontier naturalists hurried to chart and sample their vanishing laboratory. For a little while there were wild swans, cliff swallows, hoot owls and booming prairie hens. The meadows rang with the bubbling call of the bob-o-link, the musical slur of the red-winged blackbird, the swift looping song of the meadow lark, and from the groves came the dusky insistent notes of the whip-poor-will. Clean green hardwood forests stood magnificently beside shaggy swamps of tamarack. Giant catfish swam the rivers, flights of pigeons shadowed the sky, waist-high prairie grasses were daubed with long-stemmed flowers, and quiet sedges, mosses and little lace-like ferns carpeted the creek-banks.

Most of the scientists were poor, struggling, obscure in their life-times. But they left names known around the world, wherever natural history is studied. They too were pioneers, though they cleared no forests and founded no commonwealths.

With all the travelers' tales, fable and fact, lore and legend, the western country grew meaningful in men's minds. The very word "West" came to have a light and lure about it. Destiny loomed beyond the coastal mountains. There was a land of promise. In 1726, with only a few trading stations in the immense forest and the fitful fires of the Indians ringed in gloom, the canny John Ker of Kersland, Ayrshire, read its future in words that still might take our breath away. "It is a great valley, of vast extent, with such a temperate, wholesome climate and wonderful, fruitful soil as to produce anything useful as good if not better than any other country."

Part II

THE WINNING OF THE WEST

IV

The Shadow of the Rock

THE FRENCH in America took up a chain of commanding places. Quebec, Sault Sainte Marie, Detroit, Green Bay, Starved Rock, St. Louis, Vincennes—all were stations beside running water. The strategy was to control the trade and travel of the interior country by dominating the rivers and the straits between the Great Lakes. Some of their posts, like Prairie du Chien and St. Louis, were at the junctions of rivers. Others, like Sault Sainte Marie and Detroit, guarded the narrow waters that link the lakes into one continuous seaway. Still others, like Starved Rock on the Illinois, occupied high ground, upthrust from the woods and the water, dominating the wilderness for leagues around.

The most dramatic was the rock of Quebec, rising above the tidal sweep of the St. Lawrence. Between the broad channel of the river and the somber lines of the Laurentian Hills, the great gray rock is a feature that seems inevitable. The austere St. Lawrence, leading straight into the heart of the continent, calls for a landmark, a dominating height, bold enough to hold an army at bay, big enough to support a citadel and a city. If the Rock were not there the geography of the valley would seem unfinished.

The French entered the St. Lawrence portal with dreams of an empire. The Rock became a symbol of their dreams. Inevitably they made it the seat of their government and the starting place of their expeditions. Quebec in Algonquin means "the place where you go back," but it was the place whence the French went forward to the wilds. In its sheer mass the Rock stood up 330 feet from the cold St. Lawrence tides to the height of Cape Diamond. It cast a shadow all the way to the Mississippi.

At the foot of the Rock French ships stood at the quay. French

49

seamen with flashing teeth and brass rings in their ears strolled
the streets of the lower town in their rolling, salt-water step. They
devoured the crusty loaves of Quebec bakers and gulped warming
brandy. They sang old Norman songs of a sweetheart's Sunday ribbons, of gay roses in May. Down by the quayside, where birch
canoes bobbed against the hulls of French merchantmen, a circle of
Indians squatted about a fire. They boiled Indian corn, or Turkey
wheat as the French sailors called it, over guttering faggots of
pine, with a whole fish thrown in the pot to give it flavor. The
French stared at the brown-skinned Hurons and the blanketed
Chippewas. The savages stared back. Under the timeless Rock
the Old World was meeting the New.

High on the Rock, far above the topmasts of the tall French
ships, the leaded windows of Chateau St. Louis looked over the
dim forests and the fading hills. Here, within massive walls on
the brink of the precipice, sat a succession of governors—Cham-
plain, Montmagny, Courcelle, Frontenac, de la Barre, de Brisay,
Galiconniere, La Jonquiere, Duquesne, Vaudreuil. They sent their
young men out to live with the savage tribes, to learn Indian languages, to win the confidence of scattered chiefs, to map rivers and
portage paths of the unknown country. On their Rock, the governors received reports from the distant forests and sometimes they
entertained a half-clothed Ottawa or Winnebago tribesman and
heard a savage's own description of the beaver and the whitefish,
the lead and copper that made the West so rich a country. They
planned expeditions to awe the Indians and frighten the Spaniards
and the British. They mapped an enlarging web of trade routes,
by which canoe caravans should converge over many western
waters to the St. Lawrence quays and warehouses. From their
aloof citadel the French governors swayed the tribes as far away
as Minnesota and drew the commerce on the Ohio, the Mississippi
and the great, linked, westward-leading lakes.

Beside the power of the governors, there was the grace of the
Church. Above the St. Lawrence, on the gray height of Quebec
and the green height of Mount Royal, stood the New World homes

of the orders—Jesuit, Sulpitian, Recollect. There the mass was said in dim chapels with candles swaying, and there was kindled a flame of evangelism that carried the Cross to savages in the gloom of the woods and beside the rivers a thousand miles away. The missionaries traveled beside the traders and the two great incentives of men—to impart a doctrine and to push a profitable trade— were at work together. Sometimes the missionaries led the way. They learned a new Algonquin dialect and built their log chapel in the forest. Then the traders came with cheap French knives and burning brandy. Now, three hundred years later, they seem a strange company. Here were the brutal young Etienne Brulé and the gentle Rene Ménard. Both found the way into new country and both died among the Hurons in the wilderness. But one was a dissolute renegade who was killed in a quarrel over an Indian woman and the other was lost in the forests of Wisconsin when he set out to baptize a starving band of Indians.

Nicolas Perrot and Claude Allouez were both short men with muscles as tough as the roots of juniper. Both won great influence with the savages. They traveled a far country, carrying the enterprises of France. But one gathered peltry and the other saved souls. Thousands of Fox, Winnebago, Illinois and Miami tribesmen came to trade with the eloquent little merchant on the western rivers. Other thousands heard the blunt and earnest priest read the rituals of baptism and absolution. La Salle and Marquette were two well-born men who might have lived in luxury in France. But they chose the hard life of the wilderness and they marked out new domains for French trade and French doctrine. After epic toils and hardships both died in a savage country which they had made their own.

Of the two undertakings the worldly one fared better. An endless stream of peltry went in canoe caravans to the French ships waiting at Montreal, Three Rivers and Quebec, while the priests toiled over the portages with altars strapped to their backs, distributing to Indian children colored pictures of the saints. The missionaries suffered loneliness, privation and sometimes death, all for the uncertain purpose of explaining the doctrine of the Trinity to warriors with painted faces. The traders accepted the savage life —they wore moccasins and buckskin clothing and were not above mating with Indian women. But the missionaries were "black robes." Their heavy skirts filled with burrs and were torn by thorns and briars. In their minds they remained aloof, reading their breviaries by firelight, translating the Testament into tortured phrases of Algonquin, reflecting amid the noise and smell of a hunting camp on the grace of the Immaculate Mary. So they carried the gospel throughout the whole Northwest. They could count hunger, hazard and hardship a joy if a few heathen could be won for a heavenly future. *I was the more delighted . . . since I found myself in the blessed necessity of exposing my life for the salvation of these peoples.* The passing of time, and of the Indian nations they sought to save, has not dimmed the record of their long adventure in the wilderness.

The pity is that the ardor and devotion of the missionaries could accomplish so little against the long past of savagery and superstition. Often they won the trust and even the affection of the Indians. Sometimes they gained verbal adherence to their gospel. But they left the dark minds of their charges little changed. Their consolation came with baptizing savages, yet "an Indian would be baptized ten times a day for a pint of brandy or a pound of tobacco," as Parkman observed, and a warrior wore a crucifix as vainly as a necklace made of the dried forefingers of his enemies. At best they planted an alien superstition amid the fears and fetiches of heathen mythology.

At Green Bay, as Fathers Dablon and Allouez preached to the half-clothed Indians on the forgiveness of sins, a file of warriors, aping the guard they had seen outside the French governor's tent at Montreal, tramped back and forth with rigid steps and solemn countenances. At that childish mockery the two priests could hardly keep from laughing in the midst of their discourse on hell, demons and eternal flames. Afterward, when Allouez showed the Mascoutins his crucifix, they threw powdered tobacco on it as an offering. When he explained the Sign of the Cross, they all daubed themselves with crosses and went noisily to war.

So the Cross became war medicine and the patient priests plodded on to new tribes—"perhaps more tractable than those we have hitherto known, amongst whom, so far, it has been found impossible to produce any result." Hope led them through boiling rapids and over rocky portage trails, and at the next village they gave gifts of glass beads, French knives and hatchets, bribing the tribesmen to hear the articles of Christian faith—"but oh, my God, what ideas and ways contrary to the gospel these poor people have!"

They had to take their comfort from small triumphs, such as the baptizing of a dying child. "I gave baptism to several sick children, having the consolation of seeing one of these, some time afterward, leave the Church Militant to enter the Church Triumphant, there to sing eternally the mercies of God, and to be an advocate for the conversion of the people of his nation." And they had to withstand disappointment and frustration again and again. When Marquette came to an Indian town on the Wisconsin River, he was delighted to see a cross planted in its midst. But when he drew near his worn face was troubled. The naked Cross of Calvary, symbolizing the remission of sins, the Indians had hung with dressed deerskins, leather girdles, and bows and arrows as an offering to the Great Manitou of the French. Instead of a remission of sins, the missionaries had brought them one more uneasy god to placate.

In those years the mind of Christian Europe met the mind of savagery in the reeking Winnebago huts and the rude bark chapels. Allouez explained to the Wisconsin Indians "the principal articles of our Faith, the law and commandments of God, the rewards promised to those that shall obey Him, and the punishment prepared by Him for those that shall not obey Him." The Winnebagos listened politely and in return told Allouez their beliefs. They explained, earnest as any missionary, how "the Great Hare Ouisaketchak created the earth, and how the vast sea of Lake

Superior was made by beavers whose dam the Great Hare trod down in anger, so now there is the swift water pouring through the rapids that the French named Sault Sainte Marie." The Great Hare, they said, while chasing a beaver in Lake Superior, crossed Whitefish Bay in a single stride. The beavers, frightened by so mighty an enemy, fled up the rivers to the North Sea, intending to cross the wide water to France. But finding the sea bitter with salt, they turned back and spread throughout the rivers and lakes of America. "And that is the reason why there are no beavers in France, and the French come to get them here." Thus instructed, the missionaries went on among the tribes. Their doctrine had to contend with heathen mythology while the wind cried in the pine branches and the candles quaked on their rude altars. Vainly they wished that the savages could see the magnificence of the churches of France, where the incense burned on the high altar and the candles gleamed against crosses of pure gold.

The traders had a simpler traffic and a more successful one. They brought out their cargoes of knives and guns, traps and blankets and brandy, and they took back to the St. Lawrence baled peltry worth a hundred times the cost of their trade goods. It was a far-flung trade over many routes and with many Indian stations, and with its promise of fortune and adventure it lured such men as Nicolas Perrot, Daniel de Greysolon Sieur Duluth, the iron-handed and iron-willed Tonty, and the austere, empire-dreaming Rene Robert Cavelier, Sieur de La Salle.

La Salle was the greatest of the traders. He was the explorer who knew the vacant rivers and the vast silence of the interior, and the merchant who did most to erect a dominion of French trade in the Northwest. From the beginning, he had great dreams—and was mocked by men and fate. Yet he emerges, as his companion and lieutenant Tonty said of him, as "one of the greatest men of this age." The man for whom La Chine was named in derision had no humor and no scorn, and yet, failing to achieve a single one of his ambitions, he mocked his deriders by twenty years of imperial undertaking.

La Salle was the son of a rich merchant of Rouen. As a youth in France he studied for the priesthood in the Society of Jesus, but he never took orders. He needed a lonelier, more willful life than the church and a more wordly ambition than the saving of souls. He could never have submerged his individuality in the great Jesuit order. He had to create his own aspirations and shape his own campaigns. As a youth he seems to have realized his mature character—he had no love of pleasure and little taste for the enjoyments of society. Instead, he was driven by a deep and lonely ambition, a hunger for action and achievement, a need to defy difficulties and hardships. He was a man cut out for the imperial enterprises of New France.

In the spring of 1666, at the age of twenty-three, he came to Canada. Soon he was granted a tract of land on the St. Lawrence between the rapids named La Chine and the growing port of Montreal. On that estate he became a feudal proprietor and there he had two things needful to his character—solitude and power. But more than these, or along with them, he needed also struggle, hazard and far-reaching endeavors.

On his domain of three thousand acres, with the St. Lawrence always hurrying through the rapids, La Salle's thoughts went as urgently to the dark interior country. Immediately he began the study of Indian languages, tutoring with veteran voyageurs from Georgian Bay and trying the uncouth phrases on tribesmen who wandered down the river. He made occasional tentative journeys into the northern forests, like a runner practicing on the starting blocks, and there he essayed the native dialects with Indian paddlers and hunting parties squatting about a pitchpine fire. On those brief practice missions he was a man unlike the French who had gone before him. Radisson and Groseilliers were woods-rangers with wary eyes and faces burned dark by wind and weather. Their buckskin clothing smelled of fish and smoke and balsam boughs, their moccasins were caked with mud from the portages. Father Allouez donned his black robe over the powerful shoulders of a canoeman and his hands were hard as leather—often his long gown was charred with a campfire's ash and beaded with the tenacious little burrs of the underbrush.

Unlike these La Salle, in all his years in the wilderness, retained the garb of aristocracy, wearing his flaring coat crossed with sashes, his wide-brimmed hat and polished knee boots. He looked as alien to the forest as the flag of France he carried, with its white field and golden lilies. But he was no less a man of the woods for that. His mind burrowed like a muskrat into the lore of the forest, his body hardened to the demands of distant trails, and he learned the red man's nature as thoroughly as any European who had ever felt the wilderness close in upon him. After three years he had mastered eight Indian languages and had learned from a roving band of Senecas of a river called the O-hy-o. With that equipment and that incentive, he was ready to begin his claim on history.

No white man had ever seen the O-hy-o country. From the Senecas' reports La Salle surmised that the river flowed to the coast of California and would provide a route to China. He sold his La Chine estate, outfitted his expedition and set forth, in the summer of 1669, with a party of Sulpitian paddlers. Altogether they were twenty-four men in seven canoes. On the south shore of Lake Ontario they were entertained in a filthy Seneca village where children brought them pumpkins and berries and the Indian women kept their pots filled with roast dog-flesh and boiled corn seasoned with sunflower seed. But when the visitors saw an Indian prisoner tortured, killed and eaten, and when the Senecas celebrated the feast with a frenzy of drunkenness, the Frenchmen became uneasy. They could find no Seneca who would lead them to the Ohio, so under guidance of an Iroquois hunter they coasted the Ontario shore, passed the mouth of the Niagara and the distant thunder of the solemn falls, and came to the Iroquois town at the western end of Lake Ontario. Here occurred one of the surprising meetings which repeatedly took place among the French wanderers in the interior country.

As Duluth found Father Hennepin a prisoner of the Sioux in the gloom of the Minnesota woods, a dozen years later, La Salle at the Iroquois town of Otinawatawa found a young Frenchman who was already a veteran fur-trader in the Huron country. His name was Louis Joliet. La Salle was an aristocrat of Rouen and Joliet was the son of a wagon-maker in Quebec. But they met on common ground. Both were in their middle twenties, with ardent dreams of adventure. Both had studied for the priesthood and abandoned that calling for the life of wilderness trade and exploration. When Joliet produced his map of the upper lakes and spoke of the heathen tribes of that country, the Sulpitian missionaries in La Salle's small company abandoned their plan of seeking the Ohio River and set out for the western lakes.

La Salle had determined to find the Ohio, and he was never a man to surrender a purpose he had fixed upon. Perhaps he welcomed an opportunity to divorce his own expedition from the mission of the Sulpitians—he could never share an undertaking but always had to dominate it. At any rate, he feigned illness—his companions said it was induced by the sight of three large rattlesnakes gliding across a rock—and so urged the priests to go on without him. Left to his own purpose, he turned resolutely toward the headwaters of the Ohio. The dream of a passage to China leaped up again in his mind.

For two years La Salle explored country that no man from Europe had ever seen. His maps and journals disappeared before they were transcribed and so his achievement remains clouded, but historians agree that he descended the Ohio to the falls, at the future site of Louisville. There his men deserted him—as other followers were to do at other critical points in his career—and in the winter and spring of 1670, the solitary La Salle made the long journey home. But he had no home. His land on the St. Lawrence was in other hands and another man sat in his manor house. He was now a wilderness man and for the rest of his life he would have no home but forest camps and the rude stockades that he built beside the rivers.

Back in Canada, he joined a hunting party of Iroquois on the Ottawa River. There, to see the northern country that Joliet had

described, he embarked on Lake Erie, ascended the Detroit River
to Lake Huron and followed its western shore to Michilimackinac.
From that commanding strait he journeyed south over the mysterious reaches of Lake Michigan and made a prairie portage to
the Illinois River. Thus from both the east and the north he had
entered the great basin that, a century later, was designated by
the infant United States Congress as the Northwest Territory.

Having seen the immense forests of the Ohio and the broad
prairies of the Mississippi, La Salle formulated his life's ambition.
He would establish French civilization in the rich country between the two rivers. He would begin by systematizing and enlarging the fur trade, using cargo vessels on the lakes, erecting fur
depots on the rivers, establishing a chain of warehouses and magazines. It was a bold undertaking that looked to the protection of
French interests all the way from the mouth of the Mississippi to
the Great Lakes and the establishing of stations of prestige and
power at a dozen strategic points. Fortunately, there came to
Quebec at this time a new governor—a bold and ambitious man
who quickly recognized in La Salle's dream his own vision of the
power and prosperity of New France. He was Louis de Buade,
Comte de Frontenac.

Better than most of the governors on the Rock, Frontenac
grasped the extent of the interior and its promise of riches for
France. Westward in the Ottawa country stretched the dim forests
of Chateauguay and Beauharnois. Below the wide waters of Lake
Ontario stood the forests of the Five Nations. And beyond lay
leagues of dark land and shining waters all the way to the sunlit
prairies of the Mississippi. Many nations lived there—Eries, Miamis,
Shawnees, Kickapoos, Potawatomis, Foxes, Sacs, Winnebagos,
Ottawas, Chippewas. The Miamis harvested corn in the clearings
of Ohio and tilled their little fields in the Wabash bottoms. The
Sacs had their chief village on the Mississippi, the Ottawas camped
at the Straits of Mackinac and the Chippewas gathered every
spring and autumn to spear whitefish where the St. Marys rapids
poured out of Lake Superior. A fur post stood at the Soo, the gate-

way to northern "Gitchee Gumee," where the fleets paddled in with furs from the Lake of the Woods and Pigeon River. Another post was at Michilimackinac, the gateway to the west. The first post at the Straits was not on the turtle-shaped island but at Point St. Ignace, on the northern shore. To that shore, over the spaces of Lake Michigan, came canoe caravans from the south and west. By day the green point lifted above the radiant water; at night a canoeman was guided in by the flickering of campfires and the throbbing of wabeno drums.

Across Lake Michigan, Green Bay thrust its long arm into the Winnebago country. From that bay the rivers led inland—the Menominee and Peshtigo into the pine woods and the old worn ridges of the Upper Peninsula, the Wolf River into the gloom of hemlock swamps, the Fox River through grassy swales and swamps of wild rice and wild celery. From the southern end of Lake Michigan the prairie rivers led over the level lands. Where the St. Joseph and Des Plaines diminished, the Illinois River rose and wandered toward the Mississippi. To all this country only the black-robed priests and the buckskin-clothed *coureurs de bois* had come; it was known to no others. These two companies passed through without changing it, leaving it wilderness. The few marks they put upon it were soon obscured. On the northern rivers were markers at the rapids—a rude cross set up by a pious priest and a red cap hung on it by a rollicking voyageur—to warn canoemen of treacherous water. The cross was undressed fir logs, dark as the forest, and the red wool cap, warmed by summer sun and wet with rain and snow, at last blended into the thickets, faded and shapeless as lichen on a trunk of hemlock.

It was a dimly comprehended country, but La Salle saw it more clearly than any man of his age. He made the restless Frontenac envision it like a panorama from the Rock above the St. Lawrence. And he made the ambitious governor grasp his program of a commercial empire with French goods going systematically to the strategic posts and the fur caravans drawing in over the great web of rivers to the broad sea lanes of the Lakes. Together they drew up a design of occupation, fortification and settlement. As a first step, they built Fort Frontenac on the north shore of Lake Ontario at the site of the present Kingston, and La Salle was placed in command. There he launched two small sailing vessels on Lake Ontario and soon he conducted a brisk trade in peltry and supplies between Niagara and Fort Frontenac. When he counted profits of 25,000 livres a year, he was on his way to wealth. A week's journey from the nearest St. Lawrence settlement, again he had solitude and authority. But he also had unresting ambitions and a memory of distant trails. He needed enterprise and action.

So he went to France, in 1677, to seek authority to erect forts deep in the interior and to carry on trade with the western tribes. In Paris, he won the consent of the King's Minister, and then, needing money to carry out his plans, he persuaded wealthy relatives to lend him, at 40 per cent interest, the sums required. While in Paris he met an Italian army officer, Henri de Tonty, who was quickly fired by La Salle's accounts of America. Tonty had lost a hand in the Sicilian wars and he wore from his wrist an iron hook, which later made him talked about in all the Indian villages of Illinois. To the tribes he became "the man with the iron hand," and to La Salle he became the one completely loyal lieutenant ever to serve him. Now, in his quiet lodgings in Rue de la Truanderie, La Salle described the Illinois prairies and the Great Lakes ringed in forests. As he talked, the clack of horses' hoofs on the Paris streets grew dim and the silence of a wilderness country stole around them. Tonty's dark eyes burned in the lamplight. When La Salle offered him a share in his enterprise, Tonty was ready. In the summer of 1678, they sailed together for Canada. When they reached Quebec, Louis Hennepin, in his peaked hood and coarse gray robe, was there to meet them.

Hennepin was a monk badly bitten by the wanderlust. A few years before, he had eagerly sought from his French superiors an assignment in Canada, the most adventurous of the missions. Arrived in the new country, he was delighted at being sent to the remote post of Fort Frontenac. From there he first tasted wilderness travel, visiting Indian settlements in the forests above Lake Ontario. He paddled a canoe in summer and in the frozen months he tramped the woods on snowshoes, with a blanket strapped to his back. Secretly, like La Salle, he nursed his own schemes—not a design of evangelism but one of discovery and exploration. He wanted to penetrate the northwestern country where no European had ever been. Though the cord of St. Francis bound his waist, he was not a spiritual man. But he was a man of spirit. He was a dreamer, a deceiver, a man of vanity and willfulness, but he carried the excitement of discovery in him and he was unacquainted with fear.

As a part of his design of an efficient fur trade, La Salle planned to build a cargo vessel on the lakes. Previously, the peltry had come over many hundreds of miles of waterway in the slow and laborious caravans of canoes. Now he designed a vessel with billowing sails and a capacious hold, and he pictured it crammed to the hatches with baled beaver skins. Sending a brigade of men into the distant Lake Michigan country to gather furs from the Indians, La Salle dispatched his agent, La Motte de Lissiere, with Hennepin and a crew of shipbuilders to Niagara, where they began construction of a stockade. La Salle and Tonty joined them, two months later, and La Salle led the party around the thunderous falls of the Niagara to the mouth of Cayuga Creek. There, near the open waters of Lake Erie, he built his vessel.

It was mid-winter when the work began and progress was impeded by many hardships and setbacks. But one by one the timbers were laid and the frame took outline. Through the bright summer weeks of 1679, the clatter of hammers and the thudding of adze and ax sounded above the quiet creek. When the craft was finished, it lay portentous on the water and the Senecas stared at it sullenly from the shore. It was a two-masted vessel with mainsails and topsails. Above the cargo deck reared a raised poop, where La Salle could pace with his thoughts. From the prow sprang a silhouetted griffon, taken from the arms of Count Frontenac, and the stern was emblazoned with a spread-winged eagle.

The vessel was sixty feet long, of forty-five tons' burden; five cannon muzzles pointed from her portholes. This was the *Griffon*, the first ship ever to breast the empty water of the lakes beyond Ontario.

On August 7, 1679, with a salute from her cannon and a fresh breeze in her sails, the *Griffon* steered into Lake Erie. Father Hennepin was already busy recording wind and weather, the aspect of the Erie water and the Erie shores, in the journal he would one day embellish for credulous readers. On the quarter-deck, La Salle stood staring into the west, with all his dreams before him. It was an auspicious beginning. No one could have guessed that the *Griffon* would never bring a cargo home.

They passed through Lake Erie in three fine days, and stopped on the Detroit River for a day's hunting, on the site of the mile-long motor factories of River Rouge. There they picked up Tonty, who had returned from Lake Michigan where he had supervised La Salle's advance brigade of traders. With their bulkheads hung with game, they sailed on across the serene expanse of Lake St. Clair and between the low banks of the St. Clair River. The wind failed and La Salle sent his men ashore with towropes. Hour after hour they toiled with bent backs and rope-scarred hands. It was not a lordly passage but it got them through the river. Finally, in the slanting light of the August day, the *Griffon* passed the Port Huron entrance, where now the Blue Water Bridge arches over the commerce of the age of steel, and sailed out upon the blue breast of Lake Huron.

But their troubles were not ended. For a day they were becalmed. Then off Saginaw Bay they were beset by a sudden storm that tossed the ship like a bark canoe. First they were afraid the waves would drive her on the land. But the *Griffon* was well built and, despite the shabby reputation of her pilot, she must have been well handled. When the storm passed, the ship was pitching in the short steep seas with her bare masts tracing the wind-streaked sky, and the men crossed themselves in gratitude. They got sail on her and a fair wind carried them past the birch-barred shores of Bois Blanc Island and through the gleaming Straits of Mackinac. From their wigwams the Chippewas stared in wonder.

They put in at the harbor of St. Ignace, where La Salle was greeted by the Jesuits and traders who were secretly jealous and fearful of him. Hundreds of Huron canoes circled the "floating fort" with the flag of France at her jackstaff and the cannon muzzles showing in her sides. At St. Ignace, La Salle found several of his advance brigade of traders. They had disobeyed his orders, squandering the goods entrusted to them and trading on their own account. The voyage of the *Griffon* was becoming clouded.

Leaving Tonty to recruit a new brigade of men, La Salle set sail across Lake Michigan for Green Bay where some of his loyal traders had collected a large quantity of peltry. Back at Montreal, his creditors were impatient. To satisfy their claims, La Salle dispatched the *Griffon* back to Niagara laden with beaver skins, while he remained in the West. On September eighteenth, in charge of her surly pilot, the vessel sailed out of Green Bay. La Salle watched her diminish and disappear over the polished waters of Lake Michigan. He never saw his ship again. That night a storm swept over the lake, and the *Griffon* never was sighted in the Straits of Mackinac. For months La Salle knew nothing of her fate—indeed, no man ever knew how or where the *Griffon* came to grief.

Unmindful of his loss, La Salle took his party in canoes down the western shore of Lake Michigan. It was a long, arduous and hungry journey, complicated by autumn storms and the failure of provisions. Past the site of Milwaukee they paddled, nibbling a precious handful of Indian corn and finding at last the body of a deer partly devoured by wolves. Onward they pushed, around the southern shore of the lake to the mouth of the St. Joseph River (then called the Miami) in Indiana. Here, driving his sullen men to their labor, La Salle built Fort Miami, near the center of the present city of St. Joseph, and awaited the arrival of the *Griffon* on her second voyage from Niagara, and of Tonty who was bringing a party of men down the east shore of Lake Michigan from Mackinac. When Tonty at last appeared, late in November, he brought no word of the *Griffon*. Anxiously La Salle stared over the wintry water. He sent two men the long way back to St. Ignace to meet the vessel, if she should appear. Then he led his party up the ice-edged St. Joseph.

At the "south bend," where South Bend, Indiana, now occupies both sides of the river, he found the old Indian portage trail to the Kankakee. Today a paved highway, called Portage Avenue, follows that vanished trail. It leads through the pretty Riverview Cemetery and across a pleasing landscape. But La Salle's men, toiling under their portage loads, crossed a desolate prairie blackened by grass fires which the Indians had kindled. At last they splashed through the half-frozen Kankakee marshes and launched their craft in the shallow river. Christmas found them nearing the Illinois River. On the first day of January, 1680, they reached the chief town of the Illinois tribe beside the abrupt, forest-fringed height called Starved Rock. But the town was empty—the entire village had gone off on their winter hunt.

That bitter winter began La Salle's grim fortunes in the country of the Illinois. He carried in his mind his unyielding designs, but failure haunted and followed him. He dispatched his men like a strategist, to make alliances with the Indians, to set up trading stations, to erect posts at important points. He sent men out on foot to carry word from one remote station to another. He arranged rendezvous, months distant and hundreds of miles away, in that lonely country. In the branch of a tree at the junction of the Illinois River and the Mississippi he left a letter for Tonty. He sent two men to "make a circuit of Lake Michigan"—more than a thousand miles of shore line—to poke into every cove and bay and rivermouth and to scan every mile of silent sea beach in the meager hope of finding some remains of the *Griffon*.

It took a tenacious purpose to defy all the distance and darkness of that western country. In all the state of Illinois a few white men read signs of each other at the portages and they met, after months of separation, in their rude stockades. La Salle shrank from no hardship or exertion, demanding an iron endurance from himself and from his men. Though the French had traditionally depended on water routes in the new country, he had learned from the Iroquois the strategy of long swift marches over land. He was willing to go anywhere, any distance, at any season. If his men failed him, he would go alone.

In the early days of January, 1680, he paddled on down the Illinois to the broadening of the river at Lake Peoria. There he found another village. This time he faced an alarmed and wary band of warriors. La Salle assured them that he wanted only to carry on a peaceful trade. He explained his plan to build here a "great wooden canoe" which would go down the Mississippi and return with guns and traps and blankets for the Illinois villages. The warriors were satisfied. But two days later half of his shipbuilders deserted across the prairies.

Undismayed, La Salle set the remainder of his men to work, building the stockaded Fort Crevecoeur on high ground at the western end of the lake and hewing ship's timbers at the water's edge. He sent Hennepin downstream to explore the mouth of the Illinois. That errand became both legend and history. At the mouth of the Illinois Hennepin was captured by a party of Sioux and carried a thousand miles up the Mississippi. Finally, in the woods of Minnesota, he was rescued by Duluth and so he returned to France and wrote his partly fabricated *Description of Louisiana*. Meanwhile, back at Lake Peoria, La Salle saw the keel laid for his projected vessel. With the *Griffon* he had lost the sails and shrouds and anchors with which he had expected to equip his new craft. Now with the abandoning of all hope for the *Griffon*, he must return to Fort Frontenac to secure new supplies. So, leaving Tonty in charge of Fort Crevecoeur, he set out on that long journey. While the prairies were still white with winter, he passed through Illinois and southern Michigan, toiling through woods, wading rivers swollen by melting snow. Three of his companions fell ill before they reached the Lake Erie shore. There La Salle made a crude canoe and paddled toward the distant Niagara. After sixty-five days of danger, toil and privation, he entered the timbered gates of Fort Frontenac. It was the end of one of the most arduous journeys ever made.

He found more bad news waiting. In his absence his creditors had taken possession of his property. His agents had plundered him, and a laden caravan of his canoes had been lost in the La Chine rapids. Before he could reassemble his resources he had disheartening word from Tonty in far-off Illinois. His men had mutinied, destroyed Fort Crevecoeur and vanished over the prairies. But unfortunately they reappeared, and to La Salle came a further installment of calamity—the deserters had destroyed his fort on the St. Joseph, seized furs belonging to him at Mackinac and plundered his post at Niagara.

This is the way things went for La Salle. Added to the hostility of nature and the jealousy of French traders and missionaries, he had repeatedly to struggle against his own men. Nowhere do the voyageurs appear less admirable than in La Salle's service. Under other leaders they were robust, hearty, unwashed men. They were Frenchmen revitalized by the wilderness—somehow in them was restored a primitive zest long disappeared from Europe. The New World, empty and adventurous, beautiful and vast, gave them a new youth, a new boldness, a new and carefree heart. They had a great craving for brandy and tobacco, for Indian women and a rich pot of Indian stew. Jauntily they wore their Indian clothing. They ate prodigiously when they could—and they starved in silence. They carried staggering loads over rough portage trails; they paddled sixty, seventy, eighty miles a day. They lived in the solitudes hilariously, singing, laughing, telling stories—and always La Salle, in their midst, was a man on a cliff, staring into new country. He had no gift for living with them and so he could not lead them. His iron will drove them and estranged them and made them mutineers. They assassinated him at last.

But before that, he had a few more journeys to make. Now he left Fort Frontenac and voyaged up the lakes to Michilimackinac. There to his great joy he found Tonty, whom he feared dead at the hands of his rebellious men, and together they led a new party southward through Lake Michigan. This time they took the shorter route to the Illinois, making the portage from the Chicago River to the Des Plaines. It was mid winter and they hauled their canoes on sleds across the frozen flats and down the ice-covered Illinois River to Peoria, where they found open water. There was no cause to linger there. On the hill stood the ruins of Fort Crevecoeur and along the shore were the ruined lodges of the Illinois who had been massacred by a warring band of Iroquois. So they pushed on between the leafless willow fringes and, early in February, they entered the mile-wide current of the Mississippi. For two months they journeyed southward, while winter forsook the land, until at last between the marshy bayou shores the tide came in and they breathed the sea-keen air. They were at the mouth of the river, where waters born in the ice-locked lakes of Minnesota flowed into the warm, slow-heaving Gulf. There on the ninth of April, 1682, La Salle claimed possession of the entire valley in the name of the King of France, christening it Louisiana.

He had this hour of achievement, but he was still a man in debt and hated by his rivals. To establish himself commercially in the West, he still had to erect his projected station on the Illinois River —a station strong enough to provide a military bulwark against the marauding Iroquois and to draw the trade of the western tribes. The fort at Peoria was ruined. Now he planned a new post on Starved Rock, a bold height jutting above the Illinois seventy miles above Lake Peoria. On the flat top of the bluff, an acre in extent, he felled oak and maple trees, hewed out his timbers and built the stockade of Fort St. Louis. Across the river lay a populous town of the Illinois and around the foot of the bluff ranged the camps of visiting parties of Kickapoos, Potawatomis and Miamis. This was a natural location for a stronghold and a trading depot, and from the high rock La Salle renewed his dream of dominance in that country.

But no sooner was Fort St. Louis completed than a new crisis faced him. Count Frontenac was recalled to France and his successor at Quebec, Antoine Joseph De La Barre, was promptly swayed by La Salle's enemies. Soon La Salle felt the blow. His supplies were cut off, destructive reports of his activities were sent to France and he was relieved of the command of the post he had erected on Starved Rock.

La Salle's only course was to represent his own cause in Paris. Leaving Tonty in charge of Fort St. Louis, he set out for the St. Lawrence, on his way to France. Tonty never saw his leader again.

Though he could not win the loyalty of his own countrymen, La Salle had unfailing influence with the Indians. His austerity, the aloofness that kept him from a comradeship with his voyageurs, his sternness, silence and reserve appealed to the savages. They found him a chieflike man and some of them were doglike in their devotion to him. One of these was the Shawanoe hunter Nika, who followed him to Canada and to France—and back again to America on the leader's last expedition. He was killed by La Salle's own French assassins.

Now, in 1684, back in Paris, La Salle took the moccasined Nika with him on his visits to his patrons. Then, leaving the Shawanoe in his old lodgings in Rue de la Truanderie, he greased his boots and brushed his cloak and went on a final errand alone. While Nika stared out at the carts and wagons in the cobbled street, La Salle was shown into the presence of the great Louis. It was a heartening interview. The king granted more than La Salle asked, to fortify the Mississippi and secure French trade throughout the valley. That night he dreamed of his chain of forts between the Mississippi delta and the Great Lakes. Despite years of humiliation and defeat, he was young and ardent again.

With a new expedition, he sailed in high hope for the Gulf of Mexico. But his hope was not to be fulfilled. There remained a few seasons of confusion and strife, of sporadic colonization on the Gulf coast and of wandering search for the Mississippi. Twice he set out for the north, to reestablish contact with his men in Illinois and his colleagues in Canada. Each time discord among his followers defeated him. At last, in the wastes of Texas, far from the

Northwest that he had envisioned as an empire for France, he was shot by his own quarreling and rebellious men.

Months later, at Starved Rock, Tonty heard of the death of his leader. Tonty remained on the Rock above the Illinois, but the great dream had faded. Though the ensuing years saw scattered new trading posts and mission stations—at Chicago and St. Joseph, at Detroit, Cahokia and Vincennes—there was no bold design of a French civilization encompassing the whole interior country. Never again did the French governors on the Rock at Quebec see so clearly the outlines of a western empire.

V

Pack-horse Man

WHAT THE CANOE was to the French the pack pony was to the English, who had to cross a chain of mountains before they could reach the trading posts of the Ohio country. In the lush pasture lands of Pennsylvania the German and Scotch-Irish farmers bred fine horses—too fine for the rough mountain trails that led into the West. But a new country evolves its own means of transport. These fine Pennsylvania breeds crossed with Spanish pintos from the Southwest produced the hardy, trail-wise, uncomplaining pack horse that carried the first commerce over the Appalachians.

The French had access to the western country by means of lakes and rivers, and all their military and commercial strategy was based on communications by water. Water washed the naked cliff of Quebec, the bright lake currents girdled Michilimackinac, Sault Sainte Marie was a name for rushing water and all their farthest posts were erected above the moving rivers. But the English had to cross a tumbled mountain system, ridge beyond ridge, into the West. They found their way to Ohio by narrow Indian trails, threading the forest gloom and twisting up the mountains. From New York state to the Carolinas they followed rugged paths that converged on the up-curving Ohio River. The short route led through Pennsylvania. So Harrisburg became the provisioning place for a traffic that followed the ancient Nemacolin and Kittanning paths over the mounting Allegheny ridges and came down at last to the valley of the Ohio.

British trade in the West was never an instrument of empire. It had no headquarters like the compounds at Montreal and no capitol like the rock-rooted fortress at Quebec. It had no seasonal rhythm like the canoe caravans coming down the rivers on the spring race of water to the tall ships above the quaysides loading their pyramids of peltry. It had no trace of the pageantry of black-robed priests visioning by their campfires in the forest a new empire for the Church, and no imperial plan of feudal seigniories and savage nations submissive to the rule of the Rock. The British trade was sporadic, individual and motivated by simple greed. When forty dollars' worth of trade goods would secure a thousand dollars' worth of peltry, there was incentive enough to bring pack trains to Ohio.

During the hundred years of French dominance, the main trade routes to the Northwest shifted steadily eastward while retaining a commercial hold on the St. Lawrence and Mississippi systems. The first commercial route between the Lakes and the Mississippi was that of the Fox and Wisconsin rivers. In LaSalle's operations the dominant routes became the Chicago-Des Plaines and the St. Joseph-Kankakee approaches to the Illinois River. After 1700, the most important trade followed the Maumee and Wabash rivers, which connected Lake Erie with the Ohio River and so maintained the unbroken water route (except for the inevitable portage) between the Gulf of St. Lawrence and the Gulf of Mexico. And while the French trade was shifting eastward, the British were pressing over the mountains to dispute the control of the forest commerce.

By the middle of the eighteenth century the British had an extensive trans-Allegheny trade. Each season three hundred traders led their pack trains over the Pennsylvania paths. From Chautauqua Creek, at the headwaters of the Ohio River, to the mouth of the Great Miami—site of present-day Cincinnati—the English trailmen were to be found in every Indian village. They were equally established on the bays and rivermouths of Lake Erie. As their commerce grew, they set up warehouses where furs were assembled from scattered points. The first of these depots was at Logstown, a Shawnee village on the Ohio eighteen miles below the site of present Pittsburgh. This became the earliest center of

English trade in the Northwest. Another depot was set up at Pick-awillany, or Twightwee Town, as the English called it—a Miami settlement in southwestern Ohio. Though not on water, this was a strategic location, lying in an excellent hunting country at the center of trails which radiated to the Ohio River, Lake Erie and the Wabash. A third warehouse was established in central Ohio at Conchake, a Wyandot village on the site now occupied by the town of Coshocton. When the Miamis committed themselves to an English alliance, the English trade was established as far west as the Wabash. Then they were athwart the chief commercial route of the French in interior America.

To the English this vast trading ground, from Pittsburgh to the Wabash, was known as the Black Forest. It was a big, dim, silent country with its network of trails leading to the clearings and the waterways. It remained mysterious for many years. But one name was known in every village, almost at every campfire from the Chautauqua Hills to the Wabash bottoms. George Croghan, prince of the packmen, had taken the Black Forest for his domain. He was the first English-speaking man to conceive the future riches and power of the land beyond the mountains.

He was Irish by birth. But he soon became a man of the New World. Unlike most of the British in America he proved to be a skilled diplomatist with the Indians. At the same time he held the highest confidence of the governors of Pennsylvania, and when he visited London on a diplomatic mission this man of the back-woods quickly won the respect and trust of the Board of Trade. For twenty years he was a roving mediator—at council fires beside the western rivers and at the conference tables of Philadelphia and London—between the Indian nations and the Colonial government.

George Croghan never knew when he was born. But he was a young man in his early twenties, when he came to America in 1741. Some instinct made him aware that the future of America lay west of Philadelphia; some curiosity drove him over the moun-tains. Almost immediately he entered the western trade. Shrewdly he began in a region uncultivated by the French—the southern shore of Lake Erie. Between Presque Isle—now Erie, Pennsylvania —and the mouth of the Maumee—now Toledo—the French had made no attempts at either trade or evangelism. George Croghan quickly pre-empted that region as his own trading ground. Soon he was established there.

In the infrequent villages he applied himself to the Delaware and Iroquois languages, not only learning their vocabularies but adopting the figurative speech which was Indian eloquence. Though only semi-literate in his own tongue—he had great trouble with English grammar and spelling—he could address himself shrewdly to a single savage and with impressive eloquence to an Indian council. Though he never lost an opportunity to drive a good bargain, he maintained an honest respect for the Indians. From the beginning he got on well with the Iroquois, who had traditionally opposed the French, and he made fast friends of the Wyandots, a fragment of the Huron nation, whose villages were centered about Sandusky Bay.

Starting out as a private trader, Croghan repeatedly drove his own pack ponies between Harrisburg and Lake Erie. His favorite course was to follow the Nemacolin path over the Alleghenies and then take the "Great Trail" from the present Pittsburgh to Detroit. Soon he had made enough profit to hire agents and enlarge his trading grounds. He established well stocked posts at Logstown, Coshocton, Sandusky Bay and the mouth of the Cuyahoga, where modern Cleveland stands. Over extended routes he operated trains of twenty horses, each carrying 150 pounds, with one man at the head of the file of ponies and another at the rear. To the Indians they brought assorted goods—blankets and ribbons, rum and gunpowder, stockings (red, green and yellow were the Indian women's choices, in that order), knives, files and hatchets, jewsharps, whistles and bells. At the eastern terminus of his pack route, a few miles west of Harrisburg, was the 1,200 acre estate of "Croghan's Gap." Here he built stables for his pack ponies, quarters for his men, a roomy warehouse and a large tanyard. Though he called this place his home, as he later called his establishments farther west at Augwick and Pittsburgh, he was seldom there. He lived on the trails and at his scattered posts.

Amid the gloom of the Ohio forests he met his friends—Conrad Weiser, an Indian trader, translator and negotiator like himself; Christopher Gist, a surveyor and explorer who looked shrewdly over the Ohio Valley for a group of Virginia speculators; and moody Indian chiefs from a dozen tribes and nations. One of his picturesque friends, who eventually became a kind of partner, was the half-breed Andrew Montour. The son of Big Tree, an Oneida chief, and a French-Indian woman, Montour had delicate European features which he painted savagely. His love of spangles made him a good customer for a trader's wares, and Croghan's magnetism and diplomacy made him a fast friend. Though it was Croghan's business to serve the official interests at Philadelphia, he always enjoyed the confidence of the tribes and he gave some of their chiefs English names, which they bore with surprising pride. On one occasion a council of chiefs from Mingo Bottoms, including Captain Hornet, Captain Mygog-Wigo, Captain Strike-belt, Captain Pouch and Captain Slewballs, said in reference to a proposed treaty, "When George Croghan and our great men talk together, we will tell what to do."

Along with this influence over the Indians, Croghan enjoyed the full confidence of the officials of Pennsylvania. On one trip Ben Franklin sent his nineteen-year-old son to Ohio with Croghan to add to the youth's education. Croghan helped to educate Franklin himself and to heighten his already lively interest in the trans-Allegheny country. On one of his last expeditions he sent to Franklin, in London, a box of mastodon teeth and bones he had found in Ohio and he often impressed on Franklin the material riches of the interior valley. Before other Pennsylvania officials realized the future of the West, Franklin had declared: "The great country back of the Appalachian Mountains, on both sides of the Ohio, and between that river and the lakes, is now well known to be one of the finest in North America, for the extreme richness and fertility of the land, the healthy temperature of the air and the mildness of the climate; the plenty of hunting, fishing and fowling, the facility of trade with the Indians, and the vast convenience of inland navigation. From these natural advantages it must undoubtedly (perhaps in less than another century) become a populous and powerful dominion."

BUT IT WAS NOT an undisputed dominion. For a hundred years the French had considered the Ohio country their domain and they had their establishments at Fort La Boeuf on French Creek —below the site of the present Erie, Pennsylvania—and on the Maumee and the Wabash. In the imminent clash of trade the English had one advantage—their route was shorter and so they could get their goods more easily and cheaply to the Indians. But the French had been trading with the Indians for a century. Now arose two questions—Which country could win the allegiance of the tribes? And which could prepare most carefully for the inevitable clash of arms?

Far away in the citadel above the St. Lawrence sat a little humpbacked man. He had sharp features, long, bony, restless hands, and dark eyes accustomed to great distance. The Marquis de la Galiconniere, governor of New France, had been a naval officer before his arrival at Quebec. Used to the distances of the sea, he quickly acquired a conception of distance in the wilderness and he thought upon the strategy of deploying bands of men, like a fleet of armed frigates, through a dark country. He needed to deploy such a force now.

In 1749, he sent Celeron de Blainville to reaffirm the authority of France in the upper Ohio Valley. This was not to be a military adventure so much as a political maneuver, a demonstration of French force and French intentions. Celeron was to overawe the Indians, to warn off the English traders and to assert French property rights over the area into which the Pennsylvania packmen had gone.

For this errand former Admiral Galiconniere had chosen the right man. Celeron was shrewd and energetic, flexible and bold.

From a term of service as commandant at Detroit, he had a thorough knowledge of the Indians and a realistic understanding of France's diplomatic and military problem in the Ohio Valley. And he was equipped with a force of more than two hundred men— a bigger expedition than had ever passed through Ohio's woods and waters. Most of this number, however, were inexperienced voyageurs who had never seen war or wilderness and were making their first journey into remote country. Though they were willing enough at the canoe paddles, Celeron feared they would run at the first flash of a tomahawk or the quaver of a war cry.

In a fleet of birch canoes, the members of the expedition left Montreal on a blue and silver day in June, 1749. They ascended the St. Lawrence and followed the shores of Lake Ontario to the Niagara portage. With their canoes again in water they followed Lake Erie's lower shore, past Sturgeon and Van Buren Points, till they found the shallow outlet of Chautauqua Creek. That stream led them to the wind-stirred waters of Chautauqua Lake. At the head of the lake, where a quiet village now bears Celeron's name, they hauled their craft ashore for the toilsome portage to Conewango Creek, headwaters of the Ohio. Then it was good paddling with the steady June current through the great green valley of the West.

In Celeron's own canoe was an article of baggage which had added to the toil of the portages. A box, sturdily built and surprisingly heavy for its size, was packed with lead plates, on each of which was printed a declaration of possession ". . . of said river Ohio, and of all those that therein empty; and of all the land on both sides of said river." At the mouth of each important tributary to the Ohio the party moored their canoes, drew up in military ranks on the shore and buried a lead plate in the soft soil. Then to a nearby sycamore or willow trunk Celeron nailed a tin plaque bearing the arms of France and giving the location of the buried plate and repeating its inscription.

Years after the French claim to that country was forgotten, two of the buried plates were found. At the mouth of the Muskingum a group of Marietta boys dug a heavy lead slab from an eroded place on the river bank. They cut off a corner to make rifle bullets, but the remainder of that plate is now in the museum of the American Antiquarian Society at Worcester, Massachusetts. Another plate, removed from the mouth of the Great Kanawha, is now in possession of the Virginia Historical Society at Richmond. The rest are still buried at the river mouths.

Celeron made his journey without military incident, losing but one man of his party, who was drowned. But he had abundant evidence of the uneasiness of the Indians and the resentment of the English.

Ahead of him, down the Ohio, he sent his half-breed agent, Chabert de Joncaire, to prepare the Indians for the expedition's arrival and to assure them of good will. But the Indians remained suspicious and the English traders whom Celeron encountered gave no evidence of respecting the French declaration of proprietorship. At Logstown, on the upper Ohio, and at Lower Shawnee Town, now Portsmouth, Ohio, Celeron was fearful of an outbreak from bands of warriors who had been well armed by the British. But by tact and boldness he averted any incident. At the mouth of the Great Miami—now the site of Cincinnati—he buried his final plate and was ready to turn north. On the last day of August he entered the low water of the Great Miami and paddled upstream to the populous Miami town of Pickawillany. Here, after exhorting the tribe against the English traders, he abandoned his canoes and took his party overland to the Maumee River. Beside water flowing toward the St. Lawrence they built a new fleet of canoes and proceeded to Lake Erie. They were back in Montreal early in November.

Celeron was a candid man and he knew his mission had been a failure. Though his plates now posted the Ohio country like a game preserve, he did not fool himself or his superiors. "The Indian nations are not kindly disposed to the French," he reported bluntly, "and are wholly friendly to the English." His report was made not to Galiconniere but to his successor, Jonquiere. The little humpbacked governor had been recalled to France while Celeron was on the Ohio. There he proposed the only realistic plan for French possession of the disputed country—he urged the sending of ten thousand thrifty French peasants to pre-empt and settle Ohio. But in the domed chambers of Paris and the gilded halls of Versailles the ministers of France dismissed that project without a second thought. It was bright noon when the little twisted man walked away, defeated, from the Ministry. But it was the twilight hour of New France. The shadow of the Rock was fading.

ALWAYS, DESPITE the shifting policies of the British and the French, George Croghan remained a man facing the West. He chose to deal fairly with the Indians, but he, more than any Englishman of his age, saw the Northwest as a white man's country which the Indians must surrender. He lived to see that this could be only a bloody conquest, but he won as much territory by shrewd trade and negotiation as other men did by battle. He was still a young man when, in 1747, he carried his first pack train of presents to Ohio. On that trip he was not a trader but a man bearing gifts. On his train of twenty pack horses he carried a thousand dollars worth of knives and hatchets, bracelets and mirrors, blankets and ribbons, needles and thread and boxes of bone and pearl buttons for the Ohio tribes. It was not nearly enough to go around and the Indians were disappointed that there were no casks of rum among the gifts. Croghan told them that the governor of Pennsylvania had forbidden all traders to carry rum into the western country, authorizing the Indians to report any traders violating the rule and to seize the casks they brought. The idea of seizure pleased the Indians but they thought rum should have been included among Croghan's presents—they said some of their brothers had not yet tasted the English rum and would be very glad to try it before the prohibition began. Still Croghan was firm in upholding the governor's rule—he did not propose to buy western land through the Indians' drunkenness.

And he did not propose to buy it by bloodshed, as long as that could be averted.

But it could not be averted much longer. In the early weeks of 1755, an English fleet sailed from the Cove of Cork, having aboard two regiments of well equipped troops under General Edward Braddock. A few weeks later a French fleet stood out of the harbor of Brest, freighted with troops and ammunition. These forces were to meet in contest for the Ohio, four thousand miles away. The French and Indian War was at hand.

When hostilities began, thanks to some surprisingly skillful diplomacy from Quebec, the western tribes sided with the French. But the various nations of the Iroquois were loyal to the British. Some two hundred Iroquois came as refugees to Croghan's estate in western Pennsylvania. They built thirty huts around his own house and helped themselves to the corn and pumpkins in Croghan's fields. When traders came through, Croghan tried to prevent the Indians from exchanging their clothes and weapons for liquor, and finally he wrote to Governor Morris: "I am oblig'd to give them a Cag Now and then for a frolick, but that is Attended with no Expense to the Government nor no bad Consequence to the Indians as I Do itt butt onst a Month."

When Governor Duquesne at Quebec determined to drive the English traders out of Ohio, he put a price of a thousand dollars on George Croghan's head. But Croghan, confident of his standing among the Indians, moved freely even among the tribes nominally allied to the French. In Lower Shawnee Town he boldly told them of the value of his scalp and then lay down and slept soundly among them. His head remained secure, but the French moving down from Detroit made a bold attack on Pickawillany and the bloody campaign was on.

During the seesaw fortunes of the war, Croghan furnished pack trains to long-striding young George Washington and enlisted small Indian brigades to serve Washington and Braddock. In 1758, he assisted General Forbes in the capture of Fort Duquesne, which the English renamed Fort Pitt. These were maneuvers for control of the upper Ohio. But Croghan had a vision of the great rich inland basin, the entire Northwest, as the prize to be won. When the war was over and the French surrendered all claims east of the Mississippi, he tramped west on a series of Indian conferences from Detroit to the Ohio River. Like La Salle he was undismayed by distance—walking from Fort Pitt to the Wabash, paddling a canoe from Detroit to Niagara, keeping the whole dark territory in his mind, seeing it with one strategy and foreseeing its destiny as the seat of an Anglo-Saxon civilization.

This conviction took him to London, in 1764, and he convinced the British officials that they should occupy the Illinois country, which no English trader had ever entered. Though the Treaty of Paris had been signed, ceding to England all territory east of the Mississippi, the flag of France still rippled over the heavy walls of Fort de Chartres, on the Illinois bank of the river, and Pontiac's rebellious braves had taken refuge in Illinois and were defying the approach of the British. Six military missions had set out for Illinois and had come back beaten and hopeless. But George Croghan was always worth more than a garrison of soldiers. On his return from London he determined to go to Illinois himself to try negotiations. So he set out on his most memorable journey down the Ohio.

After the western shores had swallowed up his bateaux, rumor went over the mountains to Philadelphia that Croghan and his party had been captured and burned at the stake. The Indians had ambushed and slaughtered them on the Ohio shore. Pontiac had prepared a great kettle in which he was determined to boil them and all other Englishmen that set foot in Illinois.

Actually Croghan did lose some of his men and he "got the stroke of a hatchet" on his own head. At the mouth of the Wabash he was captured by a band of Kickapoos and for a time his life hung by a thread. But his old skill at negotiation was still more potent than armed force. He persuaded the Kickapoos to release him, and in a triumph culminating a lifetime of diplomacy he met Pontiac and won the "terrible chief" to English terms.

The Indians agreed to return their British prisoners and to permit occupation of English posts in the country, asking that trade be resumed on favorable terms and that they be paid a land rental for the sites of the posts. So the entire territory was opened to the British, and Croghan, with a tomahawk scar across his temple, returned to Philadelphia.

A year later Croghan made another western journey to consolidate the British interests. With a fleet of seventeen bateaux he drifted down the Ohio and ascended the Mississippi to Fort de Chartres. On the way he stopped at Big Bone Lick, examining the trampled buffalo wallow and the enormous boneyard beside the salt deposits. Some enameled bones which looked like elephant's teeth and some ivory tusks six feet long he took with him, later sending them to his friends Ben Franklin and Lord Shelburne in London. Then he proceeded with his mission. In the heavy heat of August he arrived at Fort de Chartres and met in council with a thousand Indians from twenty-two tribes. He secured their full agreement to British occupation and trade and, with their approval, he planned a system of communication from Fort Pitt to Michilimackinac, from Detroit to the mouth of the Ohio. Though he then fell ill of malarial fever and lay quaking in the heat, his heart must have beat strong with fulfillment. The whole Northwest was won by a packman who had led his ponies over the mountain trails.

VI

The Forest Conspiracy

THE BRITISH won the French and Indian War, but they did not win the Indians. The French had made a peninsula in Lake Erie, Presque Isle (Almost an Island), now Erie, Pennsylvania, the headquarters of their expeditions. They had built a wagon road to Fort Le Boeuf on French Creek, while the British pushed their forces over Braddock's Road to dispute the strategic junction of the Allegheny and Monongahela rivers which, under the hills of Pittsburgh, form the Ohio.

But like George Croghan, another man saw the contest as more than a struggle for the upper Ohio Valley. He saw the whole Northwest at stake. In his dark, deliberate and crafty mind he pictured the destiny of the entire basin from Pittsburgh to Michilimackinac, from Presque Isle to the Mississippi. He was neither French nor English, neither Colonial nor European. He was one of the tribesmen over whose ancestral grounds the powers of Europe were drawn up in arms. Now he is commemorated by two Mid-Western county-seat towns and a streamlined motor car. But when he stood under the great council elm of his tribe near the Maumee portage, haranguing his tribesmen and their allies, Pontiac was the embodiment of a power that threatened every European interest in the Northwest.

English goods were cheap, but the English were bad neighbors for the Indians. Both by the aloof British character and by the Colonial policy of making English settlements on new land, they were hostile to the tribes. The French had studied Indian languages, flattered Indian vanities, adopted the tribes as their allies and subjects. When a party of chiefs visited a French fort they were saluted with a boom of cannon and a roll of drums, they were feasted and decorated, they were fitted with French military uniforms and presented with French flags. Among the tribes French officers were not averse to mingling in social revelry and ceremony. Count Frontenac himself, painted with vermilion, ochre and soot, danced at the campfires of the Hurons. The British never learned that kind of conciliation. When an Englishman met a savage it was a meeting of hostile temperaments.

Now, at the end of the war, the decline of the French in America meant the doom of the Indians. More clearly than any man of his time, Pontiac saw the ruin ahead of his people. He schemed and struggled to avert it.

Pontiac was a chief of the Ottawas, a tribe whose home was in the forests between Lake Huron and Lake Michigan. The Ottawas were banded in a loose confederacy with the Chippewas and the Potawatomis, and so Pontiac had influence beyond the council fires of his own people.

He was a man of stern bearing and stubborn will. His shrewd, ambitious mind smoldered with hatred of the English. Though he was later reported to have led a band of his own warriors against the red-coated troops of Braddock, he first appeared in the English records when he met Major Robert Rogers on a bleak November day beside the tossing waters of Lake Erie. In the autumn of 1760, Rogers, with a party of his famous Rangers, was on his way west to take possession of Detroit, Michilimackinac and other western posts. On November seventh, the brigade pulled their fifteen bateaux into the shelter of the Cuyahoga River, where now the city of Cleveland rises. There, in the fading autumn woods before the windswept water, Pontiac appeared at the head of a file of warriors, demanding on what authority Rogers entered that country. Here were two strong men, veterans of many forays and marches in the wilderness, eyeing each other with defiance. But Rogers turned away savage wrath with a soft answer. He explained that the French had surrendered their posts and he was on his way to take possession—a possession which would bring peace and order to the interior country. Pontiac accepted that word and his chiefs smoked a solemn pipe with the Rangers. Before he pushed on west, Rogers had developed a frank admiration for the shrewdness of the Ottawa chief and his authority over his allies.

At that time the Indian population between the Ohio and the lakes was less than ten thousand fighting men and British occupation might seem to have been an easy task. But it was a vast territory and its control was entrusted to a dozen log forts separated from each other by hundreds of miles of wilderness and empty water. To these posts were assigned a bare six hundred men to hold an empire for the English king. As though completely blind to the hazards of their mission, the garrisons treated the Indians with contempt and the English traders cheated and plundered them. At the headwaters of the Ohio the English settlers were steadily intruding upon Indian hunting grounds.

Early in 1763, word went from tribe to tribe that France had ceded all the country east of the Mississippi. With the ferment which this news created, Pontiac conceived the most ambitious, audacious and fearful plot ever to take shape in an Indian mind. The chief of the Ottawas was no brash young warrior. Now fifty years old, he was a veteran of many encounters with the British and he had far-reaching influence among his people. He was known not only to his allied tribes but among the entire Algonquin race, from the mountains of Pennsylvania to the gaunt hills of Lake Superior. He was never hot-headed—he had the savage hatred and malevolence but he had also a cold patience and cunning. He could bide his time. He could control his fury while he made ready for the stunning stroke that would, between sunrise and sunset, annihilate every Englishman west of the mountains. It was a long, careful, dreadful plan.

His first step was to share his plot with a chosen circle of chiefs. These he sent out in all directions—east to the valleys of Pennsylvania, south to the villages on the Ohio, north to the tribes of the upper lakes and west to the camps on the Mississippi. With them his messengers carried the war belt of black and purple wampum and the red-stained tomahawk. Their mission was in

every camp and every village to rouse the tribes to a united strategem of war. On a chosen day in the month of May, indicated by
the changing of the moon, the deadly blow would fall. At every
British post from Pennsylvania to Lake Superior the tribes would
storm the gates, set fire to the fort and slaughter all the garrison.
By the end of that day, when the May moon silvered in the sky,
no Englishman would be left alive in all that country.

It was a simple plot, calling for action that was bold and swift
and concentrated, and so it was a remarkable plan to come from
tribes that had never known concerted action. The unified, simul-
taneous uprising of savage force was an idea never before conceived. It would render the garrisons helpless to assist each other
and it would give them no time to send to the East for aid.
Quickly the Indians grasped at the violence of the plan, but they
also caught Pontiac's craft and patience. Through the lengthening
April days they gave no evidence of their unrest. They still came
to the forts on obsequious and wheedling errands, begging tobacco,
gunpowder and whisky. Groups of them straggled in from the
winter hunting grounds, pitching their scattered camps around the
British stockades. Impassively they boiled maple sugar in kettles
still reeking of fish, and from their pots of stewing venison they
tossed bones to their quarreling dogs.

There were fourteen British posts between Pennsylvania and
the Mississippi and the attack on each of them was carefully
planned for the appointed day. Pontiac himself was to lead the
assault on Detroit. That maneuver was plotted in crafty detail—
how Pontiac and his chiefs with weapons concealed beneath their
blankets would gain admittance to the fort by asking the commandant to discuss certain matters, how at Pontiac's signal the
chiefs would strike down the British officers, how at the sound
of their war cries the Indians lounging outside would rush the
unwary sentries, and Detroit would be a British post no longer.

Detroit, in 1763, was a log stockade surrounded by the camps
and dwellings of some 2,500 persons. The garrison itself was made
up of 120 soldiers and about forty fur-traders. The river banks

both above and below the fort were spaced with Canadian cottages, each having its long strip of orchard and garden sloping down to the water. Around this settlement sprawled three disordered Indian villages, where lived bands of Wyandots, Ottawas and Potawatomis. Pontiac himself had a bark cabin on Isle au Cochon (Hog Island) now gala Belle Isle, in the midst of the Detroit River, where he lived with his squaws and a troop of children. There, in the bright days of early May, he waited for the secretly appointed time.

But the secret got out. One of Detroit's Canadian women, visiting the Ottawa village to buy venison and maple sugar, observed several warriors filing off the muzzles of their guns. When she mentioned this among her neighbors, the Canadian blacksmith remembered that a number of Indians had recently borrowed his saws and files. It seemed that weapons would be shortened in order to be concealed, but when the Canadians reported their suspicion to Major Gladwin, that commandant dismissed it lightly. Then, according to a romantic tradition, a more sobering warning came to Major Gladwin from a beautiful Indian girl with whom he was enamoured. Coming to the fort to bring Gladwin a pair of moccasins, she revealed to him the plot which was to be sprung the next day.

Gladwin immediately put his garrison on the alert. He himself spent a sleepless night watching the quiet village and the moonlit river, and hearing from the Indian camps the faint slow throbbing of the wabeno drum. In the morning, the Indians gathered in the open common behind the fort, and Pontiac, leading his file of chiefs, approached the gateway. As soon as he entered he must have seen that his plot was known—the entire garrison was drawn up under arms. But all his plans were made and he clung to them. The chiefs, holding their blankets over their hidden weapons, entered the council room where all of Gladwin's officers stood with pistols in their belts. Pontiac addressed Gladwin, formally professing friendship for the British. When he raised a hand in signal for the attack, Gladwin gave a signal of his own. A volley of shots and a roll of drums sounded from the stockade yard. Pontiac was stunned into indecision. The chiefs stood like wooden men behind him. A few minutes later, after Gladwin had reciprocated his empty words of friendship, Pontiac led his chiefs out through the gates. Detroit was still at peace.

The ruse had failed, but Pontiac immediately called a council in the Potawatomi village. New plans were drawn up and a few days later a ring of warriors attacked the fort. When the assault was repulsed, they began a long slow siege, very different from the quick decisive thrust that Pontiac had plotted.

For five months, through all the summer and into the fading fall, Detroit was under siege, and for fifteen months it remained an isolated and imperiled post. Though provisions ran low and the defenders grew haggard, the garrison held out. On starless nights an occasional bateau crept through the river bringing desperately needed supplies. By those furtive boatmen there came word of the disaster that had struck swiftly at all the British posts. Fort Sandusky on Lake Erie was captured by treachery and violence, its commandant taken prisoner. From across the Sandusky marshes he saw the burning fort under a lurid tent of sky. Fort St. Joseph on Lake Michigan had been rushed and plundered by a band of Potawatomis. Fort Quatanon on the Wabash and Fort Miami on the Maumee had fallen. Fort Presque Isle on the Erie shore had been fired by flaming arrows from two hundred Indian bows. When the water gave out the men began desperately to dig a well and they reached water in their lake shore stockade just in time to check the flames and save the outer shell of the fort. Then the Indians dug under the palisade and captured the exhausted garrison. At Fort Le Boeuf the blockhouse was fired and while the Indians danced in the light of its destruction, the little garrison of men cut a hole through the logs and escaped to the woods. They had escaped one death but most of them died of hunger before they could reach Fort Pitt. So the record of disaster ran. Of all the western posts only Detroit still flew the red cross of St. George.

Among those swift assaults, one was more crafty, merciless and dramatic than all the others. And because an English trader wrote it down while it was still etched in his memory, we have the whole lurid story of the massacre at the romantic fort beside the Straits of Mackinac.

In 1763, the turtle-shaped Michilimackinac, with its white cliffs of sandstone and its dark hood of forest, was still an Indian island. Lodges of Hurons and Ottawas were scattered along its shores. Hunting parties roamed its woods and fishing fleets roved the waters roundabout for whitefish and the famous Mackinaw trout. At that time the stockade of Fort Michilimackinac was on the mainland of Michigan, directly opposite the island, on the site of Mackinaw City of today. There the log palisades and wooden bastions stood close to the restless waters of the strait. Around the fort were a few neat Canadian cottages and a scattering of rude Indian lodges. Beside nearly every lodge or cottage fishing nets were spread on drying poles. At night the curving shore flickered with campfires and above the slow wash of the lake came the chants of the Hurons and the songs of the voyageurs. This was the capital of the whole north country, a meeting place of merchants and missionaries, a dispersal point for the voyageurs, a depot for furs and trade goods and a famed military post whose power was felt throughout the upper lakes and far down the valley of the Mississippi.

Yet the garrison was limited to thirty-five militiamen. They were all veterans of the Sixtieth Regiment, known as the Royal Americans, which had fought under General Wolfe at Quebec. Some of them had brought their families with them to this remote and romantic point. Under Commander Etherington they lived a satisfying life, varied by the rhythms of nature in a northern country —the ice-bound siege of winter, the surging spring, the long bright days of summer and then the golden autumn that ended with the cold November winds. Twice a year the trading compound was thronged with traders newly arrived from the East and with tribesmen from the remote north country. At less eventful seasons the life had a quiet spell of beauty and order. The sun rose out of Lake Huron and went down in Lake Michigan. Occasionally a fleet of canoes passed over the horizon. So it was through the month of May, 1763. After all the other forts had been assaulted, the lonely northern post remained at peace and no knowledge of the fate of the British garrisons found its way to that far place. But Pontiac's conspirators had not chosen to spare Michilimackinac. They were merely waiting.

In London, four thousand miles away, King George had a birthday, and at the post of Michilimackinac the soldiers were given a holiday because of that event. That cloudless June morning a band of Chippewas, as though to participate in the holiday, invited the garrison to watch a game of baggattaway, a form of lacrosse, between their best players and the Sacs. The garrison gladly turned out on open ground beyond the south gate of the fort and Captain Etherington placed a good sportsman's bet on the Chippewas. The game was played with scores of contestants, each team trying to get the ball to the tall post which marked its goal. It was a running, rushing, striking, tripping game, full of movement and confusion. The spectators were absorbed. Suddenly a player stepped into the clear and hurled the ball upward. It fell just inside the open gate of the fort. The whole mass of contestants milled after it. Then, according to plan, the ballgame was forgotten and a grimmer game began. Uttering their war cries, scores of Indians rushed into the deserted buildings of the fort to take possession. Others snatched weapons from the women who, seated on the sidelines, had concealed axes, knives and hatchets in their clothing. Before he could raise his voice in a command, Captain Etherington found himself bound and gagged. He was led away a prisoner.

By that time the whole settlement rang with quavering war cries. Armed Indians struck down the unarmed British soldiers and traders. In the compound the dead lay in a bloody stillness, the dying writhed under knife and tomahawk. The savages, stained with their victims' blood, shouted in rage and triumph.

In that swift and bloody assault twenty-one Britishers were killed and seventeen captured. Among the captives was the trader Alexander Henry who, by a series of miraculous escapes, remained alive and told the whole terrible story.

Two years earlier Alexander Henry, just twenty-two years old, had gone north from his home in New Jersey to the recently captured part of Montreal. All of the western fur trade promised now to pass into British hands and this young adventurer meant to claim an early share in that rich enterprise. He set out from Montreal with a brigade of canoes laden with trade goods—the first British trader to reach the northern trading capital of Michilimackinac. In fact, he reached the post before the English garrison had arrived to take over command of the fort, which had been ceded at the time of the fall of Montreal. Discovering that the Indians hated all Englishmen and would be glad to murder him and seize his goods, he disguised himself as a French voyageur until the English troops arrived.

When the British garrison took over the fort, Henry was already an established trader. He made friends with the Indians, learned their language and impressed them with his fair dealing. He made trips by canoe and on snowshoes all around the straits. He was a familiar figure in the Indian villages at St. Ignace, across the narrows, and at the Sault fifty miles to the north. He liked the country, he liked the shrewd business of trading and the orderly routine of the little British world within the stockade of Fort Michilimackinac. He was pleased with all his prospects when, suddenly on the third of June, that world came to an end.

On the day of the king's birthday Henry did not go to see the ballgame between the Sacs and the Chippewas. On the beach a canoe was being fitted for the journey to Montreal and he sat in his cottage writing letters before its departure. Through his open window he heard the shouting of the spectators around the playing field. His goose quill scratched on across the page. But that letter was never finished. Suddenly the voices changed pitch and tempo. A chorus of war cries filled the air. He hurried to his window and saw a melee of Indians swinging their hatchets on the unarmed English troops.

In that gory scene Henry observed that the Canadian inhabitants of the fort were not molested by the Indians. Seizing a slender hope he ran to the house of his neighbor, M. Langlade, and asked for shelter. Langlade, calmly watching the slaughter, shrugged his shoulders at the trader's request, but an Indian slave hid him in the garret. Through a crack in the wall he saw the massacre continue until every Englishman in the fort had been killed or captured. Then the Indians began a search of the surrounding cottages for more Englishmen. When a group of blood-stained warriors came to the Langlade door, Henry crept into a dark corner of his garret among a pile of empty birch-bark boxes which the Indians used in making maple sugar. He managed to cover himself with those *mokuks* before the stairs creaked under the Indians' feet.

Four blood-smeared figures entered the garret, stooping under its low roof with tomahawks in their hands. But their eyes were not accustomed to the darkness and, though Henry could have touched them, they saw nothing but a disordered heap of *mokuks*. When they were gone the trader sank into an exhausted sleep. He remained there all day and all night. The next day Langlade, at the fearful insistence of his wife, told the Indians there was an Englishman in his house and again Henry heard the stairs creaking. He stood up ready to meet his fate. The Indians were drunk —perhaps that saved Henry's life. One of them, named Wenniway, a six-foot warrior smeared with grease and charcoal, raised a knife over the defenseless Henry. Then some new feeling came over the befuddled Indian. He saw in Henry a likeness of his lost brother Musinigon. The knife came down and Henry was unhurt.

It seemed that Henry's life was reprieved, but as the days succeeded he was never sure. He was stripped of his clothing and with three other captives was placed in a canoe with seven Chippewas. They paddled westward. Henry was told they were to be taken to Beaver Island in northern Lake Michigan where they would be killed and eaten. The day turned foggy and instead of seeking open water they paddled along the shore in a region inhabited by the Ottawa tribe. At intervals the Indians uttered a series of shrill whoops—one for each prisoner—in a bragging announcement of the number of their captives. When an Ottawa Indian appeared on the foggy beach the Chippewas paddled ashore to tell the news of their assault on the fort. This was an Ottawa ambush. A hundred Ottawa warriors leaped out of the woods, seizing the canoe and the English prisoners. The Ottawas, angry because they had not been called upon to participate in the attack on the fort, were determined to have some prisoners of their own.

Henry and his companions were now thrown into Ottawa canoes and taken back to Michilimackinac. There the Ottawas and Chippewas disputed over possession of the prisoners. It took a full day to agree upon a division of the captives and the next morning Henry, who had been without food for four days, was returned to the custody of the Chippewas. When the Chippewas gathered to discuss the fate of their share of the prisoners, Henry saw Wawatam, a Chippewa who in the peaceful days before the massacre had called the trader his friend and brother. Now Wawatam laid an armful of presents before the chiefs and made a plea for Henry's life. It was a dignified and persuasive plea.

"Friends and relations," he said, facing the grim circle of Chippewas and then looking at the despairing Henry, "you all well know that long before the war began I adopted [this man] as my brother. From that moment he became one of my family, so that no change of circumstances could break the cord which fastened us together. . . . On that day on which the war began, you were fearful lest I should reveal your secret. You requested, therefore, that I would leave the fort and even cross the lake. I did so—but did it with reluctance. I did it with reluctance, notwithstanding that you, Minavavana, who had command in this enterprise, gave me your promise that you would protect my friend, delivering him from all danger and giving him safely to me. The performance of this promise I now claim. I come not with empty hands to ask it. You, Minavavana, best know whether or not, as it respects yourself, you have kept your word. But I bring these goods to buy off every claim which any man among you all may have on my brother as his prisoner."

This grave plea, addressed to a painted, blood-stained circle of savages, was successful. Either Wawatam's humanity or the gifts which he offered outweighed the Indians' cruelty and Henry was led away to his defender's lodge. Here, after five days of hunger and hardship, he was given food and a mound of soft furs to lie on. The next morning, peering through a chink beside his bed, he saw a group of Indians dragging the dead bodies of the soldiers who had been his fellow prisoners.

That evening, in the long June twilight, a large trading canoe appeared in the straits. While it was still distant the Indians could tell by the stroke of the paddles that it was manned by the English traders from Montreal. Having heard nothing of the fate of Michilimackinac, they steered their craft to the shore where the supper fires of the Indians were twinkling in the dusk. They had come a long, hard way and they must have been grateful to be at their journey's end, with thoughts of food and drink and eager English voices in the traders' barracks inside the palisade. But no sooner had they stepped ashore than a howling band of Chippewas surrounded them. They were stripped, beaten, and dragged to the blood-stained prison lodge.

In the slender safety of Wawatam's protection, Henry never knew the fate of these latest victims. But he became aware of a growing uneasiness among the Indians. As their stock of stolen whisky dwindled, they became fearful of the consequences of their violence. Through the camp went rumors that the English were coming in a great fleet of canoes to recover the fort and punish its attackers. After an uneasy council, it was decided to move the camp to Mackinac Island, where they could defend themselves when the British came. That day the straits were black with hundreds of canoes—behind them the fort stood over a silent shore. That night the whole southern shore of Mackinac Island, where now the excursion boats lie at wharves and visitors stroll past the curio shops, was ringed with campfires.

A few days later lookouts from the island cliffs sighted two large trading canoes coming up Lake Huron. The Indians pushed off in their canoes to meet them. When the approaching vessels rounded a point the Indian canoes swept around them and made them prisoner. The traders, like their unlucky precedessors, had come from Montreal expecting to carry on a peaceful barter at Michilimackinac.

In the captured canoes the Indians found a generous supply of rum. That night the island rang with the whoops of drunken warriors and Wawatam feared for Henry's safety. In the darkness he led the Englishman through the steepening woods to the interior of the island and pointed out a hiding place in a rocky cavern. There Henry slept till daybreak, though his bed was rough and hard. In the morning he saw that he was lying in a burial cave on a bed of human bones. That gruesome shelter, Skull Cave, is one of the landmarks of the island to this day.

When Henry returned to the sullen Indian camp he was an Englishman no longer. Except for a tufted scalp-lock his hair was shaved from his head, his face was painted with colored clay and charcoal, he wore a coarse shirt colored with grease and vermilion and carried a blanket draped around his shoulders. In that disguise he lived safely among the Indians through the summer months and went south with them on their winter hunt. He knew enough of their language and their manners to avoid suspicion and, as time went on, he learned to feel secure among them. More than most Englishmen he was adaptable to an alien life and he concluded—"if I could have forgotten that I had ever been otherwise than I then was, I could have enjoyed as much happiness in this as in any other situation."

The following spring, in company with a small band of Indians, Henry returned to Fort Michilimackinac. They found two French voyageurs the sole inhabitants of the desolate post, and with them, like any other Indian, the blanketed Henry traded his

winter furs for clothing, ammunition and tobacco. Then he bade
farewell to the faithful Wawatam and set out for Sault Sainte
Marie, where he could put off his Indian disguise and join a British caravan for the long trip to the St. Lawrence.

Standing beside Henry's canoe and looking over the wind-stirred
April straits, Wawatam lighted his pipe, puffed it in silence and
then handed it to the young Englishman. "My son," he said, "this
may be the last time you and I shall ever smoke out of the same
pipe. I am sorry to part with you." He stood there as Henry
paddled away. When his canoe was about to round an island,
Henry looked back across the wide water and saw the Indian still
standing on the shore. Now the ferry dock rises where Wawatam
watched his friend away and the merciful Chippewa is remembered by the big railway ferry "Chief Wawatam," which steams
across the deep straits from Mackinaw City to St. Ignace.

DURING ALL THE months of Alexander Henry's captivity, Detroit alone remained a British post. The rest were pillaged and
plundered, burned and stained with English blood. And Detroit,
though still flying the red cross of England, was a besieged post
with its haggard troops manning their muskets at the loopholes.
Meanwhile, violence was spreading through the valleys of Pennsylvania, where the rampant tribes were murdering English settlers and burning their cabins. By the end of the troubled year
1763, two thousand border settlers had been killed and as many
more had been driven from their homes.

Lord Jeffrey Amherst, British commander-in-chief, received the
news at his headquarters in New York. Fort Pitt faced serious
peril and the whole border was in a state of panic. Pontiac's bold
plan had been successful at every point in the western country
except for the resistance at Detroit, where Pontiac himself was
in charge of the siege. The future of British occupation beyond
the Alleghenies looked darker with each new report that reached
the commander-in-chief. At last, in desperation, the British officials talked of infecting the mutinous Indians with smallpox.

Colonel Henry Bouquet, commander of the English troops in Pennsylvania, was reported to have a plan for infecting a number of blankets with the contagion and scattering them by spies among the rampant tribes. Whether this hideous plan was carried out cannot now be determined, though it is known that a few months later smallpox made dreadful inroads among the helpless Ohio Indians.

But deliverance did not come with smallpox. It awaited a military force sufficient to put down the Indian uprising. After a year of confusion and bloodshed, the force was assembled. In impressive strength, Colonel Bouquet advanced from Fort Pitt down the Ohio, and Colonel Bradstreet, with an imposing flotilla of bateaux, set out over Lake Erie to the relief of Detroit and the rehabilitation of Michilimackinac. After fifteen months of peril and privation, the weary garrison at Detroit saw Bradstreet's vessels approaching in the river. They rubbed their eyes, raised a thin shout and fired a volley from their muskets. The Indians, already weary of the long siege, had neither the will nor the military strength to fight off that long line of well manned bateaux. Bradstreet took possession of the fort and punished a few Indian leaders who fell into his hands. But Pontiac was not there. He had fled west, before the replenished power of the English, to the wilds of Illinois. The flag of France still fluttered over the Mississippi settlements of Cahokia and Kaskaskia because the Engglish had not yet penetrated that distant country.

There the French traders, still nursing hatred of the English, sought to use the bitter chief for their own purposes. They urged him to rally the western tribes for another defiant stand, assuring him that thousands of French troops would soon arrive to take up the struggle. They dressed him in a French uniform and brought him forged letters signed by the king of France. Pontiac clutched at their promises and tried to fan the dying flame of Indian resistance. But he had no success. His own tribes were not disposed to try another alliance, and the Illinois, after a succession of defeats, had lost their taste for war. When months went by and no French troops appeared, the somber chief knew that his cause was lost.

So when George Croghan advanced toward Illinois to attempt a conciliation, the crafty, realistic Pontiac went to meet him. Solemnly he shook hands with Croghan, professing that he had been in error and was now ready to be a friend of the English. His bitterness could not have been allayed by the handful of presents Croghan brought, but he launched his canoe in the Wabash and steered for his home in peace.

Five years later, in 1769, Pontiac again visited the Illinois on what proved to be his last journey. Still considering himself an ally of the French, he went to call on the officials at the new trading post of St. Louis, across the Mississippi. On his return he fell in with a drinking party of Illinois Indians. An English trader, fearful that the great conspirator was again plotting against the English, bribed an Illinois warrior to kill him. The price was a barrel of rum. Pontiac had been drinking heavily and he was an easy victim. In a forest thicket the assassin crept up behind him with his tomahawk raised. Pontiac never came out of that thicket. When the French heard of his murder they carried his body across the wide river and buried him at the edge of the fort near the confluence of the Mississippi and the Missouri, where now the city of St. Louis stands. One era had ended in the Northwest. Another, to endure but a single generation, was beginning. The flag of Britain fluttered over every post and settlement between the Ohio and the lakes.

VII

The Redhead and the Hair-Buyer

VINCENNES, lying along the Wabash beneath the mound-
shaped hills, is a time-worn town. On the bank of the river,
beyond the quiet spire of the cathedral of St. Francis Xavier and
beside the old French cemetery with its unmarked graves of forgotten Indians, priests and soldiers, stands a handsome marble
memorial. Above the granite terraces sixteen Doric columns, more
massive than the sycamore trunks along the Wabash, support the
round entablature. Within the memorial room of French and
Italian marble is a bronze statue of George Rogers Clark. White
amid the weathered buildings of the town the memorial can be
seen for three miles down the slowly curving river—though no one
comes down the Wabash any more—and in the leafless winter it
rises white as frost across the miles of lowland, where no gaunt
regiment wades through the bottoms now.

George Rogers Clark was a man in buckskin. French and Italian
marble would have puzzled him. When he was a young man,
gaunt with a winter march through desolation, he demanded the
surrender of the British Colonel Hamilton and on the site of those
Greek columns his hungry men were fed by the cheerful French
housewives of Vincennes. The marble pile would have puzzled
him even more when he was an old man on his cabin stoop, staring down at Corn Island in the Ohio River where he had drilled
his troops for the conquest of the Northwest. A lonely, impoverished and crippled man, with only the fading comfort of whisky,
he could not have understood the bronze statue in that costly
memorial room.

A new country is youth's country. When George Rogers Clark
crossed the mountains in 1772, he was nineteen years old. But he

was a woodsman then and forever. Already he was six feet tall, with eyes quick for the flash of game or the sign of an Indian. He was hot-tempered, with a shock of red hair that a coonskin cap could not extinguish. Though he was a big man, he passed through thickets as silently as a fox. He could not get lost in the woods anymore than a bobcat. With his long rifle, he did not like a sitting target but waited for a leaping squirrel or a bird in flight. He was restless, impulsive, headstrong. His mother had married at fifteen, his grandfather had led him over the rough Virginia mountains with a surveyor's chain, and youth was concentrated in him.

For a short while, young George Clark sat restlessly under a Latin schoolmaster with James Madison and John Tyler as his classmates. But his real schooling waited for him in the border country, along its trails, its fords and its mountain passes. When he came back to Virginia, after a season in the West, his people did not know him. He was bronzed, trail-hardened, sinewy as a sapling. The spell of distance was in his eyes.

He belonged to the new country—he was the West's man. Soon he was back in the region that Virginia claimed beyond the mountains, though the British regarded all the Northwest as an unencumbered domain. Now the Colonials were becoming "Americans," and the British officials did not want them climbing their back fence of mountains to pre-empt the western country. But a process inevitable as the seasons was under way. Each year lengthening files of settlers filtered in by the trails and drifted down the Ohio. The Indians were alarmed and the British encouraged the tribes to resist the advancing settlement.

Under the celebrated Shawnee chief Cornstalk they made a systematic attack on settlers from Lake Erie to Cumberland Gap. Lord Dunmore, governor of Virginia, led an army against them and in the battle of Point Pleasant, where the Kanawha River joins the Ohio, the Indians were decisively beaten. Young George Rogers Clark was there, getting his first lessons in forest warfare, getting them well. With Cornstalk's failure, the Indians surrendered Kentucky and the creaking of the settlers' carts was a growing sound on the traces that crossed the mountains. Forts went up and log cabins grew beside them in the Kentucky cane-brakes at Harrodsburg, Boonesborough, Fort Logan. George Rogers Clark took up a plot of land at the mouth of Fish Creek on the Kanawha, sowing it to corn and rye. But he had no great taste for farming. The Indians called him Big Knife. That is not a farmer's name.

While Big Knife tended his Fish Creek fields, Colonel Henry Hamilton was appointed to the command of Detroit and was made British military commander for the entire Ohio Valley. It was the eve of the American Revolution and shrewd Henry Hamilton saw that the time was ripe for a British alliance with the western Indians. When he called a congress of the tribes, they came to Detroit in large numbers—bands of Sioux from Minnesota, Chippewas from the tangled forests around Lake Superior, Sacs and Winnebagos from the oak openings of Wisconsin, Potawatomis from the pine-fringed lakes and Menominees from the dark, timbered shores of Green Bay. Hamilton himself fired them with a fury against the Americans. He called them to the warpath and, in a rare gesture for a British official, he painted his long face, whooped their war songs with them and hurled the hatchet into the painted post of war.

He was a big man with level, calculating eyes, a long nose and a harsh mouth with a heavy underlip. From Quebec, he ordered two thousand red-handled scalping knives, which he distributed among the warriors with an announcement of a cash bounty for scalps. The State Papers of Virginia make this blunt statement about him: "Governor Hamilton gave standing rewards for scalps but none for prisoners, which induced the Indians, after making the captives carry their plunder to the fort, then to put them to death and carry in their scalps to the governor, who saluted their success with a round from the fort's cannon." The Indians called him the Hair-Buyer.

So he armed and massed the warriors for raids on the border, sending them on bloody forays against the growing Kentucky settlements. Detroit was too remote to serve as a base for these operations and he used the former French posts of Kaskaskia, Cahokia and Vincennes, strengthening their garrisons and equipping their magazines with plentiful arms and ammunition. With such rallying points, the marauding bands crossed the Ohio well armed and freshly provisioned, ready to drive the Americans from their newly broken fields. In the middle 1770s, Kentucky was the dark and bloody ground.

Promptly young George Rogers Clark became a leader of the Kentuckians. Around him he gathered a bold band of men—not soldiers but backwoodsmen, men trail-hardened and forest-wise, dressed in hunting shirts and buckskin breeches, armed like Indians with knife and tomahawk, carrying a powder horn, a game-bag and a long rifle that would shoot true for a fifth of a mile. Clark was twenty-five years old and many of his men were no older. Like him, they preferred woods warfare to farming. Clark saw that the only real defense of Kentucky was to wage an offensive war against the seats of British frontier power. Thus he developed his audacious plan—that only a young man could conceive and carry out—to march against the posts above the Ohio River and win the entire Northwest for the Americans.

First he needed to know the temper and the strength of the British establishments. In the summer of 1777, he sent two young hunters, Ben Linn and Samuel Moore, on the pretense of buying beaver skins, to spy out the Illinois posts of Cahokia and Kaskaskia. When they returned with a reassuring report, Clark was convinced his bold plan could succeed. On a hasty journey to Williamsburg he won the support of Patrick Henry, then governor of Virginia, and early in January, 1778, he was voted $6,000 by the Virginia Council and authorized to enlist 350 Virginians for his campaign. Actually he succeeded in gathering less than half that number, but it was a band of skilled woodsmen, sinewy and resourceful, that he embarked on Monongahela barges for the West. Late in May that cumbersome flotilla reached the Falls of the

Ohio, by the empty site of Louisville. Here on Corn Island, between the rushing currents of the river, he built a stockade and a storehouse and briefly drilled his troops for the coming campaign. On the long summer day of June twenty-fourth, he poled his boats into the main channel of the Ohio and shot them down the rapids on a high stage of water.

It was nine o'clock in the morning as they swept through the falls, and to their wonder the bright June sky grew dark. A total eclipse obscured the sun. Birds flew to roost in the canebrakes. The river shores faded in a sudden dusk and a white star brightened in the eastern sky. Some of the troops were shaken with foreboding—even when daylight flooded back again. They thought their campaign was starting on a day of doom. But Clark drove them on—he kept relays of men working the oars. After two days and nights in the boats they reached the site of abandoned Fort Massac. Here, to circumvent British scouts on the Mississippi, they beached their barges and began a march through Illinois' swamps and prairies to Kaskaskia.

On the evening of July fourth, that band of hungry men looked down on the town of Kaskaskia with its French cottages scattered about the British fort. Under cover of darkness Clark seized boats along the river and ferried his men across. For what happened next we have a legend, perhaps in part a myth—the kind of myth that inevitably adheres to the bold young man in a fringed hunting shirt who advanced by stealth and audacity against a superior force. According to a folktale that will last as long as the story of Pocahontas, Clark's men approached on noiseless feet until they heard the fiddles lilting inside the fort and they realized they had arrived in time for a ball. The gate was deserted. Leaving his men in the shadows, Clark strode across the empty parade ground. At the door to the assembly room he watched the dancing till an Indian, who had been lying in his blanket against the wall, sprang to his feet with a cry of warning. At the sound Clark's men rushed in with rifles ready. They were masters of the post without the firing of a gun. When the garrison was disarmed,

Clark told the officers to go on with their dance. At daylight the banner of Virginia replaced the red cross of England above the parade ground.

Immediately Clark won the villagers by his generous treatment, asking them to share the American cause of freedom and to renounce the authority of the British king. No soldier of his, he declared, should molest them. Without exception the French and half-breeds who made up the village population took the oath of loyalty to the United States. Then Clark sent a company of his men with some French volunteers to the trading post of Cahokia, some sixty miles north along the Mississippi. With the French volunteers winning their countrymen to the American cause, they passed through the outlying farms among the old blunted Indian mounds and into the heart of the settlement. Before the commander at Cahokia knew of their presence they had the fort surrounded. Cahokia was captured without bloodshed.

To the Hair-Buyer at Detroit came the stunning news. Promptly he enlisted Indians from the northern tribes and prepared an expedition against the Virginians. In October, he set out with five hundred men in a fleet of heavy bateaux. They descended the Detroit River, crossed Lake Erie and entered the Maumee, making the nine-mile portage to the Wabash. Progress was slow on the upper Wabash—sometimes they waited for beavers to build dams that would raise the shallow water. In mid-December, when ice was forming in the Wabash creeks, they reached Vincennes.

During the bleak winter Clark was in possession of the Illinois posts and the Hair-Buyer was established 240 miles away across the low-lying country. Intrenched in the strong fort of Vincennes, Hamilton sent his militia back to Detroit and dispersed his Indians, instructing them to rejoin him, with reinforcements, in the spring. As soon as the ground was dry, he expected to launch an expedition against the Virginian raiders. But Clark at Kaskaskia was not disposed to wait for dry ground and a British attack. Despite the rigors and difficulties of a winter campaign, he prepared to attack Hamilton at Vincennes before his spring reinforcements should arrive. He proposed to march overland with two hundred men, while his brig, the *Willing,* would sail by way of the Mississippi, the Ohio and the Wabash to rendezvous with him at the attacking point.

For Clark's men it was a grim and gruelling march. Late winter thaws were beginning—prairies were sodden with melted snow and swamps were wastes of water and slush ice. But they were hardened men under an indomitable leader. They slogged through the prairies, waded swamps of numbing water and swam rivers swollen with melting snow. When their supplies gave out, they tightened their belts and went on. Their march is one of the epic achievements of men against hunger, weariness and cold.

Twelve days out from Kaskaskia they reached the swollen Embarrass River, with the wide flood of the Wabash beyond it. Nine miles away, through wet woods and over desolate waters, rose the log walls of Fort Vincennes. A week was required to cross that last remaining distance. They waded knee-deep, shoulder-deep through the drowned Embarrass bottoms. At the Wabash they lashed log rafts and hollowed out canoes. Wading, poling and paddling, they made their way across the Wabash swamps. At last, fatigued and famished, they struggled to the dry ground on a wooded knoll two miles below Vincennes. Clark's scouts could not locate the brig he had sent by way of the rivers, though he sorely needed the ammunition and supplies it carried. The *Willing* had somehow failed to make the rendezvous and his men were weak for want of food. On that dire, dark day of February twenty-third, a party of Indian women appeared in a canoe. Clark intercepted them and obtained enough corn and venison to dull his men's hunger. From a half-breed hunter he learned that Colonel Hamilton was carrying on routine in Fort Vincennes, unaware of danger, but that two hundred Indians had recently arrived at the post. Clark looked over his gaunt and ragged men, less than a hundred of them still strong and able, and decided again on a strategy of boldness. With cold-stiffened fingers he wrote a message.

To the Inhabitants of Post St. Vincents:

Gentlemen,—Being now within two miles of your village with my army, determined to take your fort this night, and not being willing to surprize you, I take this method to request such of you as are true citizens, and willing to enjoy the liberty I bring you, to remain still in your houses. And those, if any there be, that are friends to the king, will instantly repair to the fort, and join the *Hair-Buyer General,* and fight like men. And if any such, as do not go to the Fort shall be discovered afterwards, they may depend upon severe punishment. On the contrary, those that are true friends to liberty, may depend on being well treated. And I once more request them to keep out of the streets; for every one I find in arms on my arrival, I shall treat as an enemy.

G. R. Clark

While this message was being sent to the town clerk, Clark put to use an old border strategem. Taking care to keep his men in sight of the Vincennes settlement but out of sight of the fort, he marched them around and around their wooded knoll so as to present a continuous stream of moving troops—he made a hundred men give the appearance of a thousand. They were still marching while the hunter delivered the message and the town official read Clark's bold words to the assembled villagers. So impressed were the French residents by that message and by the sudden appearance of an army in that desolate winter land that not one even warned the garrison of Clark's presence.

To maintain his deception of armed strength and to surprise the garrison, Clark kept his men in the woods until nightfall. In the early winter dusk he began his advance. He approached the town with two companies, one to surround the straggling village and the other to push through to the fort.

Colonel Hamilton, the Hair-Buyer, was usually a wary and suspicious man, even sending spies with the Indian bands allied to him. But on this cheerless winter evening he sat beside a wood fire in the fort, with no idea that American troops were within a hundred miles of flood-encircled Vincennes. When the first shots rang outside the fort, he thought only of drunken Indians. But the shots increased and bullets thudded into the timbered blockhouse. When a stammering sergeant stood before him, the Hair-Buyer realized that his garrison was under attack.

Clark's men had all the advantage of surprise. They had chosen their locations, crouching in darkness behind palisades and ditches, and every one of them was a marksman. The blockhouse walls were dark but each loophole was a lighted target. The Virginians poured such a stream of bullets around Hamilton's cannon that the British gunners fell back from their stations. All night the fort was ringed by American rifle fire.

At daylight, Clark demanded the surrender of the garrison. Hamilton held out for a few more hours, but his men had lost their last spark of spirit. By mid-morning he was ready to confer with Clark in the little French church that adjoined the military grounds. It was a brief conference. Clark demanded surrender of the fort and custody of Hamilton and his men as prisoners of war. At the appointed hour the British marched out of the timbered gates and the Virginians marched in. From the flagpole the American colors whipped in the chill wind. Clark renamed the post Fort Patrick Henry.

Early in March, the Hair-Buyer was sent in irons to Williamsburg. He must have been a bitter man, tramping the weary miles of the country he had hoped to govern, with an uncouth Virginia guard beside him. He had bought hundreds of scalps—perhaps he brooded about the red-haired youth who had required his surrender and whose scalp would have outweighed all the others. He had hard thoughts of failure and humiliation to keep him company, as he trudged on toward his prison. He remained a prisoner of war until the close of the Revolution. But his career was not at an end. Through British political favor he became governor of Bermuda, and he gave his name to the principal city of that tranquil island far from the war whoops of the Potawatomis and the drowned lands of the Wabash.

Clark was not to be so fortunate. At twenty-five, with a ragged troop of backwoods soldiers, he had won the entire Northwest for the future of his country. But he won no future for himself. After the conquest of Vincennes his reputation faded and his authority ebbed away. During the next years he led troops against the Ohio Indians. He burned their towns, destroyed their fields and carried off their meager stores of corn. At the Falls of the Ohio he fed his troops on the rotten buffalo meat supplied by the army quartermasters and kept the West secure. But he had no more campaigns of glory. At twenty-five his life began its long decline.

After the close of the Revolution, Thomas Jefferson proposed Clark's name as leader of an exploring party to the Pacific. The old spell of distance was in his eyes again. That was an undertaking of his size. But the project did not develop, and twenty years later it was William Clark, his red-haired younger brother who, with Meriwether Lewis, led the historic expedition to the shores of Oregon.

George Rogers Clark lived on in years of illness and neglect. A grant of land on the Ohio was the sole reward that came to the conqueror of a region as large as all the thirteen original colonies. There in his cabin he looked down at Corn Island, where he had drilled his first troops and assembled the supplies for his bold Illinois campaign, and across at the growing city of Louisville, where peaceful citizens had forgotten the fear of Indian scalping knives. He saw the rafts and barges, the flatboats, keelboats and steamers make a busy highway of the river. In those years the Ohio carried an endless stream of settlers and a growing wealth of trade. A new Northwest was shaping, but Clark had no part in it. Sometimes an old soldier came to see him and while they talked of the hard campaigns the old fire flickered in his deep-set eyes. Occasionally a moody Indian chief sat with him, smoking a pipe in Indian silence, and they were two men left over from another age. So the seasons passed and Clark grew crippled and paralyzed and speechless. At last even the memories of conquest faded in his mind.

VIII

The Two Simons

OCCASIONALLY an Ohio hunter picks up an arrowhead in the November fields. He likes the feel of it in his hand, small and thin and weighted. He likes the rough-smooth surfaces, so adamant that centuries of sun and frost have not altered the chipped flint. Then he tosses it away and looks at the shells in his gun.

Behind our sport are the hungry hunt and the wary war trail. Behind our farms and towns and cities is the dark forest with its furtive men who spent their lives in a struggle for the country. They passed over it on foot, great distances; they made fires out of white-oak bark that sent up no betraying smoke; they guided themselves by the moss on tree trunks and the cluster of the seven stars. They rendezvoused, like the great game animals, at the salt licks; they slept on disputed ground. They were borderers, living a dark and wary life between the hearth fires of their people and the council fires of the Indians. They knew the savage life and the savage languages. They knew the settler's love of land. From Indian councils they carried back word of war parties and restless tribes. They were not landowners or landseekers, but they played a dangerous game for the possession of a whole country. Most of them could not write their own names, but they were diplomats to the savage nations. They knew the chiefs—Logan, Cornstalk, Blackbird, Big Gate, Tobacco's Son, Little Turtle, Tarhe the Crane, Blackhoof, Blue Jacket, Red Pole, Captain Pipe, Tecumseh and the one-eyed Prophet. They passed through the land on moccasined feet—by art and by necessity they left no trail.

But two of them, out of many, have been well remembered—two Simons. Simon Girty and Simon Kenton learned the lore of the trail. They could withstand cold and hunger; they could set out empty-handed across hundreds of miles of hostile country. They were swift and they were patient. They could stand as still as an oak trunk or they could run for hours on soundless feet. They were alike in craft and courage. They had the same charmed life against peril—they got through again and again. They were friends all their lives—from the time in their youth when they scouted the Kanawha woods together, to the time when old Simon Kenton left a war party to call at old Simon Girty's hut on the Detroit River. They both died poor, though they had seen the waste country change to a land of riches.

They were alike in all these ways and yet one was a villain, according to our history, and the other a hero. That is to say, they served opposite sides. Girty cast his lot with the Indians and Kenton served the cause of his own people. So Girty became a name for fiendishness. Frontier mothers frightened their children with a dreadful saying, "Simon Girty will get you!" He was the fearful dark of the uncleared woods and the gliding shadows of Indians in ambush. He was the stained scalping knife and the crazed war cry. But Simon Kenton was a defender. He was the strong oak behind whom women and children might cower—he was a stockade for protection. He was the forerunner of farms and settlements in the disputed land. The two Simons were friends—in a crisis the hero's life was saved by the villain. But one fought with Clark and the other with the Hair-Buyer Hamilton. One scouted for Mad Anthony Wayne and the other for Little Turtle. One was feared over the frontier and the other was feted. The whole story of the western struggle is in their lives.

Spring came, in the year 1774, with grace and radiance to the Ohio Valley. The maple trees budded and the leaning sycamores dropped their cinnamon scales onto the river. In the woods, little wind-flowers spread their color on the dark wet ground. From settler's clearings, smoke of burning brush went up, soft columns in the tall blue sky, and in fields the moist furrows curled over in the sun. But it was an uneasy season.

All through the valleys of the Big Sandy and the Great Kanawha, Indians were restless. In soft spring nights they lurked at the edge of clearings, voicing the quavering turkey's cry. They fired flaming arrows on roofs of cabins. They came like shadows through the fields, with hatchets in their hands. They might have been placated by promises to respect their hunting grounds, or bought off with a paltry offering of kettles, blankets and Virginia tobacco. But Lord Dunmore, governor of Virginia, called his militia up and sent word through the border settlements that the Indians must be taught a lasting lesson. So on the paths where the redbud was bursting pink and the dogwood showed like white clouds in the underforest, white men waited to kill Indians. After a taste of bloodshed, the troops marched against Chief Logan's camp at Yellow Creek to destroy it utterly.

Logan had been a generous friend of white settlers, sharing his food and fire with them, helping them find their way in that wild country, persuading the Indians to accept them as neighbors. Despite that, a party of border troops swept down to Yellow Creek and massacred Logan's entire family. Later, the desolate old chief made his famous speech: "I appeal to any white man to say if ever he entered Logan's cabin hungry and I gave him not meat, if ever he came cold or naked and I gave him not clothing." Then he pointed out how his kindness had been repaid by the treachery and brutality of Virginian militiamen who "in cold blood and unprovoked, cut off all the relatives of Logan; not sparing even my women and children. There runs not a drop of my blood in the veins of any human creature."

This act called on the Mingo chief for revenge. He called his warriors together, the word going through the forest like the first fitful stirring of a storm wind. Dunmore's militia were moving into the upper Ohio and the Indians gathered along the tributary Kanawha. So Lord Dunmore's brief, inglorious war began.

In that season two scouts served together, seeking the disposal of the Indians, carrying messages between the two divisions of Dunmore's troops. One was Simon Girty and the other was Simon Kenton. Kenton, a beardless youth of nineteen, bore litheness in his six-foot frame. He had clear blue eyes and a soft voice, but he was already a skilled and fearless borderer. Girty was fourteen years older, a short man beside his young comrade, powerfully built, with eyes as black as darkness. Their paths were to cross and recross in the future, but from the first they were drawn to each other. Both had forsaken civilization. Now they shared a campfire and their craft of the wilderness. And sometime, in a mood of almost feminine feeling, while the dark and peril lay around them, the two bold men made a vow of friendship. "Girty and I," Kenton said many years later, "two lonely men on the banks of the Ohio, pledged ourselves one to the other, hand in hand, for life or death, when there was nobody in the wilderness but God and us."

In the glow of their furtive campfire they told each other their stories—what had turned their faces from home and hearth, what had sent them over the border. They were both fugitives.

Simon Kenton grew up at the foot of Bull Run Mountain, in the back country of Virginia. He attended school but half of one day —that taste was sufficient for him. So he was a boy ranging the country, learning to take his directions from trees and streams and stars, finding resources and reliance in himself, becoming acquainted with solitude. Along the stream banks, on the rough mountainsides and in the twilit woods, he learned his lessons.

At sixteen he fought with an older rival for a girl, and left his opponent limp and bleeding on the ground. Thinking that he had killed him, Kenton fled the country. An old farmwife had told him, in his childhood, that the moles on his neck were a sign that he would be hanged at an early age. Now the long-legged youth remembered that prediction and he pushed on grimly over the mountains. His age was sixteen years and seven days. He had neither gun nor provisions, he was barefoot, bareheaded and empty-handed. Thus he began his career in the wilderness.

To escape detection he changed his name to Simon Butler—it was only as Butler that Simon Girty knew him. He voyaged down the Ohio, when that was a mysterious river, into an unknown land.

He hunted and trapped and learned the tongues of the western Indians. He took his furs up river to Fort Pitt and went back again to the hunting grounds. By the time of Dunmore's War, he was nineteen and a veteran of the western country. He was well prepared to serve as a scout for the Virginia militia. Years later he discovered that his rival was not killed that April day beneath Bull Run Mountain, so he resumed the name of Kenton. But he could never resume the tame life of the settlements.

Girty was a man who left his own people for the Indians. He should have been an Indian-hater, but life is not logic and Simon Girty followed instinct rather than conviction. He grew up on the Pennsylvania frontier at the rude little settlement of Chambers Mill near Harrisburg. When he died, the frontier had crossed the Mississippi, and Illinois was ready for statehood.

To the huddled log huts of Chambers Mill the Indians brought their furs to trade for blankets, fire-arms and whisky. Girty's father was a small-time trader, somewhat favored by the Indians because he drank with them in his cabin. In these sessions the savages muttered and shouted and thumped each other till the whisky stupor overcame them. But sometimes they had a fit of rage. On a dark December day in 1751, an Indian named The Fish drank himself full of whisky and split the trader's skull with a tomahawk. At that time Simon Girty was ten years old. His mother soon married again. Five years later the entire family was taken captive by a raiding band of warriors. On the banks of the Allegheny, Simon's step-father was tortured, scalped and toma-hawked before the eyes of his wife and four step-children. For three years Simon Girty lived as a captive in a village of Seneca Indians. It was not an arduous captivity. He learned the Senecas' language and fitted easily into their life. When a treaty required the Ohio Indians to give up their prisoners, he went, half reluc-tantly, back to the settlements. There he met his brothers, who also had been living among savage tribes.

Simon Girty, then, at eighteen, had acquired a taste for the care-less life of the camp and could not share the ambitions of his own

people. He was content with a simple existence—he felt no desire to acquire land or property. He knew no trade but he knew
the Indians. Soon he drifted into the services of the Pennsylvania
traders, acting as Indian interpreter at Fort Pitt, where the tribesmen came in with their packs of peltry. He was more at home
among the Indians than the traders and he spent more time talking
their tongue than his own. He was quick to master new dialects.
Soon he became the best Indian linguist on the frontier. Not only
did he talk their language but he seemed to think with their minds,
and so the Indians liked him—a leader of the Delawares even
adopted his name and became Chief Simon Girty. In that casual
life, going on roving hunts with the tribes, living at the frontier
post, he passed the years of his young manhood until he took the
oath of allegiance to the British king and went to serve as a scout
in Dunmore's War.

So now, beside their campfires in the great woods of the Ohio,
the two Simons met on common ground. Both had turned their
faces from civilization.

Lord Dunmore's War was quickly over. Where the Great Kanawha joins the Ohio, a wedge of land thrusts between the two
rivers. It has a smiling name—Point Pleasant—and now a monument stands quietly above the peaceful land. There it was that the
Virginians were encamped when the Indians, under Cornstalk,
Logan and Blackhoof, burst on them in the uncertain light of
dawn. But the Virginians were seasoned fighters, incapable of
panic. Quickly they spread out in a two-mile line among the trees.
All morning long the Indians pressed the attack, but the Virginia
rifles took a steady toll. In the end, the Indians weakened and their
attack waned. That night they fled, leaving a quarter of their
number dead on the dark field of Point Pleasant.

After that victory, Simon Girty was sent into Ohio to negotiate
with the bitter and defeated Logan. At Pickaway Plains he met
the desolate chief under a massive elm tree, its branches bare
against the autumn sky, and there Logan made his famous speech
of harsh conciliation. "I have killed many," he said, in retaliation

for the massacres of all his kinsmen at Yellow Creek. "I have fully glutted my vengeance. For my country, I rejoice at the beams of peace. Yet, do not harbor the thought that mine is the joy of fear. Logan never felt fear. He will not turn on his heel to save his life. Who is there to mourn for Logan? Not one."

With the Indian uprising put down, Girty remained at Fort Pitt. There he resumed his easy life, interpreting for the Indians who came to trade, going out with an occasional hunting party, caring nothing for personal acquisition. Meanwhile, Kenton had gone down the Ohio to resume his forest life of hunting and trapping in the valley of the Licking River, where he once counted fifteen hundred buffalo pacing in single file to the salt beds. He explored all the game trails and the Indian paths—he kept that great mysterious web like a map in his mind, never to forget it. So he came to know the western country as no man, white or red, had ever known it. Every stream of running water, every ridge above the level land, every forest glade and tangled canebrake he remembered. Now he was a hunter, following the game trails. But soon he was to be engaged in a grimmer stalking, on a mortal pursuit.

In the middle 1770s, the Kentucky settlements were building. From time to time Simon Kenton served as a hunter to provide meat for the growing villages. But the Indians, incited by the British Hair-Buyer at Detroit, crept across the Ohio to raid their lonely settlements. When George Rogers Clark recruited his force for the conquest of the Northwest, he found a man ready for his most exacting service. Simon Kenton became a scout for Clark.

Four borderers were among Clark's recruits, four men who could find their way through hostile country, observing the British garrisons and the movement of Indian parties. Samuel Moore, Ben Lynn, Si Harland and Simon Kenton were to go, in their own way, to spy out the situation in Illinois. That was Clark's plan. But among themselves they decided that two would be more effective than four. They drew lots. Lynn and Moore won the draw and set out as casual hunters to spy at Kaskaskia. When Clark was ready to launch his expedition, Simon Kenton was at his side, floating down the river and marching across the Illinois ridges to Kaskaskia. When Kaskaskia was taken, Clark sent three scouts on a dangerous spying mission to Vincennes. They were three lean, long-striding men with Old Testament names—Shadrach Bond, Elisha Batty and Simon Kenton. They reached the British post on the Wabash, hid their hats and guns in a thicket and with blankets around them, and a hand on a concealed tomahawk, they stalked the streets of Vincennes like half-breed hunters just in from the woods. For three nights they mingled with the French and the Indians. When they left the town, they knew everything that Clark would need to know to plan his bold attack. So they strode back across the winter prairies.

Meanwhile, Simon Girty had joined the British. Disgruntled by his treatment from the revolutionary Virginians and Pennsylvanians, he had decided to cast his lot with the enemy. With him were other disaffected men. Secretly, on the night of March 28, 1778, they crossed the river below the palisades of Fort Pitt and set out for the distant post of Detroit. Seven men made up that party, turning their backs on the cause of Independence. One was a lean, shrewd, calculating Pennsylvania Scot, Alexander McKee. He stood six feet three in his moccasins. His big-nosed face, weathered to the color of beech leaves in fall, gave him an Indian look—he had been Indian agent at Fort Pitt. He met a strange death a few years later. In the West, he raised a fawn which remained a household pet even after it became a full-grown stag. One morning, as McKee was getting out of bed, the animal sprang at him, goring him fatally with its horns. He died within an hour.

But that March night, striding through the Ohio woods with two Negro servants at his side, he was full of a proud and bitter life. Like Girty he was driven by hatred for the military authorities at Fort Pitt. With McKee was his cousin, Robert Surphlit. Another of the party was to become famous as a renegade—a short, pugnacious Irishman, Matthew Elliott. Like Girty he was an experienced borderer who knew the Indian languages and the interior country. The last member of that band of fugitives was a man named

Higgins, who has left no record and seems to have been swallowed up in the western woods.

From Pittsburgh to Detroit was a long journey for men on foot in a time of war. Spring had moved on to the fullness of summer before they reached Detroit. Mid-June had arrived when Colonel Hamilton, the Hair-Buyer, welcomed them to his service. He soon had plans ready for them, and Simon Girty began the career that made him infamous in border history. With a three-fold mission he went to live with the Ohio tribes, keeping them friendly to the British, seeing that British gifts were distributed among them, leading their war parties against the Kentucky settlements.

At this time, Simon Kenton was in Kentucky, hunting game for the settlements and defending them from Indian attack. In the summer of 1778, after a few Indian skirmishes in company with Daniel Boone, Kenton was idling about Boone's Station. Growing tired of inaction, he decided to recover some horses stolen by the Indians and taken across the Ohio. With two companions he crossed the river and soon came upon a herd of horses grazing in a meadow. They haltered the animals and led them back to the river. But a strong wind sprang up and the horses refused to take to the roughened water. While Kenton and his companions waited there for better weather, a party of Shawnees attacked them. One was killed, another escaped and Kenton was taken captive.

This began the most famous episode in Kenton's eventful life. Knowing the scout to be a great prize, the Shawnees resolved to take him back to their village. For transport they chose a young and half-wild horse, lashing Kenton face-upward upon the animal's back. The horse reared and kicked and writhed under the unnatural burden and then plunged wildly through the forest. Kenton was lacerated by branches and briars, and the Shawnees roared with laughter. After three days' journey, they reached the village of Chillicothe. There Kenton was released—to run the gantlet. Half way down the long line he ran with clubs and sticks flaying his head and shoulders. Then in a desperate effort, he lunged aside and broke the close-order line. Summoning all his famed swiftness of foot, he left his pursuers behind. But an Indian, lounging at the edge of the village, appeared in his way. Exhausted as he was, he could not elude the Indian, who threw him to the ground. The Shawnees swarmed around him and he was quickly stunned with their kicks and blows.

In a solemn ceremony the Shawnee warriors voted to kill their famous captive, but only after he had been carried on a tour to the various villages of the tribe. The tour was a prolonged torment for Kenton. At each village he was forced to run the gantlet and he was always subject to whatever torture short of death the tribesmen could devise. Finally, battered and weak and hopeless, his face blackened by the Shawnees as a mark of doom, he lay at the village of Wapatomica.

That day there passed through the village a war party, led by a white man, returning from a foray in Kentucky. Simon Girty saw the prisoner, bound hand and foot, with the children jeering at him. But he did not recognize the scarred and blackened Kenton. For a while he questioned him, as a military prisoner, on matters of warfare. At last he asked the prisoner's name. Kenton had known Girty from the moment of his appearance in the village, and he had waited for this question. When he spoke his name there was a silence between them—perhaps their memories went back to the pledge they had made years before by the flickering light of their campfire. Then, as Kenton told it years later, Girty flung his arms about him and cried like a child.

Old border historians have quoted Girty's eloquent speech to the Shawnees, pleading for the life of his friend. No one can know how that speech went, but whatever he said was sufficient. The Indians released Kenton to his defender, to be Girty's prisoner. That night he slept in Girty's quarters, on a bed of deerskins. In the morning he was fed as much as he could eat. In a few weeks his wounds had healed and he went with Girty on visits to neighboring tribes. Then the tide of Indian feeling changed again. A group of warriors took the prisoner from Girty, tortured him anew, and set out for the Indian town of Sandusky, where he was to be burned at the stake. But when they stopped at the winter hunting lodge of Logan, the old chief recognized Kenton and promised to intercede for him. At Logan's behest a British officer came to Sandusky and bought the prisoner with British gifts, explaining that he was wanted at Detroit for the information he could provide. So Kenton arrived at Detroit while Colonel Hamilton was on his fruitless errand to Vincennes, and there he remained a prisoner of the British for six months. As time went by, he was given the freedom of the settlement and by patient and crafty preparation he managed to escape. Avoiding the Shawnee lands, he went by a wide arc, west of the Wabash, through unexplored country to the Falls of the Ohio and so back again to Kentucky. It was just a year since he had gone on his brief errand to recover stolen horses.

Along the Ohio the sporadic warfare went on. The Indians crept through the woods and murdered farmers in their fields. Kenton scouted the war parties and aimed a deadly rifle from the log stockade. It was a struggle between an old order and a new one, full of bloody incidents, and American destiny hung on violent little episodes hidden in the forest. A family just settled in Kentucky was attacked by a raiding party. An Indian bullet took the life of the father and an Indian raised his tomahawk above the head of a six-year-old boy. At that instant from the doorway of the cabin an older brother shot the Indian. The raiders fled. The boy over whose head the tomahawk had lifted was named Thomas Lincoln. His own son, born twenty-five years later near that scene of border violence, was Abraham Lincoln. Simon Kenton never thought about destiny, but the future of America was quickening into life in the cabins and clearings that he defended.

IN ALL THAT warring West there stood one island of peace and harmony, for a little while. In 1772, a band of Moravian missionaries, Christian Frederick Post, David Zeisberger and John Hecke- welder, had christianized the Delaware Indians in the gentle Ohio country at the head of the Tuscarawas River. They established sev-

eral tranquil villages—near a spring of sparkling water was Schoenbrunn (Beautiful Spring), amid wide fields of Indian corn was
Gnadenhutten (Tents of Grace), on a sun-bathed plain was Lich-
tenau (Fields of Light). Now the village of Schoenbrunn, restored
as a museum on its original site, shows the timbered cabins and
the grassy street where once the Indian brethren lived in serenity.
There were no firearms in their villages—they had no use for the
tomahawk but to chop firewood and they carried no scalping
knives.

But their villages lay, unfortunately, on the path of war between
Fort Pitt and Detroit. Fearing that the Moravian towns were giving aid to Revolutionary spies and that the missionaries sent reports of British movements to the American authorities at Fort
Pitt, the British took military action. In the fall of 1781, a band of
Wyandot Indians under British leadership rounded up the Delaware brethren and drove them west to "Captive's Town" in the
dreary Wyandot country near Upper Sandusky. There Simon
Girty spent the winter with the Wyandots, keeping surveillance
over the missionaries whom he suspected of complicity with the
Americans at Fort Pitt. All that winter the converted Delawares,
torn between the exhortations of the Wyandots to return to their
Indian beliefs and their trust in the Moravian teachers who were
so wise about the Great Spirit named Jehovah, huddled in their
smoky lodges nibbling their daily ration of a pint of corn.

By early spring provisions were so low at Captive's Town that
the Delawares were permitted to return to their Tuscarawas villages to gather the corn left standing in their fields. There they re-
opened their cabins, and each day they went to the fields to strip
the corn from the tattered stalks. In the midst of that peaceful task
a company of Pennsylvania militiamen arrived. There were a hundred of them, roving the country for marauding Indians. The
Delawares in their fields were the Indians they found. Quickly
they took action. They surrounded the Delawares and drove them,
their arms still filled with yellow corn, into the village of Gnadenhutten. There they herded the whole number into two cabins, the

men into one and the women and children into another. After debating whether to kill them or take them as prisoners to Fort Pitt, the militiamen under Colonel David Williamson proved that they could be more savage than the Indians. They marched into the crowded cabins and massacred ninety-six men, women and children. Two Delaware boys, cowering in a corner, were overlooked—they were the only remnant of those peaceful Brethren. Then the Pennsylvanians burned the cabins above the dead bodies, and the "Tents of Grace" was a blackened ruin among the withered cornfields.

Meanwhile, Heckewelder and Zeisberger had been taken from Upper Sandusky to the forest-shored Sandusky harbor on Lake Erie, where a boat was to take them to the British authorities at Detroit. They were still there when Simon Girty came in from a scouting expedition. He disliked the missionaries, and a bottle of rum put him in a bad humor. He threatened their lives, but he sank into a harmless stupor before he could execute his threats. The next day, two bateaux appeared over the flat rim of Lake Erie. The missionaries were taken to Detroit.

By that time the Pennsylvania militiamen were moving west against the Wyandot towns. Wary Indian scouts observed their approach and when they neared Upper Sandusky the Wyandots were ready. In a brisk encounter the militia was defeated and Colonel William Crawford was taken prisoner to Half-King's Town. There, on a soft June night, Colonel Crawford and Simon Girty met. They talked a while—quite possibly Crawford asked Girty to intercede for his life and possibly Girty agreed to try. But Crawford had been leading an expedition to wipe out the Wyandots and Delawares, and his men had committed the massacre of Gnadenhutten. There was little reason for the Indians to spare him.

Crawford's fate was horrible, and because Girty watched it in silence he has been called a fiendish man. But Girty was helpless to intervene. And Crawford took his torture and death with great courage. For three hours he endured an agony of slow death. The

Indians cut off his ears, stripped him naked and beat him while
he hobbled about a blazing fire. They burned and shot and hacked
him until at last he fainted and fell into the embers and the fire
burned out. Two white men saw it—Dr. John Knight, a prisoner
who later escaped, and Simon Girty. If Girty watched with less
than John Knight's anguish, it was because he had lived a rough
life and he knew the ways of savages and the wilderness.

When Girty reached Detroit, the war was over and the border
grew quiet. Girty lounged about the fort, vaguely discontented
with idleness. In the summer of 1784, he started on an aimless tour
of the Ohio country. In a Delaware town he found a white girl,
half his years, who since being captured four years earlier had
lived with the Indians. When Girty left the town, Catherine Malott
walked beside him. Together they went north to Lake Erie and
around the shore to Detroit. There Simon Girty made her his wife.
He took her to a little farm on Indian land across the Detroit
River, he built a cabin and tried briefly to farm a strip of ground.
But his heart was not in it.

Though the British had surrendered the West, there was still
an Indian border and the British still retained control of the western trade. The interior country had to be won again and again.
Sullenly the Indians watched the westward-moving Americans.
Settlements were under way north of the Ohio. The Ohio Company had planted its town of Marietta and claimed the entire Muskingum Valley, and a hundred miles farther west a group of New
Jersey speculators had contracted for the land between the Great
and Little Miami rivers and had begun a settlement where Cincinnati now stands. Incited by the British traders the Indians rallied
to defend their lands. By 1790, Simon Girty was the father of two
children and approaching fifty years of age. But when word came
that General Josiah Harmar at Fort Washington—now Cincinnati
—was ready to march north with a thousand men, he was off to
the wars again. At the Indian camps he was welcomed with feasts
and dancing. He sat in the councils of the Miami Little Turtle
and the Delaware Captain Pipe, of the Wyandot Tarhe the Crane

and the Shawnee Blue Jacket—a white man who had lived among the Shawnees since his boyhood and had become a chief—and he discussed with the bold young Tecumseh the strategy of ambush and surprise.

The Indian strongholds were in the valleys of the upper Wabash and the Maumee, close to the source of British supplies at Detroit. Early in the autumn of 1790, General Harmar, with nearly fifteen hundred troops, set out from Fort Washington for the Maumee. In a victorious march he destroyed villages from which the Indians had retreated and he felt that he had overawed the hostile tribes. But when he turned back toward the Ohio, the tables were reversed. The Indians struck swiftly and savagely from the woods along his line of march, taking toll of his troops again and again. Bands of warriors followed the army down to the Ohio, attacking white outposts in the Miami Valley. Harmar got his humiliated force back to Fort Washington, but his campaign had only stirred the tribes to a new pitch of hostility.

The next year, General Arthur St. Clair, governor of the Northwest Territory, organized a punitive expedition with which he meant to push the Indians permanently out of Ohio. But this time the Indians reversed their tactics. Instead of retreating, they advanced to meet the northward-moving army. St. Clair was ill with rheumatism and gout, he had poorly trained troops and no scouts in advance of his expedition. In what became Mercer County, Ohio, on a bleak November day, the Indians burst upon him. Simon Girty was in their foremost ranks, along with the chiefs whose councils he had sat with when their strategy was being planned. It was a disaster for the Americans. Six hundred of St. Clair's men were left dead on the field and when the battered, tattered files tramped back to Fort Washington, Ohio was still Indian country.

Not until two years later, in 1793, did the Americans try again. Then it was Wayne, the Big Wind, that did it. He could bluster, he could be brazen, brash and bold—he was Mad Anthony. But he became coldly careful when care was needed. He trained his

troops till obedience was instinctive and he taught them every detail of every maneuver in his battle plans. Then he moved north,
building strong forts that the Indians could not oppose. He went
into winter quarters at Fort Greenville. From there he sent scouts
into the Maumee country.

That winter, in the villages along the Maumee, Simon Girty con-
ferred with his dusky colleagues. Carefully they planned their
strategy, but it was they who were surprised by Wayne's powerful
force and by his methodic advance that gave them no opportunity
to engage his forces piecemeal. During the winter, Wayne built a
stockade on the site of St. Clair's disaster, calling it with full confidence Fort Recovery. In the spring, keeping his force compact
and his supplies at hand, he advanced to the head of the Maumee
and there, at the edge of the Indians' own stronghold, he built Fort
Defiance. Finally, on August 20, 1794, Wayne's army met the full
force of Indian resistance. The place was chosen by Wayne, in a
ruined swath of forest where a cyclone had left a wreckage of
"Fallen Timbers." A big wind had prepared the battle ground for
Big Wind, and it took just sixty minutes for Wayne's crouching
files of infantry and his swift flanking cavalry to rout the Ohio
Indians and end forever their armed resistance to American
authority.

A year later, in August, 1795, a congress of 1,130 chiefs and warriors came peaceably to Greenville to sign Wayne's historic treaty.
The Indians had sold their land again and again. Now, at Greenville, Wayne paid in trade goods and annuities for territory that
had previously been purchased three times over—at Fort Stanwix,
in 1784, at Fort McIntosh, in 1785, and at Fort Harmar, in 1789.
The difference was that Wayne had firmly planted American military power across western Ohio. In reality the Treaty of Greenville
opened interior Ohio to peaceful settlement.

While Simon Girty shared these final defeats with his Indian
colleagues, Simon Kenton had been scouting the disputed country
for the American generals. He led forays against marauding bands
of warriors. He intercepted Indian sorties. And along with these

martial errands he located land warrants for venturesome settlers and helped them survey their boundaries. He disapproved of Governor St. Clair as a military leader, tersely and shrewdly reading his character—"He was a minister-looking man. He had no briar-look—no keenness in him." But when Wayne took command of operations, Kenton felt different. At Wayne's request he raised a band of scouts who went ahead of the army's methodic advance, taking Indian prisoners, getting information, keeping the tribes anxious. Though he was restless during Wayne's deliberate halts for the building of forts, he came to see that Wayne's way was the way of a complete and lasting victory.

So, after many years of border warfare, there came a term of peace. When war loomed again in 1812, Simon Kenton, fifty-eight years old, was slowly recovering from a broken leg. His family objected to another campaign, but he could not miss it. From Urbana, Ohio, where he now lies buried, he rode off to join the Americans moving on the British at Detroit. When the American troops reached Detroit, the British had retreated across the river and the Americans followed, overtaking them on the banks of the little River Thames. Kenton, as he had done in his younger years, was ahead of the army, scouting British movements, and he was present at the sharp skirmish in which Tecumseh, the Shooting Star of the Shawnees, was killed. At the end of the war the whole Northwest was won from the Indians and the British, and the border was pushed on across the Mississippi.

On that last campaign, in enemy country across the Detroit River, Simon Kenton took a day off from military duty to visit his old friend Simon Girty on the little farm near Amherstberg. Girty was away and so Kenton missed him. That was just as well, for it would have been a sad meeting.

Girty had become an old man, crippled and rheumatic. His hair had turned white, his skin hung loose on his once bull-like neck and his eyesight was dimming. For a few years he lived on beside the river, waiting for the end. Sometimes a restless, moody Indian stopped to visit him, but there was no more strategy to plan against the marching troops, no traps to spring upon defenseless settlements. The Big Wind, General Wayne, had been dead for twenty years. Chief Blue Jacket was buried beside the Auglaize River in Ohio. Old Tarhe the Crane was in his grave beside the Sandusky, and Little Turtle, dead, surprisingly, of gout, lay under the grass of Kekiong-gay near Fort Wayne, in the new state of Indiana. In February of 1818, while a swirling snowstorm hid the fields and the river outside his door, old Simon Girty died. So ended the days of the border's most notorious renegade, a man with a kind of savage greatness. As though the earth were reluctant to receive him, they had to hack the frozen ground for his grave.

Simon Kenton lived nearly twenty years longer, until 1836. He had claimed great tracts of land and lost them through legal confusion and complication. The wilderness he had scouted became valuable before his death, but he had no share in its new era. He drew a pension of twenty dollars a month, a scarred and dented man, sometimes living over the forays and perils of his youth. Then he gave up, playing games with children in the sun and dozing by the fireside in his last winter. The April woods were greening, the dogwood shining white when he died.

IX

The Echo of Tippecanoe

THE WEST had to be won again and again. The French won it by the infiltration of trade and evangelism among the Indians. The British won it by siege and foray from the French. Then the Americans won it from the British by forced marches and bold attack. And still it was the Indians' land. In the ensuing years, Americans won it from the Indians in a sporadic and protracted war that continued from the rout of Cornstalk on the Upper Ohio, to Black Hawk's defeat, sixty years later, on the Upper Mississippi. Point Pleasant, Fallen Timbers, Tippecanoe, Bad Axe Bottoms—these are names for gunfire, the quavering war cry and the driving of the tribes from a land where history could not leave them in possession.

The most resounding name, though it was a brief and meager battle, is Tippecanoe. It is a name in a high voice, a prolonged and echoing name. It has a halloo-ing timbre, like a word called across a distance or a span of time. It is a word that could come from but one country in the earth—it is as American as Yankee Doodle. It became remembered—partly for its sound, and partly because the savage syllables make a kind of grotesque English sense. It also calls to mind the clash of two leaders of their people—the great Shawnee Chief Tecumseh and the old Indian fighter and brief-term President, William Henry Harrison.

Mad River, in western Ohio, is, except in the time of spring freshets, a tranquil stream, taking a leisurely way toward the Great Miami and the Ohio. It could not have been much different in 1768 when there stood on the wooded bank of the river, near the present city of Springfield, Ohio, an Indian village of Shawnees and Delawares. Here in that year a Creek woman, lying in a hut made of round saplings chinked with clay, bore to her Shawnee husband three male children. One of those triplets was to lose his life in a raid against white settlers in the mountain coves of Tennessee. Another became the "Prophet," the one-eyed sachem whose religious zeal fired the tribes from Ohio to beyond the Mississippi. The third was Tecumseh, the Shooting Star, the greatest Indian of history.

It is not surprising that this leader sprang from the Shawnee people. They were a small tribe—a hundred and fifty warriors, perhaps six hundred people all told—in Tecumseh's time, but they had a long history of independence and a proud tradition. According to their legends the Shawnees were the first people created by the Master of Life, and all other red men were descended from the original Shawnees. They had come from the sunny pampas of Florida, where the Suwanee River retains the tribal name. By stages they had lived and hunted through the middle ground. Through many wanderings and resettlements they retained their freedom and their identity. With their nomadic life, their patriarchal traditions and their pride of race, some early Americans speculated on their being descendants of the Lost Tribes of Israel. They believed themselves superior to the sedentary tribes—they had the flexibility and the imagination of wanderers. This was the line that might produce a national leader—a man who could dream of a confederacy of all the jealous and warring tribes of the troubled Indian race.

When Tecumseh was a lad of six, his warrior father was killed in Cornstalk's clash with the Virginians at Point Pleasant. When he was twelve, his home was destroyed by raiding Kentuckians under George Rogers Clark. He fled with the women and children into the woods. When the Americans were gone, he stared at the ashes of the Indian town and the smoking ruins of their storehouse. He was early learning the mortal rivalry between his people and the white men. Even then he must have seen that warfare as the life-struggle of his race, yet when he became the leader of that struggle he proved chivalrous and magnanimous, opposing torture of white prisoners, sparing lives whenever possible.

Tecumseh's life had the quality of legend and its events and surroundings seemed to be preparing him for a destined role as leader of his people. Born a Shawnee, of the proud and unprovincial tribe, he grew up in the strategic, cosmopolitan town of Piqua, a center of Indian life in the Ohio country. Piqua lay on the trail from Lake Erie to the Ohio River. It was a halting place for families on the move, a meeting place for tribes in council. To its council fires came members of the Ohio tribes—Miamis, Wyandots and Delawares, the Michigan Ottawas and Chippewas, the Illinois Kickapoos and Potawatomis, the Foxes and Winnebagos from Wisconsin and the Sacs from beside the Mississippi. In Piqua the boy Tecumseh learned the languages and traditions of the scattered nations. He thumped time to their songs and dances. He heard their disputes and problems. He came to realize that they had a common cause and a common destiny.

When he was nineteen, Tecumseh set out with a roving party on a three-year wandering. This was his coming-of-age, his *wanderjahr,* that would give him experience, perspective, maturity. The little band of young men set out west through the forest trails to the Wabash and over the Grand Prairie beyond it. They crossed the Mississippi and hunted buffalo—already diminished on their own lands—with the restless, pony-mounted Osages. Back on the east side of the Mississippi, they allied themselves to a war party of Cherokees that was harrying the settlements of American squatters in the valleys of Tennessee. Now Tecumseh tasted the diverse passions of war. He knew its grief when a triplet brother was killed by a white man's bullet and he knew its exultation when he led a victorious attack through a bullet-swept clearing. Before he left the southern tribes, the young Tecumseh had won their lasting respect. He fought beside the Cherokees like a blood brother and in a friendly hunting contest he brought back more game than the veteran hunters of the hills. They remembered his long stride, his quiet, confident voice, his far-seeing eyes.

Twenty years later they still remembered him and unquestion-ingly accepted his leadership in the Indian Confederacy. When he returned to his own people in 1790, he was not a boy but a man.

The three years of Tecumseh's wandering had seen important changes in Ohio. Under the Land Ordinance of 1785, Congress had granted to the Ohio Company and the Scioto Company extensive tracts along the Ohio River east of the Scioto. In the spring of 1788, the first caravan of Yankee settlers had arrived from Massa-chusetts and were erecting their town of Marietta at the mouth of the Muskingum River in the Ohio Grant. In the same year John Cleves Symmes and a company of New Jersey speculators con-tracted for a million acres between the two Miami rivers and built their first settlement on the site of Cincinnati. The new Ohio set-tlers called for military protection and the government increased the strength of the garrisons in the recent grants. Treaties were made with the Indians, and settlers soon pushed beyond the treaty lines. The tribes were bound to resist.

Tecumseh, in his early twenties, took a strong part in the spo-radic warfare. He fought against General Harmar's expedition in 1790, helping to drive it back in defeat to the Ohio. He led small parties against the Kentuckians under George Rogers Clark and Simon Kenton. He was in the front of the attack that slashed to pieces St. Clair's unwieldy army. When Wayne advanced into the Indian grounds, Tecumseh led the Shawnee warriors. After the defeat at Fallen Timbers, he accepted the hopelessness of further resistance. But he did not attend the treaty congress at Greenville, and when rich hunting grounds six days' horseback journey in width were ceded for a pile of perishable trade goods and annuities of $250 to $1000 to the tribes, he denounced the chiefs who signed the treaty.

In the next years, Tecumseh ranged widely as a hunter. But he was really on another mission. He sat with leaders of the tribes, discussing the sale of land to white settlers and the loss of tribal hunting grounds. He ranged the whole Northwest and, as he visited the scattered tribes, he began to develop his idea of an Indian Confederacy. Before him Pontiac had conceived a common uprising, but Tecumseh dreamed of a unified nation. He saw all the tribes, from the lakes to the Gulf, from the Alleghenies to the Rockies joined in a permanent union, like the new-formed union of the American Colonies. They would act in one accord on matters of warfare and diplomacy, and they would agree to a joint ownership of all the interior land so that there could be no piecemeal cession by petty tribal chiefs.

While Tecumseh was working with patience and foresight for his confederacy, his remaining triplet brother came into great influence among the Indians. He (Laulewasikau) announced himself as the successor of an aged medicine man who had recently died. So he took upon himself the role of a prophet, and as The Prophet he became known to history. He had a striking appearance—one eye socket was empty, from an accident in hunting, and the remaining eye was enlarged and commanding. He wore heavy brass rings in his ears and an elaborate headdress that added to his uncommon height. He was an eloquent orator. Indians who had heard him describe the new future for his race spread his fame wherever they went. Soon hundreds were coming to his village on the Wabash to hear him for themselves. He preached a return to Indian ways and a renouncing of the white man's trade and treaties. He prophesied a new age of power and prosperity for the tribes. This doctrine fitted in with Tecumseh's political conceptions and for several seasons the two brothers traveled together from tribe to tribe. They pictured how in the near future the Indians would gain back their surrendered land, game would multiply and thickets would close over the roads that the white men had slashed through the forest. The Indians listened gladly. Crowds of warriors came to hear them and returned to their villages with a new and burning purpose.

In 1808, the Shawnee brothers set up a kind of diplomatic capital at the point where Tippecanoe Creek flows into the Wabash. This place, the former site of a Miami village which had been destroyed by American troops, soon became a center and stronghold of In-

dian life. It was called Prophet's Town. When news of the inter-
tribal gathering at Prophet's Town reached Vincennes, young
William Henry Harrison, governor of the Northwest Territory,
was alarmed.

William Henry Harrison could not then have known what the
name Tippecanoe was to mean in his varied life, but he knew that
any gathering of Indians must be suspected. Harrison, at twenty-
seven, was governor of all the Northwest. As a youth of aristocratic Virginia ancestry he had gone into the army, served under
Wayne and risen rapidly to prestige and influence. He was a
shrewd negotiator and a stubborn foe of the Indians. In 1795, he
married the daughter of John Cleves Symmes and he shared his
father-in-law's conviction that the Indian claim to traditional lands
should not stand in the way of civilized occupation.

From the leafy little town of Vincennes, Harrison conducted his
office of territorial governor. In a walnut grove beside the Wabash
he built a mansion, impressive for that time and place—a solid
brick house of twenty-six rooms in the Virginia plantation style.
This dignified place, with its lawns and gardens sloping to the
river, was the social capital of the entire Northwest. He called it
"Grouseland." The house still stands today, preserved as a museum,
beside the slowly-curving Wabash.

To Grouseland, between 1808 and 1811, Harrison summoned
Tecumseh three times for council. Each time he told the Indian
leader that his people must make way for the American occupation of new country. Each time Tecumseh was dignified and defiant—and between times he tirelessly ranged the western country,
cementing the new alliance of the tribes. Harrison wrote with a
kind of baffled misgiving: "You see him [Tecumseh] today on the
Wabash, and in a short time you hear of him on the shores of
Lake Erie or Michigan, or on the banks of the Mississippi, and
wherever he goes he makes an impression favorable to his purpose."

In the fall of 1810, while Tecumseh was on a southern journey
winning the support of a distant tribe, Harrison decided it was

time to strike. With the arrival of fresh troops at Vincennes, he sent out a general demand for the surrender of all Indians accused of killing American settlers and called upon the Miamis in particular to renounce the leadership of Tecumseh, to disclaim the Prophet and to reject the Indian confederation. When it was reported that a party of warriors had stolen horses from a white settlement, Harrison began his march on Tippecanoe.

Sixty miles above Vincennes, near the site of the present Terre Haute, the governor built a fort on the Wabash, named Fort Harrison for himself. Ahead of him to Prophet's Town on Tippecanoe Creek he sent twenty friendly Miami chiefs who were to appeal to the Prophet to accept Harrison's demands. The Miamis did not return—Harrison later learned they had fallen under the spell of the Prophet's eloquence and joined the confederation. Harrison drew up his force of nine hundred men a mile and a half from Prophet's Town, where it was arranged that he should meet the Prophet in council the next day. But Harrison's movement to a camp ground nearer the town, and his disposal of his troops in the hollow-triangle battle order, made the Indians suspect that he was planning an attack before daybreak. In Tecumseh's absence the Prophet urged the chiefs to prepare for attack. Hidden in willow clumps and thickets, the Indians waited through a night of intermittent rain for the first hostile move across the field. In the faint dawn, when Harrison's orderly beat the drum for reveille, the anxious Indians thought the attack was on. Swiftly they charged upon the camp.

So with the ring of riflefire and the thud of gunstocks and tomahawks began the tragic battle in the half light of a November morning, At first the Indians broke the American lines and poured into the enclosure. Harrison had to regroup to preserve his shattered lines. But when daylight broadened, his mounted troops became effective and the Indians had to give way. The Americans outnumbered them and were better armed. Once the Indians began to yield, the pressure increased against them. By mid-morning they were in full flight across the Wabash bottoms. The next day

Harrison marched into the deserted Prophet's Town. He destroyed it completely and set fire to the stored harvest of five thousand bushels of corn. After three days' rest for his troops, he turned back to Vincennes. When he arrived there he was a hero. "Tippecanoe" had a bitter sound to Indian ears, but to the Americans it meant deliverance.

Tecumseh returned to a town in ruins. His cause seemed lost with his defeated and scattered followers but he was not yet ready to give in. With a new war impending between the Americans and the British, he crossed the Detroit River and joined forces with the British. From their stronghold of Malden he went out to win the Indians of the lakes region to the British cause. "Tippecanoe" had begun to bear bitter fruit.

To the West the War of 1812 brought a brief reign of terror. Just five garrisoned posts lay between the Ohio and Canada—Fort Harrison, Fort Wayne, Detroit, Fort Dearborn and Fort Mackinac. The first American strategy called for an invasion of Canada from Detroit. General William Hull, commanding in the West, reached Detroit on July fifth and looked across the river to the British post of Malden. While he waited indecisively, a hard blow was struck the American cause far to the north. Where Lake Huron narrows to the island-studded strait, on its humped, turtle-shaped island, the new Fort Mackinac stood—under Lieutenant Porter Hanks with fifty-seven men. The monotonous garrison life went on in that stockade on the edge of the island's southern cliff. They did not know that war had begun. But from St. Joseph's Island, in the St. Mary's River, a force of six hundred Indians under British leaders was approaching. The leaders landed their fleet of canoes in the dead of night on the north shore of the island, at a point still called British Landing. In the darkness they hauled two cannon up to a height above and behind Fort Mackinac. By daylight they had the fort surrounded. It fell without a shot.

When word of the fall of Mackinac came down Lake Huron to Detroit, Hull feared that the victorious British and Indians would attack his rear. While he waited, still indecisive, the British moved

forces from Niagara to Malden and launched them at Hull across
the river. That bold move caught Hull off balance—he surrendered
Detroit and all of Michigan Territory.

On the sandy shore of Lake Michigan, beside the sluggish
Chicago River, Fort Dearborn stood, isolated now that Detroit
was in the hands of the enemy. Fur-trader John Kinzie had already grown fearful. He had left his cabin under its two poplar
trees, put away his fiddle, untied a dugout from his landing and
rowed his family across to the fort for protection. A growing camp
of surly Potawatomis assembled around the post. Summer came
lush and lovely over the prairies and the lake, but in Fort Dearborn it was an uneasy season. Then in early August, 1812, came a
dispatch from Hull ordering evacuation of the post. Captain Heald,
the commandant, gave his provisions to the Indians and secretly
dumped his ammunition in the river. He got his baggage wagons
ready, loaded in the women and children, and at 9 A. M., on
August fifteenth, the stockade opened and the procession filed out
on the rutted road, that became Michigan Avenue, between a low
ridge of sandhills and the sandy beach of the lake. For a mile the
Potawatomis lurked along in the rear of the procession. Then
they disappeared. Half a mile farther their heads thrust up, like
turtles—a survivor later remembered—over the ridge. It was
ambush.

A burst of riflefire began it. Then it was melee. In its midst a
young Indian climbed into a wagon and scalped twelve white children. It didn't last long—there were sixty-nine whites against five
hundred Indians. Within an hour half the whites lay grotesquely
on the sand—their bones whitened the beach for years—and
the rest were captives. Next day the Indians plundered the fort
and burned its buildings to the ground. So, for the first time,
Chicago went out in fire and there was a smoldering mound of
ashes where the river flowed around its sandbar into the tranquil,
sunlit lake.

With these failures and disasters in the West, the Wabash-
Maumee line became the limit of American military authority.

Most of the Northwest was lost when William Henry Harrison was given chief command. He had to win the territory back. And he did. His strategy was to drive the British off the lakes and to march for the recovery of Detroit. To fulfill this plan, Perry built his fleet in the forest at Presque Isle and sailed out to win his resounding victory on Lake Erie. At the same time Harrison stormed Detroit and pursued the British across the river into Canada. With the British were Tecumseh and six hundred warriors. The British commander was reluctant to make a stand but, at the banks of the Thames River, Tecumseh declared that his warriors would not retreat another step.

Harrison crossed the Thames with his men keen for action and faced the British drawn up in open order. Shrewdly he sent his horsemen to break the line of British infantry in a wooded area between the river Thames and swampy ground. At the command, his horsemen spurred forward. Once they wavered in the British fire, but a second rush carried them through. In two minutes the British first line had surrendered. The Indians were more stubborn. Crouching behind logs and trees they raked the Americans with riflefire. But the American line was stiffened by reinforcements. Soon the battlefield grew still and the outnumbered Indians faded like shadows in the brush and swamp. The engagement lasted just twenty minutes. When it was over Tecumseh lay dead among the scarlet autumn leaves.

When Harrison's men found the famed chief's body, they took from it bits of clothing and even strips of Shawnee skin, as souvenirs of battle. That was the end of the Indian confederacy. Harrison marched his troops back to Detroit and embarked them on Perry's victorious ships, with the purpose of retaking Fort Mackinac four hundred miles away. But when the ships grounded on the shallows of the St. Clair River, that expedition was abandoned. Instead, the fleet sailed down Lake Erie to Niagara for the final battles of the war. Tecumseh was dead, the British were beaten and Harrison was a hero to his nation. In that aura he resigned from the military and governmental service and settled on his farm at North Bend, Ohio, above a great curve of the river.

Tippecanoe was past but it was not forgotten. To the rolling farm above the river came admirers of William Henry Harrison. He was commissioned to make new treaties with the Indians and he journeyed west to meet the tribes in negotiations which opened all the country east of the Mississippi to American settlement. Politics took him to Congress and a diplomatic mission sent him as United States Minister to Colombia. And in 1840, nearly three decades after the battle by the Wabash, the hero of Tippecanoe became a Presidential candidate.

It was a hectic, hilarious campaign, full of rollicking, roistering and rolling the cider barrel. Harrison was the Northwest's candidate, the Northwest's hero, against the suave New Yorker, Van Buren. The old fighter's associates in the Indian wars rallied round him and new admirers flocked to his support—"Tippecanoe" they began to call him. He made a speaking tour by steamboat down the Ohio River. At every landing odes were read in his honor, torchlights flickered, monster mass meetings assembled. The Westerners were behind their man and they carried on a campaign with all the color of a county fair and the fervor of a crusade. If the contest contained no political ideas, no single trace of thought, they made up for that lack by parades and band concerts, by nicknames and slogans.

Early in the struggle the opposition made a fatal error. In attacking General Harrison they charged that he was poor and ignorant, that he drank hard cider and ate crackers and knew no better than to offer his guests that simple fare. They said he was a log-cabin and hard-cider farmer who worked with his own hands. That jibe was a boomerang. It provided the Whigs with all their rallying cries. If Harrison was poor, more credit to him. In Van Buren's administration there had been two panics—in 1837 and 1839—and it was the lot of a good American to be poor and to work with his hands at such a time. And if Harrison remained poor after handling millions of dollars as governor of the Northwest Territory, his was a proud and honorable poverty. But the greatest shout went up in support of the man who lived in a log cabin and liked hard cider. Almost overnight thousands of log cabins were set up in cities, towns and villages, in courthouse yards and beside railway stations and in public parks and squares. At Whig rallies log cabins, live coons and kegs of cider took the place of political doctrines, and the chant of "Tippecanoe and Tyler too" was heard from the Atlantic to the Mississippi. It was the most laughing, shouting, singing campaign ever held. It was a prolonged, hilarious jamboree.

Immense crowds gathered—twelve thousand at Springfield, Illinois, fifteen thousand at the historic town of Greenville, Ohio, thirty thousand at Fort Meigs on the Maumee, where Old Tip had withstood the British and the Indians, forty thousand on the Tippecanoe battlefield beside the Wabash. At Tippecanoe the meetings lasted for three days and more than three thousand wagons were counted on the grounds. As the election neared, the excitement mounted. Where Harrison took the stump for an address, the crowds were counted not by hundreds, or thousands, but by acres. Political parades, miles in length, passed over the roads, canals and rivers of the West. And everywhere was the log cabin, the cider barrel and the shout of "Tippecanoe!"

Here was the beginning of the log-cabin sentiment in American politics and folklore. At every mass meeting there was a log-cabin "raising," with coonskins on the walls and live coons climbing the roof, and a cider barrel beside an old oaken bucket dripping cool well water. Sixty thousand persons paraded behind a movable log cabin in Boston, another sixty thousand marched in Syracuse beside canoes and log cabins mounted on wheels. At Springfield, Illinois, young Abe Lincoln spoke to a crowd that had gathered from a hundred miles around. In fact, one log cabin had been hauled on wheels all the way from Chicago by thirty yokes of oxen. A fire burned on its hearth, real smoke issued from its chimney and the latchstring hung conspicuously out. That traveling cabin had a live hickory tree growing in its dooryard, with live coons climbing in the branches. At Dayton, Ohio, then a town of six thousand, an estimated seventy-five thousand persons milled around the ubiquitous log cabins and shouted for Old Tip.

Actually it was a symbol and a myth that fastened the log cabin onto William Henry Harrison, who had lived in his Grouseland mansion at Vincennes and in a fine residence on two thousand acres at North Bend. But it was a deeply American symbol, as "Tippecanoe and Tyler too" was an unstoppable American slogan. Farmers named their teams Tip and Ty—"Git up Tip, go it Ty!" was heard in unnumbered harvest fields, on all the roads and at every village hitching rack. And people who had no idea what Tippecanoe was or where the outlandish name came from went to cast their votes for the log-cabin candidate. So when the votes were counted, Van Buren, who ate soup from a silver tureen and drank imported wines, carried only seven states, and Old Tip went to Washington. "We have been sung down, lied down, drunk down," said the Democrats.

But the victory was brief for General Harrison. Though he had gone robustly through the frenzied campaign, he fell ill immediately after his inaugural. Within a month he was dead. This was the shortest Presidency in our history.

On his farm at North Bend the old Indian-fighter was buried and over his tomb a tall shaft was raised as his monument. At its top it carries a beacon light seen far down the river. For a century now, steamboat captains have saluted Old Tip with a soft, hoarse whistle as they pass the quiet point where he lies.

Tecumseh had no monument, but his name was not forgotten. In taverns in Illinois and Indiana, when winter snow lay deep on the prairie, men told a tale of Tecumseh's skin being stripped from the body and dried and made into razor strops—though some doubted it would serve that purpose. On the Ohio and the Mississippi, a hundred years ago, a handsome paddlewheel steamer named "Tecumseh" carried crowds of people from Cincinnati to Vicksburg and New Orleans. It was decorated like a feted warrior, with a sunburst on the paddle boxes, brass rings on the monkey braces and red collars on the tall twin chimneys. In Annapolis, a long way from the inland waters of the Shawnee country, an Indian figurehead recovered from the sunken U.S.S. *Delaware* was set up on the Naval Academy grounds shortly after the Civil War. Though it represented the Delaware chief Tamenend, the midshipmen called the bold Indian head Tecumseh and began a lasting tradition of saluting it on their way to recitations, to ensure a passing grade.

THERE IS a familiar irony in America's treatment of the Indians. They were feared and hated, driven out and extinguished, and then idealized. After he was safely dead, Tecumseh became the subject of romantic writing and romantic painting. He was made the hero of a poetic drama—five acts in heroic couplets—and artists painted him as a man of delicate yet commanding features, with poetic face, noble bearing and far-seeing eyes.

Tecumseh saw the doom of his race and perhaps he thought of himself as the last resisting leader of his people. But another leader emerged and the Indians made one more stand before they were forever driven beyond the Mississippi. Looking at those romantic portraits, you may think of another bitter and beaten chief—the last in all the Northwest Territory to resist—who after his death was commemorated by a great granite statue, fifty feet tall, on the land that he failed to defend.

Black Hawk's land lay five hundred miles west of the Shawnee country. It was safe for a generation after the Battle of Tippecanoe. The chief village of the Sac Indians occupied a tableland on the Mississippi three miles south of Rock Island, where the Rock River joins the Mississippi. Here on a V of land between the rivers, the Sacs had their wide cornfields, their clustered lodges and their national cemetery. In the summer of 1832, those few square miles of earth, amid a sweep of empty country, became the cause of a foolish and tragic war. It could have been avoided by a paltry payment in trade goods and it could have been averted by a modicum of white man's patience and coolness of mind. But in that troubled summer a fear and a fever swept over the Middle

Border. Tales of Indian savagery spread like fire over the frontier and troops were summoned to protect the Illinois settlements. Then, in a series of fiery proclamations, volunteers were rallied to reinforce the regulars and an expedition was organized to drive the tribes forever beyond the Mississippi. In the end, the campaign cost two million dollars and four hundred lives.

Years before, when there were no white settlers anywhere in the domain of the Sac and Fox tribes, the Indians had sold the land between the Illinois and Wisconsin rivers for an annuity of $3,000, but the government had stipulated that as long as the lands remained public domain the Indians should be free to farm and hunt upon them. So their life went on unchanged. But when restless bands of squatters, pushing ahead of the government survey, found the fertile fields of the Sacs, they took a fancy to that region. The Indians, returning from their winter hunt, found their fields and their cemetery under the plow of the squatters. Black Hawk appealed to American officials, who advised him to move his people permanently across the Mississippi. Then the short, lean, quiet-spoken chief, sixty years old, made the decision that he afterward put into memorable words: "Rock River was a beautiful country. I liked my town, my cornfields and the home of my people. I fought for them."

It was a brief, one-sided war. Black Hawk's allies, the Wisconsin tribes, never fulfilled their pledges to him and a powerful force of United States Army troops and Illinois militiamen marched against the ill-prepared Sacs. The campaign became a pursuit as the whole Sac tribe—men, women and children—straggled in flight through southern Wisconsin. Many of them died on the way, of wounds and starvation. The remnant reached the Mississippi alongside the mouth of the Bad Axe River. There they were cornered. General Atkinson's troops were on their heels and an army transport, the *Warrior,* barred their way across the river. In that hard place, on the second of August, 1832, the Indians fought their last battle east of the Mississippi. It was a fight in weed-choked ravines and bottom lands, a blind and hopeless struggle amid mud-encrusted driftwood and underbrush. The Indians, weak from hunger and flight, fought and died within a closing circle of gunfire. Some turned and plunged desperately into the river, but only a few survived the Mississippi currents and the deadly aim of Atkinson's sharpshooters, to crawl exhausted on the Iowa shore. By noon, in the sullen heat of that August day, there were only the dead lying in the trampled brush of the Bad Axe bottoms.

With Indian resistance completely at an end, population streamed west, over the Great Lakes and the Ohio River, into the empty counties of Illinois and Wisconsin. Caravans of settlers' wagons creaked over the old Indian trails and towns sprang up wherever two rutted roads crossed on the prairie. What Indians were left east of the Mississippi were enclosed in reservations. Even these were to be taken from them when the tribes were herded forever out of their traditional country.

In 1838, the last pathetic band was led across the state of Indiana. Early in September, with the heat of summer still lying close over the country, 800 mingled tribesmen were gathered at Twin Lakes, near the head of Tippecanoe Creek, which was one of the Indian villages permitted to remain after the treaties of 1832. But settlers looked greedily on their reservation land and President Andrew Jackson had promised to drive the Indians west of the Mississippi. So the tribes were ordered to evacuate and soldiers arrived at Twin Lakes to escort them out of the country. Chief Menominee fought a futile skirmish with the troops of General John Tipton, but the warriors were soon surrounded and the stubborn old chief was taken prisoner. (Now his granite monument stands where his hopeless people were rounded up for their long journey to the plains of Kansas.) A cloud of dust hung over the thirteen army wagons loaded with provisions and the four hundred horses of the troops. The Indians were permitted a last look at the graves of their dead. Then the long march began.

It was a desolate band of exiles that shuffled toward the West, but many of them never left their native Indiana valleys—malaria was bad that year. After a feverish summer, the water lay stagnant and green-scummed in the creeks. Every day men, women and children died; each night from the edge of the camp came the thud of mattocks and the thrust of spades where the troops on burial detail dug a common grave for those who would not journey farther. When the dusty, heartless caravan reached Logansport, on the Wabash, a government doctor declared that half of them were not fit for travel. But the army had its orders and the weary file moved on.

There remained one pathetic scene at Tippecanoe where once the chiefs had met in council to plan their great confederacy. On a hot September night, the Indians pitched their camp where Prophet's Town had stood. General Tipton had fought with Harrison on that field twenty-seven years before, but now he was a sober man in charge of a wretched people. All night he heard the wailing of sick children and the troubled sleep of the exiles. The next morning he lined them up, the old and the young, the sullen and the weary, the sick and the hopeless. He distributed $5,000 worth of gifts, and still their eyes were desolate. Then he ordered his men to their places. The drivers cracked their whips and the wagons creaked away and the long file of Indians straggled on. Behind them they left only the lasting music of their names to be a part of the new America—Wabash, Wawasee and Mishawaka, Nappanee, Miami and Tippecanoe.

X

Chain and Compass

No OTHER COUNTRY has been so conscious of the surveyor's chain and compass as has America. Within a span of three generations a whole continent was surveyed. That was the first task in the vast process of occupation. While it was under way, surveying became an everyday science. "Navigation" appeared in the meager curriculum of schools and academies far inland. Handbooks of practical astronomy circulated in country stores and were studied by firelight in settlers' cabins. Surveying manuals were packed in the tin trunk beside the *Emigrant's Guide* and the family Bible. Gibson's *Theory and Practice of Surveying,* Gummere's *Treatise on Surveying,* Telford's *Elements of Surveying,* Simms' *Principle and Practice of Levelling*—these were the scientific literature of the unsettled country. Countless young Americans began their careers as members of a surveying crew and thousands who went on to other pursuits had followed surveying as their first profession.

Take the surveyors out of American history and the gaps become appalling. George Washington handled the chain and compass in the rough valleys of western Pennsylvania. William Clark, discoverer of the Columbia River, ran county lines in the Blue Ridge Mountains before he was nineteen years old and was surveyor-general of Illinois twenty years later. Abraham Lincoln ran section lines over the low hills that hem the Sangamon. Even Henry David Thoreau, a transcendentalist at heart, measured the strict bounds of Concord township and located many farmers' corners. Hosts of men shared in that task that was as broad as the continent, using the light of Aldebaran and Polaris and the sun's rays to fix a net of invisible lines across America.

It must have left a mark on them as well as on their maps. They pushed ahead of settlement into new country, not roving like traders and hunters but methodically following a compass needle, taking measurements, calculating elevations, fixing exact and unalterable benchmarks. They waded the swamps and climbed the ridges, they set up their tripods in creek beds and hacked a way through thickets to run their uncompromising lines. So they learned a way of doing. There were no detours, no evasions and circumventions in their profession. They learned a way of thinking. Their lines ran straight over rough, confused and difficult country. They learned a way of living. For long seasons they took the fortunes of weather and isolation. They waited, sometimes weeks on end, for an observation of the stars to clinch their meridian. They fought wolves and camp rats and mosquitoes, they shook with ague and bled from the furious little wounds of the black fly, they counted their chain links over quaking swamps and snow-bleak prairies. They advanced into a country that was land merely, and they left it invisibly and forever changed. Their field notes were the basis of a future civilization. With every sight and measurement they gave the land a pattern as fixed and final as the ordered stars. No men in America did more lasting work than theirs.

WHILE THE Northwest was British, American colonists looked across the mountains as across a fence at an inviting land. King George's Royal Proclamation of 1763, forbidding American settlers to go beyond the forks of the Ohio, was like King Canute's asking the tide to stop. Men who had seen the western country were fired to possess it; men who had not seen it had heard of it and were determined to see whether its fabled riches were real. Traders had already tapped the riches of the country, squatters were filtering onto the fertile lands beside the Ohio, speculators were calculating the future of vast tracts over which the Indians roved as aimlessly as the deer and the buffalo, and hosts of hardworking farmers on tight little fields from New Hampshire to

North Carolina wondered about the wide and fertile earth beyond the mountains.

The speculators had already looked enviously at the interior tracts. The Ohio Company of Virginia, a partnership of Virginia gentlemen, had organized in 1747 for the purpose of securing territory in the West. Having petitioned the Crown for a grant of 500,000 acres, they hired Christopher Gist to explore the Ohio Valley for good level land suitable to settlement. Gist was well equipped for such a mission. A surveyor by profession and a veteran woodsman of the frontier of North Carolina, he knew Indian languages and understood the problems of new settlement. He began his famous trip in the autumn of 1750, when the Ohio hills were colored with the russet of beech leaves and the gold of maples. He found George Croghan at an Indian village on the Muskingum and, in company with the trader, he struck across country through the naked woods of winter to the Indian town of Pickawillany on the Great Miami. In the radiant western spring he returned to the Ohio River, at the mouth of the Scioto, then followed the Ohio down to the falls at the site of Louisville. On his return to Virginia, he reported strong Indian opposition north of the Ohio and suggested a settlement on territory south of the river. (Kentucky was never settled by any Indians, being used by the tribes as a common hunting ground. But the north shore of the Ohio remained the "Indian side" for more than two generations.) Gist's suggestion was shrewd and practical, but the outbreak of the French and Indian War put an end to the Ohio Company's project.

When the war was over, feverish speculation began. Large tracts were sought for sale and colonization. In 1765, George Croghan proposed to organize a company to buy the land of French settlers still living in Illinois. But William Franklin, Ben Franklin's restless son, had a better idea—to petition the British Crown for a tract of 1,200,000 acres between the Wabash and Mississippi rivers. In London, Benjamin Franklin urged this plan with Lord Shelburne and the Board of Trade and he doubtless would have put it through had not diplomatic responsibilities called him across the channel to France. In 1770, George Washington, who had explored, scouted and fought in the hinterland with a shrewd eye for likely land, toured the Ohio country with George Croghan. Eventually he acquired 33,000 fertile, river-side acres, with sixteen miles fronting on the Ohio River and forty miles on the Great Kanawha.

Meanwhile, a large land company had been organizing. In 1764, the famous Philadelphia firm of merchants, Baynton, Wharton and Morgan, had launched a project known as the "Grand Illinois Venture" to establish themselves in trade beyond the Wabash River. Their "Venture" failed to win approval from the British authorities, and Samuel Wharton, convinced that fortunes were to be made in the West, turned to land speculation. In 1769, in partnership with the English capitalist Thomas Walpole, he formed the Grand Ohio Company with the design of purchasing 2,400,000 acres between the Alleghenies and the Upper Ohio. This project grew in its founders' minds until it included twenty million acres spreading into the Southwest and was pictured as a new colony to be known as Pittsylvania. Later, the name of this non-existent colony on its unowned lands was changed to Vandalia. Its actual organization was still pending when the War for Independence brought the whole project to an end.

When, after the troubled years, the war was fought and won, the infant Republic had a vast western domain to brighten the future. Land in the newly won region was promised as a bounty to thousands of unpaid Revolutionary soldiers. Here was the beginning of America's largesse to her military veterans. There was no rich national treasury—the "Continental" scrip, issued by the Continental Congress, had about the value of shin-plasters—but there was a rich domain to be settled. So Virginia promised land to her soldiers—to major generals, fifteen thousand acres; to brigdier generals, ten thousand acres; to lesser officers, less land in proportion to their rank, and to enlisted men a hundred acres each. This was the first soldier's bonus, and to pay it the colonies reasserted their claim to western territory. The Virginia Military Tract comprised the whole area between the Little Miami and the Scioto rivers, and the Firelands, with which Connecticut proposed to reimburse her soldiers and citizens who had suffered during the Revolution, took up a deep strip at the western end of Lake Erie. After the War of 1812, the United States created Military Tracts, of two million acres each, in Michigan, Illinois and Arkansas. When it was found that the Michigan military lands were poorly drained and unsuited to farming, the Illinois tract, between the Illinois and Mississippi rivers, was increased to 3,500,000 acres, and a tract of five hundred thousand acres was established in Missouri. Veterans of the War of 1812 received by lottery their plots of 160 acres.

But in 1783, the Ohio country, vaguely extending to the Wabash, and the Illinois country, extending to the Mississippi, were still hunting grounds of the Indians and there was no legal means of land distribution in the public domain. To provide such a means was the purpose of the Pickering Plan. In 1783 Timothy Pickering, serving as scribe for a number of army officers with their restless men still in camp at Newburgh on the Hudson and awaiting military discharge, wrote out a proposition calling for the purchase from the Indians of the land between Pennsylvania's western boundary and a line running south from the western tip of Lake Erie, and the disposal of this tract as bounty lands to Revolutionary soldiers. While this proposal was being debated in Congress, a steady stream of squatters was moving up the valley of the Muskingum. Obviously, it was high time for an ordinance that would provide some legal means for the sale and settlement of the public lands. At last, in 1785, after much debate and controversy, Congress agreed upon a Land Ordinance, which stipulated that as territory was purchased from the Indians it was to be surveyed into townships and subdivided into sections and opened to private ownership.

So the first western survey was begun. It affected the map of the United States all the way to the Pacific. East of the Alle-

ghenies county and township divisions were systemless and irregular, following natural contours and the whims of landowners
and local officials. But beginning in Ohio and continuing through
the old Northwest and across the continent, the boundaries are
regular almost as a checkerboard. Except in the Virginia Military
Tract, where the United States did not control the land, Ohio was
surveyed in straight lines and right angles. The map shows where
Thomas Hutchins first leveled his transit and ran his lines, laying
off systematic townships of six miles square. That plan became
the pattern for land survey across the country.

Thomas Hutchins was orphaned at the age of fifteen in New
Jersey, and he spent his youth on the western frontier. He knew
the trails and waterways of the Upper Ohio and he was familiar
with the Indian tribes of the region. During the French and
Indian War he served as an officer in Pennsylvania's Colonial
troops. He was Colonel Bouquet's engineer in western campaigns
and, after the Peace of Paris, in 1763, he made the first hydro-
graphic survey of the Ohio River. Not only did he measure length
and width and depth and currents of the river, but he noted
camping sites, contours of the shores, the character of timber and
soil throughout the valley, and he traced the portages between
the headwaters of the Ohio and the rivers that led to Lake Erie.
When his survey was completed and his detailed map was published, it showed the river and its tributaries and also the overland trails that threaded the interior. From his long, careful, calculating journey he brought back a blueprint for the Valley's
occupation.

During the War for Independence, Hutchins served as military
geographer, using his knowledge of the country to support the
desperate strategy of the Colonial troops. After the war, he carried
his chain and compass into rough country, surveying new roads
in Pennsylvania, running state and county boundaries. When the
first survey was ordered in the newly created Northwest Territory, Thomas Hutchins, "geographer to the United States," was
ready to measure land that had never known a deed of entry.

Hutchins was commissioned to survey the Seven Ranges—the first seven rows of townships west of the up-curving Ohio River—according to the rectangular system of surveys provided in the Land Ordinance of 1785. His "geographer's line" ran forty-two miles due west from the intersection of the Ohio River and the boundary of Pennsylvania and his western meridian dropped south over the wooded hills to the Ohio River, near the site of present Marietta. A post was set at each mile and every six miles a township corner was indicated by a monument. The townships were six miles square. Each township contained thirty-six sections of one mile square, or 640 acres. Thus began the square plotting of the public lands, which makes the map of the western states so different from the map of states east of the Alleghenies.

This was a simple and lasting reform. The traditional practice in the Colonies had been to require each man to survey his own land, in his own way. As a result, a patent to a simple, four-sided tract of land sometimes read with a complication and ambiguity that no court could make clear. One such tract of 400 acres was located in this manner: "On the waters of the Rocky Fork of Paint Creek, Beginning at Two Sugar Trees and a poplar South seventy Degrees West two hundred poles from two Beeches, and a black Oak northwesterly corner of Benjamin Wynkoop's survey No. 3019, running North twenty Degrees East two hundred and sixty poles crossing a Branch at forty and one at eighty-six poles to three Sassafrass, thence North twenty Degrees West one hundred and sixty poles crossing a Branch at sixteen poles to the beginning." When a sassafras tree, or even three of them, served as a point, the survey was at the scantest mercy of time. But the new system conceived boundaries in relation to unalterable benchmarks and monuments. Given a specific quarter of a specific section in a specific township in a specific range (SW¼ S17, T21N, R27W) the tract could be simply and clearly identified as long as records endure.

Actually, the plan of a rectangular survey came from Thomas Jefferson, who had a sense of the long future of America and wanted, in a survey as well as in a Bill of Rights, to lay a lasting foundation. He distrusted rivers and ridges as lines of demarcation, knowing that ridges wear down and rivers carve new courses. It was said that he discussed with Thomas Hutchins a survey like that of Holland, where the country was too flat for natural divides. So Hutchins ran his lines as straight as light over the tumbled hills and through the devious valleys.

His experience was to be relived many times by other men pushing on to the Wabash, to the Mississippi, and at last to the white-ribbed surf of the Pacific. They advanced upon new country like a small expedition against formlessness, armed with transit, compass and measuring chain. The field crew was directed by a deputy surveyor, often called the Land-Looker, who received his commission from the surveyor general. They went into the territory with instruments and provisions, barrels of flour and pork, bushels of beans and dried apples, bags of sugar, salt, oatmeal, rice and coffee. Often they drove a few head of cattle with them, to be slaughtered for fresh meat. Besides axes and guns, pots and pans and kettles, they carried their special instruments—theodolite, compass, a standard chain, flags, tally pins, field books, mapping paper, pens, pencils, bottles of ink and glue. Sometimes the instrument box contained a dozen wild goose feathers for making quills, and when the ink ran out after a long season in the field they drew their maps with a russet ink made from forest bark. The flagman, wearing a red shirt to be seen in thickets and cane-brakes, carried his rods and flags. The chainmen bore their chains and tally pins. The ax-men, or moundmen, carried their marking tools. The Land-Looker himself, the deputy surveyor, led the way with his transit over his shoulder and his compass at his side.

To determine the true meridian, the surveyor had to supplement his measurements with observations of the stars—sometimes he had to wait weeks for a clear night sky. Meanwhile, there were the dangers of Indian attack and the lurking perils of new country. Night after night the surveyors lay in their blankets with the howl of wolves around them. Wolves were especially numerous in the

Ohio and Indiana country until the 1820s, when they disappeared with mysterious rapidity—some thought they were carried off by hydrophobia. So the field crew pushed on, leaving behind them the posts numbered with the marking iron, the cones of earth with the stakes driven in, the benchmarks that would identify the claims of a new race.

Often the surveyor burdened himself with specimens of earth and rock. In the mineral-bearing regions his pack grew heavy and his task was freshly complicated, because his magnetic compass became useless in the vicinity of bodies of ore. In Wisconsin and Upper Michigan the surveys could not be made at all by the old instruments, and because only Indians knew the way through that dense and forbidding country the field crews included Chippewa hunters who never thought of land as personal possession. "My reason teaches me," wrote the defeated old Black Hawk in his famous autobiography, "that land cannot be sold. Nothing can be sold but such things as can be carried away."

In 1844, with a couple of Chippewa chainmen among his crew, the surveyor William Burt ran one of the final surveys in the Northwest Territory and made one of the famous discoveries in America. While running a section line near Teal Lake, in the rough hills below Lake Superior, Burt watched his compass needle swing like a weathervane in a storm. He sent his men to look for the cause. They found a rusty purple outcrop, the color of a grackle's wing, and William Burt had discovered the iron that rings Lake Superior in a crescent of treasure. But he was a surveyor rather than a prospector and what delighted him most was the demonstration of his solar compass, which he had patented eight years before. Now, while the magnetic compass veered around to a quarter circle from magnetic north, his solar compass pointed steadily northward. With that unswaying needle to mark his course, Burt surveyed the rugged northern wilderness. Then another woodsman, George Stuntz, ran the boundary lines of Minnesota and Wisconsin in the big dark country at the tip of Lake Superior. That was in 1850—seventy-five years after Thomas

Hutchins had marked the sections of his Seven Ranges beside the up-curving Ohio. At last the whole Northwest was surveyed.

THE SURVEY opened the land to settlement. Behind the chain-man who left his invisible lines came the farmer who set up his rugged rail fence. While Hutchins' first survey was in progress, a new land company was being formed. The story dovetails here, like pieces of a picture. General Benjamin Tupper of Massachusetts was one of Hutchins' deputies and he was excited by his observation of the Ohio country. Back in Massachusetts he stopped in the quiet village of Rutland to visit his old friend, General Rufus Putnam. Before a hardwood fire they talked long past midnight, Tupper describing the western country and Putnam prompting him with pointed questions. It was not talk about benchmarks and section lines, but about field and forest, soil and water, temperature and rainfall. Outside in the darkness lay the cramped stony fields of New England hemmed in by the New England hills. But the land that Tupper described was wide and free and gentle, with deep soil that had never been stirred by a plow.

Out of that midnight talk grew the Ohio Company of Associates. They called disbanded officers and men of the Revolution to meet in Boston at the Bunch of Grapes Tavern on the first day of March, 1786. There they organized the Ohio Company, to promote a settlement in the western country. By March of the following year they had raised sufficient funds to send an agent to Congress to apply for the purchase of lands. Their agent was well chosen—in the person of the Rev. Manasseh Cutler, a whaling agent, botanist, lawyer, doctor, minister, who had served as a chaplain in the Revolutionary army. Cutler talked with Thomas Hutchins and was assured that the location to apply for was on the Muskingum River, "the best part of the whole western country." With his broad interests and his persuasive manner, Cutler was granted the purchase of 1,500,000 acres north of the Ohio River from the seventh to the seventeenth range of townships. Meanwhile, the famous Ordinance of 1787 had been enacted, providing for the settlement and organization of a territory larger than any country in Europe except Russia.

This Ordinance created the Northwest Territory, bounded by the Ohio and Mississippi rivers and the Great Lakes, and provided that eventually it was to be composed of five states, which would be admitted into the Union with the full powers and privileges of the original states in the federation. Its settlers were promised political and religious freedom, universal educational opportunities and responsible citizenship in the nation. Here were the principles on which all the future states across the continent would be founded. In 1787, the survey was limited to a few ranges on the Territory's border. But the township lines would extend into every mile and acre of the wilderness, as the chain and compass men took the first step in creating a country where there was none.

Part III

THE RESTLESS NATION

XI

Where the Rivers Meet

APRIL SEVENTH, 1788, was a rainy day with the chill of winter lingering over the great bend of the Ohio and in the bare woods that framed the Muskingum. Where the rivers meet, Fort Harmar stood up with its picketed palisades surmounted by block-houses that surveyed the empty waters and the lifeless earthworks of the vanished Mound Builders. The fort was two years old, and in those slow months its garrison had seen only occasional bands of Indians who came down the Muskingum to trade their winter furs for traps and hatchets, blankets and beans. Some fifteen hundred Indian warriors roamed the land between the Ohio and Lake Erie. It was, till now, their land, and had it been divided among them in the white man's way, each would have owned a domain of seventeen thousand acres.

But on that rainy seventh of April it became a part of America. Out of the cold fog, over the rain-pitted Ohio, past the rounded point of Kerr's Island, in the slow current of the river came a dark shape. A galley its builders called it, but it came down the river like a floating shed—flat-roofed and slab-sided, dark with rain. It bore no name. Some of its builders called it the *Adventure Galley,* and some the *Union Galley.* Later, remembering that landing on the shores of wilderness, some called it the *American Mayflower.* In the April rain, followed by its companion flatboat and three heavy canoes, the *Adventure—Union-Mayflower* missed the mouth of the Muskingum, for which it was headed, and came alongside the Ohio bank beneath the log walls of Fort Harmar. Here the pioneers first stepped upon Ohio soil, and in their galley stalls the horses and oxen stamped restlessly. There was time for a noisy welcome in the fort and a hot meal around the messroom tables, before the troops towed the flatboats into the Muskingum and moored them on the east bank at the foot of a raised terrace that the Mound Builders had once used as an avenue between their temples and the river. There the forty-eight men landed—their wives and children were to come when dwellings were ready—and the first settlement of the Northwest Territory was begun.

TODAY MARIETTA is a spacious, leafy town, with layers of memory kept alive by the mounds of a forgotten people and many monuments to people whom it cannot forget. It is a town of shady river front and of many open squares and broad green terraces. It has the composure of time. In the quiet Mound cemetery the great Conus Mound, bearing a canopy of forest trees, rises above the graves of the first families—more Revolutionary officers are buried there than anywhere else in America. The spacious "Sacra Via" still connects the raised square of a temple mound with the Muskingum landing. Now, on the broad temple square—the Quadranaou, as the classical-minded founders named it—Marietta boys bat out a baseball and fly their kites. Down the "Sacred Way" four lanes of elms and maples march to the Muskingum, and in their shade children with toy shovels build little mounds of earth. So time moves round again. At the foot of Sacra Via, beside the Muskingum, stands a replica of the *Union Galley,* built at West Union, Pennsylvania, and floated down the Ohio to land at Marietta in the cold rain of April 7, 1938, one hundred and fifty years after the first settlers began the claiming of the continent beyond the mountains.

Modern Marietta has broad streets of substantial houses under rows of arching elms. It is on the great graceful curve of the Ohio, but the town really belongs to the Muskingum, the more intimate river with its hilly, wooded shores. The river front is parked and gardened, with churches and solid New England houses looking across the shadowed grass to the bright Muskingum shore. Here is one of the few towns in America that have known how to use a river, to encompass its beauty and borrow its light. Marietta has preserved the leafy river shores as it preserved the time-softened earthworks of the Mound Builders who first lived on that pleasant land. And it has preserved its own beginnings. The Land Office— a one-room, hand-hewn building, brown with weather and green with vines—still stands on Washington Street. Here were made the first maps of the territory, and the first land claims were filed of the country that stretched to the western sea. Across Washington Street, now enclosed in the brick walls of the Campus Martius Museum, is the two-story house of General Rufus Putnam, a house that was part of the original stockade that the settlers built in 1788. At the foot of Washington Street one of Marietta's many monuments marks the landing place of the first families—the women and children who came in the summer of 1788 to join the men who had made the beginning of a settlement. Along Muskingum Park, Front Street is framed by the handsome North-west Territory gateways, and under the elms the six stone figures of Gutzon Borglum's memorial commemorating the "Start West-ward of the United States" stands where Arthur St. Clair was inaugurated first governor of the Northwest Territory, on a sunny summer day in 1788. That seems long ago and far away, and the original palisaded square, guarded by blockhouses, seems far dis-tant from the prosperous dignified Marietta of today. But the rivers have not changed since the *Union Galley* drifted through the rain. As the graceful town now spreads over the fields those first families plowed and planted, there is a slowly deepening dimension of time in Marietta.

THE MOUNDS beside the Muskingum had been silent for cen-turies, but in the spring of 1788 they came to life. There was the thud of axes and the ring of mallets in the warm May air, as the forty-eight pioneers built their first cabins and their blockhouse square. It was a beautiful setting. As spring came on, the stately tulip trees bore their lofty blossoms and the magnolias flowered white. Over the mounds rambled the flowering honeysuckle. Locust trees grew fragrant in the warm June nights. At the point where the Muskingum joins the Ohio, across from Fort Harmar, rose a row of cabins. Around them was planted a protecting stockade of sharpened poplar logs. Picketed Point it was called, running along the site of the business blocks of Front Street in modern Marietta. On somewhat higher ground was built the military stronghold, the Campus Martius as the New England settlers called it. General Rufus Putnam, superintendent of the affairs of the community, had erected West Point and other fortifications. Here he planned an impregnable fort to safeguard the new colony. It was built of heavy poplar logs, with blockhouses at the corners and dwelling houses making up the side walls, and was surrounded by a formidable log palisade. Standing on a rise of ground, with cleared fields around it, the Campus Martius could defy attack from any direction.

Here was the first capital of the Northwest Territory. Governor St. Clair had his residence in the stronghold, as did General Putnam and other officials. Though designed for seige and warfare, the Campus Martius quickly became a center of civil and social life. The southeast blockhouse was used as a social hall and the northwest blockhouse as a place of religious worship. In these timbered rooms, pierced with loopholes for rifle barrels, were held the first Sunday school and the first day school in the Northwest Territory. But before many seasons passed the fort served its martial purpose. During the Indian Wars it sheltered hundreds of refugees from plundered and imperiled settlements along the Muskingum.

In the Campus Martius the first detailed plots of Marietta were drawn. Laid out in the New England manner, each settler received an in-lot for his dwelling and an out-lot of eight acres for cultivation. A town common, now the beautiful Muskingum Park, provided grazing ground for the community's horses and cattle. A decision was made not to lease the land occupied by certain mound formations and to preserve forever the broad, raised Sacra Via which connected the mounds to the river.

That summer, in 1788, the first families arrived and domestic life began. Marietta was a camp no longer but a community of families, with women carrying their water pails to the well and children scampering off to pick wild grapes and wild cranberries. They must have looked with wide eyes at the Indian mounds, the curving waters, the green forest enclosing the newly cleared acres already patterned with beans and corn and pumpkins. In the autumn the forest turned scarlet and gold on the hills and rivers ran blue and clear. Men staggered in with great fish from the rivers and whole carcasses of deer and bear from the woods. The new country was a land of plenty. Yellow mounds of pumpkins stood beside every cabin and bushels of bright cranberries gleamed inside doorways. Venison sold for two cents a pound, bear meat for three. Hundreds of cords of firewood were ricked up along the palisade.

That winter, when the rivers were locked in ice and the snow lay deep against the cabin walls, well worn paths connected all the cabins. At night, while the wind roared loudly in the trees, the men gathered around the hearthfires. Their talk went forward to the next season's clearing and the new colonists who would swell their settlement, and to the years to come when their settlement would be but the first of many and the Territory would be five strong commonwealths in the federated nation. Then, like all old soldiers, they looked back to the campaigns of the Revolution. It was good to call up the past as well as to foresee the future. These men had fought through seven years and many times seven battles, from that April morning on Lexington Common to their final restless bivouac at Newburgh on the Hudson, where they had waited, with their arms stacked in the trampled company street, for the peace terms to be known. Even then they were thinking of the years of peace, of the life of a new nation, of new lands over the mountains. War, always precipitating change, had jostled them out of their New England farms and villages. Now with a new era ahead for the nation, they sensed a future for themselves in a new and distant country.

They talked about it vaguely in Newburgh and more definitely in Boston, when Rufus Putnam called them together not as soldiers but as citizens. When the Ordinance of 1787 was passed by Congress and the purchase of Ohio lands was assured, they planned the long journey to the shores of the Muskingum. Forty-eight of them were ready and eager to go. Though winter approached they thought of their arrival in the Ohio spring when the first crops should be planted. Early in December, they gathered at Ipswich, Massachusetts, at the church of Manasseh Cutler. At dawn, with a cold wind blowing from the Atlantic a few miles away, they listened to Cutler's farewell words. Then they fired a volley from their guns and took their places. The oxen leaned into their yokes and a covered wagon lurched ahead. "For the Ohio Country" was lettered on its towcloth hood.

For eight weeks and eight hundred miles they trudged over turnpike mountain roads and at last by the old Glade Road over the high ridges of Pennsylvania. On January twenty-third, they reached Sumrill's Ferry—now West Newton, Pennsylvania—on the Youghiogheny River, thirty miles southeast of Pittsburgh. There the axes rang in the woods and the pale chips scattered on the snow as they built the craft that would float them down the river—the variously named galley, an open flatboat called *Adelphia*, and three heavy canoes. The boats were built under the direction of Jonathan Devol who, a score of years later from his Marietta shipyards sent vessels down to New Orleans and into the Atlantic trade. Now in the dead of winter on the ice-fast Youghiogheny, he was getting his craft ready to launch onto the spring crest of water. So the men who started from Ipswich with a covered wagon arrived at Fort Harmar with two flatboats. In retrospect, around their winter firesides, the men of the first forty-eight made that long journey many times.

In its first season the new settlement was known by four short-lived names—first, the Indian name Muskingum; then a Greek word, "Adelphia," meaning "Brethren," and two other Greek names, Castropolis and Metropolis. These classical names were

pleasing to the taste of New Englanders who named the Mound
Builders' earthworks Quadranaou, Capitolium, Cecelia and Sacred
Via, and who called their stockade Campus Martius and a creek
that flowed past it the Tiber. But before a year was past, they
chose a new name for their town, calling it Marietta in recogni-
tion of Marie Antoinette's influence in directing French aid to the
Colonies during the Revolutionary struggle. It was a musical and
friendly name.

Marietta was the Plymouth of the Northwest Territory. There,
at the meeting of the rivers, was repeated the experience of planting new life in a wilderness. The stern and rockbound coast had
become a wooded river bank but it was as remote as though it
lay on a new continent. During the first years there was only
a tenuous communication over the mountains and only a difficult
and meager trade to link them with the seaboard. Farmers who
wanted to buy a pound of tea or a few iron spoons had to exchange
100 pounds of pork or flour. So they learned to depend upon themselves and their new country. They were like the founders of the
Plymouth colony, God-fearing, truth-loving, inflexible of purpose.
They bore Old Testament names—Phineas, Jabez, Hezekiah,
Jonas, Simeon, Josiah, Ebenezer, and so on. To the wilderness
they brought integrity, purpose and a patriarchal sense of the
future. They built sound, solid houses, laid out broad streets and
gave their town the dignity of ancient names. Though far from
books they had a love of learning. Settlers like these, a few years
later in the Muskingum woods, gathered the famous "Coonskin
Library," the first community library in the Northwest Territory.
Wanting books but lacking money, they trapped raccoons and exchanged peltry for literature. To their home-made shelves—still
preserved in the Ohio State Museum—came Locke's *Essays*, Schle-
gel's *Philosophy of History*, Smollett's *History of England*, Good's
Book of Nature, Thompson's *Travels*, Rollin's *Ancient History*
and Gibbon's *Decline and Fall of the Roman Empire*. They built
their learning on solid foundations, like the foundation timbers
of their log schoolhouses.

ON APRIL 7, 1788, little more than a century and a half had
passed since the *Mayflower* had hove to in Plymouth harbor and
its company stepped ashore on the rock thrust up from the chafing
tide. When another 150 years had gone, on April 7, 1938, the anniversary was observed by the Northwest Territory celebration. It
was an elaborate and far-reaching celebration, with activities in
the schoolrooms and colleges, the newspapers and State Houses
throughout the Old Northwest. But it focused in Marietta where
the rivers meet, and its notable feature was the re-enactment of
the arrival of the first settlers.

A caravan of forty-eight men, mostly college students, was recruited to make the winter march from Ipswich, Massachusetts,
to western Pennsylvania. Two yokes of oxen were taken from the
hill fields of West Virginia and broken to highway traffic and city
streets. Five cavalry horses were borrowed from the United States
Army and an authentic Conestoga wagon was assembled from old
relics found in barns and carriage sheds in the Conestoga Valley.
The party was equipped with tools of the Revolutionary period
and clothing of the time. In every detail the 1938 "settlers" dupli-
cated the pioneers of 1788.

But the land they journeyed over was a different land. Fifty
thousand persons watched them depart from Ipswich where Manasseh Cutler had blessed the first party in the winter dawn. They
passed through Cambridge, Worcester and Springfield; they
crossed the Hudson at Newburgh, where the troops had first
dreamed of a settlement in the West; they went on through Easton,
Allentown, Reading and Harrisburg, and up the steep roads to
Burnt Cabins and Top of Ridge. At every town and city the
streets were deep with people. Spectators came scores of miles
to watch the men in coonskin caps and buckskin breeches, with
powder horns at their sides, driving oxen over the motor highways of the twentieth century. On the way three dogs attached
themselves to the expedition. "Buck" joined at Allentown, Pennsylvania, and completed the entire celebration tour through the
Mid-Western states. "Bones" disappeared at Pittsburgh after trav-

eling with them for three hundred miles, and "Stogey" dropped off some months later in a friendly town in Indiana.

Sumill's Ferry was gone from the Youghiogheny when the modern caravan arrived, and the modern town of West Newton, Pennsylvania, had grown up beside the river. There the party spent ten cold winter weeks building their replica of the *Union Galley* and its companion flatboat. The camp in the snowy woods these college students called "Shangri-La," but the tools they used were the broad-ax, the adze and the whipsaw of 1778. While their craft were building, the river bank was far from the remote and empty place it had been a century and a half before. More than a hundred thousand visitors came to see the *Union Galley* taking shape at the edge of the ice-bound river. The modern pioneers built their vessels in two weeks' shorter time than Rufus Putnam's men required, though every log was felled in the forest and every timber was shaped with the tools of the eighteenth century.

When the ice was gone, they launched their craft and drifted past the great steel-mill towns which Rufus Putnam's men could never have conceived. They reached Marietta on a day of chill fog and rain, just four minutes late of schedule, on April 8, 1938. The original party was watched by a band of Delaware Indians, who had come down the Muskingum to trade furs at Fort Harmar. The new arrivals were greeted by uncounted thousands who stood in the cold rain and watched a party of "soldiers" come down from the site of the vanished Fort Harmar and use rowboats to tow the flatboats to their landing place on the Muskingum. Here a group of Delaware Indians, descendants of the tribe that once roamed the Muskingum valley, met the modern pioneers.

From Marietta the modern caravan set off on a trek which the men of the Ohio Company never dreamed of making. They traveled throughout the five states of the Northwest Territory presenting a historical pageant in parks and amphitheaters in nearly two hundred towns and cities. Their route lay north and west through Ohio to the level distances of Indiana and Illinois and then to the lakes and fields and woods of Wisconsin and north past the tip of Lake Superior and through the woods of Minnesota to Lake Itasca, where the Mississippi River rises. Here they made their camp at the extreme northwestern point of the Northwest Territory. The return route followed the Mississippi, through Minneapolis, Winona and La Crosse, then passed through the prairies of central Illinois, crossed the Wabash at Vincennes and reached the Ohio at Evansville, Indiana. They followed the Ohio through Cincinnati, Portsmouth and Gallipolis and ended their tour at Marietta, after ten months and three thousand miles of travel. The boys in buckskin had signed autographs all the way.

Tom and Jerry, the ox team that hauled the covered wagon, had made a long journey and been applauded by ten million people. That winter they went back to a brush farm in the hills of West Virginia.

XII

Frenchmen's Landing

THE OHIO COUNTRY was a strong magnet. While Rufus Putnam's men were clearing the first streets of Marietta, a fleet
of flatboats floated down the river. Late in August of 1788, they
passed the mouth of the Muskingum, where the axes were thudding at the base of sycamores and the first Marietta cornfields were
tasseling on the cleared ground. This was the party of John Cleves
Symmes, a New Jersey speculator who had negotiated with Congress for the purchase of a million acres between the Great and
Little Miami rivers in western Ohio. Included in the contract was
the location of a college township, which eventually became the
foundation of Miami University. Haphazardly, without the reso-
lute leadership and careful plans of the Marietta colony, the Miami
Purchase was settled, its chief center known as Losantiville. This
fanciful name, coined by a Pennsylvania schoolmaster in Symmes'
party, designated "the town opposite the mouth of the Licking
River"—by means of L for Licking, *os* Latin for mouth, *anti* for
opposite, and *ville* for town. Situated at the mouth of the rich
Miami Valley, on the strategic, long-established Miami-Maumee
Trail, it quickly became the dominant settlement in the Symmes
tract. Within a generation, as Cincinnati, it had become the "Queen
City of the West."

But the pull of Ohio lands was felt farther away than New Jersey. Across the Atlantic, under the sunny skies of France, the
summer of 1778 was a tense and troubled season. Revolution threatened to sweep the country like a tempest and no Frenchman knew
where to turn for refuge in that storm. Add to that situation the
fact that French poets, novelists and philosophers had for a generation idealized the "natural man" and had pictured the New

167

World wilderness as a land of promise for the oppressed and harried peoples of Europe, and the vast empty acres of Ohio seemed an inevitable haven for French refugees. Further, there were in France considerable quantities of Continental Certificates of discounted value. Their holders would grasp at the prospect of exchanging that dubious currency for indubitable land.

With this as a background, there were lively prospects in France for the sale of western territory. In June of 1788, while the Marietta settlers were awaiting the arrival of their families and while Symmes was outfitting his Ohio caravan at Morristown, New Jersey, a young Connecticut Yankee arrived in Paris as an agent of the Scioto Land Company. Already, at the age of thirty-four, Joel Barlow had pursued a varied career. A Yale man, classmate of Noah Webster, he had tried law, journalism, politics and poetry, and had served as a chaplain, preaching to ragged troops in Washington's army. His chief success had come to him as a poet. The most gifted of the "Hartford Wits," he enjoyed a limited fame as the author of a 5,000-line epic on "The Vision of Columbus." But he had to make a living and so he turned to the promotion of the Scioto Company's scheme for the sale of western lands in France.

It was easy to sell American lands to anxious Frenchmen after the storming of the Bastille in July, 1789, and Barlow was aided by a winning and unscrupulous Englishman named William Playfair. Capitalizing on the unrest of France, Playfair issued alluring and assuring descriptions of lands he had never seen. He pictured the Scioto country as already surveyed, cleared and partially settled. He predicted that in twenty years the population beyond the mountains would equal that on the Atlantic slope and that by then the national capital would be located on the Ohio. His pamphlet promised rich crops of cotton, tobacco, wheat, sugar and grapes, and declared that along the Ohio, French custard grew like fruit on the trees and candles grew in the swamps. The accompanying map showed the location of prospective mines for lead, coal and salt.

The French, forgetting that a "Mississippi Bubble" had burst two generations before when the Illinois prairies did not yield the gold and silk that the Mississippi Company had promised, turned eagerly to the prospect of a prosperous life in the New World forests. Within a few months a hundred thousand acres of Scioto lands were sold, and in February, 1790, five hundred French colonists embarked at Havre for America. Barlow wrote that twenty thousand others would follow the advance five hundred. Five years later he was made an honorary citizen of France, a tribute to his cosmopolitanism rather than to his part in a shabby and sorry venture.

There was folly in the hopes of the five hundred, folly in their going unprepared for life in a wilderness and in their flight from the crisis in France. All of them were of the upper bourgeoisie—ten of the company had been members of the National Assembly. Among them were skilled artisans who would find no use for their talents in the dark Ohio forest—goldsmiths and watchmakers in a land where men told time by squinting at the sun, glassblowers in a settlement where women stretched greased pigskins over their window openings, hairdressers in a country whose native mode was the scalplock, carriage-makers in a region without a road, dancing masters in a country where the Indians stamped around the painted war post. There were landscape gardeners, but no one knew how to grow a crop of wheat, wood-carvers but no one who could swing a bladed ax.

They made a miserable crossing, three long months on the wintry ocean, and the first boatload landed at Alexandria on the Potomac in the mild month of May. But new difficulties soon began. Arrived in the New World, they discovered that their engraved "land deeds" were worthless—the Scioto Company had failed to make payments on its grant and so it had no lands to sell. In fact, the lands "deeded" to the French colonists lay within the Ohio Company's grant and were not in the Scioto tract at all. Fortunately, the American Congress was sympathetic and the Ohio Company desired new settlers on its lands. While the French waited in bewilderment on the Potomac, fifty expert woodsmen, recruited in

New England, were at work clearing land and building log houses on the Ohio River opposite the mouth of the Great Kanawha.

In October, when the shores of *La Belle Riviere* were colored with wine-dark oaks and golden hickories and autumn haze softened the far blue curves of the valley, the French company arrived. The flatboats came to rest against the shelving bank and the emigrés hurried up the fifty-foot slope to see their city. They saw on that level plain, still studded with stumps of oak and sycamore, four peak-roofed blockhouses and four rows of low log huts. Beyond, like a confining wall, began the dark forest that stretched unbroken to Lake Erie.

It was far from the cobbled streets, the leaded windows, the friendly squares of Lyons and Paris. It was far from the cafés and flowering gardens. But it was home, after months of homelessness. And the French made the best of it. That night they tuned their violins and danced a minuet on a puncheon floor.

Chicamango had been the Indian name for that level plain above the river. The French called their town Gallipolis—city of the Gauls—and so it remained. The French were not to stay there. In a few years it was a Yankee town, like Marietta and Manchester and Maysville and Portsmouth. But it is still today Gallipolis, pronounced "gallop-police," with its tree-canopied park fronting the river and a faint trace of France in an occasional iron balcony on an old stone house.

The emigrés had hardly unpacked their trunks and boxes when November winds stripped the forest. Soon their plain was bleak with winter's snow. They sat by their smoky fires and wondered how things were going in the troubled land they had fled and what was their future in this cold land of promise. Congress, to make amends for the Scioto Company's deceit, granted seven acres to each family. But out there, across the drifted snow of the compound, stood the naked forest. They had a wild, lost land to bring to harvest.

In the first thin sunlight of spring they began their task. With awkward, unsure strokes they hacked at the forest. They injured and killed themselves with crashing trees. They planted a tag of cornfield and set out fruits and flowers. When Rufus Putnam visited the settlement he was delighted at the formal gardens framing the rude rows of dwellings. But he was alarmed at their scanty fields of grain and vegetables.

The second winter was more bitter than the first. The Ohio froze from shore to shore and no flatboat could swing in to the landing with pork and potatoes and flour. Huddled in their huts, the French stared grimly at the ice-locked river and the leaden sky. In every household someone lay burning with intermittent fever. When at last spring came, many of them left, worn and wan and beginning to be ragged, finding their way back over the eastern mountains. Those who remained were the patient, persevering ones and the totally hopeless. According to their temperament they grieved over their hardships or busily enlarged their little gardens and set up shops in their houses. Some turned to their old crafts, making watches, compasses and sundials, chiseling stone for sculptured mantles—Rufus Putnam boated a carved mantel-piece back to Marietta, where it went into his own parlor—making thermometers, barometers, tobacco pipes. One ingenious carver fashioned a graceful lamp from bear and buffalo bones dug up at the salt lick.

The most cheerful man in the lowly settlement was the twinkly-eyed little physician, Dr. Sangrain. Happily he worked in his bare office, making thermometers and barometers with the scale neatly painted and the frames deftly carved—some of his instruments are thought to be still in existence along the Ohio. He had a large golden peach in a small-mouthed bottle—a wonder he had waited all summer to accomplish, for he had tied the bottle to the limb of a tree when the peach was no bigger than a marble. That curiosity was a marvel to the children and to the occasional Indians who came to stare at it, and their wonder was an endless delight to the doctor. He was a small, slight man with a gentle voice, but he had killed two Indians in a close encounter. In his office he made phosphoric matches that were miraculous to red men and white on that frontier. Dr. Sangrain lived happily in the shadow of the forest.

Most of his countrymen were of another disposition. Lonely, bitter, disillusioned, they stayed at Gallipolis only because they had no means to get away. They worked half-heartedly in their fields and pottered in their shops, carrying on a petty trade with the growing traffic of flatboats on the river. From season to season their numbers dwindled. After fifteen years a traveler remarked that the place was returning to the gloom of its primeval woods.

But Gallipolis was not through. Though it declined as a city of the Gauls it rose as a city of the Virginians and the New Englanders. By 1820, it was a busy, cheerful place with fruitful orchards, wide fields, a lively river landing and a prosperous street of shops and stores. There were schools, churches, a newspaper and a solid brick courthouse. To care for visitors who came by the early steamboats on the Ohio, Henry Cushing built a hotel of bricks brought from England as ship's ballast. This cheerful proprietor stood on the landing and greeted travelers with a friendly "Come up to our house!" and so his place became the "Our House" Inn, famous up and down the river a century ago and still standing today.

The Our House faced the tree-shaded river-front and from its windows a visitor could watch the endless life on the Ohio. Around the river's bend passed arks and flatboats, pirogues and bateaux, broadhorns and keelboats, laden with families, livestock, poultry, wagons, implements and house furnishings, bound for the western settlements. Great white steamboats churned in to the landing and passengers strolled First and Second Avenues and State and Court Streets, while the stevedores trundled freight on the levee. By 1825, Gallipolis was an important river town and Lafayette called there on his triumphal tour of the Valley. The great Frenchman was feted by a crowd of cheering Yankees, among whom were a few aged settlers who remembered over a gulf of years the leafy squares of Paris, the stately tree-lined avenues and the bridges arched above the Seine.

But Gallipolis became known to America not because of Lafayette or any Frenchman—rather by a descendant of Scotch settlers in America. In a roomy frame house on Court Street, sixty years ago, Oscar Odd McIntyre grew up under the watchful eye of his grandmother. He was a boy who liked the river with its big boats from Pittsburgh and Cincinnati, the winding country roads beyond the Indian mounds and the friendly life of First Avenue on Saturday evenings when the band played concerts in the river park. He was expelled from school for chronic absence. He worked at a few jobs and then became a reporter for the Gallipolis *Tribune*. Twenty years later he was a New York newspaperman whose "New York Day by Day" was the most widely read column in the world. In Gallipolis they set up a bronze marker to indicate his boyhood home.

In his column he was a New Yorker second and a son of Gallipolis first. He was famous and wealthy, with a gourmet's palate and a glittering limousine, but he was still a small-town boy, a Mid-Westerner, writing about the breathless beauty of New York. In his column he brought together the big town and the little town. He wrote of the New York skyline at sunset and also of the old-time coffee-grinder, of his grandmother's jellies, of hoghead cheese and the Barlow knife he whittled with on the landing, while the ferry boat chuffed across the wide river from West Virginia. In the midst of the glitter of Manhattan nights he remembered the fireflies winking in the willow fringes along the Ohio, the smell of clover from the hills and the idlers drowsing under the trees across from Our House.

When he died, in 1938, they buried him on Mound Hill, one of the haunts of his boyhood when he should have been in school. His memorial is a marble bench, and there a visitor can sit in the warm and friendly afternoon and gaze on the place that Odd McIntyre liked best, where the French landed with heavy hearts in a wilderness that seems so long ago.

XIII

Treason Island

IN THE LONG slow days of summer, when the Ohio lies languorous between its curving shores, sometimes a picnic party sets out from Marietta to the Island. Not Kerr's Island, abreast of the town with the Williamsburg bridge looking down at its tangled shores, but the larger, lovelier island, steeped in memory, that the romantic Harmon Blennerhasset called the "Isle de Beau," though it became an isle of ruin in the end.

The route lies down the river fourteen miles from the mouth of the Muskingum and a mile below Parkersburg on the West Virginia shore. A motorboat will get a party there, or they can drive the winding road to Rockland and follow a dirt road to the old Rockland Cemetery, on the brow of the bluff that overlooks the river and the tree-fringed island. At the foot of that steep bank they can find a rowboat that will take them across.

Blennerhasset Island is three miles long, the largest island in the Ohio River, and it curves a little with the stream. Willows make a frieze along its banks and at places the pale trunks of sycamores slant up through the lesser growth. These are great trees, a full hundred feet in height and forty feet around at their base. They have been growing there since Harmon Blennerhasset strolled with Aaron Burr beside the river, deep in treasonous speculation on their empire in the West. No other talk quite like theirs ever sounded in America, before or since.

Now the island is innocent, untroubled, well disposed for picnicking. A field of corn rustles in the summer air—the earth is deep with the silt of repeated floods—and at its upper end a grove of trees makes a rich shade on the grass. One finds an open place for baseball games and a stone oven for a cooking fire, and under a forked maple tree the cool well that Harmon Blennerhasset drank from—with a moss-green bucket on a moss-green rope. Also, under the trees, making a good bench to sit on, lies a little block of cut stones—all that is left of Blennerhasset's once famous mansion.

A picnic here is a holiday and a glimpse of history. Down the south channel comes a towboat, with its soft quick panting like a dog on a summer day, pushing a long string of barges. And, half-real and silent on the river, starting no wake of water and seen only with the eye of memory, are other craft—Aaron Burr's four-room houseboat with its railed promenade and Margaret Blennerhasset's barge with her saddle horse erect in the bow and her Negro groom at the steering oar. On the island, like mingled streams of water, the past and present flow together and something like a legend comes to life again.

In the autumn of 1797, Harmon Blennerhasset, a tall, careless, gifted, aristocratic Englishman, arrived by keelboat at Marietta with his nineteen-year-old wife, the daughter of a celebrated Irish statesman who was a governor of the Isle of Man. They had eloped and married, to the consternation of Margaret Agnew's family. Restless Harmon Blennerhasset resolved to take her far beyond their reach. He sold his inheritance, packed his books, musical instruments and chemical apparatus, and sailed with his beautiful bride for America. In New York they were entertained by prominent families, but Blennerhasset's romantic mind, filled with the forest fancies of French and English poets, felt the call of the frontier. He wanted to live in harmony with nature, beyond the discords of society. So they journeyed to Pittsburgh and there embarked on the keelboat that landed them in the growing town at the mouth of the Muskingum. For a season they liked Marietta's frontier hospitality and restless Blennerhasset had found the place where he could enjoy the pursuit of happiness. When he saw Backus Island, a dozen miles down the river, he fell in love with it. He took Margaret to walk in its stately groves and to watch the river current through its screen of willows. It seemed like paradise. For a little less than four thousand dollars he bought it from

Elijah Backus, a newspaper editor of Marietta. Then Blennerhasset hired a master builder and a troop of carpenters from Marietta.

For two years they were busy on the island, building a U-shaped mansion with a central house of two stories flanked by low-curving wings. The central unit contained drawing room, dining room, sleeping rooms; one wing comprised quarters for ten servants and the other accommodated Blennerhasset's library and laboratory. From the East came boatloads of furnishings—silver, glass, linen, curtains, carpets—that made the mansion an island of elegance among the crude cabins and hand-hewn furniture of the frontier. From the colonnaded doorway a carriage drive curved through the woods to the river, where visitors could moor their boats at Blennerhasset's landing. A network of graveled walks spanned by ornamental gateways led through the pleasant grounds. When the landscaping was complete, there were acres of flower, herb and vegetable gardens, young orchards snowing white petals on the spring grass, a pasture of fine cattle and blooded horses and spreading fields of grain.

Life was pleasant there. Blennerhasset walked his land in knee-breeches, silk stockings and silver-buckled shoes. Margaret cantered over the bridle paths, attended by a Negro groom. Blennerhasset read in his library, dallied in his laboratory with chemistry and electricity. Both of them studied the stars through a portable telescope. In the drawing room, Mrs. Blennerhasset staged with her guests impromptu performances of Shakespeare, and her husband played his own compositions on the violin and cello. Blennerhasset was so gifted and versatile a man, so removed from the grubbing life of the river settlers, that his contemporaries made up absurd stories of his cultivated taste and refined accomplishments. They said that he paced his terraces repeating the entire *Iliad* in the original Greek.

The fame of this gardened island with its white mansion showing through the trees passed up and down the Ohio. The Blennerhassets' friends came from Marietta and Belpre to visit them, and visitors arrived from farther away. One visitor showed up in a houseboat on a soft May day in 1805, and from the first he left a shadow there. Aaron Burr, then forty-nine years old, had known the flood tide and the ebb of fortune. A soldier in the Revolution, member of the New York Legislature, Attorney General of New York, Commissioner of Revolutionary Claims, then a member of the United States Senate and Vice President of the United States —he was perhaps most famous, or most infamous, as the man who had killed Alexander Hamilton in a duel at Weehawken on the Hudson. Brilliant, ambitious, energetic, he was designed for boldness of action—he must court either triumph or disaster, there was no middle, routine way. Restless, romantic Harmon Blennerhasset would find a fatal charm in such a man.

It was a treasonous scheme that brought Burr to the West where he had a political popularity in contrast to the bitterness he had won for himself in the older Colonies. At Pittsburgh he embarked in a commodious houseboat on a journey down the Ohio and the Mississippi. Ostensibly he was going West to further a land speculation beyond the Mississippi. Actually he meant to explore the possibilities of establishing a southwestern empire of his own. Though the details of the plan remain nebulous, its outlines are clear, shrewd and bold. Burr hoped to provoke a war between the United States and Spain along the lower Mississippi. In the confusion of that conflict, he could use a small force of men to detach the Southwest from the Union and set it up as his own principality.

So, with vast plans and conjectures to keep him company, he set out from Pittsburgh on his long journey. During a brief stop at Marietta he heard impressive accounts of Harmon Blennerhasset and his island paradise. A man who lived so lavishly must have money to invest in a large enterprise, and a man who ruled an island might be attracted to an empire. With thoughts like these Burr approached the island. This was the first of three visits he paid to the Blennerhassets, and the third visit found the two men deep in their conspiracy. By that time Burr had been down the Mississippi, where he had won the friendship of influential people, and he had been back East, where he had raised a part of the

money the undertaking would require. Now he was more confident than ever. As he unfolded the plan to Blennerhasset, that
curving island must have shrunk beside the vision of an empire
from the Mississippi to the Rio Grande. Perhaps to Blennerhasset's extravagant nature the island life had grown a little tame. At
any rate, he went in all the way. He mortgaged his island and his
mansion, sold his remaining securities and ordered a fleet of transport barges from a Marietta boat-builder. It was a substantial fleet
—ten craft of forty feet length, five of fifty feet and a keelboat of
sixty feet to carry firearms and ammunition. One of the barges
was to be fitted with glass windows, a fireplace and a canopied
promenade for Blennerhasset's own family. At the appointed time,
when Burr had his strategy ready to spring, the fleet was to bring
men and supplies down the Mississippi to a rendezvous with Burr.

But Burr in his effort to win followers and supporters had talked
too freely. While he toured the Ohio towns to enlist men for his
expedition, he was watched with vague and growing suspicion.
At the same time, Blennerhasset was writing anonymous letters to
a Marietta newspaper, asking why the eastern and western areas
of the United States should not be politically divided. This naive
propagandizing helped to arouse questions over Blennerhasset's
activities and his mysterious order of fifteen barges then building
on the Muskingum was reported to government officials. Then
President Jefferson issued a proclamation declaring that unlawful
enterprises were on foot in the western states and commanding all
civil and military officers to use their immediate exertions to bring
the offenders to punishment. Within a few days the Ohio legislature, in session at the old capital of Chillicothe, authorized calling
out the militia.

This action, early in December, 1806, came on the eve of Blennerhasset's departure. Marching to the Muskingum, the Ohio
militia seized his boats and supplies. On Treason Island, Blennerhasset had gathered a band of recruits. At the turn of events many
of them deserted the cause, but a few determined followers went
to Marietta, planning to wrest the flotilla from the militia troops.

By boldness and stealth they succeeded in escaping with one barge. They floated it down the river in the long December night and took Blennerhasset off the island to make the voyage down river to his rendezvous with Burr. His wife and children were to follow later.

The next day a troop of Virginian militiamen landed on the island. Finding the conspirator gone, they proceeded to despoil his property. They billeted themselves in the mansion, broached Blennerhasset's pantry and his cellar of wine, and in the excitement of sumptuous food and drink they carved the furniture with their sabres and fired their muskets into the chandeliers.

Meanwhile, Blennerhasset was both conspirator and fugitive. Sailing down the river on an errand of insurrection, he also was fleeing the authorities who attempted to intercept him at Point Pleasant and again at Gallipolis. By a combination of good luck and thick December weather, he eluded capture and met Burr where the Cumberland flows into the Ohio, three days before Christmas.

They escaped down the Mississippi, barely managing to keep ahead of their pursuers. Meanwhile, Blennerhasset's family made the voyage down the rivers, overtaking Burr and Blennerhasset at Bayou Pierre, Louisiana, in the middle of January. For two weeks more they eluded the Federal forces. Then they were taken into custody and transported to Richmond for trial. Though it was certain that their plans were treasonous, they were released for lack of material evidence. Burr had been too shrewd to leave tangible witness of his scheme, and all his activities could be explained by his interest in settling the western lands in which he had speculated.

That spring, when the willows were green and the grass was lush in the meadows, Blennerhasset returned to his island. But he could not regain his paradise. After the Virginia militiamen had violated the estate, nature had given it a harder blow. A spring flood had swept over the island, drowning it beneath sullen waters —as has happened many times since then. So the house was in ruin

and the gardens were buried in silt and debris. But for Blennerhasset that didn't really matter. All movable property had been
seized and sold by his creditors, and the island itself was in possession of a mortgage-holder. A few years later, on Christmas Eve,
1811, the deserted mansion took fire—perhaps from the camp some
riverman had made there—and burned to the ground. Only a
mound of ashes and the gutted foundation walls remained where
the white mansion had stood. Slowly grass and greenbriar, running woodbine and wild blackberries softened the gaunt ruins.

Harmon Blennerhasset made two more unsuccessful ventures—
first as a cotton planter in Louisiana, then as a lawyer in Montreal.
Finally, leaving a trail of failure and ruin in America, he crossed
the Atlantic again. He settled on another romantic island, the green
isle of Guernsey in the English Channel, and there, far from the
woods and hills of the Ohio country, he died in 1831. Burr, after
a period abroad to escape political and financial pressures, returned
to New York and resumed the practice of law. He too lived on an
island—Staten Island—and died there in 1836.

It is quiet on Blennerhasset Island now. As evening draws on, a
picnic party can look across to the lights of Parkersburg on the
West Virginia shore. In the summer darkness fireflies flicker in the
willows and wind rustles the long ranks of corn where once the
flowering gardens spread. A whistle sounds, a roar of wheels in-
creases and on the railroad bridge, like a moving chain of lights,
the "National Limited" streams to the East. The fire dies down
and the rowboat pulls away. Then the island is tranquil under the
summer stars and its winter of treason is as remote as legend.

XIV

A Long, Uncertain Road

ROM CUMBERLAND GAP, where the knobs of Kentucky shoulder the hills of Tennessee, came the restless men of Virginia and the Carolinas, striding the rock-strewn roads with their women and children in the lurching wagons behind them.

> *Cumberland Gap is a noted place—*
> *Three kinds of water to wash your face.*

The best kind was the water that flowed to the Ohio, and the settlers followed it. Over the steep Pennsylvania roads came ped-dlers, traders, merchants and another stream of families in sway-ing wagons under a canopy of towcloth. Through the Mohawk Valley passed settlers from New York, Massachusetts and New Hampshire, traveling roads that in a few more years would lose their traffic to the long lines of barges on the Erie Canal. All these ways converged on Ohio and all these many people had a flush of fervor—an excitement of heart, a purpose burning in their eyes.

It was called "Ohio Fever." It swept through communities from New Hampshire to the Carolinas. It left farms abandoned and villages lifeless. But it gave as much life as it took away. So the trails of Ohio were scarred by the deep print of settlers' wagons and the blue Ohio sky was feathered with the smoke of settlers' fires. Whole counties echoed with the thud of the clearing ax and the sun warmed new furrows where the forest had made a twilight for fifty thousand years.

Ohio was the Far West in those years, and whatever way the settlers followed, it was a long, uncertain road. But they came, season after season, first by hundreds, then by thousands, then by hundreds of thousands. Each family had its own experience of loneliness and toil, of struggle, of failure or fulfillment. But all had the same hope and the same hardship. Here is one family among all the rest——

IN THE BLEAK winter of 1809, in the kitchen of their farmhouse in the township of Clinchfield, Connecticut, the Greenup family watched the snow fall deep on their stony fields. Fleming Greenup was a silent man that season and Hannah Greenup wondered how a growing family could live on potatoes and cornmeal—it had been a scant harvest last autumn. In the early twilight, Sally bent over her schoolbooks beside the lamp and little Georgie and Ruth Ellen tugged at their mother's skirts as she mixed another pan of cornbread for supper. Flem Greenup put on his coat and cap and mittens and stamped off to the stable with a milk pail at his side. With his head pressing the cow's warm side and the milk streams rhythmic in the pail, he kept turning a question in his mind. He had a problem to decide.

He needed more land than the sixty rock-veined acres out there in the falling snow. But beyond his stone walls another man's fields began and beyond his slope of woods rose another man's timber. And the taxes. Connecticut farms were taxed by acre, regardless of land values, and Flem Greenup had seen many helpless farmers sold out by the state. More land meant more taxes, and even if he had more land——

He dug his head deeper into the cow's flank. He didn't like to think of being dispossessed of land that had been in the Greenup name since it was first claimed from the Indians.

That evening, when the table was cleared and the dishes were washed and put away, Fleming Greenup called his family together. They sat around the empty table with the lamp glowing on the red-checked cloth. Sally closed her spelling book and Georgie squirmed in his home-made high chair and Ruth Ellen nodded in her mother's arms. The lamplight held them in a quiet circle while the wind beat at the window and a kettle sighed on the stove.

Fleming Greenup opened a small calf-bound book and laid it on the table. "There's a place out west in Ohio," he said slowly, "described in the *Western Gazetteer and Immigrant's Guide*. Listen close now while I read about it."

When he put on his steel-rimmed glasses he looked like a schoolmaster, his lean face long and solemn in the lamplight.

Ross County, he read, *is situated on both sides of the Scioto, which divides it about equally. It is watered by Paint Creek on the west side of the Scioto; Kenniconie and Salt Creeks on the east. This is a rich and healthy country.*

He paused and looked up earnestly at his wife. "Go on, Flem," she said, one hand slowly patting the baby.

The inhabitants are mostly wealthy, and have elegant buildings, large and well improved farms; the traveler approaching a farmhouse is forcibly struck with the indications of PLENTY, which are presented at every step; such as immense fields of grain, large stacks of wheat, capacious corncribs well filled even in summer; numerous herds of stock, cattle, horses, hogs, sheep, common and merino; yards swarming with poultry; and should he have occasion to enter the hospitable mansion, he will find there the same proofs of abundance and perfect independence; everything is on the scale of external wealth, a plenteous board, elegant and costly furniture, and well dressed children.

He lifted his eyes to the bare walls and the rough-hewn kitchen shelves. In his gaze were also his two lean calves in the barn where the mows were already shallow and the grain was shrinking in the bins even with the harvest just four months past. Hannah Greenup stared at the mound of clothing in her hamper, worn and patched and mended and waiting to be mended again.

"So you think things might go better in the western country," she said.

Sally looked up with wondering eyes. "You mean we're going West, like the movers, mother?"

"That is for your father to decide," Hannah said.

Flem bent over the page again. *The country abounds in game and there is a constant supply of excellent fish. The surface is free from stagnant waters, which insures health to the inhabitants. Although it has already a prosperous settlement, Ross County offers many eligible situations to industrious immigrants.*

Sally drew a great breath and her eyes came back from the imagined country. "When are we going, father? When do we start?"

He closed the book as solemnly as though it were the family Bible. He looked into his wife's quiet face. What he saw there reassured him. "We start as soon as the snow is gone," he said, "and the roads are fit to travel."

THAT SPRING many families were on the move. Some of them came through Clinchfield with their wagons groaning under loads of tools, provisions and household goods, bound for New Connecticut in the Western Reserve. But Fleming Greenup liked the description of the Scioto country, where the land was partly settled, with good sites still plentiful along the tributary streams. Terms were easy and in that rich region a man could conclude his payments in a few seasons. It was that journey, through New Jersey and across Pennsylvania and down the broad Ohio, that he had traced on the map of the *Western Gazetteer* those winter evenings. So the family made ready.

Picture them on a gray March day, with the snowbanks shrinking in the fields, driving out of the farmyard with their wagon creaking—Flem and Sally on the wagon seat and Hannah between the smaller children on a tin trunk, with all their goods around them. But at the crest of the hill Flem stopped his team. They looked back at the house in the valley, and the rocky fields and the hill pasture and the white churchspire above the distant trees. Eleazer Greenup had settled that farm a hundred years before, when Connecticut was a Crown colony, with the seal of King George stamped upon its charter. Hard-won land—four generations of

Greenups had carried rocks to the edge of the plowfield, two generations had fought the British at Clinchfield Meadows and had seen their own barn go up in smoke from Indian arrows tipped with fire. Flem stared in silence. Now a new generation was going to a country that would always be different, a country without memories, a land that could never be so tightly cherished as that little stone-studded field in the valley. The house stood lifeless in the gray March weather. No smoke curled from the chimney. In the kitchen the kettles were gone from the shelf and the fire was dead in the stove. Four generations of Greenups had sat in that room on winter evenings and had watched the summer twilight from the doorstep, while the thrush song faded in the woods. In the bedroom beyond the kitchen the old had died and the children had been born. For a moment Flem was afraid to face his wife.

"Wait, Flem," she said suddenly. She handed the baby to Sally and stepped down from the wagon. She walked fast down the hill and to the house where Fleming Greenup had brought her as a bride. She opened the kitchen door. There she had rocked her babies to sleep, there the relatives had gathered for Thanksgiving and Christmas—those bare walls almost echoed with hymns and ballads and lullabies. She put her face against the doorframe— and then Flem was beside her.

She looked up at him. "Will we have a home again?"

"Yes," he said. "My great-grandfather left England to come here. Another time has come for moving. But not if you've set your heart——"

She closed the door upon the silent house. "No. I'm ready."

Together they walked back to the wagon. Flem lifted the reins. "Giddap," he said to his horses.

Their route was west and south, across the Hudson and down through Orange County. A false spring warmed the meadows of New Jersey as they journeyed between orchards and pastures where the grass was greening in the sun. In fine weather they passed through Springfield, Chatham, Morris and Chester. Then the roads grew rough and the hills loomed in their way. The sky was gray and sunless.

"Is it the Pennsylvania mountains?" Hannah asked.

"No," he said, "these are only the Jersey hills. It's a long way yet to Pennsylvania, and we'll have to get a mountain wagon before we try General Forbes' road over those mountains."

At night they made their camp beside streams or at the edge of woods. Hannah and the children spread a pallet on the wagon floor and Flem made his bed on the half-frozen ground, for the nights were sharp with frost. So they passed through Dutch Valley, Batestown, Mansfield, and across the river to Easton.

"Now look around you," Flem said to his family.

"Is it Ohio?" Sally asked.

"No. But we're in Pennsylvania."

It was a different country that they saw, passing through Bethlehem and Northampton. The apple orchards of New Jersey had given way to broad fields, where men drove teams of oxen hitched to home-made wooden plows. Set solidly along the road were stone houses and spacious stone barns of the "Pennsylvania Dutch."

They crossed the Schuylkill River, swollen by spring water, on a bridge of logs chained to trees on either bank. Under the wagon's weight the log road sank beneath the water and the horses splashed through a swift current. Flem watched the water with narrow eyes, his reins held taut, till the stream was crossed. Then the road was smooth and level. Steadily the miles flowed under the horses' hooves. Around them now were fields like carpets of green—by mid-summer the wheat would ripple golden in the wind. The road grew more populous and the voices of burly wagoners rang out in songs and curses as the red and blue Conestogas swayed like ships over the hoof-churned highway.

"There," said Flem, "that's the kind of wagon we'll outfit with at Harrisburg. That's what we need to take us over the mountains."

It was a marvel to see the skill of the drivers and the strength of the horses—six or eight or even ten hitched to a freighter's wagon. The heavy loads rocked over the road, bells jangling, wheels tossing mud, drivers snapping their long whips with a sound like pistol fire.

In the busy, bustling, horse-smelling town of Harrisburg, amid the rattle of harness and the creak of wagons, Flem took his family to the friendly homelike tavern called the "Travelers' Rest." While they bathed and rested, he went to see a firm of wagon makers. He sold his farm wagon and bought a heavy, high-wheeled Conestoga, and he counted gold pieces from his leather pouch and bought another team of horses, mountain-wise, to hitch ahead of his own team. Men assured him he would find ready buyers for the added pair in Pittsburgh where mountain horses were always in demand.

Early in the April morning they loaded their implements and utensils, their chests and seeds and medicines, into the curved Conestoga wagonbed with its canvas canopy. They took their places in an impromtu caravan of settlers, like themselves bound for Pittsburgh and the Ohio. At the bank of the Susquehanna they waited their turn and were ferried across on a large flatboat worked by nine men with setting poles. Then, with the harness bells jingling and the wagons swaying, they were on their way. The April sun shone brightly and the road was hard and dry. With four horses the big wagon rolled along like a buggy. There were other wagons before and behind them. They were part of a company.

Hannah's eyes were as blue as Sally's and a flush of eagerness glowed in her face. It had done her good to have a rest at Harrisburg.

"Will it be like this in Ohio?" she asked, gazing out at the fine farms of Cumberland County. With the thud of hoofs on the road and the music of harness bells, she could believe in promises they had wondered at back in a winter-bound farmhouse in Connecticut.

"I guess it will," Flem said, "though Ohio is still two hundred miles away."

The next day, beyond Carlisle, they traveled in a cold rain through poor and stony country. It was slower going then, and slower still when they began the long grade up South Mountain. Soon the road was framed in dripping forest. Occasionally they passed dark little clearings, with wet black woods around them. They saw children, pigs and poultry huddled together about dilapidated cabins.

"Will Ohio be like this?" was the heavy question in Hannah's mind, but she left it unspoken.

At Shippenburgh, over the mountain, the caravan halted and Flem climbed down in the mud to tighten the traces on his teams and to pad a chafing collar on one of his new horses. Through the rain he had occasionally glimpsed the dark looming ridges in the west. There was hard work ahead.

They camped that night at the foot of First Brother, the first big barrier of the Alleghenies. The afternoon had cleared but when the sun dropped below the lifted skyline the hills rose up immense and lonely. Ahead of them rose range after range, height after height, some covered with pine forest, the dark shadow of others leaning bleak and naked on the sky. The narrow road was like a knife-cut slashed in the steepening forest. That night they piled wood on their campfire while wolves howled from the dark. Connecticut seemed far away.

The road over First Brother was rough almost as a streambed. Up the long grades the caravan crawled with a grating of wheels and a creaking of leather. Now the drivers' voices were sharper than the slow jangle of the harness bells. But from the height they looked down into the fair prospect of Path Valley with the village of Rymersburg showing through the trees.

"Father," Sally breathed at Flem's side, "it's beautiful!"

Wild and still and romantic, broken by a brook of silver, the valley seemed an omen of all that lay before her in the wide world of America. But her father had another picture in his mind.

"We want broad fields," he said, "level and open to the sun."

At Rymersburg they stopped while a blacksmith shod a team

that had found trouble holding back the load on the downgrade. While the caravan was halted, people got down from the wagons and walked through the friendly street.

"You're over First Brother," the villagers told them, "but there's the Second and Third to come."

Again their gaze climbed up the tumbled ridges, and the men talked together about handling their teams on steep curves and slippery ledges. So far they had come through well. Their wagons were sound and their horses were strong, willing. But before they started on again, they saw signs of the hazards that lay before them. In a trampled stable yard they stared at wagons sagging on broken wheels and in the dim stables they saw horses stained with mud, their heads hanging.

"Some have to be shot," said the stable keeper, "but these are only lamed and winded. They'll take to the road again."

Back at his wagon, Flem looked soberly over his harness. He made sure that the heavy collars fitted snug on his horses' shoulders and he took up a link in the traces to keep their pull even and steady. He tested the brakerod, seeing that the shoes clamped firmly on the big wheel rims. The wreckage in that stableyard was not entirely a surprise to him. He knew that on that journey wagons broke down and overturned. He knew that horses fell in their harness and that loaded wagons passed over them while the brakes squealed noisily on the wheels. Some wagons plunged from log bridges into swollen rivers and others overturned in treacherous fords. He had heard a traveler grimly describing the ascent of Sidling Hill, where the road leaped down the ledges with rain making a torrent under the wagon wheels, and concluding soberly, "The reason so few are willing to return from the western country is not that the country is so good but the journey back is so hard."

Flem looked at the shoes on his horses and then he went to the blacksmith shop. Though the other drivers were restless to be started, Flem said quietly, "We'd better lose an hour here than a day up there on the mountains. I'm going to get these shoes tightened and I think you'd better do the same. There's no use risking a lame horse or a crippled one, and it's a long way to the next town after we put this one behind us."

They agreed, reluctantly, and the smith went from wagon to wagon, examining each horse, lifting the hoof to his leather apron and driving a few nails in. When he had finished with the last team he reached up to the hames and shook the harness bells.

"Now you're ready for the road," he said. "Every shoe on these animals is sound and tight. If you've got a good driver, put him at the head. Let him set the pace. Pull hard on your brakerods on the downgrades and don't take the turns too sharp. Then you'll get through to Pittsburgh and go floating down the river."

When the caravan climbed Second Brother, Fleming Greenup was at the head. The long climb was a test of strength for the horses and of skill for the men. From his youth Flem had been a good teamster, driving a lofty load of hay or a heavy load of lumber with a sharp eye for the boulders in the Connecticut fields and a quick, firm hand for his team. Now he learned to judge mountain roads—where the bed was firm and where it might prove treacherous, where the rocks were merely rough and where they might snap a heavy Conestoga wheel like kindling. He learned the strength and resiliency of that sturdy wagon and how it could sway on an uneven road in rhythm with the horses' pulling. And he learned more than he had ever known about horses. He pushed them, he drove and urged and lashed them—he had to have their last frantic strength on the abrupt, pitched grades and around the perilous turns. But he never made demands beyond their power. He breathed them after every heavy grade. He stood beside them and stroked their corded necks till their trembling left them. And always from the wagonseat he watched the road as carefully as though he were planting his own feet on its rugged surface. His horses never slipped or stumbled.

Sometimes he unhitched his team and drove them back, the iron traces jangling dully in the mud, to help a driver who was mired hubdeep. At other times he stopped the caravan to water the horses at a mountain stream and to let the travelers stretch their legs.

The mountaineers came with eggs and milk and bread to sell, and with friendly greetings. All those mountain people "rickoned"— a strange word to Yankee ears—and they talked in drawling voices that made the Greenup children stare.

"Rickon you'ns are goin' into the back country."

"Rickon you'll find some good land if you keep goin'."

"Rickon Ohio must be fillin' up, cause a heap of people are headin' there this spring."

That became a familiar speech, repeated in every town and tavern on the way.

"A sight of people are on the roads."

"A pile of people are goin' West this year."

"A powerful parcel of people are bound for the 'Hio country."

It was monotonous but comforting, to Hannah under the arch of towcloth with sober Georgie beside her and restless Ruth Ellen in her arms, and to Flem on the wagonseat with wide-eyed Sally at his side. It was a reassurance when the road seemed endless and the wet wind lashed them and a new range of hills rose up to bar the way. It was good to know they were part of a great company, on their way to the future.

At Bedford they crossed the beautiful Juniata, but Flem had eyes only for the swift current flowing over a sagging bridge of logs. Beyond, the road followed the river's bank, and for half a day they had the rush and glint of water to set a pace for the teams. It was a bright blue day with April smiling on the hills and the bells rang like music from the horses' hames. Later they crossed the Juniata again, at a treacherous place where a wagon lay like a foundered ship on a ledge along the shore. Flem's eyes narrowed when he saw a pair of men digging a grave under a tall pine tree.

It was fourteen miles to the crest of Allegheny Mountain, a hard pull over roads studded with stone and pitted with holes. Flem drove grimly, with his mouth set and his gaze never lifting from the road. But at the crest, while he rubbed the breathing horses, he gazed over a fine prospect of diminishing hills. In the slanting sun the western horizon was radiant with light.

"That's the last big mountain," he said gratefully. "We're over the backbone now."

Three days later they came down the long grade, with the brakes rasping and the horses jogging loosely before the load. "There," Flem pointed. In the distance they saw the smoke of Pittsburgh and the gleaming of the rivers. Then the woods closed in again and their eyes were cheated. But soon the broad valley opened before them. From Grant's Hill they looked down on the triangle of land between the Monongahela and Allegheny rivers and beyond the point they saw the Ohio, broad and free and shining in the April light.

Pittsburgh was then, as now, a dramatic place. With four thousand instead of four hundred thousand people, it was even then a metropolis. On the river banks stood sawmills, gristmills, a slitting mill, ropewalks, sail lofts, a boatyard, a nail factory—the first in America—cotton and woolen factories, an anchor smithy, brickyards, potteries, breweries, a foundry and a glass factory. That V of land between the rivers was one of the busiest places on the continent. Streets were thronged with traffic—lumber wagons, brick wagons, farm wagons, great creaking freight wagons and swaying Conestogas. Among them were gigs and carts, buckboards and buggies, and sometimes a man on horseback leading a string of pack ponies. On the rivers moved another stream of traffic—arks and skiffs, flatboats and keelboats, rafts of every shape, size and description. From taverns came the hearty voices of teamsters about to start back over the mountains and of rivermen about to start for the Mississippi.

After a day of looking about, because a Yankee does not hurry at a trade, Fleming Greenup sold his mountain horses and his Conestoga wagon. On the next day he bought a flatboat that had come down the Monongahela with a load of lumber. He moved his family into a small stern cabin and tied his horses in the open bow. A plow and a bed wagon went upon the cabin roof. Then, with a copy of Zadok Cramer's *Pittsburgh Navigator* to guide them, they started on the strange new portion of their journey.

It was a blissful way to travel, after the toil and strain of the mountain roads. Hannah sang while she washed clothing and hung it on the rope rail that Flem had stretched to hold the children in. The children romped on the cabin roof and Flem lounged at the big steering oar, watching the spring-rife shores slip past. Always some craft were in sight—rafts, flatboats, keelboats, skiffs—and friendly greetings rang across the water. Twenty times a day Flem called, "Look, Hannah! Over there!" and they stared at some special wonder, a keelboat with a penful of Negro slaves on the cabin roof, a deer swimming the river with branched antlers lifting above the water, a big raft bearing a hut at one end and a haystack at the other, like a barnyard, with pigs and chickens roaming in between.

Besides the river there was the endless variety of the shores— hills and plains, woods and meadows, lonely cabins and friendly settlements and an occasional bustling town. Past Steubenville with its steep streets they drifted, past the busy river front of Wheeling, past the graceful town of Marietta where the Muskingum came down between green hills, past Gallipolis on its broad, elevated plain and so to Portsmouth at the mouth of the Scioto. They had been just a week on the river when Flem steered his boat into the Portsmouth landing.

Again they traveled to the sound of wagon wheels, this time over winding Ohio roads through a country lush with spring. They found a location in Ross County, near Paint Creek, above the prosperous town of Chillicothe, capital of Ohio in those years. There Fleming Greenup entered his tract and made his initial payment. He had chosen a plot of level ground with an open meadow fringed by hardwood forest. In the clearing, near the site where they would build their cabin, stood a row of young apple trees ready to burst into bloom.

It touched Hannah to see that sign of home in this distant empty place, before their cabin walls were raised. "How did they get here, Flem?" she asked.

"Man named Johnny Appleseed," Flem said. "I heard in Ports-

mouth how he went through all this country planting apple orchards wherever he found good soil and a sunny clearing."

"Johnny Appleseed!" Sally cried. "Is that his real name?"

"That's what they call him. He travels afoot with a sack of apple
seeds for planting. He's everybody's friend—even the Indians'."

Sally's eyes were bright as bluebells. "I'd like to see him some
day."

"Maybe you will," her father said. "They say he keeps an eye
on all his orchards."

IN THOSE YEARS Chillicothe was a noted place. Settled chiefly
by Virginians, its main thoroughfare, Paint Street, was lined with
solid stone houses with deep verandas. To its cupola-crowned
State House came the legislators from every organized county
in Ohio and its stores drew trade from many miles around. Over
busy Paint Street passed farmers hauling corn, wheat, potatoes,
turnips, the loads lurching in the rutted road and the axles creaking. Zane's Trace, a new road hacked through the forest, led
over the hills to the east and Paint Creek and the Scioto made
a water route to market with the county's wheat, pork and turkeys.

The Virginians had made a pleasant and dignified town deep
in the western country. But Virginians were not its only settlers.
Three German hunters, named Ruffner, Belans and Behrle, had
trapped on Paint Creek before Chillicothe was founded. As the
settlement grew, it attracted many Germans from Pennsylvania
and also direct from Saxony and Westphalia. Scores of German
immigrants came to Chillicothe as indentured servants, having
their passage money paid by some Ohio resident. After working
for three years, they won their "free" papers and then established
themselves as equal and independent citizens. Besides, there were
New York families—"York Yankees is the meanest," said the
Virginian who was bested in a trade—and others from New Jersey and Massachusetts. It was a mingled stream that poured into
the western country, and each year the stream was growing. A
"powerful parcel" of people had the Ohio fever.

Ross County, on the Scioto, offered a different life from the stony fields of Connecticut. Around them Fleming Greenup's family saw a land of wooded hills, dominated by Mount Logan— which still appears on the great seal of Ohio—and of grassy meadows and forested bottom along the watercourses. Fields demanded great toil when they had to be widened by ax and grubbing hoe. But the land had great fertility, and its corn and wheat, its rye and barley, were a wonder to a Yankee farmer who had tried to cultivate rock-studded hillsides. On the uplands toward Mount Logan roamed deer and bear. Though the buffalo were gone, their bones still whitened the salt licks and their wallows still yawned by the creek beds. Along the streams were ducks, geese, cranes and herons; in the woods gray squirrels, turkeys, partridges.

Young George Greenup was to grow up a Buckeye boy with an itch for a rifle trigger and the lore of the woods more real than book-learning. He found turkeys' nests in the forest and brought the eggs home to hatch under a patient hen. He learned where the big trout lay in the quiet pool under the leaning willow tree. He found secret places in the woods where ginseng grew. He dug the roots and took them in to Paint Street, where a storekeeper kept his account till he had money enough to buy a shining, long-barreled Deckhard rifle. With his cheek against that gun barrel he could soon hit ducks on the wing and was ashamed to shoot a squirrel anywhere but through the head. For target practice in that country they had no concentric circles with a bull's-eye center but only a nailhead in a board 100 steps away. Three bullets were enough to drive the nail home.

A new family spent the first season in a cabin of sycamore or poplar logs—a room twelve feet by sixteen, chinked with moss. Rafters were held by wooden pins driven through auger holes. A roof of bark and split shingles was weighted down by poles. The floor was puncheons—rough boards split from forest logs—and doors were puncheons hung on wooden hinges. If it did not resemble the "mansions with elegant furniture" described in the *Western Gazetteer,* it was still their own, and they had not gone

in debt to build it. Fleming Greenup had a Yankee knack for
using tools. His entire cabin, and its beds, tables and benches, he
built with an ax and an auger.

Ohio fever attacked young men chiefly—the West was a young
man's country. When the Ohio Legislature first met in Chillicothe in 1803, more than half the lawmakers were under forty.
As late as 1840, 80 per cent of the Ohio population was under
forty and 30 per cent was under ten. Boys became men early in
that society. When the state of Michigan was admitted to the
Union, its governor was twenty-one years old. Stephen A. Douglas, the Little Giant, who had come to Illinois from Vermont,
was a United States Congressmen at thirty. Before that he had
been an auctioneer, a schoolteacher, a lawyer, a land commissioner,
a state's attorney and a judge. Sometimes the Ohio fever became
another, mortal, kind of fever—gravestones in the old cemeteries
of Ohio and Indiana show a high death rate for infants and for
young men and women in their twenties.

In those years a haze of smoke hung over all the valleys. Soft
blue vapor drifted up from ten thousand clearings where settlers
burned logs, roots and stumps at the margins of their fields.
Brush burned out with a leaping fury but great stumps smoldered,
making a slow cloud in the sunlight and a glow in the dark night
sky. For hundreds of miles the air was tangy with that burning.
Land offices were spaced across Ohio, at Marietta, Chillicothe and
Cincinnati, across Indiana, at Jeffersonville and Vincennes, and
across Illinois to the banks of the Mississippi at Quincy. To every
office the settlers swarmed. They saw the land agent mark their
claim on his survey maps, they signed their name or made their
mark, and hurried back to drive deeper their corner stakes.

After 1818, large tracts were set aside as Military Lands and
offered as bonuses to the veterans of the War of 1812. Some of
the soldiers came with their campaign rifles in their wagons, their
campaign hats jaunty on their heads. But many chose to sell their
patents to speculators. So there were four kinds of owners of
newly opened western lands—the Federal government, military

veterans, speculators and squatters. Speculators prospered most. Vast tracts of vacant land came into their possession. Some of them operated from a distance, like Romulus Riggs of Philadelphia who named his daughter "Illinois" and offered at one time 226 quarter sections—nearly forty thousand acres of Illinois prairie. Others bought, sold and traded in the raw western towns. Arvertising each new section as "the Mesopotamia of the West," they competed with the government for the purchase money of settlers from Virginia and New York, from Scotland and Germany, from Sweden and Wales.

Through the 1820s the immigrants streamed west by way of the Ohio River. When the Black Hawk War ended, in 1832, and the Indians were pushed across the Mississippi, a new rush began by a northern route. For twenty years the Erie Canal and the Great Lakes carried to the vacant country around the lakes the founders of new cities and new commonwealths. This movement reached a climax after the momentous year of 1848, when famine and revolution in Europe sent hundreds of thousands of immigrants to the upper Mississippi Valley. In the spring of 1851, Ralph Waldo Emerson left the graceful village of Concord, Massachusetts, to lecture in the log schoolhouses, the raw academy halls and the drafty frame churches of the frontier. He traveled on a steamboat down the Ohio, slept under buffalo robes on the floor of canal barges and drove in buckboards across the prairie roads of Illinois. Two days he spent in the spreading capital town of Springfield, where farm wagons rutted dirt streets, and then he went north and west through horse-high prairie grass and oak and maple forests to the Mississippi and to the steep little shipping town of Galena. There, in his tavern room, with a scratchy pen on paper he described that river-bordered country to another philosopher, Thomas Carlyle, beside the Thames five thousand miles away. "On all the shores interminable silent forest. If you land, there is prairie behind prairie, forest behind forest, sites of nations, no nations."

But nations were coming. On a summer night soon after his

words were written, the palatial steamer *Atlantic* was running in dense fog over Lake Erie, westward bound. Head on, through the darkness, drove the strong new steamer *Ogdensburg*. There was no glimpse of danger, no cry of warning—only a crashing impact and the grinding of ship's timbers. The *Atlantic,* with her side torn open, quickly filled with water. Five hundred dazed and battered passengers floundered through the flooding passageways. Some of them leaped into the water, others clung to the upper rails of the stricken ship. In the gray, fog-shrouded dawn the *Ogdensburg* saved 250 of them before the big liner sank from sight. Many of those survivors were Norwegian immigrants and they finished their journey to take up claims in Wisconsin and Illinois beside the Germans and the Irish, the Scots and the Swedes, who every day streamed off the big immigrant boats at the western lake ports.

In the winter of 1853, fourteen steamboats lay ice-bound at the junction of the Ohio and Mississippi rivers, and in their crowded cabins two thousand German and Irish immigrants fumed over the delay that kept them from pre-emption lands along the Upper Mississippi. That summer double-header passenger trains daily brought long chains of immigrant cars to Chicago, and throngs of persons, in homespun garments and with bulging carpetbags, fanned out across the prairie in wagons, on horseback and afoot. Nine thousand immigrants changed trains in Chicago in a single day. At the same time, the Milwaukee and Mississippi and the Milwaukee and St. Paul railroads were carrying other thousands to river ports. They filled railway stations and steamboat offices, covering the floor with a solid mat of chests, trunks and bundles, and lying down to sleep in the midst of their goods.

When Henry Clay made his last journey from Washington to Kentucky, according to legend, he stepped out of his stagecoach, walked over to the roadside and bent down till his ear touched the ground. "What are you listening for, Mr. Clay?" the driver asked. "I am listening," said Henry Clay, "to the tread of unnumbered thousands of feet that are to come this way westward."

Writing of his travels through the valley of the Ohio, Charles

Dickens referred to towns and villages, and then he corrected himself: "I ought to say city; every place is a city here." The poorest crossroads was a metropolis in expectancy. Out in Illinois the name of Stone's Landing was changed to Napoleon, because it had great expectations. Goose Run became the Columbus River. A cluster of log houses on the prairie dreamed of its future as a leading city of Illinois and took the name Illiopolis. Some said Cairo, at the mouth of the Ohio, would surpass New York and Boston. They talked about a future capital city on the Mississippi.

For half a century new states received the motley multitudes. The movement was one of the most momentous in history, with a drama too vast and too familiar for Americans to understand. New citizens came wearing many garbs and costumes, speaking various languages, with a dozen different memories and traditions behind them. But the land was large enough and the tasks were big enough for all, and the West made them its people. The Greenups from Connecticut and the Werthheimers from Saxony, the Flynns from Ireland and the Lloyds from Wales, the Sandersons from Scotland and the Breckenridges from Virginia—they had followed a long, uncertain road to a long and certain future.

XV

Autumn Rains Were the Curtains

Before the land was fenced and tame, when there was room for a wanderer to tramp the meadows and thread the woods and steer his canoe in the running waters, a legend grew up in the new country. It is the only legend in a land that quickly filled with sober people. But Johnny Appleseed had his seasons when the settlements were still far apart on roads marked only by a white blaze on the bark of trees. Then a family in their clearing, hungry for a new face and a stranger's voice, would welcome a ragged man who planted apple trees while he talked of the road to heaven.

Johnny Appleseed was the name by which people knew him from Pittsburgh to the bends of the Wabash, from the Ohio River to Lake Erie. He had a Christian name—Jonathan Chapman. He was born in Massachusetts. There, in his boyhood, he often wandered off in quest of birds and flowers. In the autumn of 1801, he floated down the Ohio in two canoes lashed together and laden to the gunwales with apple pulp from the cider mills of western Pennsylvania. He went west, not to locate land but to plant apple orchards in the clearings where people would come. For forty years he wandered the country with a deerhide sack rustling on his shoulder. Along with apple seeds he scattered seeds of healing herbs—catnip, hoarhound and pennyr'yle, to serve the settlers of the future. Wherever he wandered he made friends— with Indians and whites alike, with the men on the early traces, teamsters, peddlers, itinerant preachers riding their forest circuits, with all the settlers, Yankee and Hoosier, Irish and German, and with little children playing dolls with corncobs and old men sitting in sunlit doorways.

Johnny was something of a circuit rider himself, with the whole country for his parish. He preached more often than any doctrine a text of apple blossoms on the warm May wind. One story said he was kicked in the head by a horse and had a vision of heaven as a vast orchard of blooming apple trees. By belief he was a Swedenborgian—among his apple seeds he carried ragged copies of *Heaven and Hell* and left them for people to read till he should call again. Sometimes he tore pages from his books to make them go farther. So he circulated the visions of Immanuel Swedenborg by installments, from cabin to cabin in the lonely country. When night found him on the trail, he read his tattered texts by firelight and saved crumbs from his supper for the squirrels and partridges. One rainy night he took refuge in a hollow log and found it already occupied by a bear. The two slept peacefully and in the morning parted on good terms. Some have called him St. Francis of the West. He was the only saint the busy western country ever bred.

No one knows certainly when Jonathan Chapman died—though it was in the 1840s in Allen County, Indiana, not many miles from the site of the old Battle of Fallen Timbers. But Johnny Appleseed never died. He went on wandering the country, in people's memory. He was blessed every spring when the orchards bloomed white on the hills and every autumn when the ripe fruit bowed the branches down. Even after those orchards were old and decaying by the rivers, his memory stayed green. By that time he belonged to the whole Middle West, and an Illinois poet, Vachel Lindsay, made a song about his crossing the Appalachians to wander the wide country—*He ran with the rabbit and he slept with the stream*—and leave it blossoming behind him.

Johnny Appleseed became a subject for stories. That is the way he was remembered, and it is the way to tell about a man who found a place in the affections of people who gave him a night's lodging in return for his gentle gospel, and of others who never heard his voice or saw him ragged in the twilight. So here is a story about Ike Hyar's barndance, more than a hundred years ago.

NOBODY WHO was there ever forgot Ike Hyar's barndance, because it was a dance, a fight and a wedding, almost. Besides, a sermon was thrown in—a curious, remembered kind of preaching, about apple trees and the green fields of Ohio and the years of America still to come.

In those days, settlements grew on the Ohio and fine farms spread up the wide valley of the Scioto, where the buckeyes dropped white petals at the edge of clearings and the sycamores leaned above the water. Young Link Barren, just turned twenty-one, was new to that country. He had come from the dark mountains of Pennsylvania and you can imagine how his gray eyes lighted over a land of oak-clad hills and green valleys flashing with streams on their way to the Ohio. But he was bound for a newer country still—to Illinois, he said, where the prairies rippled in the wind and the unfenced earth was waiting.

Bound on that long journey, he had no mind to halt by the Scioto. But when Fleming Greenup asked him to give a hand with the harvest, he stopped. There was something about those golden fields, or maybe it was Sally Greenup's corn-colored hair, that persuaded him.

"I can stay a week," he said. "Long enough to get the fodder in."

He was a tall fellow, slim at the waist and wide as a steer across the shoulders. In the cornrows he set a pace that darkened the shirt on Flem Greenup's back. At dusk, when they came in, his voice rang across the meadow where Sally looked out from the kitchen door.

"That's good corn you've got, Mr. Greenup. But I mean to have better corn and a bigger field out there in Illinois."

Flem smiled. "There's no rooster can crow like a young rooster."

At evening he sat in the firelight like a member of the family, only he talked more than a son or brother would. Hannah brought in a bowl of apples—Pippins, Russets, Red Astrachans and Seek-no-farthers. "Thanks to Johnny Appleseed," she said, "all our trees are bearing."

"Who's Johnny Appleseed?" Link asked.

"He's the man who started all the orchards hereabouts," Flem said. "He wanders the unsettled country planting apple seeds."

"Maybe he has been to Illinois," Link said. "Maybe I'll find apple trees——"

"No," Hannah said quickly. "That's too far distant."

"Johnny never goes beyond the Wabash River," Flem said. "He has orchards for three hundred miles. That's enough to keep him busy."

"Well," Link bit into an Astrachan, "he's missing the best country. I've heard the soil is ten feet deep in Illinois and fine as buckwheat flour." He was off again with his future on the prairies.

While he talked Flem sat working tallow into a pair of boots, Hannah rocked with her sewing basket in her lap and Sally sat in the shadows watching the firelight play on Link's strong, youthful face. Even Georgie and Ruth Ellen, up in the loft, peered down like two 'possums.

"I want a place in the new country. I mean to mark my corners and choose my land. A spring, a grove of timber, a wide prairie ready for the plow."

He had a shock of sun-bleached hair and a pair of laughing-sober eyes. But he wasn't laughing then. A far look came in his eyes that made Flem Greenup remember how he had left Connecticut six years before.

Hannah said over her work, "There's land here. There's land left up the fork above us."

Link shook his head and his shadow moved emphatically on the wall. "I want a place where other men haven't come. I mean to be there from the beginning."

Hannah's hands were still while she studied him a moment. "You're uncommon certain what you want."

"Yes'm," Link said.

He had been a stable-hand at a tavern in Rymersburg, Pennsylvania, where the life flowed west, freighting teams and Concord coaches, buckboards and carryalls, traps and carts and Conestoga wagons with arched hoods swaying and bells ringing from the harness hames. Month after month, season after season, that stream pressed on, urgent and unending, to the west. Finally he knew that he would have to go.

Hannah rocked steadily, her chair creeping across the floor to where Sally sat in the shadows. She put a hand on the girl's arm.

"It's a wild, wide country—Illinois," she said, going on with her work. "Weeks away and uncertain. Lonely, too, I've been told. The McDavids came back from there last year."

"There's grass waist-high in the meadows," Link said. "And earth as black as gunpowder."

Sally sat motionless against the wall. Her gaze never left his face.

On Sunday, Isaac Hyar came. He was a widower, a tall, broad, assured man of thirty years, standing there in his Sunday black with his dark mustache curling above a straight, determined mouth. He looked sharply at Link and then turned to Fleming Greenup.

"See you got some help."

"Man from Pennsylvania," Flem said. "Link Barren. He's on his way west."

Ike turned to Link with a new trace of approval. "Good country, west. A young fellow can get a real start out there."

Link looked at him levelly. "That's what I mean to do."

Ike had a big, roomy, deep-mowed barn, just completed. "I'm having a barndance," he said. "Saturday night. It'll be a whole moon then." He walked over to Sally and flashed his white smile at her. "I want you all to come."

Hannah closed the oven door and smiled across at him. "We'll be there, Ike. Now can't you stay for dinner?"

Ike stayed. All through the meal he talked about his new barn, the new kitchen on his house and his new team of Morgan horses. "I want you to see those Morgans, Flem. I'll match them against any team in the country."

Hannah looked satisfied. "You're doing well," she said. "You've got nearly everything."

His pleased smile fixed on Sally across the table. "Almost every-thing," he said.

After dinner, they sat hearing about Ike Hyar's cattle and the hay his bottom field had made. Link slipped out of the house and roamed off alone up the back pasture. That evening he said, "I guess I can stay a few days longer. Till we get that corn all shucked."

So he was there for Ike Hyar's dance. The fiddle twanged as they stepped into the barn and the floor creaked with the lively step of the dancers. The big Y-beams were outlined strongly by a row of lanterns around the wall. Above them, dim and empty, the deep mows waited to store Ike Hyar's hay.

Sally's eyes lighted with the music and Link took her hand in his big paw. "It's like I've known you all my life," he said, "but we never have danced a step together."

"No, we never," Sally said.

A hand gripped hard on Link's shoulder. It was Ike Hyar, proud and possessing, in his Sunday clothes. "Help yourself to the cider," he said, pointing to the knot of people gathered at the barrel. "It's free."

Then Sally was gone in his arms and Link walked off the floor with his hands deep in his pockets.

"Have some cider," said Flem, coming from the barrel. "It's needled just right—sharp as a cockleburr."

Link shook his head. "I'm not dry."

The fiddle kept twanging and the dancers made a tangle of moving shadows on the floor. Link wandered around the barn, the open stalls and the box stalls, the granary and the seed room, the harness room and the deep dim mows. It was a handsome barn, all right.

After a while the music stopped, while old Ferris Melish went to wet his throat. Ike Hyar stepped over to the bench and took up his fiddle. He twanged it with his fingers, then raised the bow and began to play "The Wind that Shakes the Barley." He sawed sharp and fast, swaying to the tune, keeping his right foot beating on the floor. Ike was proud of his fiddle-playing, like everything else.

Then Link was on the floor dancing with Sally. Folks stood around to watch them—the big, fair-haired man with laughing-sober eyes and hands that could span Sally's slim waist—or nearly —and Sally Greenup with two wild roses in her cheeks, blue youth in her eyes and something else that came in them while Link swung her to the music. Ike Hyar looked darkly at them above his fiddle bow. Hannah Greenup sat against the wall talking to Mrs. McDavid and looking troubled. It was a wide, wild country Link Barren was bound for, and Sally was just eighteen.

Around them, as they danced, was Isaac Hyar's security. Broad fields stretching away, a frame house newly painted, and this big barn, still smelling like new lumber, ready to house his grain and fodder, his horses and cattle. And that new kitchen waiting for a wife.

But Link's eyes were seeing something else. "I mean to have a bigger barn than this, and better fields, in the new country."

Sally looked up at him with pure belief. "Yes. You will have them, Link."

"But not alone," he said. "You must go with me."

Her eyes were troubled with the future. Dimly she saw the long journey, the unknown land, the loneliness and struggle. "I'm half afraid——"

His hand had tightened round her and his voice was at her ear. "There's not a thing to fear for."

The music stopped. Ike Hyar stood, stropping his bow with a marble of rosin, while they called for another tune. Link peeled off his jacket, hanging it on a peg in the wall. When he got back, Ike Hyar was at Sally's side. He had come in such a hurry that he still held the fiddler's rosin in his hand.

Sally looked from one to the other—the dark, assured face of Isaac Hyar in his big new barn, the fair, boyish features of Link Barren on his way to an unknown place. Her eyes wavered. Ike Hyar put a hand on her shoulder. He had a tight, possessive,

muscled hand and now his mouth was a thin straight line beneath
the curl of his mustache.

"Have some more cider," he said to Link.

"No," Link said. "I'm dancing."

The fiddle stopped and people's voices all at once were still.
There wasn't any movement or any change except the burning
in two pairs of eyes. Ike Hyar's restless hand still held the lump
of rosin. His fingers kept rubbing it till you could see the white
powder sifting to the floor.

"Get out of the barn," Ike Hyar said. "Get off this place and
on your way."

He caught Sally in the curve of one arm. "Strike up a tune!"
he called. "We're here to dance."

When Link put a hand on his shoulder, Ike Hyar flung his
right arm, hard. Had it been a blow it was short, but it was not
a blow. It was that ball of rosin, hurled into Link's face. It struck
his cheekbone and it stunned him for a moment. The rosin rattled
on the floor. A white ring stood out on Link's dark face, a white
ring slowly flushing. Then Link lunged and Ike threw up his
hands. But Link charged past them. They grappled. In that powerful embrace Ike's back began to bend.

Out in the barnyard a dog barked sharply and there came the
sound of a stranger's voice. As Link turned to look over one
shoulder, Ike slipped out of his hold.

A stranger, thin and ragged as a cornstalk, stood in the wide
door. He waited there a moment, his eyes on the two men, wary
and breathing, in the center of the room. He stood still as a new-
leafed tree, and the soft winds, the little whispering alder leaves
and murmuring watercourses were around him.

"Peace to this place and all its people."

Gentleness sounded in his voice, like wood doves on a hawthorn
branch at twilight. Twilit gentleness shone in his bearded face.
He wore a knapsack on his shoulder.

"Why——" said Fleming Greenup. "It's Johnny Appleseed!"

The stranger went to the center of the floor, facing the two men there. "Put away your anger, friends." He stooped and picked up the ball of rosin. "I looked for gladness in this place. I heard music across the fields, and here's the fiddler's rosin stone."

Ike Hyar took the rosin from him. There was no fighting now, though two pairs of eyes still smoldered.

Link rubbed the swelling lump on his cheek and stared at the newcomer. He had never seen such a scarecrow. A tramp, he looked like—or a man out of the Bible. In a quiet voice he asked: "Where might you come from, stranger?"

All around the circle they answered for him.

"Where does Johnny Appleseed come from? He comes from everywhere."

"He comes from the cider mills along the broad rivers."

"He comes from the wagon ferries and the landings."

"He comes from the orchards by Blossom Creek."

"He comes from the clearings in the Military Lands."

"He comes from the deer pastures where the Indians hunt."

"I've heard it told," said Flem admiringly, as if Johnny Appleseed were a thousand miles away, "he ran from Mad River to Germantown to warn the settlers from the Indians. Thirty-five miles he ran, between dark and daylight. And when the Shawnees came, the town was empty as a last year's robin's nest." He turned to the visitor. "Where you from now, Johnny?"

The people gathered round.

Johnny Appleseed began to talk in his soft voice. As he talked they forgot the cider in the barrel, the fiddle in Ferris Melish's hands, the unsettled question of who would dance with Sally Greenup. Johnny Appleseed was a man to charm all hearers. He was as good as a long letter from the folks you knew, he was a newspaper in a country that didn't have a printing press in fifty miles, he was a church meeting and a town meeting and a school meeting all in one.

"There's a new settlement at Harmer's Bend. . . . The Butterfield family was burned out. They have moved on west to Darke County. . . . The apple trees, praise God, are bearing all along the Whitewater. . . . A new blacksmith has settled in Lucasville with a floating barge and a barrelful of horseshoes."

"A barrelful of horseshoes? That's good. But you came on foot, Johnny. Where's your horse?"

"I gave him to a family moving west. They lost a horse in high water at Third Crossing. They needed a team."

"That horse——" old Ferris Melish said. "The Indians never stole him. The renegades never stole him. The horse thieves never stole him. There was an apple twig in his bridle and everybody knew it was Johnny Appleseed's horse, and they never touched that animal." He said it almost reverently. "Where you traveling this season, Johnny?"

Johnny Appleseed's voice was like the rivers flowing. While he talked, you began to see that great mysterious western country —the dark forests and green glades where deer nibbled the mint leaves, sunny prairies that sloped toward Lake Erie's blue and steep hills that held the curving Ohio. You saw him going down the Cuyahoga with two canoes lashed together, heaped to the brim with apple seeds. You saw him paddling up White Woman Creek and turning into the Black Fork and so entering the wild green heart of Ashland and Richland counties. You saw him, barefooted or in moccasins, tramping the old Indian trail from Fort Duquesne to Fort Sandusky. You saw him finding his way south and west into new country, planting orchards where settlers would come in time. They would find no booted print before them, but the white blossoms would blow in May and the red fruit would star the brown grass of October. You saw him always moving, like a river—rivers were in his talk. Their names rolled like Indian music off his tongue—the Scioto, the Muskingum, the Great Kanawha and the Little Kanawha, the Raccoon, the Olentangy, the Licking, the Great and the Little Miami. While he talked you saw green shores and clear waters, smooth bends where clouds lay mirrored and the sunset flowed. You saw deep woods where bloodroot flecked the dark ground and wild anemones lifted fragile faces, and April fields where windflowers bloomed like a pale blue drift of snow. But most of all you saw young apple orchards waiting for settlers who would gather the fruit of years to come.

Then someone remembered that a traveler might be hungry. "Here's crullers and cider, Johnny. It's not much for a man that's been traveling, but here they are."

Johnny Appleseed slung the deerskin pack off his shoulder. There was a dry rustling sound, along with the solid clink of metal.

"That sounds like the jingle of gold, Johnny. Maybe you're in business now."

Johnny reached in and brought up a handful of apple seeds with gold coins glinting among them. "Campbell Ayres is the blacksmith at Ford's Crossing. I'm taking some money to his old mother down the river." He hung the pack on a wall peg and accepted a mug of cider. A sprinkling of apple seeds glinted on the floor where he had spilled them through his fingers.

"What luck with the orchards, Johnny?"

"Fine," Johnny said. He scooped some up from the floor, plump and bright as blackbird's eyes. And while they all stared at the dark kernels in his hand he told his parable.

"It's seed and it's soil," he said, his pale eyes growing distant in the lantern light, his face looking beautiful as a fox and almost as thin. "There is no luck more bitter than poor seed, but one as bitter. The planting of plump dark seed in soil that fails—that nourishes for a season and is spent forever. Look to your seed," he said, turning his grave eyes on them. "Look to your seed," he repeated, "and remember your soil."

He poured the seed back into his pack and raised his mug of cider.

It was simple, but it left them all silent. Even grinning old Ferris Melish twisted the top of one ear and kept on nodding, over and over. Sally looked across the room to the wide door framing the darkness. Her face was distant and earnest as dreams. Beside her Hannah sat with hands folded and head bent. Hearing Johnny Appleseed was nearly like church.

All this time Ike Hyar's eyes were on the deerskin pack, hanging from the wall. His fingers kept turning the ball of rosin in his hands. Now he spoke up: "I've got a new barn here, Appleseed Johnny, and a new kitchen on my house. I'd like to have an apple tree planted to mark this night and this visit."

"I'll plant an apple tree," Johnny said, "for any man. I'll plant a whole orchard."

"I haven't room for an orchard," Ike said. "It wouldn't pay to give up all that ground. I want just one tree, beside the kitchen door. If you'd plant it now, in the moonlight, it would be sure to grow."

Johnny led the way and they filed out behind him in the silver night. Link stood beside Sally Greenup and while Johnny was digging the ground with his knife-blade, Link whispered: "When he talks, it's like the place I'm going to—the new country, that has to be. And when he talks I see you going with me, plain as daylight."

"I know," she whispered. "I know."

"You'll go, then, tomorrow?"

"I want to, Link. I want to go." But there still was trouble in her eyes.

The planting was quickly done and Johnny Appleseed smoothed the earth, leaving a little whittled stake to mark the place. He closed his eyes and bent his head for a minute, while the moon silvered his ragged shirt and his tangled hair. When he led them back to the barn the fight was forgotten and the dancing was forgotten. They gathered about him while he told of the rabbits that sat around his campfire and the bear that shared its cave with him one early snowstorm.

From the timber floated an owl's hollow cry.

"Crotch hemlock!" said Ferris Melish, pulling out his heavy silver watch. "It's past time for going home!"

They began to say good-bye to Johnny Appleseed, pressing his hand and hoping he would stop their way. Link went to the wall to get his jacket. He put his arm in the sleeve and as he swung it over his head a dull clinking sound made people turn. They stared at him in silence.

Ike Hyar reached up for the deerskin pack and handed it to Johnny. "I'd think it might be risky," he said in a loud voice, "to be carrying gold dollars in your sack."

Every person under the dim roof knew there were no gold pieces left among the apple seeds. Link stood with his jacket half on and the rest of it hanging heavily against him. He saw the repeated look in all those eyes, the reproach, the contempt, the shame that anyone should steal a man's gift to his aged mother, a gift in the keeping of gentle Johnny Appleseed. And he saw Sally Greenup's eyes, stricken and struggling.

Link's thoughts ran blindly through his head. He saw Ike Hyar's thin, triumphant smile and the pity in Johnny Appleseed's soft eyes. He put a hand into the sagging pocket and his fingers tightened on a coin. He was ready to fling the pieces on the floor and stride off—in dark night, beneath the stars, toward the far and unknown country. Then he saw Sally's eyes again—appealing. She wanted to believe him.

Something at his fingers' ends sent a swift thought through him. He drew out a gold coin, his eyes sharp upon it, feeling the coarse dust on his fingers.

Then his shoulders straightened and his eyes flashed a message to Sally Greenup. Three strides took him to Ike Hyar's side. His hand went out, not threatening but swiftly, with a gold coin glinting in his fingers. In one downward motion he wiped it across Ike Hyar's coat front. The lantern light glinted on a mark of rosin dust across the dark lapel.

Link scooped out the coins. "These came from your pack, Mr. Appleseed."

Already the accusing circle was tight around Ike Hyar.

"Rosin dust—off that fiddler's ball."

"He left his mark on those gold pieces."

Voices swelled and Ike Hyar stood like a coon with the dogs around him.

"It's worse than thieving—to take the gold out of Johnny's pack and plant it in another's pocket."

"While Johnny was planting his apple tree——"

Slapping angrily at the rosin dust on his coat, Ike Hyar stamped out of his own barn. Beside him, gentle and persistent, walked Johnny Appleseed.

"Have you heard the doctrine of Swedenborg, my friend?"

Ike Hyar's voice came back from the barnyard, rasping, "I don't hold with doctrines."

And Johnny's patient voice. "They are very simple. The oneness of all things. The kinship among men."

But two in that company didn't hear that gentle sermon, being busy with another matter.

"I mean to go tomorrow, Sally. Nothing can stop me. Will you be going too?"

Her eyes were shining. "When they stared at you like that, I knew I'd have to go. But it does seem a long, uncertain way."

Hannah Greenup read the look that passed between them. She turned anxiously to the ragged man just entering the door.

"Here are two," she said, "bound for the distant country. Can you hold them back, Johnny Appleseed?"

"Hold them back?" Johnny repeated with his eyes on the two of them. "They are young, with life before them. There is no power of earth or heaven to hold them back."

"But it's a far journey—all the way to Illinois. A long, uncertain road."

As Johnny Appleseed turned to her his eyes grew distant in his thin, illumined face. "The future is always a long road," he said softly. "But the young make it certain. That's the way it has been in our country. That's the way it will be. There must be trials and troubles, sadness and separation, but the young will not shrink from the way before them." He turned to Link. "Where do you mean to go, with this girl beside you?"

"To the new country," Link said. "Beyond the fence lines and the traveled roads."

Johnny Appleseed nodded. "Beyond safeguard and comfort. Maybe you will go beyond the rivers that have turned me back." He reached into his pack. "Here. Take some seed and plant your orchard when you get there."

But first he bent over and cupped his hand, taking one kind of kernel from what he gave them. "Look well to your seed," he said.

Hannah Greenup, with Flem at her side, peered at the black kernels. She put out a hand to touch them, as though they were good omens for her daughter's future. Now her eyes had lost their darkness.

"There's one kind of seed I never give the young," Johnny said, putting the few selected kernels back into his pack.

"What kind of apple seed is that?" Flem asked.

"Seek-no-farther," said Johnny Appleseed.

Outside, the moon stood big as a barrelhead over the timber. Link saw the silver in Sally's eyes.

"We'll stop at the preacher's at Ford's Crossing."

"Tomorrow," she said.

He nodded. "We'll be already on our way."

Now THERE are monuments and memorials to the ragged man who carried a sack of apple seeds on his shoulder. At Ashland and Mansfield, in Ohio, and at Fort Wayne, Indiana, he is commemorated in stone. He has other memorials where people plant new orchards, thinking of the barefoot man who first brought apple blossoms to the wild new country. He never fought a battle or founded a town, but memory holds on to the gentle wanderer who came at last to rest where Mad Anthony had scourged the Indians. Eighty years later Vachel Lindsay chanted:

In the four-poster bed Johnny Appleseed built
Autumn rains were the curtains, autumn leaves were the quilt;
He laid him down sweetly and slept through the night,
Like a stone washed white,
There by the doors of old Fort Wayne.

XVI

Smoke on the Western Waters

IN THE LONG-AGO summer of 1791, John Pope made a voyage from Pittsburgh to New Orleans in a keelboat named the *Smokehouse*. A fireplace was built into its crude little cabin and it smoked its way, like a later generation of steamboats, down the Ohio and the Mississippi. Aboard the clumsy craft, taking turns at its heavy steering oar, were six men—a Kentuckian, a Virginian, a German, an Irishman, a Welshman and a man born at sea. From the beginning of its commerce the Ohio drew men of many nations.

The Ohio is a river without a source. In the high valleys of the Appalachians rise the Allegheny, the Conemaugh, the Youghiogheny, the Monongahela. These all make the Ohio which springs full-grown at Pittsburgh under the timbered hills. Neither does it have a mouth. Instead of finding the tidal-heavy sea, it finds the Mississippi, still a thousand miles from tidewater, where the brown hills of Illinois look across to the brown hills of Missouri. It is a river between rivers. It carries the springs of Pennsylvania to meet the melting snows of Minnesota and Montana. It is the one great river in the continent, until you get to the far-off Columbia hurrying down between its mountains, that flows west—in line with the march of America.

For fifty years the Ohio was more than a river. It was a highway, broad and free and majestically moving, that led through the mid-continent wilderness. Like a highway it supported settlements —from Pittsburgh to the Mississippi it was spaced with fertile farms, busy towns and yeasty young cities that grew so fast a traveler could not recognize them after five years away. That highway carried every kind of man—pirate and preacher, settler and soldier, trader and tourist. Floating gristmills used the river current to grind the settlers' corn. Floating tinsmiths kept shop on flatboats and mended pots and kettles in all the riverside towns. Every spring a smithy came floating down with its glowing forge. When they heard the clang of the anvil, farmers led their teams to the river to be shod. Itinerant furniture makers sowed the current with yellow sawdust, and store-boats did a brisk business in salt, soap and muslin at the river landings. The first newspaper in the western valley was set up and printed on a flatboat.

A book-boat joined the motley river traffic and people browsed along the shelves of a floating library before there was a public reading room beyond the Alleghenies. To the landings and to the roads that ended at the river bank came floating museums, exhibits of wax works and penny peep-shows advertising "the world in a box." A hundred years ago floating dramshops plied the Ohio and luring "love boats" were moored at St. Louis, where the raft crews ended their long voyage down the Upper Mississippi. The first theatrical troops in the West played on flatboats, with the audience on the terraced river bank. Later, in the age of steam, the calliope-proud showboats filled the hills with music and drew the settlers for miles around.

To begin with, the Ohio was a military road. Though it was never gashed and trampled by the freight of war, it carried the expeditions that won the West for settlement. All the men and arms and supplies for the Indian Wars passed through Pittsburgh and were floated to the disputed country. George Rogers Clark built a fleet of flatboats on his island, near the site of Louisville, and set out by water for the strongholds in Illinois. In 1793, a hundred flatboats streamed down the river, carrying Mad Anthony's men and horses, his provisions and equipment. During Wayne's campaign a hospital boat operated between Pittsburgh and the embattled West. Hurrying past it with brawny men at the setting poles, an express boat carried military dispatches. When the campaigns were done, those military barges were still sturdily serving the frontier. Fort Washington, from which the city of Cincinnati sprang, was built from the lumber of fifty flatboats that had carried the freight of war.

Before the wars were over, the Ohio began to carry settlement
and trade. Down from the Pennsylvania mountains the immigrants came to the Monongahela River towns of Brownsville,
Elizabeth and Morganstown. At each of these places, as at Pittsburgh, were busy boating yards where the thud of the ax and the
hammer never ceased. Here one stream of commerce ended—great
wheels rumbling over mountain roads, gay Conestogas with their
red sideboards, blue running gear and white arched canvas, and
bells jangling from the hames that stood up like horns from the
horses' collars—and another stream of commerce began. Its sound
was the mellow note of the boatman's horn and the halloo of a
voice over the mist-hung river. It was a grateful change—after
toil, peril and struggle there came this moving, tranquil road that
took men to their destination. On raft or flatboat, horses grazed
around their little haycock and chickens scratched in the chaff
at their feet, a woman rocked her baby's cradle and a man smoked
his pipe while he leaned on the steering-oar, with the tireless river
carrying them to the future. In late spring, lindens and honey
locusts blossomed on the shores, over the water in the drowsy
sunlight came the hum of bees and the strong sweet smell of wild
thickets of muscadine. Banks of willow and hornbeam framed
the river in a changing frieze, and wide-winged herons passed
over in lazy flight. It was a pleasant thing to be at ease on your
journey, to watch the shores move by and to think of the land that
waited to be bounded by your corner stakes. That was the immigrant's blissful daydream.

At evening, when the boat was moored to a willow clump, a
man could throw his fishing line into the current or take his rifle
ashore to hunt fresh meat. Savory odors came from the supper
fire—wild turkey, wood ducks, catfish, white perch, sunfish. Sometimes after supper, the moon brightened like a silver dollar above
the hills and a family could float all night on the polished river
with fireflies flickering along the shores and an owl calling from
the top of a tulip tree.

Flatboats ranged from twenty to a hundred feet in length and from ten to twenty feet across. Some were open arks or "sneak-boxes"—mere barges fitted with a steering-oar. Others had a roofed shelter of varying size. "Kentucky boats," designed for a voyage of but a week or two, were never more than half-covered. Craft wholly covered, called "New Orleans boats," were more heavily built and offered more commodious shelter for the long voyage down the rivers. On a spring crest of water the journey from Pittsburgh to Cairo took fifteen days; in the slow current of midsummer it might require ten weeks. Some settlers moved west on rafts with a haystack at one end and a tent at the other. There was room on that slowly moving island for horses, pigs and poultry, and sometimes a wild turkey settled down to feed with the hens.

On the river, a flatboat was called a "broadhorn," perhaps from the occasional custom of ornamenting the blunt bow with a pair of spreading cattle horns, or perhaps because many flatboats were fitted with horn-like sweeps which pivoted in a forked stick at either side of the boat and were used to keep the craft on its course. Broadhorns were often lashed together—boatmen said broader surface gave them more advantage from the river current. But boatmen were seldom in a hurry. They had a better motive for traveling in company. People felt a comradeship on the river and it was natural to cast their lots together. With their boats lashed, families could exchange past experiences and future hopes. By pooling their provisions, they could vary their fare of cornbread and fried catfish. Professional boat crews often lashed their cargo-laden craft together to guard against attack from Indians and river pirates, and to enjoy swapping and yarning, eating and singing, napping together like a litter of pigs in the sun. Timothy Flint, a veteran Ohio River traveler, once traversed eight flatboats at a time. On one, men were killing hogs; on another, men were sampling a cargo of apples, nuts and cider; on a third, men were patronizing a dramshop—already Flint had found that string of broadhorns better than most river towns for variety and diversion.

The flatboat was a one-way craft. It could travel only with the current, so its life was brief. Arrived at his destination the owner might sell it to someone wishing to carry goods farther down stream—by relays of owners some flatboats went all the way from the Monongahela to New Orleans. Often the builder loaded his boat with lumber for Pittsburgh. There a settler bought it for the journey to Portsmouth or Cincinnati. Then a merchant loaded it with pork for Louisville, where it passed to another merchant who sent it laden with tobacco to Madison, Indiana. From there it might carry a load of barrel staves to New Orleans. But more frequently the Monongahela broadhorn ended its marine life at an Ohio landing. Sawed lumber was precious and many flatboats were taken apart and hauled inland for material. Many pioneer schoolhouses along the Ohio were built from flatboat timbers and an occasional flatboat was reassembled as a church.

Like flatboats, rafts served both for transportation and building purposes. As sawmills increased in the West, rafts came down the rivers by thousands. Big rafts were unwieldy in narrow channels—sometimes they wedged into bends and if not broken up promptly, other rafts would add to them until the mat of logs reached fearful proportions. This was a popular subject of pioneer legend. One legendary raft was said to have begun forming about 1530 and by 1830 it was more than 150 miles long. In that time it had become so solid that vegetation flourished on it and travelers crossed the river without suspecting that they were near water.

Keelboats first appeared on the Ohio tributaries, carrying salt from the licks and the drying kilns to settlers on the Ohio, and freighting lumber from the sawmills to the river landings. These were two-way craft—they drifted with the current and were poled or "cordelled" against it. They made possible a regular commerce on the river. The first line of keelboats was established before the Indians had relinquished the valley. In 1793, a fortnightly service in goods and passenger transport was begun between Pittsburgh and Cincinnati—commonly called Columbia until 1800—and early in 1794 this became a weekly service. The boats

were protected against Indian attack by heavy bulwarks pierced
with portholes for gun barrels. Each boat carried six small cannon
and a complement of muskets. In a few years the Indian menace
was ended, but there remained the threat of attack by river pirates
who infested the Indiana hills.

The first two decades of the nineteenth century were the keelboat age on the western rivers. An endless throng of persons waited
at the head of the Ohio for passage west and mountains of trade
goods piled up on the landings. Flour, salt, iron, cider, peach
brandy, barrel staves—all went west and south on the rivers.
Molasses, sugar, coffee, lead and hides came back upstream with
the boatmen laboring at the poles. So began the river trade that
today is steel, sand, coal, oil, limestone and sulphur. Cincinnati
in the early years had a large trade in flour, for the land between
the Miami Rivers was "mellow as an ash heap." In the first four
months of 1802, more than two thousand barrels of flour went
aboard the broadhorns and keelboats at the Cincinnati levee. Also
from there went pottery, bricks, woven goods, wheels, and door-
and window-frames. Louisville grew rapidly because hundreds of
workmen were needed to portage goods and haul boats over the
falls of the Ohio. The settlement soon developed its own exports of
bacon and tobacco. The Indiana towns furnished a prodigious
quantity of barrel staves. This was the barrel age, when a cargo
was measured not in tons but in barrels. Salt and flour, pork and
whisky, coffee and molasses all moved in barrels. The Indiana oak
forests became barrel-staves piled house-high on the landings at
Madison, New Albany and Evansville.

A keelboat loaded with three hundred barrels carried some fifty
tons of freight. That was easy to move downstream, but it was
back-breaking work against the current. Two lines of boatmen on
either side of the craft thrust poles against their shoulders, lifting
or setting their poles to the cry of a steersman. It was a treadmill.
By virtue of bent backs and feet endlessly plodding the runway,
the load crawled upstream. An Irishman who had agreed to work
his passage on a keelboat expressed himself after a few miles at the

pole: "Faith, if it wasn't for the name of riding, I'd about as soon walk." When the river was too deep for poling, a cordelle or towline was used. The crew swam ashore, one carrying the cordelle in his teeth. Then they fought, hacked and waded along the shore, hauling at the towrope. It was labor that only rugged men could stand. And when the deep water was past, the gruelling toil went on at the poles. In a swift current the struggle was desperate—shoulders bending, poles quivering, the captain's profane voice roaring. There were similar crises with snags, reefs and bars. As he got his breath after one of these terrific efforts, the boatman spat over the side and remarked. "I'll be fly-blowed before sundown to a certingty, if the snags ain's so thick that a fish couldn't swim without rubbing his scales off."

In the keelboat age, the riverman was as lusty a breed as any that the labors of America have produced. By 1815, three thousand of them lived on the rivers, making a legend that would outlast their violent lives. They were restless, ribald, weather-darkened men, collected from the waning Indian trade and the disbanded pioneer armies, already schooled to toil and hardship. Arrogant, swaggering, boisterous, they ruled the rivers for a generation. They routed pioneer camp meetings; they even stampeded military musters, putting the militiamen to flight when they came roaring across the drill field. The riverman was "Billy Earthquake," and the ground trembled when he stepped ashore. He crooked his neck and neighed like a stallion. One squint of his eye would blister a bull's heel—when he was an infant he had turned from his mother's breast and called for a bottle of old rye. When Davy Crockett woke up a riverman with an oar, Billy Earthquake bawled, "Halloe, stranger, who axed you to crack my lice?" For recreation after all day at the setting pole they gambled, drank and wrestled, or got a pack of dogs and went coon hunting through the bottom timber. Then they spread their blankets on the riverbank, threw green wood on the fire to drive off the mosquitoes, and slept like the dead till daybreak.

The boatmen had a hard life and little reward, beyond adventure and hardship, for their prodigious labors. Many of them were maimed by accidents and bloodshed, many were drowned or died of disease, a few lived to an impoverished old age. In 1805, the city of Natchez, on the Mississippi, established a hospital "for the relief of paupers and boatmen." In 1816, Louisville had a boatman's hospital. In 1837, when keelboat and steamboat accidents were a familiar story on every stretch of river, the Federal Congress established marine hospitals at New Orleans, Natchez, Napoleon, St. Louis, Paducah, Louisville and Pittsburgh. Some reports state that it was not uncommon for half of a keelboat's crew to die during the course of a long voyage. Sometimes entire crews perished —of drowning, cholera, water poisoning or the mysterious milksickness—leaving a derelict boat and cargo among the willows along some lonely reach of river.

In the keelboat age camaraderie reigned on the river. A steamer is an aloof craft with its raised decks and its impersonal paddlewheels, but a flatboat or keelboat was close to the river and the boatmen felt akin to each other. They were always curious about other craft and other crews. As soon as a boat appeared around a bend, the cupped voices hallooed across the water. At Limestone, Kentucky—later Maysville—a famous greeting was exchanged between passing keelboats.

"Where you from?"

"Redstone."

"What's your landing?"

"Millstone."

"Who's your captain?"

"Whetstone."

"Where you bound?"

"Limestone."

They shouted greetings and information, nonsense and banter, and sometimes they exchanged curses till the rival craft was out of sight. Every boat had a horn to signal with and the soft clear notes, varying in pitch, made the music of the keelboat commerce. On foggy days or in darkness the horns sounded over the murmuring water, "to scare off the devil and bring good luck." In silent fog or in night's stillness, mellow notes of the horn echoed weirdly from the unseen hills.

In 1811, the first steamboat was launched in the Ohio. By 1825, steamboats carried the bulk of the trade and the keelboat age was over. Though the clumsy boats were still used on tributary rivers and some were towed behind steamboats on the Ohio, their day was past. The mellow horn gave way to the steamer's bell and setting poles were replaced by churning paddlewheels. So the race of boatmen came to an end. But one of them lived on in river lore and frontier memory. Like Paul Bunyan of the woods and Buffalo Bill of the plains, Mike Fink, king of the rivermen, became a frontier hero and a frontier myth.

Mike Fink was born beside the Ohio, near Pittsburgh, in the perilous years of the 1780s. While still a gangling boy he served as a scout in the Indian Wars. After that he took to keelboating, when the trade was just beginning. He grew to be a man like the cargo barrels he carried—burly and thick-chested, broad as a bull and just under six feet tall. Even as a youth his fame spread up and down the river. When he became a captain, he gathered a rowdy crew but Mike was more than a match for his men. He had a roaring voice, a fist like a blacksmith's hammer, a deadly aim with a rifle and a boundless appetite for strong food and straight whisky. Many times he made the long journey from the hills of Pennsylvania to the Louisiana bayous. He was known and talked about in every riverfront tavern from Pittsburgh to New Orleans. On the Mississippi he was called "The Snag," on the Ohio, "The Snapping Turtle." He was as strong as three men on a setting pole and when he was at the steering-oar a heavy keelboat obeyed like a canoe. He took his boat through impossible waters and over impassable bars. When there was a hard run ahead, Mike was a tyrant to his crew; when it was smooth sailing, he skylarked with them, wrestling and playing cards and shooting off the corkscrew tails of pigs along the shore.

By 1820, the Ohio Valley was filling up with settlers and the river was cluttered with steamboats and Mike was ready to move on to a better country. In the spring of 1822, in St. Louis, Major William H. Ashley was advertising for ENTERPRISING YOUNG MEN to go on his expedition to the far Northwest and establish the Rocky Mountain Fur Company in the Country of the Yellowstone. This was a project to Mike Fink's liking. With two veteran river-mates, Talbot and Carpenter, he presented himself to Major Ashley. The three signed on as boatmen, hunters and trappers. In long, shallow-draft Missouri River boats the expedition set out on the long journey to the Yellowstone. Winter overtook them in the bleak Mandan country of Dakota. There, in restlessness and irritation, while the boats were ice-bound and the country was a waste of snow, Mike and his comrade Carpenter developed an ugly quarrel. They had wrangled many times, over many matters, but this was different.

This was over an Indian woman. Often in the past they had held rifle practice by shooting whisky glasses off each other's heads. Even after emptying a jug of whisky, Mike would propose to "shy" up a copper to see who would take the first shot. Now their quarrel smoldered through the winter and when spring came to the wide plains of the Missouri, they agreed to a shooting match. Mike won the toss and took the first shot. His bullet passed dead-center through Carpenter's head. Talbot sadly unstrapped his comrade's pistols and buried him on the prairie. Afterward, when his tongue was loose with liquor, Mike boasted that he had killed Carpenter deliberately. Talbot listened with narrow and hating eyes. He drew one of Carpenter's pistols and fired at Mike point-blank. So Mike Fink died beside another river, and the king of the Ohio boatmen was buried in an unmarked Dakota grave.

THERE WERE perils of many kinds on the Ohio—reefs and snags and bars, swift water and shoal water, collisions and fire—but the greatest peril was of men. At first it was Indians. After they were gone, it was a worse peril of boat robbers and river pirates. For a generation they preyed upon the river trade.

First of the boat-wreckers was a New Hampshire Yankee named Pfluger, known in the West as "Colonel Plug." With a vicious band of men, Colonel Plug went into the business of piloting boats through dangerous channels on the Ohio. But instead of piloting them through, they wrecked the craft or drove them onto shoals. When the crews abandoned the boats to seek help or to wait for high water, Colonel Plug and his gang robbed the cargoes at their leisure. If a captain refused the Colonel's offer of pilotage, the gang boarded the boat in the middle of night and dug caulking from its bottom seams. Next day, when the boat was sinking in mid-river, the robbers swarmed out from shore to salvage the cargo, which was never seen by its owners again.

In one of those episodes, Colonel Plug met his death. On a stormy night he was aboard a deserted boat digging caulking from its keel. With the strain of wind and tossing water the mooring line parted. So he was alone aboard a storm-driven boat with her bottom seams laid open. It sank in the wind-lashed river and the villainous Colonel Plug sank with it.

On the Illinois shore of the Ohio River, some twenty miles below the old settlement of Shawneetown, a deep cave still opens into the sheer limestone bluff. From this high eyrie an infamous succession of pirates scanned the curving river and swooped down on passing craft. For ten miles the channel was narrowed by bars and islands and the crews could never know from what hidden cove or thicket they might be attacked. Crew and cargo were taken up to that high cavern and there disposed of at the pirates' leisure. Cave-in-Rock it was called, an innocent name, but it was a term of terror for thirty years.

In 1797, when the first slow trading barges were passing the sharp bends of the Ohio, a Virginia gentleman named Samuel Mason arrived in frontier Illinois. In the lawless country he took up a lawless life. He built himself a stronghold in "Cave-in-Rock" and painted a sign above its entrance "Liquor Vault and House of Entertainment." That lure brought unsuspecting river travelers and flatboat crews up the steep path to the cavern, where Mason and his followers robbed them of all their possessions. When the nature of his "Entertainment" became known along the river, Samuel Mason left the cave and fled the country.

But piracy still flourished at Cave-in-Rock. Mason was followed by other outlaws—Duff, Sturdevant and Philip Alston. At first they practiced a primitive method of decoy, like that of Indians who had forced white prisoners to hail passing boats asking for help or for passage. There were women in the Cave-in-Rock gangs and few flatboat captains would sail past a solitary woman calling for help on a lonely shore. But when the boat touched land, a pirate crew swarmed out of the willows. They captured or killed the boatmen and ransacked the cargo. Plunder and captives they carried up the bluff into the deep passages of the cave. Years later sixty human skeletons were found in a remote room of that extensive cavern.

One band after another infested Cave-in-Rock, but the most feared was that of "Big" and "Little" Harpe, two brothers who arrived on the river after a career in outlawry in Kentucky and Tennessee. Micajah (Big) Harpe came to the Ohio in the guise of a Methodist circuit rider. He was entertained at homes of pious settlers and he said grace with one eye closed and the other appraising the silver spoons laid out for the minister's coming. When he left the house, in the dead of night, he took the silver with him and anything else his roving gaze had settled on. Joined by his brother at Cave-in-Rock, Micajah Harpe organized a ruthless and powerful band of pirates. They plundered river commerce, murdered flatboat crews and defied the authorities in the growing river settlements. But at last a band of vigilantes routed them from the cave and pursued them across the country. After a desperate chase through hills and bottom timber, Micajah Harpe was shot. The vigilantes cut off his head and impaled it on a sapling beside the river. There the skull, whitened by sun and rain, remained for many years.

Now Cave-in-Rock is the property of the state of Illinois and that notorious portion of the river shore is preserved as a state park.

The hills are laced with harmless "nature trails" and picnic tables overlook the once perilous channels of the river.

IN THE EARLY 1800s, at country stores in the Muskingum and Scioto valleys, Ohio farmers sometimes stared at a Spanish coin the storekeeper handed out in change. The Spanish "levy" and the "fip" remained in circulation in those regions until the Civil War. Neither the farmers nor the storekeepers knew where those coins came from, but rivermen had sailed deepwater brigs down the Ohio and the Mississippi to the seaports of the Caribbean. They had brought back Spanish coins along with memories of tropic ports and cargoes. They had even sailed Pittsburgh and Marietta ships across the Atlantic to Liverpool and the harbors of the Mediterranean.

Settlers who came over the mountains were inlanders leaving the seaboard far behind. But flowing water led west and south and at last it joined the open sea. The western country gave its people arrogant ideas—later they were to have big farms, big buildings, big cities. Back there when the bear still scrambled through the river bottoms they conceived a bold idea—to build ocean-going ships two thousand miles from tidewater and send their inland goods to the seaports of the world.

The first sea-going vessels were built on the Monongahela where the first crude keelboats had been knocked together. But these new sloops and schooners were graceful craft with strength built into their trim lines. The western forests held fine timber—white oak and black walnut—and New England shipbuilders had come over the mountains. So they launched their sturdy hulls and stepped in the lofty masts and the jib-boom that rode proudly above the flaring bow. They rigged spars with shrouds from Pittsburgh rope-walks and fitted snowy sails. Then Ohio sailors ran up the masts, and through the river, in the spring of 1801, with canvas spread to the wind, passed the *Monongahela Farmer*, carrying 750 barrels of flour, whisky, hides, hemp and flax. Three months later she lay at the wharves of New York discharging western cargo. Soon after, the *Louisiana* and the *Duane,* both built at Pittsburgh, sailed down the river with cargoes for far-away Liverpool.

In this bid for sea-borne commerce, Marietta took the lead. With her Yankee shipwrights and seamen, with fine timber that framed the Muskingum and low-price farm products of the valley, Marietta men saw their town not as a remote and isolated settlement but as a port with access to world markets. In the Devol shipyard, at the foot of Monroe Street on the Muskingum, there rose the framework of a proud, strong ship. She was the brig *St. Clair,* named for the first governor of the Northwest Territory, of 104 tons burden, the first square-rigged vessel ever built away from tidewater. On a warm spring day in 1801, her holds filled with barreled pork and flour, she cast off her lines and stood into the river while the populace of Marietta shouted farewell from the Muskingum shore. Other Ohio citizens cheered as the *St. Clair* swept down the river, towering above the laborious keelboats and barges. Two months later she discharged her cargo in Havana and took on 100 tons of sugar for Philadelphia. Marietta had become a port of entry.

For the next eight years the shipyard at Marietta rang with the ax and the hammer and the calking mallet. In 1802, the imposing square-rigged ship *Muskingum,* 220 tons, with yardarms braced against her masts, and the sturdy brig *Eliza Green,* 130 tons, began their long voyages. These big ships went down the river in ballast, in order to pass the shallows and the Falls of the Ohio. On the Mississippi, with a deeper channel to the sea, they loaded cotton for Liverpool. Months later they passed through St. George's Channel, under the bold Welsh mountains and around the sunlit dome of Holyhead into the wide sea-mouth of the Mersey. Then they lay, with the name *Marietta* on their fantails, among the ships of many nations at the long gray docks of Liverpool.

In five years, more than twenty deep-water ships were built at Marietta—as the shipping men grew bolder the craft increased to 300 tons' capacity. But the Ohio River had bars and bends and barriers, and as the vessels grew, the river passage became more hazardous and difficult. The hardest barrier was the Falls of the Ohio at Louisville, where a ledge of limestone thrust across the channel causes a series of rapids in which the river drops twenty-two feet in a distance of two miles. In high water the falls were passable, but they were never without threat to a big and heavy vessel. Boatmen had their choice of three chutes through the falls. The best one—Indian Chute—offered smooth water framed in perilous rock sides. A big vessel bound down river waited at Louisville for a rising crest of water. Then, with an iron hand at the wheel and a quick eye for a frothing current, it ran the rapids. With good luck along with good management, it might rub the rocks a few times and still sweep through to safe water. So one by one, the brigs and barques and full-rigged ships passed the barrier and went on to the Mississippi and the sea.

But at last luck ran out. In April of 1807, four big Marietta vessels, bound for New Orleans and the ocean trade, lay in the Louisville basin waiting for a rise of water. When April was nearly past and the river did not rise but began to fall, the captains realized that they must try the passage then or wait at the falls all summer, and perhaps all the next winter as well. They took soundings and prepared to run the rapids. The first ship drifted into the current and with the men tense at their stations bore down swiftly toward the chute. It scraped the rocks and staggered in the rush of water. For a few tense moments its tall masts swayed against the sky. Then it rode the current steadily and coasted through to safe water. But the other three ships came to grief. They rolled in the churning water, their timbers shuddered from the blows of unseen ledges, they lost steerage way in the swift current and were thrown upon the rocks. They never saw the salt water they were built to sail.

This disaster was a reason for the sudden decline of deep-water shipbuilding on the Ohio. Another reason was the Embargo Act, which Ohio shipping men ruefully read backward as the O-grab-me Act. This law, prohibiting all foreign trade, threw its long shadow over farms and villages two thousand miles from the delta of the Mississippi and put an end to a vigorous young industry on the Ohio.

But there was a revival, forty years later. In 1846, Captain Asa Waters of Marietta came back from a visit to Phildelphia with a report of dreadful famine in Ireland. A Philadelphia merchant, John Farnum, had told him that thousands of Irish peasants were facing starvation. In their western land of plenty the Marietta shippers remembered that they had once sent laden vessels across the Atlantic. Now Captain William Knox sat down at his drawing board and made plans for a three-masted barque. It was named for the Quaker merchant who was so concerned about the hungry peasants of Ireland.

In February of 1847 the *John Farnum* loaded a cargo of mercy—10,600 bushels of Ohio corn. Without lightening cargo and without difficulty or delay she passed the falls at Louisville, for a canal had been completed in 1828 and boats no longer had the boiling chutes to run. In March, she sailed out of the Mississippi delta and steered for the Atlantic. After a stormy two months' passage, the tall ship entered the hill-framed harbor of Queenstown where throngs of Irish people cheered with tear-filled eyes.

While she lay at the wharf, hundreds of Irish peasants came to stare at the mercy ship, and at the strange, musical name *Marietta* on her curving fantail. They asked questions about America, about the fields that produced the rich yellow grain, about the country beyond the mountains where a tall ship could depart for a hungry port in Ireland. When he sailed out of pretty Queenstown harbor, Captain Knox carried a load of Irish immigrants. Eventually Marietta received some new citizens in return for her cargo of corn.

One other period of deep-water shipbuilding came to the Ohio. In the 1940s when a war on African, European and Asiatic beachheads called for thousands of landing craft, the shipyards of the Upper Ohio produced whole fleets of strange new vessels. Not white oak and black walnut went into them, but a later product of the valley—steel. They were designed for a somber cargo of tanks and guns and battle-helmeted men; they were shaped not for the docks of commerce but for beaches on fortified shores. In their coat of war gray they hurried down the river, in snow and rain, in fog and sunlight, and at last their ramps opened in the midst of thunder and their cargo was delivered on the coasts of Sicily and Normandy and the islands of Japan. For a century and a half Ohio River craft have touched the far places of the world.

THE RAPID spread of the steamboat on inland waters is one of the prodigious developments of America. Before Fulton's grotesque *Clermont* sailed the Hudson, in 1807, the idea of steam navigation was almost universally ridiculed. Within ten years after that first steam-driven voyage, there were steamboats all the way from the Atlantic to the Missouri and the Gulf of Mexico.

The Ohio River, with its great and laborious keelboat commerce, was an inevitable highway for the steamboat. Within three years after the *Clermont's* trial run, a steamboat was building in Pittsburgh. It was arrogantly named the *New Orleans* in token of the destination three thousand miles away which the vessel was to reach on its maiden voyage. When launched into the Ohio, it was an impressive craft, 138 feet long with a beam of 26½ feet, towering above the motley arks and keelboats along the Pittsburgh shore. It was built with a jutting bowsprit and was painted blue as the Ohio sky. All summer it was fitting and in October, on a high level of water after autumn rains, it set out on its long voyage.

Aboard were an engineer, a pilot and six hands, and also the family of N. J. Roosevelt, one of the vessel's owners. All along the Ohio the craft created wonder and misgiving. At Cincinnati and Louisville, while wood was loaded for the hungry boilers, citizens trooped aboard to see the marvel for themselves. At village landings people stared in silence as the sky-blue boat steamed past and farmers ventured that the craft would blow up before it rounded the bend. It arrived serenely at Louisville and waited there for high water. On a crest of current it ran the falls, quivering but untouched by the sharp limestone ledges. So it passed down to Cairo and into the Mississippi and at last arrived triumphantly at New Orleans.

Eight miles an hour this boat had traveled down stream. Scoffers who had declared it would never reach New Orleans now vowed it could not voyage up river. Actually the *New Orleans* did not return to the Ohio but remained profitably plying the lower Mississippi, where cargoes were abundant and the channel was free from the perils of the snag-infested Ohio.

But the Ohio soon had other steamers. The *Comet* in 1812, the big, fuming *Vesuvius* in 1814, and the *Enterprise* (a favorite name on the western waters—there was an *Enterprise* on every river and a succession of them on the Great Lakes) in 1814. This pioneer *Enterprise* was the first steamboat to voyage back up the Ohio, overcoming the strong current and picking its way through the tortuous channel. Then Captain Henry M. Shreve built his famous *Washington,* a double-decked steamer with a shallow draft made possible by the use of a high pressure engine with horizontal cylinders. This was the type of craft made famous on the western rivers and its fundamental design was never superseded. Up and down the rivers the *Washington* trailed its plumes of smoke. It made a round trip between Louisville and New Orleans in forty-one days, and men began to talk about ten-day service between Ohio River ports and New Orleans. A fever of excitement and a rush of trade came to the Valley. In the keelboat age eastern goods were brought over the mountains and delivered at Cincinnati at a cost of eight dollars a hundred pounds. Now, up-river from New Orleans, the same goods were delivered at a cost of one dollar a hundred-weight.

Quickly the steamboat age came to a country without roads. Shipyards sprang up at scores of Indiana towns. Seventy-six steamers were launched into the Ohio between 1815 and 1819; by 1830, more than two hundred were churning the Ohio and the Mississippi. Pork, whisky, cheese and flour went down the rivers; coffee, sugar, molasses, and eastern manufactured goods came back. The population of Ohio doubled in a decade; Indiana's population quadrupled in the ten years following its statehood in 1816. Hundreds of thousands of new settlers thronged the steamboats and the river landings. Hills of trade goods rose on the levees. On every stretch of river appeared the white steamboat trailing woodsmoke from its tall twin stacks, and for miles over the water came the notes of its melodious bell.

By 1830, steamboats began to be palatial. Cabins grew lush and plush. The long halls were filled with crystal chandeliers and polished mahogany. Before luxury came to the frontier towns and cities, it was lavished on the steamboats that served them. Tapestry and mural paintings lined the walls of the great interior saloon, and gilded statues were spaced in niches along the wide, carpeted stairways. In the 1840s a polished clientele traveled the steamboats— Cincinnati and Louisville families going to New Orleans for a winter holiday, Louisiana planters coming North for a summer social season. Then there were rows of gleaming glasses in the mirrored barrooms and stacks of silver coin on the green-covered tables in the gambling cabins. At night, there was dancing in the long saloon where orchestra music overlaid the rush of the paddle wheels.

The 1840s proved a decade of speed records. Railroads were coming to the western country and steamboat men advertised new fast schedules on the river. In 1844, at the old keelboat building center of Elizabeth, Pennsylvania, on the Monongahela, was launched the famous *J. M. White*. Built for power and speed this big boat became the pride of the rivers. Its record run from St. Louis to New Orleans in three days, twenty-three hours and nine minutes made rivermen forget for a little while the rivalry of the railroad and was talked about across the country. An ornamental model of the *J. M. White* stood in Secretary Stanton's office in the War Department at Washington throughout the Civil War.

After the middle of the century, there were many famous Ohio River steamers. The *Telephone*, built by Maddy Brothers near Gallipolis and named for Bell's new invention just two months after the first telephone exchange in the world was opened at New

Haven, Connecticut, was queen of the Upper Ohio until it was sunk by an ice floe on New Year's Day, 1885. But a sister vessel, the *Telegraph,* carried the houseflag proudly between Pittsburgh and Cincinnati. Scores of other boats, each with an individual splendor and a proud tradition, plied the river. They carried on river trade when railroads paralleled the shores and the locomotive engineer waved a friendly, derisive hand from his cab window. The river was losing to the railroad, but the steamboatmen did not give up quickly. Fine new boats went into the water and men were proud to serve them. In Cincinnati twelve bell foundries kept on casting great bells for the pilot-houses of steamboats, and the melodious pilot's bell and the hoarse voice of the whistle were more stirring than a locomotive's clangor. Now the big white boats are gone— the *Gray Eagle,* the *Tacoma,* the *Wild Wagoner,* the *Highland Mary,* the *Guiding Star,* the *Ben Hur,* the *Valley Gem,* the *Goldenrod,* the *Tecumseh,* the *Sunshine,* the *Magnolia,* the *Tempest,* the *Chesapeake* and the *Andes.* But their records are preserved in the River Museum at Marietta and their memory still haunts the grass-grown landings at every town from Pittsburgh to the Mississippi.

In 1820, while commerce swarmed on the Ohio and the Lower Mississippi, the Upper Mississippi lay a wilderness valley with the river flowing vast and vacant between unpeopled shores. Cairo, at the confluence of the Ohio and the Mississippi, was a place of two rude buildings. St. Louis, metropolis then as now of the Middle Mississippi, was a trading town of 4,900 people—the first steamer had churned into its primitive levee in 1817 and now an occasional steamboat stained its sky with a blue-gray drift of smoke. But above St. Louis no steamboat had ever passed. The only traffic was an occasional keelboat delivering goods to the fur posts at Prairie du Chien and remote Mendota, or carrying military expeditions to the lonely northern country. The site of Quincy, Illinois, was marked only by the rough cabin where John Woods, later governor of Illinois, was clearing bottom land. At Hannibal, on the Missouri side, one settler, John S. Miller, kept a blacksmith shop and shod the squatters' oxen. When he moved to Galena, at the news of lead mining, the site of Hannibal became deserted. On up the river, Fort Madison was an abandoned post, with wolf tracks in the company street—the fort had been erected in 1808 and abandoned five years later. The site of Dubuque, formerly a trading post where Indians gathered, had grown up with brush and brambles since the death of Julien Dubuque, in 1810. An Indian village occupied the site of Moline and Rock Island where, a century later, factories turned out an endless stream of plows and wagons, tractors and harvesting machines for the farming empire of the Middle West. Just above the mouth of the Wisconsin River, on a terrace that faced the Mississippi, stood the fur-trading post of Prairie du Chien. Except for a few weeks of activity in the spring it was a drowsy place between the silent forest and the solemn-flowing river.

There was, however, one busy post on the upper river. Beyond the expanse of Lake Pepin and the lofty palisades of Trempeleau, Sugar Loaf and Diamond Bluff, on a height above the meeting of the Minnesota and Mississippi rivers, stood the strategic post of Fort Snelling. It was established in 1819, when that headland dominated trade and communication in the northern wilderness. In its early years the fort commanded the great sweep of the Mississippi and the trading settlements of Mendota and St. Anthony along the river shores, as today it commands the busy areas of Minneapolis and St. Paul. From the northern woods the Indians brought rich peltry to the traders' warehouses. From the Canadian prairies the half-breed trappers came with caravans of creaking Red River carts laden with furs, pemmican, moccasins and dried buffalo tongues. Up the Mississippi from far-away St. Louis crept an occasional keelboat, bringing military supplies and trade goods. Here, at the remotest corner of the Northwest Territory, Colonel Josiah Snelling, brusque, convivial, improvident, drilled his men on the lofty parade grounds and on festive winter nights, in the big cleared messhall, led them, with his lady, in quadrilles and Virginia reels while the rivers were locked in ice and snow lay deep over all the northern wilds.

The steamboat had quickened the life of all the Ohio Valley. Now it brought life to the far rim of the Northwest. In May, 1823, between the spring-rife shores of Illinois and Missouri the stern-wheeler *Virginia* under Captain John Crawford poked her way up the uncharted channel, past the many islands and the mouths of northern rivers. She made her way under the bold bluffs of Wisconsin. Her smoke drifted over the broad face of Lake Pepin and her wake washed the shores where the Indians were camped. At sight of the smoke-puffing Great Medicine, the tribesmen fled to the woods.

The *Virginia* bore a small but notable company. At St. Louis, while a crowd of Indians, immigrants, teamsters and fur traders watched from the levee, the last of the ammunition and supplies was loaded and then the passengers filed across the gangway. There was Giacomo Constantine Beltrami, a romantic Italian adventurer who was planning an expedition to discover the source of the Mississippi in the deep woods of northern Minnesota. There was also Major Lawrence Taliaferro (pronounced "Tulliver"), famous Indian Agent at Fort Snelling—a courtly, magnetic, judicious man whom the tribes called "Four Hearts" in respect of his fair-mindedness and impartiality. Sharing the narrow cabin with these two gentlemen adventurers was a stolid Sauk chief, Great Eagle, who had overcome his fears of the Great Medicine that moved on the water and was ready to try a voyage up the river whose banks his people had trod for many generations. On the steamboat's open deck, surrounded by their cats, dogs, hens and turkeys, sat a family of Kentuckians—first of a great stream of immigrants from Illinois, Kentucky and Tennessee, from Germany, Ireland and Scandinavia, that would throng the Upper Mississippi steamboats in years to come.

Not all of this small company arrived at Fort Snelling. Great Eagle waded ashore in disgust when the *Virginia* grounded on a bar. Traveling the rest of the way on foot, he beat the steamer to the mouth of the Des Moines River. The Kentuckians got off in northern Illinois and squatted on a fertile patch of prairie land. But Beltrami and Taliaferro stayed aboard till the *Virginia* turned at last into the Minnesota River, under the cliffs of Fort Snelling. The little steamer had come eight hundred miles in twenty days, lying up nights, stopping along the wooded shore while the crew went to work to cut her firewood, fighting her way through the Des Moines and Rock Island rapids, laboriously freeing herself from bars and shoals. But with her arrival, steam commerce had begun on the Upper Mississippi.

That was in 1823. Time brought swift changes to the outlying country. By 1830, the steamboat age had come on the upper river and there were busy landings and growing settlements spaced all the way from St. Louis to St. Paul. By 1840, Eastern and European tourists were following a "fashionable tour" of the West, a tour which took them by steamboat down the Ohio River and up the majestic Mississippi and East again by means of a Great Lakes steamer passing Mackinac, Detroit and Niagara. The "fashionable tour" encircled the Northwest Territory.

But it was not without difficulty that steamboats mastered the Upper Mississippi. The Ohio had troublesome falls and bars and evil snags, but the upper river was far more perilous for navigation. Between St. Paul and St. Louis more than five hundred islands, besides uncounted bars and ledges, complicated the channel and bewildered the pilot on thick nights and foggy days. Just above the mouth of the Des Moines River lay the nine-mile stretch of Lower Rapids, and abreast of Rock Island the current boiled over the dangerous Upper Rapids. Both barriers haunted the minds of pilots and captains and were cursed by sweating roustabouts in the back-breaking toil of shifting cargo and poling their craft off submerged ledges. The upper river had a long list of lesser "nightmares" that filled cub pilots with dismay. Stretches at Cassville, Brownsville, Trempeleau, Point Douglass, and Beef Slough, with their narrow channels and shifting bars, demanded nerve, vigilance and lightning judgment. It is not strange that long after their day on the river, men remembered the pioneer pilots like Louis de Marah, Louis Moreau and Pleasant Carmack, who took the first steamboats up the river.

But in time the channel was surveyed and charted and the river's landmarks had meaning in terms of deep and shoal water, cross-currents or a sluggish stream, and skilled pilots took their boats through safely and on schedule. Then the Upper Mississippi steamers grew in size and splendor. They had gleaming white cabins and tall black chimneys joined by a monkey-brace spangled with brass balls. Their paddle boxes were ornamented with coats-of-arms and colored portraits and the long mahogany lounges were graced with mural panels depicting dramatic points along the river—Mt. Trempeleau, Maiden Rock, Diamond Bluff and the Falls of St. Anthony.

Some of the most impressive boats came from the Ohio. The side-wheeler *Phil Sheridan,* the pride of the "White Collar" Line running out of La Crosse, was built in 1865 at Cincinnati, for operation between Cincinnati and Wheeling. But the Civil War was barely past and Phil Sheridan was a hated name on the south bank of the Ohio. At every landing in Kentucky and West Virginia the handsome steamer, showing on its paddle-boxes a portrait of Little Phil astride his charger, was pelted with mud and hooted from the levee. At last the owners sold their fine new vessel to Commodore William F. Davidson, who needed a fast boat to compete with the lavish Northern Line steamers on the Upper Mississippi. So for ten seasons General Sheridan galloped between the shores of Wisconsin and Minnesota on a packet's paddle-boxes. Other large boats, such as the *Belle of La Crosse* and the *Alex Mitchell* launched at Paducah, Kentucky, were built on the Ohio for the trade of the northern river, because boat-building timber was not at hand on the Upper Mississippi. Fine stands of oak grew in Wisconsin, but until the middle seventies no railroad linked the hardwood forests to the boatyards on the river.

Railroads brought boat timbers to the Mississippi and in turn a steamboat carried the first locomotive—the high-stacked, brass-

fitted *William Crooks*—to the little stub railroad line, bravely
named the "St. Paul and Pacific," that ran between St. Paul and
St. Anthony (now Minneapolis). So the river and the railroad were
cooperators for a while. When railheads had first reached the river
in the fifties, the steamboat lines were overwhelmed with a traffic
of settlers bound for the northern towns and produce from the
newly settled counties of prairie land. Just before the Civil War
and again just after the war, not enough vessels were available
to carry the multitudes of people crowding the steamboat offices and
the mounds of merchandise on the levees. But when the railroads
reached north along the river and the locomotive whistle echoed
under the hills, a bitter and losing rivalry developed for the steamboats churning up the Mississippi.

One by one the big boats dropped out, wrecked or sunk or laid
up, and no new ones took their places. Then the dominant traffic
on the river was the vast rafts of pine logs floating down, under
guidance of squat little towboats, from the Wisconsin forests to
sawmills at La Crosse, Clinton, Hannibal and St. Louis. The older
river life was a fading memory: the music and dancing, immigrants talking in many languages on the crowded lower deck and
tourists at the upper rail watching the moonlight on the water,
while people in all the river towns boasted of the big steamers—
the lavish *Metropolitan,* the *Excelsior* with its steam piano, the
swift *Gray Eagle* and the splendid *Northern Light.*

WHILE COMMERCE grew on the rivers, a vaster commerce had
come to the Great Lakes and the smoke of steamboats streaked the
sky for a thousand miles from Buffalo to Chicago and to remote
Duluth. The pioneer steamboat *Walk-in-the-Water,* with a handful of passengers and a few tons of barreled cargo, first plied Lake
Erie in 1818, when no one could even dimly foresee the prodigious
fleets that, within a century, would carry coal and grain and iron
and limestone between the Great Lakes cities. The *Walk-in-the-
Water* sank in the water, near the eastern end of Lake Erie, at the
end of her third season. But she was followed by other vessels, the

Superior, the *Chippewa,* the *Pioneer* and the *Enterprise.* By 1830, a regular schedule of steamers trailed a haze of woodsmoke over Lake Erie. At first, the steamers were confined to the growing trade between Buffalo and Detroit, while tall schooners sailed the long stretches of Lakes Huron and Michigan, supplying fur posts and bringing down barreled whitefish and baled peltry. But when, in 1825, the Erie Canal began to pour its motley commerce into the West, the lakes trade pushed on from Erie to Huron and Michigan.

For thirty years a never-ending throng of immigrants gathered at Buffalo, restlessly waiting passage on the immigrant ships that would take them to the lake ports of Michigan, Wisconsin and Illinois. During the single month of May, 1836, ninety steamboats arrived at Detroit and one of them carried seven hundred settlers in its crowded cabins. In those years, the harbors were white with the sails of schooners freighting wheat and lumber, corn and lard, cheese and flour, whisky and tobacco, between Lake Erie and the western lakes. But the steamers, trailing their plumes of smoke past Lake Erie's green islands and over the blue solitudes of Lake Huron, through the forest-framed Straits of Mackinac and down the long sea-lanes of Lake Michigan, were engaged in the fastest-growing business in America—the business of carrying immigrants to the West. Steamers brought the founders of new cities and the citizens of new commonwealths—men who plowed the prairie sod and felled the northern forests. They gave back to the lakes another commerce—holds heaped with wheat and terraced with lumber. The wheat went to Buffalo and the Atlantic; the lumber went down Lake Michigan to build prairie cities and over Lake Erie to supply the East with famous Michigan pine. The Erie Canal had brought multitudes of settlers to the docks at Buffalo, and within a few years canal barges were loading Great Lakes wheat and Great Lakes lumber for their plodding journey back to the Hudson.

Lake Superior, cut off from the lower lakes by the mile-long rapids of Sault Sainte Marie, was a lonely sea surrounded by a wild and lonely land. A few small schooners, lost as seagulls on that

"Big Sea Water," called at the scattered fur posts and brought
their peltry down to the Soo. There Sheldon McKnight, with his
old gray horse, hauled it over the portage and another schooner
took it down the St. Marys River and to the lower lakes. But in
the middle forties the minerals of Upper Michigan emerged from
red men's lore to white men's geological surveys. A rush began
to the wildest, loneliest, most rugged region in all the Northwest
Territory. Roads did not exist in that region—it was a generation
before roads penetrated the woods and swamps of the iron and
copper ranges. Access to the ranges was by water, and there were
no vessels on Lake Superior capable of carrying the new trade in
men and supplies. But at the wharves of Sault Sainte Marie, just
a mile from the lower end of Lake Superior, ships called regularly,
having come up the beautiful St. Marys River from Lake Huron.

The logical thing was to transport some of those ships around
the rapids and launch them into Whitefish Bay. In the winter of
1845, six schooners and two steamers inched their way on rollers
down Sault Sainte Marie's Water Street, while shaggy horses
tramped dark circles in the snow around a creaking capstan. That
spring Lake Superior had a fleet of vessels ready to trade between
the Soo and the lonely copper camps on the wild cape of Keweenaw. Ten years later, St. Marys Falls Canal was opened and
Superior became one in commerce with the lower lakes. Then
vessels from Lake Erie whistled under the hills of Marquette and
Copper Harbor, and steamship smoke blew over the stump-studded
waterfront of Duluth and across island-studded Chequamegon Bay.

By the time of the Civil War, steamers had come up the
Mississippi to Fort Snelling and up the lakes to the head of remote Superior. The western commerce that had started with keelboats at Pittsburgh had gone a long way in sixty years. That water
transport was to be rivaled by highways and railroads. But the
great water routes remained vital to the inland country. The vessels changed. On the Ohio and the Mississippi, the gleaming steam
packets disappeared, and now it is an event to see the excursion
boat *Gordon C. Greene* calling at a grass-grown landing. (That

sturdy steamer makes excursion cruises every year, between April and December, on the Ohio, the Tennessee, the Upper and the Lower Mississippi.) But the traffic goes on, through regulated pools of river, in barges pushed by diesel-powered towboats.

Now it is a vast traffic in the heavy goods of industry. A single tow of coal barges has covered eight acres of water and carried a tonnage equal to that of twelve miles of freight cars. During the hectic early 1940s all the steel sheets for the Quonset huts that sprang up in every latitude of the earth where fighting men were in need of quarters, from Tunisia to Kiska, from Iceland to Saipan, were freighted down the Ohio. In March, 1944, thirty fully equipped four-room houses for war-plant workers passed down the river in a single tow pushed by the towboat *Arthur Hider*. Over the Upper Mississippi passes a barge trade in oil and sand, flour and wheat, soy beans and lumber, scrap-iron, coffee, rice and fertilizer—a greater tonnage than was ever carried by the spangled steamboats. On the lakes, from April till December, there moves a prodigious, never-ending commerce—a big ship passes Detroit's Windmill Point Light every twelve minutes, carrying coal and iron, wheat and limestone for the industrial basin of America. The west-running river vitalized the valley and the westward-leading lakes opened the northern states to settlement and trade. The Northwest Territory was framed in water and it has been girdled by shipping from the beginning of its civilization.

XVII

The Prairie's Dreaming Sod

ARLY IN THE SUMMER of 1815, while the locust trees were flowering at the river's edge and the sycamores leaned their pale green crowns above the water, a chain of Pennsylvania flatboats drifted down the Ohio. Moving among the river's motley traffic, past the scows and skiffs and rafts, the arks and broadhorns and the first fuming steamers of the West, they presented a curious sight. They carried George Rapp's colony of eight hundred religious followers, still speaking their Wurttemburg German and singing in unison across the water the old German hymns.

Though bound for Posey County, Indiana, where Father Rapp had purchased 30,000 acres bordering the Wabash, they were not like the other Hoosiers, dressed in butternut clothing with long rifles cradled in their arms and a wad of tobacco in their cheeks. The Rappites looked like another race—the men wore steeple-crowned hats, sky-blue smocks and knee-length leggings; the women wore white shawls over their shoulders and sober black bonnets that tied under their chins. They looked forward not to the prosperity of Indiana but to the coming of Christ.

The Rappites were sturdy, industrious and undeviating in submission to their leader. Though they lived in daily expectation of the Millennium, they had a practical realization of the tasks of a new country. They were as familiar with the ax and grubbing hoe as with the Book of Revelation. When they arrived at their site, a few miles up the Wabash from its confluence with the Ohio, they found a wilderness of forest, swamp and tangled bottom land, where for many generations the Indians had hunted bear and trapped beaver. Under their blue smocks the Rappites had powerful arms and shoulders and under their steeple hats they carried

243

a stern and stubborn purpose. In three years they had cleared land, drained swamps and set up solid buildings that awed their frontier neighbors. Then they laid out extensive vineyards, filled the rich meadows with herds of cattle and flocks of sheep, and built their town, Harmonie, as substantially as though they had never heard of the Millennium.

They labored from dawn to dark, winter and summer—they lived lives of toil and self-denial. At the edge of their village they built a labyrinth of dark and shaggy hedges that led to a soft green bower with a blissful little summer-house in the center. It signified their belief that suffering and self-denial in this world are preludes to the bliss of the life to come. The Rappites kept watch by night, and a sleepless colonist could hear the solitary watchman cry the hours and intone a grave reflection: "Again a day is past and a step made nearer to our end. Our time runs away and the joys of Heaven are our reward."

Beside the Wabash they built their community houses of stone, brick and clapboard—stone that they quarried and brick that they baked and clapboard that they sawed in their own mill. Two of their four community houses stand beside the Wabash today. In one of them, the Tavern, a traveler may find lodging and he can see in his bedroom the oak and walnut timbers that Father Rapp's men hewed out of the dark Wabash forests. They built their granary strong as a fort and its four-foot walls of stone and brick promise to stand as long as anything in Indiana. They built a church where Father Rapp preached to them. Its roof was lifted by twenty-eight pillars of walnut, cherry and sassafras.

For ten years the colony of Harmonie prospered. The Rappites lived as a community, working together in the fields to the music of their German band, living together in the large community houses, sharing equally in the fruits of their fields and mills. Bright flower gardens bordered all their houses and matched teams of horses hauled their wagons to the granary. They had five meals in their long working day, with breakfast before daylight and supper after dark. In winter, while their fields lay frozen, they were busy

at their stone quarries and brick ovens and in their spinning and
weaving mills. Their fame as a progressive colony traveled up and
down the Ohio, and beyond.

So they lived in harmony—or in all harmony except one, for
Rapp had persuaded his people to accept celibacy. Four thousand
miles away, in England, Lord Byron gave the colony on the
Wabash two stanzas in *Don Juan:*

> When Rapp the Harmonist embargoed Marriage
>   In his harmonious settlement (which flourishes
> Strangely enough as yet without miscarriage,
>   Because it breeds no more mouths than it nourishes,
> Without those sad expenses which disparage
>   What Nature naturally most encourages)—
> Why called he "Harmony" a state sans wedlock?
> Now here I've got the preacher at a deadlock.
>
> Because he either meant to sneer at Harmony
>   Or Marriage, by divorcing them thus oddly.
> But whether reverend Rapp learned this in Germany
>   Or no, 'tis said his sect is rich and godly,
> Pious and pure, beyond what I can term any
>   Of ours, although they propagate more broadly.
> My objection's to his title, not his ritual
> Although I wonder how it grew habitual.

In ten years' time the Harmonists built a town and created a
community worth vastly more than the $150,000 that George Rapp
sold it for. He sold it because it was too successful. Primitive Chris-
tianity was a doctrine for the poor and oppressed. Life on the Wabash
was making his people prosperous and secure. "Rich and godly,"
Byron called them, but as their riches grew their godliness diminished. As the discipline of pioneering softened and relaxed, they were
growing restive and worldly. So Rapp commissioned Richard
Flower, a resident of the English colony of Albion on the Illinois
side of the river, to sell the entire property. And he prepared to lead
his colonists to a new home in the wilderness.

George Rapp was apparently a devout man—certainly he was a shrewd one. He knew that his people would not easily be persuaded to leave the rich land and the pleasant town of Harmonie. So he resorted to a religious ruse. At the close of a summer afternoon, when the colonists filed in from the fields, he called them all together. Silently he led them down to the river bank and pointed to a rough slab of limestone imprinted with the marks of two large naked feet. Here, he said, the angel Gabriel had appeared to him, commanding that he take his people to a new place. When the angel rose to heaven, George Rapp saw that he had left his footprints on the stone.

That miraculous demonstration stilled all the rebellion among his followers. Solemnly, sadly, and with the awe of those whose coming and going is decreed by God, they packed up their household goods, boarded their weathered fleet of flatboats and poled them slowly up the Ohio, leaving their peaceful village deserted on the Wabash. During another period of toil and self-denial they built their new town of Economy on the Ohio riverfront under the steep green hills eighteen miles from Pittsburgh.

George Rapp's limestone slab is still on view in the village of New Harmony. It stands in the yard of the commodious house built for Father Rapp in 1815, with the two large footprints showing plainly—the left print, after being badly weathered, was repaired by a workman with hammer and chisel a few years ago. Where the stone came from is a mystery, though there was a rumor that Frederick Rapp, the leader's adopted son, had brought it back as a souvenir from a visit to the Indian mounds of Illinois. If so, some prehistoric savage left the imprint which sent a band of German peasants from the place and made possible the undertaking there of one of the famous social experiments in the restless history of man.

THE RAPPITES at Harmonie were only the first of the sects and societies that raised their temples, tabernacles and community halls on the prairies. The West was hospitable to new people and new ideas, and so the colonies came. Some were religious communities —Mormons, Shakers, Zoarites, Amish, Mennonites, Separatists, Jansonists—taking their doctrines from the Old Testament and the Book of Revelation and following a special dispensation which came on golden plates to Joseph Smith, or by a voice from heaven to Eric Janson, or by a gift of prophecy to George Rapp. With belief in their leaders and in the will of God, they went into the wilderness to plant their various versions of the Christian society. Others were socio-economic societies—the Fourierists, the Owenites, the Icarians—each group seeking to set up an ideal community of justice, equality and brotherhood.

The Mormons came to Kirtland, Ohio, in the Western Reserve, in 1831. There they built the first of the great gaunt temples that marked their long and troubled wandering from New York State to Utah. They believed that the Millennium was imminent and that at the coming of Christ the wicked would perish and the Mormon Saints would inherit the earth. Though they had a zeal for gospel, they were not above the love of land. Some of them carefully figured the tillable areas of the earth and dividing that by the number of Mormons to be saved, they calculated the acreage that each Saint would receive. Meanwhile, they had inner dissensions and outer conflicts with their frontier neighbors. So they moved on from Ohio to the banks of the Mississippi at Nauvoo, Illinois. There the leader, Joseph Smith, was killed by mob violence after he had defied the authority of the state of Illinois and from that handsome site on a broad curve of the Mississippi the Mormons moved on again, in 1846, to the far-away valleys of Utah.

While one sect moved out of Illinois, another came in. From Sweden, in the same year that the Mormons ferried their thousands of wagons across the river and began the long journey to the West, the fanatical Eric Janson led a band of four hundred followers into the prairie country. Disembarking from lake steamers at Chicago, they marched across one hundred and fifty miles of level land to Edwards Creek, which flows to the Mississippi. There they built their town, named Bishop Hill, around a great log tabernacle shaped to form a cross, and there they farmed their thousand-acre fields. For a few years they prospered, while Eric Janson preached to them—with his maimed, three-fingered hand outstretched in exhortation—and conducted the colony's affairs with shrewdness and foresight. But when a young Swedish adventurer wandered into the colony with a knife in his belt and a long rifle on his shoulder, an uneasy feeling went through the community. His name was John Root. He had no taste for earnest labor or for Jansonist doctrine, but he lounged on the benches in the big dining hall and talked of his wanderings on land and sea. His most rapt listener was the shy and lovely niece of Eric Janson.

When the leader tried to separate them, John Root's eyes flashed dangerously. One day he came in from target practice and shot Eric Janson dead. Then the leadership of the colony passed to Eric Janson's widow. She was a strong-willed woman who had now outlived four husbands—a drowned seaman, a Swedish schoolmaster, a devout Bishop Hill farmer and the fanatical religious leader. She knew the affairs of the colony and was capable of administering them, but St. Paul had said, "Let your women keep silence in the churches," and it was difficult to govern in silence. So the business of the colony was conducted by a group of seven trustees and the community grew stronger and more prosperous. But when a Jansonist missionary came home to Bishop Hill preaching the doctrine of celibacy to which he had been persuaded by the Shakers, conflicts began. Many of the colonists moved away and there was no community of worship among those who remained. In 1861, the property was divided among its four hundred shareholders. The religious community was at an end and Bishop Hill became another prairie town on the banks of a creek in Illinois.

The Shakers made four prosperous settlements in Ohio. One of them was located on the "heights," which later railroad and real-estate men made a handsome suburb of Cleveland. Other settlements, with their big barns and barrack-like community houses, and their shops, mills and offices, were located near Dayton and Portsmouth. The largest of them, Union Village, occupied three thousand acres of land in southwestern Ohio. The empty brick barracks, which once housed the five hundred people of the colony, still line a Warren County road just outside the dignified old town of Lebanon. In those silent and decaying buildings the Shakers lived in groups, of thirty to a hundred, called families—the "family" members were called brothers and sisters and they lived on separate floors. A sister was appointed for each brother—she mended and washed his clothing and reproved him for disorderly ways. The brothers and sisters marched in pairs to the dining room, but in the Shaker community men and women were not allowed to meet alone.

Their celibacy required that they maintain their numbers by proselyting and Shakers energetically visited the frontier camp meetings to win converts. This activity aroused the hatred of their neighbors, and bands of wrathful men repeatedly threatened the Shakers with violence. As proselyting diminished, their numbers dwindled and the spacious fields grew up in dog fennel and wild mustard. Union Village was finally dissolved in 1907, after 102 years of existence. Now its rich acres are an Ohio prison farm with convicts working the fields that the celibate Shakers first brought to harvest.

The Zoarites were a community of two hundred simple, stolid German Separatists who settled the town of Zoar—named for the place where Lot found safety after his flight from the iniquities of Sodom—in Tuscarawas County, Ohio. Doffing their flat hats to no one, they paid for five thousand fertile acres by working on the Ohio Canal, which bisected their land. Under the leadership of Jacob Bimeler, they prayed and sang, raised bountiful crops of corn and wheat and operated a sawmill, brick ovens, a flour mill and a tannery. They affirmed a doctrine of celibacy, but when a comely young woman entered the community, Jacob Bimeler received a new revelation. His own marriage to the new convert marked the abandoning of celibacy. With hard work and peaceful cooperation, the Zoarites flourished for eighty years. But gradually they lost the fervor of Separatist doctrine and they grew restive under the restraints of communal life. In 1898, they agreed to divide their property and substitute separate granaries for the common storehouse.

The Icarians were economic rather than religious separatists. A colony of French immigrants, they were followers of Etienne Cabet who, while imprisoned in France for his political beliefs, wrote a book called *Le Voyage en Icarie* describing his idea of a perfect society. The book won him a number of ardent followers, and Cabet organized a colony to found their Icaria in the New World. The attempt was begun in Texas, but fever and famine made it a failure. In 1848, Cabet took his three hundred followers up the Mississippi to Nauvoo, Illinois, from which the Mormons had recently departed. There, in the houses the Mormons had built and the fields they had broken, the Icarians prospered for a few years. They farmed the rich black prairies and tended the orchards which the Mormons had set out. On the river bank they operated a lumber mill, a flour mill and a distillery. They began to rebuild the ruined Mormon temple, which a band of Hancock County rowdies had burned on a November night in 1848, and Cabet had visions of a great Icarian community with that massive temple at its center. But when construction was half completed a spring cyclone leveled it to the ground. That took the heart out of the project and the walls were never raised again. In the middle fifties dissension broke the colony in two. Cabet himself was expelled in 1856, along with a minority of members who had remained loyal to him. The colony survived a few more years, though dogged by financial difficulties. It was disbanded in 1860.

In those hopeful years a century ago, there were more than forty Fourierist "Phalanxes" in America, spaced all the way from the Transcendentalists' Brook Farm outside of Boston, to Ripon, Wisconsin, where the Wisconsin Phalanx named its town Ceresco, after Ceres the goddess of grain. Eight phalanxes were formed in Ohio. Others appeared in all of the other states of the Northwest Territory. All were founded on the theories of the French scientist François Marie Charles Fourier, who believed that the universe was governed by laws which man could discover and apply to the organization of society. Human society, he thought, was still in an infant and primitive state, with time and opportunity for development. He believed the human race was destined to live for eighty thousand years, of which five thousand had been spent. The race, therefore, was like a five-year-old child with seventy-five years still before him. An analysis of human nature revealed the existence of twelve passions. Five of these he called sensitive, four affective and three distributive. Society, he reasoned, should be organized in units small enough to be manageable and large enough to allow the play of all twelve passions in all combinations. Two thousand persons, thought Fourier, constitute a minimum society, or phalanx, which should exist as a social unit in a single building.

His scheme began with this local unit and extended to a world unity. Four phalanxes form a union, four unions a district, four districts a province. Beyond these are the larger federations—nations, empires, regions, continents, and finally a world confederacy, embracing all in order and harmony. In the individual phalanx, which was the only step of the Fourierist organization to become realized, property would be held in common and work and reward shared equally by the members. Each person would choose his occupation by aptitude and to everyone work would yield pleasure. Rather illogically, then, Fourier emphasized the fact that by the benefits of association and communal property an individual would need work but ten years of his life.

The surprising spread of Fourierism in America was the result of the enthusiasm and conviction of three literary men. In his New York *Tribune,* Horace Greeley carried on a vigorous newspaper campaign, praising Fourier's science of society and urging the founding of colonies based on his concepts. He even sent his own newspaper men to organize phalanxes in the West. The cause was aided by Albert Brisbane, who had studied in Paris the theories of social reform developed by Fourier and Saint-Simon. Brisbane's *The Social Destiny of Man* was an eager elucidation of Fourierism, and his *Concise Exposition of the Doctrine of Association* became a kind of handbook and gospel for Fourierites in America. Then Parke Godwin published his simple and practical *Popular View of the Doctrine of Charles Fourier*. By the middle 1840s Fourierism had a lively press in America. As the theories circulated, phalanxes sprang up at more than forty different places, from Massachusetts and New Jersey to Wisconsin and Illinois.

The average life of these scattered phalanxes was two years. Many of them did not endure past their first winter. None except Brook Farm, with Nathaniel Hawthorne and Margaret Fuller among its members, left a literature to trace the pattern of its hopes and its frustrations. Most of the western phalanxes sprang up in enthusiasm, withered in disappointment and were soon forgotten. Failure was common enough in the new country—individuals, families and communities accepted failure and moved on to a new beginning. There was no particular reason to remember the failure of a phalanx.

But the fortunes of a few of them can be traced and doubtless the others fared no better. There were two Ohio Phalanxes on the Ohio River. One failed financially in its second year of existence, the other came to a tragic end when the ruinous flood of 1847 washed away its buildings and took the lives of seventeen of its one hundred members. A stronger society was the Phalanx Company organized in 1844 near Warren, Ohio, by N. C. Meeker, an editorial associate of Horace Greeley. On fifteen hundred acres the members built a tannery, a wooden bowl factory, a wagon-shop, and a shoeshop, in addition to their community buildings. This colony flourished into the 1850s, by virtue of hard work which did not always yield pleasure and from which there was no prospect of retirement.

Dissension eventually arose over the rates of pay of managers and laborers, and that quarrel led to the disbanding of the colony. Now the old Phalanx mill and a red-painted granary and cheese factory along U. S. 422 are all that remain of the Phalanx Company.

The power of the printed word was evidenced by the forming of the Wisconsin Phalanx when, in 1844, a group of young settlers at Kenosha, Wisconsin, after reading one of Horace Greeley's Fourierite editorials, were fired to found a community of their own. They purchased six hundred acres in the present township of Ripon, in Fond du Lac County, and there built their long community lodge and their barns and granaries. For five years they carried on their communal life. But quarrels among themselves and disagreements with a settlement of neighbors on a hill nearby caused them to disband their society. Now the fields of "Ceresco" are built up with the streets of Ripon, but at the western edge of the town there still stands the "Long House" where the Fourierites lived.

All these sects and societies represented some strand of hope or faith or optimism which had sought realization in the broad new country. All through the West ran currents of ardor and idealism. The *Southern Illinois Advocate* of Shawneetown, the old flatboat landing on the Ohio, was the only newspaper in ten counties in its early years. But it had sanguine and far-reaching principles— "Universal liberty abroad and an ocean-bound republic at home." In 1852, wrote the editor of the Cincinnati *Gazette:* "There are no people in the world so ready to make experiments in social relations and domestic arrangements as those of the western country—none so little fettered by established habits or less disposed to consider hereditary prejudices as heirlooms which cannot be parted with."

The new country was hospitable to men of all races and all doctrines. It offered a new chance for the old search for perfection. If all its experiments failed, if the seeking was not fulfilled, if the old compromises were made again with error and human frailty, it is still good to remember that the fair and fertile lands had a welcome for men's minds as well as their muscles. American society was too young and restless to accept the restraints of communal life, and the wide American land lured people into the pursuit of individual possession and accomplishment. Utopia was the dream of a tired and downtrodden people; it faded in the strong light of opportunity and western enterprise. But the passing dreams of Utopia are a part of the prairie landscape, as much as its willow-fringed creeks and its groves of maple trees.

HARMONIE ON THE BANKS of the Wabash had enjoyed ten years of peaceful and prosperous community life when Father Rapp led his people away from the pleasant Indiana home. The town was deserted for a year. Then, as New Harmony, it became the scene of a second Utopia. Though that experiment was short-lived, it made a village on the Wabash one of the memorable communities in all the American past.

Robert Owen, a cotton manufacturer of Lanark, Scotland, was as aware as Fourier himself of the evils of the factory system. He tried to mend them, not by abolishing factories but by improving the living and working conditions of his employes. He earned the ardent enmity of his business associates by establishing schools, hospitals and recreation centers and improving the housing in his mill town. He vigorously supported reform legislation but when, in 1819, he stood for Parliament in Lanark borough, he was defeated. Then he began to doubt that the new society could be born in the Old World. So in 1824, when Richard Flower of Albion, Illinois, came to England with a commission to sell the Rappite property, he found Robert Owen in a mood to listen to his description of the town of Harmonie on the banks of the Wabash. Owen had already developed a plan for a perfect society, which was to give man a new existence by surrounding him with "superior circumstances." In this society all possession would be held in common by the people; all would share equally in labor and the fruits of labor; work would be made pleasant and attractive; the family would be replaced by community association. There was little opportunity to try out this lofty plan in England or Scotland with their age-old abuses and superstitions. But on the sunny prairies of America, beside the rivers of the West, men might achieve the happiness and harmony of which he dreamed.

Richard Flower, the real estate agent for Father Rapp, knew something of reform himself. He was originally an English gentleman who had followed his son, George Flower, to a new colony in Illinois where it was hoped that living conditions could be vastly improved for a community of English working people. George Flower and his associate, Morris Birkbeck, had found the location, just fifteen miles from the Rappites' Harmonie, and had acquired 26,400 acres of land.

Then George Flower returned to England and brought back fifty colonists, including the members of his own family. This was the beginning of the quiet and industrious settlement of Albion. But now, offering the Rappite property for sale, Richard Flower had doubts about its fitness for a community such as Owen pictured, where science would win new triumphs over superstition, where art and music would refine the community's emotions and philosophy would illuminate its life. Though Flower had been promised a commission of five thousand dollars for selling the Rappite town, he warned Owen that the interior of America was a tangled and unreflective place and that its people were crude, boisterous and afflicted with chills and fever. But reformers dare not easily be discouraged.

So Robert Owen arrived on the banks of the Wabash in December, 1824, to see for himself the town that the Rappites had built. With kindly eyes, steel spectacles, cape over one shoulder and tall hat above his flowing hair, he looked more like a schoolmaster than an industrialist. But he had the hundred and fifty thousand dollars which Father Rapp had set as the price of his domain. It seemed an ideal setting for his ideal community. Even its name he approved. He paid over the money and considered it a bargain.

In the spring of 1825, in Washington and Philadelphia, he described his plans for New Harmony and invited all who sympathized with his aims to join in the undertaking. He asked no investment of money, he cared nothing about people's failures or difficulties in times past. Anyone who aspired to the life of liberty and brotherhood would be welcome at New Harmony. His invitation was published and circulated widely, and people began

streaming into the town on the Wabash. By the end of a year
nearly a thousand colonists had come from every corner of the
United States and from a dozen countries of Europe. Some were
cranks, some were curious. Some were earnest, some were lazy. A
few came with their pigs and poultry but more came empty-
handed and starry-eyed with the Utopian dream.

For a while New Harmony was the most polyglot town in
America. In a single block of Tavern Street one heard the Hoosier
drawl and the Yankee twang, the clack of Irish and the burr of
Scotch, and other voices raised in French, German, Russian and
Italian. He saw Kentuckians in hunting shirts, New Englanders
in broadcloth, Scotchmen with plaid mufflers across their throats,
German scholars with capes over their shoulders, impoverished
English gentlemen with walking sticks, Illinois farmers with black
mud on their gumshoes, Indiana backwoodsmen chewing a cud
of slippery elm and hoping to beg a bite of tobacco. Each day new
arrivals stalked up from the river landing—more ruthless and ec-
centric men, more discontents and dreamers. It would indeed be a
triumph for reason and benevolence if Harmony could be made
of that motley aggregation.

Meanwhile, Owen was enlisting trained specialists from both
sides of the Atlantic. The most important of his associates was
William Maclure, a wealthy Philadelphia geologist who had posi-
tive and progressive ideas about education. Maclure responded
whole-heartedly to Owen's plan, investing a hundred thousand
dollars in it and preparing to go with Owen to direct the organization of the community. His interest in the colony was primarily
educational—he confidently believed he could make New Harmony the center of education in America.

Using his money and his influence, William Maclure enlisted a
score of philosophers, scientists and trained educators, and had a
keelboat built at Pittsburgh to carry them down the Ohio. They
began their river journey in the unlikely month of December,
1825, and with the delay of ice jams in the river they did not reach
New Harmony until the end of January. That keelboat, named

The Philanthropist but variously called *Noah's Ark, Maid of the Mist,* and *The Boatload of Knowledge,* brought to the frontier a greater accumulation of learning than had ever been assembled in America before that time. Among the twenty passengers there were authorities on everything from earthworms to eclipses of the sun and on all matters of social, moral and political philosophy.

There was Thomas Say scanning the wintry shores with his mind on mollusks and crayfish. A young man, a bachelor, he was a veteran of extensive field trips and the author of works which began the science of entomology and conchology in America. For the Philadelphia Academy of Natural Sciences he had collected specimens from the hills of Georgia to the Florida keys. He had served as naturalist to Major Stephen H. Long's expedition to the Rocky Mountains, and had returned from that high country with hundreds of new insects, shells and butterflies, and a long list of newly discovered birds and animals. As he traveled toward New Harmony with his eager face and quickly lighting eyes, he was the foremost naturalist of North America. Beside him was sharp-faced Charles Alexander Lesueur, naturalist and painter, an outdoors man looking worn and weatherbeaten and yet ready at a half hour's notice to take the trail again. A Frenchman by birth, he had become a citizen of science. He had made a four-year trip around the world, he had explored the wilds of Australia. When Maclure brought him to America, he had achieved international renown as a zoologist and painter. Now he was bound for New Harmony, but that was not his destination so much as his jumping-off place. During the next seasons he roamed far and wide from the Wabash. He published the first account of the Indian Mounds of Indiana and he made the first classification of the fishes of the Great Lakes.

There were others—Doctor Gerard Troost, a native of Holland, known wherever mineralogists assayed samples of ore, John Chappelsmith, artist and engraver, Professor Joseph Neef, musician and educational reformer, and Robert Owen's four sons, all gifted scientists and educators. In the *Philanthropist's* cabin, away from the blowing snow and the ice-clogged river, the women of the party discussed science, education and rational morality, along with less severe questions of the cutting of shirtwaists and the embroidering of reticules. Frances Wright, author of a Byronesque play, "Altdorf," which had delighted audiences in London, New York and Philadelphia, was a magnetic Englishwoman, a brilliant lecturer and an ardent crusader for the abolition of slavery.

Madame Marie Louise Fratageot, a woman of cosmopolitan learning and distinguished bearing, had been persuaded by Maclure to bring a group of her well-bred schoolgirls from Philadelphia to New Harmony, where they would grace the town's social life and refine its manners. The prettiest and most vivacious of her girls was Miss Lucy Sistaire, who found more of her future beside the Wabash than anyone could have foreseen. Just a year from the time of their arrival at New Harmony, Lucy Sistaire and Thomas Say were married, and there they remained until Thomas Say's death, eight years later.

With the arrival of the *Philanthropist,* New Harmony became the most notable center of learning in America. At that time sixteen-year-old Abe Lincoln, in his faded hickory shirt and high-water pants, was working on a riverside farm and sculling a ferryboat across the Ohio at the mouth of Anderson's Creek. He ferried Kentuckians with ox-teams and pack horses bound for New Harmony, and he ferried other persons—travelers on business with Robert Owen and frontier scholars and scientists going to consult the masters on the Wabash. Hearing that in New Harmony there were thousands of books and a school and men who knew everything, Abe Lincoln wanted to go to that place himself. But they needed him to cut rails and mow grain on the riverside farm and to scull the ferryboats across the broad Ohio.

With all his teachers, lecturers, musicians, artists and scientists on hand, Owen believed his colony was ready for permanent organization. He called a meeting in the Hall of Harmony—the old Rappite church—to establish the "Community of Equality." The constitution declared his basic principles—equality of rights, equality of duties, community of property, freedom of speech and action, sincerity in all proceedings, kindness in all actions, courtesy in all intercourse, order in all arrangements, the preservation of health, the acquisition of knowledge, and obedience to the laws of the country. Here were brave new words, a redundancy of faith, hope and good will. People went home that starlit night with an unheard music round them.

For a season New Harmony was busy, fervent, attractive. Maclure planted exotic trees he had brought from China—Trees of the Golden Rain—at the gateways of the old Rappite houses. Every night people streamed to the Hall of Harmony for concerts, lectures, balls. A lively literary club discussed Pope's *Essay on Man* and Shaftsbury's *Characteristics* under the direction of beauteous Frances Wright. A Thespian society presented French and English drama. A newspaper kept the citizens informed in current science and philosophy, as well as in the doings of the Wabash Valley. Owen's building program went unrealized—he had planned a great four-sided phalanstery, forming a hollow square a thousand feet long, to house an academy and a university as well as the various departments of the community life. It was to stand on an elevated terrace and the four corners of the building would be marked by four towered halls of culture. Though this Shangri-La existed only under Owen's tall black hat, the institutions of New Harmony were real enough. Schools were established on a plan far ahead of conventional education of the time, with interest replacing compulsion as the incentive to learning. Workshops, museums and laboratories were used to supplement classroom instruction. A library bulged with books in various languages. The first kindergarten in the United States enrolled the five-year-olds of the community. Meanwhile, the educators worked on their theories and the scientists pursued their researches and from time to time both delivered lectures to the laity.

One of the superintendents of "general economy" in the settlement was Stedman Whitwell, a London architect who had been induced to come to New Harmony to design the new community buildings. Fortunately, he found other pursuits. He wrote verses, theorized about social reform and devised a simplified system of geography. Being worried about the number of Washingtons and Springfields that were multiplying in the states, he worked out a system of place names which would be a key to geographical location. Using letters to indicate numbers he would spell a city's latitude and longitude and thereby provide its name in the new system. By his method Washington became Feilli Neivul and Pittsburgh became Otfu Veitoup. Some critics of Whitwell's system suggested applying it to the name of a neighboring Indian Chief, Occoneocoglecococachecodungo.

The New Harmony *Gazette,* edited by two of Owen's sons, became the official paper of the community. It was less interested in news than in essays on moral responsibility and human happiness and articles on natural science and agriculture. Another publication was the fortnightly *Disseminator,* or to use its complete title, *The Disseminator of Useful Knowledge: Containing Hints to the Youth of the United States from the School of Industry.* This periodical outlasted the School of Industry which Maclure had established and continued in existence for ten years after the dissolution of the community. As the local journal it published the findings of Thomas Say and other scientists, who remained at New Harmony and made their field trips from that base. In ten installments, in 1829, appeared Say's exhaustive *Descriptions of Some New Terrestrial and Fluviatile Shells of North America,* and in the following year appeared the six installments of his *Description of New North American insects, and observations on some already described.* Maclure contributed sociological letters on conditions in Mexico, where he had gone because of failing health after the disintegration of the community in 1827. The *Disseminator* also printed discussions of education, geography, agriculture, natural history and political economy. Sample titles: "A Double-Headed Child," "Origin of Volcanoes," "Cure for Rheumatism," "Swedish Method of Breeding Turkeys," "Canals and Railroads," "Cure for the Maggot in Sheep," "Methods of

Restoring Persons Apparently Drowned," "Methods of Preserving Peas Green for the Winter." It was read by farmers in their kitchens and geologists in their laboratories.

New Harmony had a brief duration, followed by an enduring wonder that it could have existed at all. Despite the glowing colors of Owen's charter and the ardent beginnings of organization, the commune lasted just two troubled years. During that time there were complaints, conflicts of opinion and a crucial quarrel between Owen and Maclure. Out of discord were born several dissenting settlements—Yellow Springs, Macluria and Feiba Peveli— a group supporting Whitwell's geography—that set up makeshift existence near New Harmony. In the parent community, the ideal of cooperation was never fully realized. Differences in previous social background continued to separate aristocrats from commoners and European émigrés from Hoosier clodhoppers. While groups disagreed, cattle strayed, factories were idle, fields went untended, pigs ran wild in the woods. Robert Owen had expected to work a miracle, and no miraculous transformation occurred in New Harmony's assorted varieties of human nature. So, in the summer of 1827, the noble experiment was abandoned. The property of the settlement passed into private hands, family life was resumed and, like a horse settling into accustomed harness, the people took up the old competition with each other. Many of the colony drifted away, a few to try other experiments in society, the rest to plow their own fields and sow them to their own grain.

Probably the men of science were the least disillusioned of all the Harmonists. Their passion was phenomena, rather than perfection, and the prairies still waved with many grasses, swamps were still scummed with algae, clouds of passenger pigeons still cast mile-long moving shadows on the land. Thomas Say remained at New Harmony, as did placid Gerard Troost and restless Charles Lesueur. In the next years Say wrote his great work on Conchology, Troost tramped off to collect rocks, Lesueur explored the mounds of southern Indiana and trudged along the Great Lakes and the Mississippi classifying fishes. For thirty years the village on the Wabash remained a leading scientific center. To see the thousands of classified specimens, to use the libraries collected by Maclure and Say, to consult the men in their museums and laboratories came many visitors.

Constantine Rafinesque, the wandering scientist who took all nature for his province and made astonishing discoveries in diverse fields, came in his mud-stained boots and tattered jacket. Jean Jacques Audubon arrived with dark and restless eyes and a mind filled with the prodigal species of the forests. Sir Charles Lyell journeyed from Scotland to see the geological collections and to talk with the men who had gathered them. Using New Harmony as his base, David Dale Owen, the reformer's son, conducted a geological survey of the Northwest. For seventeen years the Wabash village was the headquarters of the United States Geological Survey. The old Rappite granary was turned into a storehouse for geological, archaeological, botanical, biological and entomological collections, and for a generation that dim and massive building, still harboring a malty smell of grain, was one of the great museums of the world.

After the Civil War, New Harmony settled into the drowsy life of an Indiana village. But its memories stayed alive as in few places in the Middle West and there remains today a faintly incredulous pride in its curious past. If an angel had not alighted on the river bank, if Utopia had not been established on the Wabash, still an ardent impulse had been given to social justice, to progressive education, to the emancipation of women and the pursuit of scientific knowledge.

Now the quiet town retains its past. Street names go back to the Rappites—Granary, Church, Tavern and Steam Mill streets; the west entrance to the modern high school is the fanlit rose door which once opened into the Rappite church and the Owenite Hall of Harmony. The old granary still stands like a fortress defying time. Two of the old community houses still flank Church Street, and around the dignified house built for Father Rapp and later occupied, successively, by William Maclure, Thomas Say, and David

Dale Owen, the Trees of Golden Rain flower each June with their long yellow tassels. Now the state of Indiana has begun a restoration of the old community, and New Harmony will be remembered as one of the ardent failures and generous impulses of the West when it was young.

XVIII

The Trampled Towpath

THE FIRST ROUTES of travel in the new country became the final routes. The great game animals and the roving Indians trod out paths which marked the routes of inland commerce. Beneath many a modern cement highway is a forgotten buffalo trace and beneath ballasted railroad beds are war and hunting trails of the Indians. By instinct, herds and tribes found the strategic cross-country ways, which later the surveyor's transits located.

Between Lake Erie and the Ohio River ran four canoe routes, each with its laborious carry over the almost indiscernible height of land. The Cuyahoga-Tuscarawas-Muskingum, the Sandusky-Scioto, the Maumee-Auglaize-Miami, and the Maumee-Wabash were routes by which trappers and traders crossed the country before a wheel turned anywhere in that wilderness. Above Detroit, Lake Huron swings north, away from the central river systems, but Lake Michigan loops back, parallel with the Mississippi and pointing toward the Ohio. Two historic routes of discovery and exploration linked Lake Michigan with the Mississippi River. From Green Bay, the course of the Fox River lies south and west and its final curving shallows are within a mile of the westward-flowing Wisconsin. And from the extremity of Lake Michigan the Chicago and Des Plaines rivers lead back through prairie marshes toward the westward-flowing Illinois.

Each of these canoe routes became a canal route in the twentieth century. The vanished portage trail, where packmen sweated under boxes of trade goods and bales of peltry, was replaced by a canal bed over which the barges moved with corn and wheat, lard and whisky, coal and iron. The Fox-Wisconsin Waterway, the Illinois and Michigan Canal, the Wabash and Erie Canal, the Miami and

Erie Canal, and the Ohio and Erie Canal made a system of water transport between the Great Lakes and the western rivers. For a generation horses plodded on the towpaths and canal horns sounded through the streets of inland towns and over prairie fields.

Of all these water routes, the Ohio and Erie Canal was the first in operation and the most prosperous and important. With its feeders and branches it ran for 335 miles. It brought to central Ohio a tremendous flow of trade and population. Least significant was the Fox-Wisconsin Waterway—the actual canal ran for a bare two miles and it carried a few wheat cargoes toward Lake Michigan before it passed into disuse. Now they are all abandoned and only one modern route—the Illinois Deep Waterway—links the lakes with the rivers. But a century ago, each of them carried the urgent commerce of a rich new region. Eventually this region developed the greatest network of railroads in the world. But in 1825, the railroad was yet unborn and so canals were carved beside the rivers and over the old portages. Then the commerce of the lakes had a flowing link with the commerce of the rivers and a million western settlers had a trade route to the sea.

The dream of linking the Great Lakes to the western rivers began with the discoverers themselves. Late in the year 1673, Father Marquette, portaging through the weary swamps of Illinois, foresaw a canal between Lake Michigan and the Illinois River. A hundred years later Thomas Jefferson traced on his map of Virginia a canal route between Lake Erie's Cuyahoga River and Big Beaver Creek which flows into the Upper Ohio. In his retirement at Mount Vernon, George Washington mapped a waterway through the Pennsylvania mountains, connecting the Ohio River with the Potomac and the sea. Early in the nineteenth century, when the only market for the growing Ohio River trade was New Orleans and the Gulf, repeated proposals were made for a canal across the Appalachians to bring western products to eastern markets. But more practical plans focused upon a canal route between the Ohio and Lake Erie. And when Governor De Witt Clinton began his momentous canal from Albany to Buffalo, it

was inevitable that a canal should link the Ohio with Lake Erie.
So Ohio trade could find its way to the Hudson River and the
Atlantic.

In 1823, when the Erie Canal was nearing completion, the governor of Ohio sent to New York for engineer James Geddes,
who had surveyed much of the route of Clinton's Ditch. With
his tripods and transits, his chainmen and rodmen, Geddes tramped
the wilderness of central Ohio and found five practicable routes by
rivers which led from Lake Erie and the Ohio to a portage on
the watershed. The best route crossed the central part of the state,
linking Cleveland on the lake with Portsmouth on the river by
way of the Cuyahoga, Tuscarawas, Licking and Scioto rivers.
Another strategic route connected Cincinnati and Toledo by way
of the Great Miami, Auglaize and Maumee rivers. Either of these
canals was a prodigious undertaking, but the West had great energy and great expectations. In 1825, the Ohio Legislature authorized the construction of both projects.

At that time just one sixth of Ohio was cleared and cultivated,
and the canals were mapped through great tracts of wilderness.
Work on the Ohio and Erie Canal began with a brave ceremony
at Licking Summit, outside Newark, Ohio, on the Fourth of July,
1825. With bands playing and troops at rigid attention, Governor
De Witt Clinton of New York and Governor Jeremiah Morrow of
Ohio each dug a spade of earth. Then the first crews of Irish workmen spat on their hands and seized their mattocks and shovels,
mule teams strained at scoop buckets, the ditch began to yawn.
Three weeks later, at Middletown, Ohio, the same ceremony inaugurated construction of the Miami and Erie Canal. Within a
generation that process was repeated in Indiana, Illinois and Wisconsin. In swamps, woods and prairies, construction camps sprang
up and the forty-foot gash, framed by berm and towpath, grew
across the land.

In those years, the West resounded with many labors. Forests
came crashing to the ground, sawmills snarled and clanged, towns
grew up amid a furious clatter, and over the long dry canal ditches

rang the teamsters' voices and the thud of ax and mallet. Faint and far away, that uproar was heard in Europe, and the lure of work and wages brought thousands of new immigrants to the canal shanties in the West. At some places the ditch was dug by farmers and farmboys, earning thirty cents a day to use on their land payments. But to the great unsettled areas contractors brought in gangs of immigrant workmen. Soon after the ceremony at Licking Summit two thousand men were toiling on the Ohio Canal. It was a sweating, swearing job—dragging heavy dredges, heaving at rooted stumps, prying up boulders. Like many of America's big undertakings the canals were built by men not yet American, by men serving their time in makeshift camps before they acquired a settled citizenship. In the yawning canal bed men called to each other in German and Norwegian, and the fierce shouting of the Irish was like a foreign tongue.

Teamsters shouted, mules bunched their muscles, and with a sound like warfare, exxplosives thundered under rock ledges and roots of trees. Ten hours a day the gangs kept at it, grubbing and clearing, mucking and ditching, heaping up the embankments, building locks and culverts. At night they ate enormous suppers and sang rowdy songs and drank their ration of whisky to fight swamp fever and forget their aching bones. The shanty camps were knocked down and set up again at the next location. The big ditch wormed across the land.

One section of the Ohio Canal was dug by men who sang hymns. Through Dover and Zoar the Zoarites built the canal to pay for the twelve thousand acres of their community. In their flat-brimmed hats, with the red and blue star of the Separatists on the shoulders of their blouses, they dug the ditch across their spacious fields. At the same time, the older brethren at Zoar built their Garden of the New Jerusalem, with its Tree of Life sur-sounded by the twelve shrubs of the Apostles and radiating from it the twelve paths of the twelve tribes of Israel. From their construction contract on the canal, the Zoarites earned twenty thousand dollars, enough to build their tannery, brickyard and ore furnace. Soon the canal barges were carrying their leather, bricks and ironware to market.

More than a thousand miles of canal was surveyed or under construction in the late 1830s. These were prodigious undertakings for a new area with no wealth in the state treasuries and with a still meager population. Inevitably work was sporadic—sometimes it stopped altogether and weeds grew in the empty cut while new loans were floated, new investors were sought, and new canal lands were sold to incoming settlers. English speculators paced the raw earthworks along the Wabash and sent back to London and Liverpool recommendations about the purchase of Indiana bonds. But the financial crash of 1837 put a sudden end to all public works in Indiana, where three canals, a system of turnpikes and a railroad were being built by a state with little more than the present population of Indianapolis. In Ohio, at that time, canal construction was carried on by convicts from the state penitentiary. But with economic recovery in the middle 1840s, work was resumed on all the western projects. Again the brawny, red-faced Irishmen labored in the winter cold and through the stifling heat of summer. To stave off fever they had their daily dose of whisky and on Sunday a double dose, as a canal foreman had observed that fever renewed its ravages every seven days.

Canal building cost money and it cost lives. Malaria, known as "canal chills" and "canal fever," laid uncounted victims in little excavations beside the yawning ditch. Hundreds died of cholera when the epidemic swept the West, after being brought to Detroit and Chicago by the troopships sent from Buffalo to put down Black Hawk's Indians. Other men died from powder blasts and the kick of the big mules that hauled the scoops and dredges. Besides the hazards of disease and accident, there was the "Irish War"—for the men of Cork and the men of Northern Ireland brought their rivalries across the Atlantic and carried on a protracted, furious warfare along the canal ways. When a band of "Corkians" ran afoul of a band of "Fardowns" from Ulster, fever and cholera seemed mild disorders. From one cause or another, the mortality rate was high. For every six miles of canal construction a man died. But still the Irish came, and with them came the big, gentle Norskies and the hard-working Germans. So, despite feud and fever and financial panic, the canals were all completed and from thousands of creeping barges the horns rang over the prairie.

Pressure for new markets had been felt along the rivers as well as in interior counties. In the spring of 1826, 152 flatboats passed Vincennes on the Wabash, loaded with 250,000 bushels of corn, 100,000 barrels of pork, 10,000 hams, 2,500 live cattle, 10,000 pounds of beeswax, 3,600 venison hams, besides hogs, oats, meal and chickens. All had to go South for want of transport to hungry Eastern market places. Before the canals were operating, the middle states were full of produce which had almost no value. In Licking County, Ohio, ham was worth 3 cents a pound, eggs 4 cents a dozen, flour 1 cent a pound, whisky 12½ cents a gallon, chickens 5 cents each or 50 cents a dozen. When the canal was ready for commerce, the value of these products multiplied five and ten times.

So canal trade began with a triumphant excitement. Treble of bugles and bass thunder of cannon welcomed the first barges through the locks. At a hundred different places, as new sections of the canals came into operation, military parades formed, with fireworks, band concerts, and multitudes of persons cheering as the first horses tramped the towpath with a bunting-decked barge behind them. When that celebration was over, a more lasting activity began. At scores of towns and cities, bargeyards were established and warehouses grew like cliffs beside the canal bank. Wheat, corn, oats, coal, iron, lumber, pork, flour, bacon, lard, whisky passed up and down. At Cleveland, Akron, Portsmouth, Toledo, Fort Wayne, Evansville, Chicago, La Salle, St. Louis, hundreds of canal boats lined the landings and mile-long caravans of wagons waited to unload the grain from prairie farms. By 1840, 420 barges operated between Cleveland and Akron on the Ohio Canal. The first cargo over the Miami and Erie Canal arrived at Toledo from Cincinnati in June, 1845. Two years later, 417 boats were on the canal, carrying candles, flaxseed, scythe-stones, ginseng, ice and cheese, along with the bulk products of grain, pork and flour.

The great canal commerce was in wheat. Before the Red River Valley and the plains of Kansas were golden with ripened grain, the nearer West was famous for its wheat. Ohio was a wheat state when machine tools and rubber tires were unknown. Indiana and Illinois were corn and wheat states. Wheat cultivation moved west with the frontier. In the 1850s Wisconsin was the second wheat state in the nation. Then the short Fox-Wisconsin Canal was opened and wheat barges moved up to Green Bay on Lake Michigan. Though the canals carried many different cargoes, the primary purpose of their building was to get Western wheat to Eastern markets. When the water routes were opened wheat rose from ten or twenty cents to as much as a dollar a bushel at canal ports.

In 1838, before the Illinois and Michigan Canal carried wheat to lake water, Chicago sent exactly seventy-eight bushels of grain eastward. Twelve years later Chicago was the grain center of America, shipping twelve million bushels annually. The second grain port was Toledo, at the head of two canals, the Wabash and the Miami, which brought flour, wheat and corn from all the central counties of Ohio and Indiana. In those years caravans of creaking grain wagons lined the streets of the canal towns. Families rode in with their grain and waited cheerfully for their turn at the loading platforms. Women climbed down from the high wagon seats and chatted under the trees; children raced along the canal and sometimes hopped a barge-ride to the next lock; men found their way to the taverns that surrounded every canal station. Day and night, horses plodded towpaths and heaped barges crept on toward the lakes. At Chicago, Toledo, Cleveland, barges were emptied while the holds of schooners were filled, and under a white spread of canvas prairie wheat moved on to Buffalo and the East.

In the mid-century, five hundred Lake Michigan schooners

brought an endless stream of lumber to Chicago, which promptly became the largest lumber port in the world. Some of that lumber built Chicago, but more of it went on, by canal and river, to the treeless prairies of Illinois, Missouri and Kansas. It built the barns and houses of prairie farms and the newly created farms sent back a golden flow of grain in the same canal barges that had delivered building lumber. In 1848, the first year of full operation on the Illinois and Michigan Canal, Chicago's trade quadrupled. It multiplied many times in the years that immediately followed.

Besides the freight barges, every canal had lines of packets to carry passengers on an excursion or a journey. Usually the packet had a cabin divided into men's and women's quarters, but providing a common lounging and dining room. Sleeping quarters were lined with bunks three feet wide, softened by straw-filled mattresses. But in busy seasons, passengers overflowed the bunkrooms and stretched out at night on tables and floor. Sleeping on a packet was not a simple matter—because of the noise of the drivers and lockmen, the hardness of beds and distraction provided by clouds of mosquitoes. If there were a stern wind, a barnyard smell hung closely over the cabins, as spare horses were quartered on the boat. Packet business was best on the Ohio Canal and thousands of passengers made the eighty-hour journey from Cleveland to Portsmouth. On a few de-luxe packets, meals were provided; others stopped at mealtime and the passengers went ashore and patronized a tavern or cooked their own meal over a campfire while the horses were being fed. Larger packets carried seventy-five passengers and were propelled by a file of three horses at a rate of four miles an hour.

Many celebrated travelers paced the narrow decks and slept in the unyielding beds of the packetboats. John Quincy Adams, William Henry Harrison and William McKinley all knew the discomforts of a journey on the Ohio Canal. James A. Garfield in his youth worked on the canal as a driver and a bowsman. But the real traffic on the packets came with thousands of immigrants seeking homesteads in the middle states. Coming ashore from Erie

Canal boats, they crowded steamship offices at Buffalo and then overflowed landings at Cleveland, Toledo and Chicago. There they took packet passage to the inland counties. Alone, in families, in whole colonies they traveled the canals. Some traversed the entire state of Ohio and went on to a destination on the Ohio River, or even on the Mississippi.

It was a slow way to travel, and to these wondering people with their chests full of Old World goods and their minds full of Old World memories, it must have seemed a vast land that unrolled, at the rate of a horse's plodding, from the deck of a canal barge. Sometimes it was a forest country, dense with tulip, walnut and sassafras trees; sometimes it was prairie as vacant as a summer sea; sometimes it was farmland with fat cattle in the pastures and long fields of grain ripening in the sun.

They passed bustling young cities where heavy wagons rumbled to the landing, market towns with hogs and cattle herded in the streets and villages drowsing in the shade of ash and walnut trees. Sometimes the packet ran through a cut, twenty or thirty feet deep, with the horses plodding up against the sky; sometimes it followed a ridge where a wondering immigrant could look far off in all directions over farm and field and forest. They passed silent mounds and earthworks, ages old, and noisy new settlements where the sound of saw and hammer quickened the restlessness to find their place in the young and yeasty land. From the deck of a canal packet they saw the whole changing pattern of a frontier country, from vacant wilderness to teeming settlement.

Like vines across the land, the canals sprouted towns and cities. A lock was a site for a store, then for a sawmill, and soon the cabins of a town grew around it. A few seasons brought flour mills, brick ovens, salt works, foundries. Canal boats hauled out lumber from clearings and brought in steam engines for gristmills. And they brought people to fill the towns. Cleveland grew from five hundred to five thousand in the ten years following the beginning of canal construction. Its first industry was a bargeyard with a mounting backlog of unfilled orders. In those years, Erie Canal barges were towed across the lake from Buffalo and added to the fleets on the Ohio Canal. At first the canal route below Cleveland was framed in silent forest, but soon the scream of sawmills filled the air and the forest became canal towns, feverishly growing. Long before the age of rubber tires, the town of Akron, located on the old Tuscarawas portage, owed its existence to the canal. The name is Greek, meaning "high place." Akron was the highest point on the Ohio and Erie Canal. It began with a cluster of shanties housing Irish teamsters and shovelmen. Just beyond Akron the canal traversed Portage Lake with a long bridge for the tow horses. Akron was the center of some of the most difficult construction of the entire canal, and the whole town cheered on the July day, in 1827, when behind Job Harrington's team of black horses the towrope tightened and the *State of Ohio* inaugurated canal commerce to Cleveland.

Over the old portage were twelve locks in the space of six miles. Each lock became the site of stores and taverns, and the lockage of barges made the town's first business. In 1840, a branch canal, the Ohio-Pennsylvania, was completed to Pittsburgh. Then Akron, with water transport in three directions, was the leading inland port in the West. On the cupola of the vanished Empire Hotel a watchman called the approach of canal packets and hotel attendants lined up at the lock to welcome visitors. Now Main Street of Akron lies on the old canal bed and part of the canal flows under the pavements of the city. Other towns, like Massillon, Ohio, laid out on a crossroads in 1826, grew up with the canal trade. A hundred years ago Massillon was one of the great grain markets of the world, with long lines of farmwagons creaking in from the surrounding counties. It was much the same at Fort Wayne, Indiana, and La Salle, Illinois, where the canal boats discharged Michigan lumber and loaded millions of bushels of prairie wheat. The southern areas of Ohio, Indiana and Illinois had an early and substantial settlement supported by the river. But the northern areas were transformed by the canals. Before 1830, Cleveland was closer to New York and Cincinnati to New Orleans than these Ohio cities were to each other. The canals turned the prairie commerce toward the lakes and the Atlantic. They made the Midwest a unified region.

But, suddenly in the 1850s, the vine began to wither. Hardly were the canals completed than their age of usefulness was gone. The West might have waited for the railroads, but when the canals were planned no one dreamed that by 1860 a network of iron rails would lace the midland country.

Longest-lived of the canals was the Ohio and Erie, called the "Grand Canal" in its peak years. Through the 1840s it carried a vital commerce, but even in those years the railroads were reaching out for canal trade. In 1835, the first thirty-five miles of the Mad River and Lake Erie Railroad were completed in western Ohio. By 1860, Ohio led the nation with three thousand miles of railroad between the river and the lakes. The great era of railroad building was the 1850s, and that decade saw the doom of the canals. In 1850, the Ohio canals carried twenty-six times as much freight as the railroads. Ten years later the railroads carried twice the tonnage handled by the canals. In 1856, revenue from the "Grand Canal" fell below the cost of operation and from that year canal trade was limited to local business between points not connected by rail.

By that time, passenger traffic had deserted the four-mile-an-hour packet. So the old canal boats were left to rot at the landings, except when the Sunday school trooped aboard for an excursion to Canal Fulton or Canal Winchester. At the canal stations the locks grew green with moss. Taverns closed and warehouses no longer rumbled with baled and barreled goods. At the old town of Canal Fulton, the great grain elevator on Canal Street was converted into an opera house. On its opening night the "Famous Blakeney Troupe" from New York presented "East Lynne" to a crowd that came for miles around. But some of them missed the sound of canal horns on the barges and the rush of water through the opening locks.

To other canals, which later came into operation, the decline arrived while the lockgates were still new and the towpaths not yet grooved and hollowed. The first canal boat arrived at Evansville, southern terminus of the Wabash Canal, in April, 1835. Within a month the first train steamed in over the newly built railroad. The barge ran a losing race with the locomotive. The last canalboat tied up there just seven years later. The lock gates never opened again. The same sequence appeared in Illinois. In April, 1848, the Illinois and Michigan Canal was at last completed, and the canalboat *General Fry,* with a festive crowd of public personages, passed triumphantly from Lockport to Chicago. A few days later the barge *General Thornton* soberly arrived at Chicago with a cargo of sugar from New Orleans, and a history-making commerce had begun. But in October of that year the first locomotive in Chicago, a high-stacked stubby-tendered engine named the *Pioneer,* was unloaded from a Great Lakes schooner's deck. In that first year the rivalry began.

A decade passed before the canal felt the tightening pressure of steel rails across the prairie and a half century before it gave up entirely. But when the long cattle, coal and grain trains streamed in to Chicago and the trains of lumber, leather, and manufactured goods streamed out, the canal's years were numbered. The Little Fox-Wisconsin canal was the shortest-lived of all. During the construction it passed like a lead dollar from public to private hands and back to the public again. When it was opened, the Fox River proved to be inadequate to float a profitable commerce. Some cargoes of wheat went through in seasons of high water but the Michigan and Mississippi Railroad soon took the trade away. Then the Fox shallows filled with wild celery and the idlest man in Wisconsin was the superintendent of the lifeless canal, who opened the locks once in a decade to save a Menominee Indian a carry with his canoe.

For a time the larger canals remained in operation. When the states found them unprofitable, they were leased by private companies or taken over by investors in canal bonds, who did not know what to do with their new property. In Ohio, a private company with a low-cost lease operated the Miami and Erie Canal for half a century at a modest profit. At one time track was laid for the running of motor cars to tow the barges at a more efficient rate than the plodding pace of towteams. The "electric mule" was widely advertised, but the company went into receivership before its plans were realized. Eventually an electric interurban line occupied the canal bed.

Now for hundreds of miles the vanished canals have become the site of other means of transportation. The railroad put the Whitewater Canal, in Indiana, out of business, and today a railroad uses the old towpath for a roadbed. Where once coal barges crept up the Ohio Canal, long coal trains thunder toward Lake Erie ports. In many places the canal bed has become a highway. Through the heart of Cincinnati, a six-lane parkway occupies the old Miami Canal route, curving under the city's hills. Toledo took over the other terminus of that canal for street and sewer purposes—part of the canal bed there is webbed with railroad tracks. In Cleveland, railroad yards cover the site of the old canal bed and the barge basin.

But in hundreds of other places the long straight channel still stretches across the land—sometimes empty, sometimes with enough water to make good swimming holes in summer and smooth skating rinks when the fields are blank with snow. In southwestern Indiana, the old Whitewater Canal, a branch of the Miami, still curves through the valleys, leading through the village of Laurel and down to Metamora with its covered bridge and the old stone watermill. Here, a sagging, covered aqueduct still carries the canal over the Whitewater River. Near Toledo, at Side-Cut Park, heavy locks of the Miami Canal are slowly rotting. At La Salle, Illinois, near the shaggy mesa of Starved Rock, the old canal property has been made a recreation ground and for a hundred miles the towpath serves as a pleasure drive. At the quiet old town of Canal Fulton, ten miles of the Ohio Canal have been restored by the state. Each summer its quiet water and green banks attract thousands of visitors. Now there is good swimming and fishing where Canal Fulton's three hundred barges once loaded cargoes of wheat and coal. So the old system of transport remains in earthworks and basins, like the works of the vanished race that heaped up time-defying mounds above their dead.

Now, in the mid-twentieth century, there is talk again of a barge canal to carry coal from the Ohio to Lake Erie ports and to bring iron ore from Lake Erie to the steel cities on the river. And there is one waterway in vital use between Lake Michigan and the Mississippi. The Illinois Waterway is a successor to the abandoned Illinois and Michigan Canal which, after its opening in 1848, made Chicago the commercial center of the Mid-West, and was outmoded by the railroads. A more recent canal, the Illinois and Mississippi, which cut across the prairies from the Great Bend of the Illinois to the Rock River and the Mississippi, proved too small for modern commerce and was abandoned shortly after its completion in 1907.

But there remained a need for the linking of waters that Marquette, Joliet and La Salle all dreamed of as they portaged through the weary Des Plaines swamp. On the second of January, 1900, after years of construction, control gates at the mouth of the Chicago River were opened and the river began to flow backward over the continental watershed, or through it, and toward the Gulf of Mexico. Thus was opened the Chicago Drainage Canal, one of the great engineering projects of half a century ago. There had been an urgent need for a sanitary canal to carry Chicago's waste away from Lake Michigan. In 1917, with the demands for war-time transport of heavy materials, the Federal government deepened the channel from Chicago to Lockport on the Des Plaines River and from Lockport to Utica in the shadow of Starved Rock. Now a public waterway, it was called the Sanitary and Ship Canal and it carried the commerce of the Federal Barge Line between Chicago and the Mississippi, though the limited channel of the Illinois River required the use of shallow-draft barges.

For miles the modern channel, 20 to 26 feet deep and 160 to 300 feet wide, parallels the old Illinois and Michigan Canal, which looks insignificant beside it. Finally, in 1933, improvements were completed on the Illinois River, providing a minimum depth of nine feet throughout its length. A great modern barge trade began. Over canal and river channels bulk cargoes move between Chicago, Minneapolis, St. Louis, Kansas City and New Orleans. Steel barges, as many as ten in a tow, pushed by Diesel-powered boats with hinged smokestacks that lie down at the approach of bridges, carry a vast tonnage of coal, sugar, sulphur, lumber, steel and limestone. With its low-cost handling of bulk materials it has taken millions of tons of business from the railroads.

In the second World War, this Illinois waterway became a vital channel for goods and ships of conflict. Scores of naval and merchant craft built in yards on the Great Lakes sailed by this route to tidewater and to the remote theaters of war. Submaries, escort vessels, cargo ships passed through the stone canyons of Chicago, between the prairies of Illinois and so to the Mississippi and the Gulf of Mexico.

One memorable passage through the waterway was made during a series of driving snowstorms in January, 1945. That event began months earlier with the construction of three deep-water merchant ships at the head of Lake Superior and with the launching at Toledo of the world's most powerful ice-breaker, the egg-shaped, 5,000 ton cutter *Mackinaw* of the United States Coast Guard. The *Mackinaw*, with two propellers at her stern and one at her bow, was designed to break the thickest ice in the lakes and at the same time to tow the biggest lake freighters.

Her first task was a war task. Construction was finished in mid-winter on the cargo ships at Duluth harbor. Though the northern straits were locked in ice, those ships were needed at Atlantic ports to load war cargo. The *Mackinaw* battered and crunched her way up the ice-sealed St. Marys River and, for the first time in the history of the Soo Canal, the locks were opened in the month of January and the three ocean-bound freighters, *Pemiscott, Hidalgo* and *William L. Nelson,* passed through. Then, with the powerful *Mackinaw* shattering a path through solid blue ice, the three ships steered down the winding, wilderness-framed channel of the St. Marys. Past Sugar Island they went with Chippewas peering out from tar-paper huts in the snowy woods, through Neebish Channel where Finnish farmers were cutting firewood at the edge of their snowy pastures, past Lime Island, white and silent. The St. Marys River is the only place in the world where a farmer hauling cordwood can be run down by a steamship—all winter the river is a hard, white road for teamsters and truckmen. As the *Mackinaw* sheared through the ice, a truck on the way from the Canadian to the American shore was marooned by the seventy-foot channel that the cutter cleft in the solid ice. The driver switched off his engine and lit his pipe, while the three cargo ships, trailing black smoke over the ice-white straits, churned past —that narrow channel would soon be hard again and his road mended.

The fleet filed on, over the silent plain of Hay Lake and around Point Detour with its lifeless light-tower marking the ice-sealed reef. West of Mackinac Island lay a ragged field of windrowed ice and the Mackinac Strait was locked in ice that could carry a train. But the *Mackinaw* was made for such a passage. Sucking out water with her forward propeller and shattering the shelf-ice with her weighted bow, she lunged on. Fifteen miles west of Beaver Island, on the ninth of January, she cracked through to open water. Then the cargo ships diminished over the cold blue seaway of Lake Michigan.

Thirty hours later they passed through the Outer Drive Bridge with the vast façade of Chicago lifting against the winter sky. Their masts and deckhouses had already been taken down to clear the fixed bridges on the inland waterway. In the black waters of the Chicago River, while a snowstorm whitened their decks, pontoons were fixed to the ships' sterns so that they could navigate the nine-foot channel of the Illinois River. Then their whistles echoed among the steel cliffs of Chicago and their smoke drifted up the lofty walls. The next day they were steaming through the snowy flats of Illinois, with the Mississippi before them. Five more days brought the languorous air of Louisiana and the sunlight flashing on the Gulf. Then the ships that had left ice-locked Superior were on their way to the long supply routes of a world-wide war. They had passed from freshwater to the sea by the route Marquette had dreamed of three centuries ago in the swamps of Illinois.

Some of the western canals are obliterated and all but forgotten, but the urge to open new ways for transport still lives in the minds of Middle-Western men. Now a new canal project, as bold as any of the past, traces a water route between Lake Erie and Lake Michigan, across northern Indiana. Already hearings have been conducted by the U. S. engineers' offices in Toledo and Chicago, and surveys have been called for by way of Maumee, Ohio, and Fort Wayne, Indiana, "or any other practicable route." Soon the project will be ready for debate in Congress. Perhaps in the years ahead a waterway will lead straight west from Lake Erie to the smoke-stained skies of Gary and South Chicago.

XIX

The Open Road

BETWEEN SPRINGFIELD, Illinois, and the graceful old prairie
town of Jacksonville, on U. S. 36, is a two-mile stretch
of highway containing sixty-three different kinds of paving surfaces. It is a road of many colors—red, black, brown, gray and
cement white. It contains brick, stone, gravel, tar, asphalt in many
combinations. Each year those sixty-three segments of surface are
minutely studied for evidence of weathering and wear. The Bates
experimental road is evidence of the science of roadbuilding in a
region that, from the beginning, has launched its commerce on
wheels. It is a culmination of experience that began with the first
road in the Northwest Territory, a hundred and fifty years ago.

Ebenezer Zane was in the Ohio country before the Revolutionary War. He knew the ways through the deep Muskingum
woods and he got along with the Indians. In 1796, he was authorized by Congress to build a road from the Ohio River opposite
Wheeling, West Virginia, to the Ohio River opposite Maysville,
Kentucky—a road that would cut the southwestern corner of Ohio
and provide communication in the interior. In two years, Zane's
Trace was completed, over a dogleg course due west from Wheeling to Zanesville and then southwest through the old towns of
Lancaster and Chillicothe to Aberdeen, on the banks of the Ohio.
It was a rough and narrow road walled in forest. None of the
sixty-three varieties of modern paving surfaced it. The trace was
the raw forest floor, ribbed with the roots of giant ash and hack-
berry trees.

In autumn it was carpeted with red and golden maple leaves,
in winter it was paved with rigid ice. In spring it was not paved
or carpeted at all. It was bottomless with mud and frighteningly

rutted by the heavy wheels of traffic—one traveler spoke of ruts deep enough to bury a horse. In summer it was velvety with dust and every wagon stirred up slow smoke that hazed the windless air. But in every season strings of pack horses plodded through the Ohio woods and wagons lurched over roots and boulders and splashed through bogs and streams. To hundreds of families, lonely and remote in the wild country, Zane's Trace was a great highway. For a time it was the only road in the whole Northwest.

But a longer, wider, smoother and more luring road was to follow—leading straight as a rifle bullet to the West halfway between the lakes and the river. To multitudes of Middle-Westerners in the second quarter of the last century, the National Road was the course of opportunity and of the future.

The National Road began on the headwaters of the Potomac at Cumberland, Maryland, and led over the mountains to Wheeling on the Ohio River. It was truly a national road—though early called the Cumberland Road—as it was authorized by Congress, paid for by the Federal Treasury, and built under supervision of the War Department. The road was begun in 1811, was completed to Wheeling in 1818, and there was immediate anticipation of its extension into the western country. It was seven years, however, before legislative enactments and engineering surveys made way for the next stage of construction.

July fourth, 1825, was a memorable day for transportation in America. On that day, at the very hour when the governor of Ohio and the governor of New York broke the ceremonious first spadefuls of earth for the Ohio Canal at Licking Summit, a similar ceremony took place before the tall-spired Belmont County courthouse at St. Clairsville, Ohio. From St. Clairsville, road construction was pushed both east and west. To the east the National Road followed the course of Zane's Trace. But the new road was no gash through the forest. Eighty feet wide, its cleared and graded way ran straight across country. Its traffic lane was surfaced with successive three-inch layers of broken stone. Massive stone bridges spanned the streams, and culverts carried the road over ravines and ditches. It was a highway built to outlast its builders, and today the streaming traffic over U. S. 40 uses the roadbed graded by gangs who carried the first open road into the West.

Across Ohio the construction went and eventually across Indiana and Illinois to its terminus on the Mississippi, opposite St. Louis. A clamor of construction crept, year by year, across the middle land. First went the chain and compass men, leaving a trail of boundary and grading stakes behind them. Then came the burly men with grubbing hoes and double-bitted axes. Within sound of their thudding blades came swampers who trimmed fallen trees, dragged out logs, uprooted stumps and burned vast mounds of brush and slashing. Then teamsters' voices roared, mules strained, scoops bit into trampled ground and drags began to iron out a broad traffic lane. Behind them lay a graded roadbed, ditched and leveled and mounded slightly at the center. Behind the grading gangs came the surface crews with shovels and wheelbarrows and wagon trains of broken stone. They left a solid road ready for traffic. But the rivers were not yet bridged or the ravines spanned. One last troop of workmen came—skilled stonemasons who built the famous S-shaped bridges (legend says to slow runaway horses) and the solid culverts. As a finishing touch, they set the mile-stone markers at the roadside—where some of them remain today.

From the Ohio River this broad new highway followed the old narrow path of Zane's Trace west through Cambridge and Zanesville, where it crossed the singular and surprising Y bridge—"Go to the middle of the bridge and turn right"—over the Muskingum. Beyond Zanesville it ran west for a hundred miles without so much as a jog, except in Columbus where it crossed on High Street from Main Street to West Broad. This kink in the straight highway represented a compromise between the north and south sides of Columbus, each of which wanted to contain the new pike. As a result, the National Road passed the Ohio capitol and turned the corner of Broad and High streets, which is still a transportation axis of the Mid-West. On that windy corner, where now moves the heaviest stream of transcontinental motor traffic, there passed, when a forest darkened the capitol grounds and foxes lurked on the site of the Deschler-Wallick Hotel, the most traveled trail of Indian days connecting Kentucky's hunting grounds with Lake Erie's fishing waters. To the Shawnees it was no less significant than a National Road—it was "Athiamoiwee," path of the armed ones. Painted parties followed it, for a deadlier business than hunting, to the dark and bloody ground of Kentucky.

The National Road reached Columbus in 1833. A busy life flowed over the completed portion, while crews carried construction on, straight west, to Springfield and the Indiana line. The pike was completed across Ohio in 1840.

Indianapolis was the center of operations in Indiana. From the Hoosier City the road was built both eastward and westward across the state. Laborers worked from daylight to dark for 50 cents a day. A yoke of oxen was worth 45 cents a day, and a single horse dragging a scoop bucket over the endless mounded roadbed earned 20 cents a day for its owner. The road became Indianapolis' main street. When it was carried across the state, in 1850, with a plank surface on which the freight teams pounded and the wagons rumbled, a busy and boisterous traffic rolled through the Hoosier capital.

From Indianapolis the road led west by south and crossed the Wabash at Terre Haute. From there it ran on across the Illinois grasslands, through Effingham and Vandalia, through pretty Looking Glass Prairie and the dusty coalmine town of Troy. At last it ended on the banks of the mile-wide Mississippi. Then, in the mid-century, travelers in the hurrying stagecoaches could travel the longest, straightest and smoothest road in America, from Washington to St. Louis, in 94 hours.

In the 1830s and '40s there streamed over the National Road a motley and restless traffic. Like the barges, keelboats and packets on the Ohio, there were big swaying freight wagons, light, fast-moving express carts—called Shake Guts by the drivers—and the stagecoaches that used a fresh relay of horses every dozen miles. There were farm wagons, market wagons, democrat wagons, buckboards, carts and buggies, besides droves of cattle, sheep and pigs that sometimes occupied the entire 80-foot roadway. A century ago the middle states were one of the great pork and wool producing areas of the world. Hill pastures between Columbus and Zanesville were dotted with tens of thousands of sheep and in the meadows of Indiana great herds of hogs and cattle browsed. In those years a farmer drove his animals to market on the hoof and stagecoach drivers often had to make their way through a milling stream of livestock.

The Conestoga wagon, already grown famous on the roads of Pennsylvania, became the great freight carrier of the middle states. Loads of 8,000 or even 10,000 pounds were lashed under its canopy of towcloth and hauled by powerful six-horse teams. For those heavy loads, the wagoners used massive harness with leather back-bands 10 inches wide and traces of iron chain—it took a strong man to throw that gear over a horse's back. Brass bells jangled from the harness hames, and the wagon's red wheels, blue sideboards and white canopy made it a kind of moving bunting on the road. In the deep wagonbeds, rounded at the ends to keep the load from shifting, passed the boxed, baled and barreled commerce of the inland country.

The wagoners were a breed of robust, hardy, jovial men. Usually they devoted their lives to the freighting trade. They knew all there was to know about horses, roadbeds and tavern keepers. Unlike the coach drivers who traveled back and forth over a local segment of highway, the wagoners followed the road for hundreds of miles. They knew the hills and the plains, the populous sections and the empty country. They were weeks away from their home station, like seamen on a voyage. Their business set them apart from other travelers on the road. They wore a garb of their own—blue denim trousers and blue flannel hunting shirts trimmed in red. They spoke a language full of terms of horses, harness gear and wagon houses. They did not mingle with other travelers but put up at freighters' inns with spacious wagonyards and stables.

All day the teamster was alone, swaying on his high seat, watch-

ing his horses on the grades and gazing over the wide-flung country when the way was level and straight. All day he heard the plod
of hoofs and had the horizon to ponder. At night he wanted other
company. So it was good, as dusk was thickening, to see a wagon-
yard already half-filled with freighters, to hear horses stamping in
long stables, and to smell pork and cornbread where yellow candle-
light showed the landlord's kitchen. In every gathering of wagoners old friends met with gusty greetings. They ate vast meals at a
long table and drank straight whisky from pewter mugs. Certain
old wagoners carried a fiddle with them, tied up in a feedbag
under the seat, and after supper there would be music around the
barrel stove and a stamping of feet. There were tales to tell and
another drink of hot rum or hot whisky on a cold night. Then the
wagoners rolled out their blankets on the floor and slept till daylight.

It was a rough and roving life, back and forth on the great road
through the restless country. It must have had a spell, for wagoners
rarely tried another trade. Past them unrolled a panorama of
change and opportunity—land being settled, towns springing up
and cities growing. But these were not enough to tempt them from
the driver's seat, with the hoofs pounding and a brassy music
shaking from the horses' hickory hames. Like old seamen, they
kept to their craft. When their days were over, they settled down
somewhere on the highway. They sat on the doorstep and waved
to the wagons going past. When their gray heads nodded and they
napped in the sun, their dreams must have been of great loads
lumbering and the long straight road before them.

Freight wagons rumbled behind plodding teams, but stagecoaches rattled to a staccato beat of hooves. Thousands of travelers
—merchants, land speculators, politicians, preachers, immigrants
and their families—saw the flying landscape from the windows of
the western stages.

The stagecoach had evolved new lines and new dimensions, like
the boats on the Ohio, by the time it reached the level pike of the
Middle-West. The old Cumberland coach, originally used in Mary-

land, was a big, sturdy, square-built vehicle with space for sixteen passengers. But it was heavy to haul and hard to handle on steep roads and it proved too cumbersome for general use. It was replaced by the lighter, egg-shaped models—the Trenton coach and the Troy coach. The Trojan models, made at Troy, New York, became exceedingly popular. By 1850, five thousand of them were on the roads of North America, from Yucatan to Nova Scotia. Hundreds were used in the old Northwest. Painted deep red and lined inside with red morocco, they were a bright fleck of color in the dusty commerce of the early roads. They cost a thousand dollars each, and many of them earned their cost many times over. On the National Road they were advertised as "Trojan Carriages."

More famous still was the historic Concord coach, first built at Concord, New Hampshire, by Lewis Downing, in 1826. In the following decades the Abbott, Downing Company built many thousands of coaches and sent them into service in every part of the United States. They were soundly and compactly built, stripped of all excess weight but fitted out with elegance. Beside the old Cumberland coach they were trim, jaunty and somehow spirited— like a Morgan horse beside a Percheron. To the bullwhackers and freighters, the Conestoga wagon was an exalted vehicle. To stage-drivers nothing on wheels could compare with a shiny Concord coach. They praised its lines and its balance as a yachtsman praises the sheer and cutwater of his craft. Concords were built in various sizes, with a capacity of from four to sixteen passengers, but the lines of the structure were basically the same. All were fitted with the same specifications, including mudboxes, sandboxes, leather curtains, brakes, fluid lamps, side candle lights and boot and bag footboards.

There was an excitement about stage coach travel like that of the steamboats. On his high seat the driver sat like a captain, the horses were well matched, the harness was always freshly oiled and its metal fittings polished. A brass horn was part of the driver's equipment and its long high note announced arrival and departure. Coaches were individualized by distinctive names and decorations.

Many names were romantic in the fashion popularized by Godey's Lady's Book—over the National Road raced the "Lady of the Lake," "Gentle Annie," "Rosa Lee," "Sultana," "Loch Lomond," "Queen Victoria," "Pocahontas," "Highlander," along with coaches bearing more robust and western names, "Rough and Ready," "Enterprise" and "Henry Clay." On the square panel of the door were brightly painted pictures, often bearing such titles as "Pleasant Journey" and "Won't You Come Along?" A favorite decoration showed a large, black Newfoundland dog standing guard over the safety of the travelers. Standard colors for Concord coaches were canary yellow on wheels and under-carriage and a bright red body.

In the 1840s keen rivalry developed among the stage lines. The National Road Stage Line was the aristocrat, but it felt a growing competition from the Good Intent Line. Then the strong new firm of Neil, Moore and Company, with headquarters at Columbus, established lines that webbed the state of Ohio and fed their growing business on the National Road. Other lines flourished while the railroads were building—the Citizens' Line, the People's, the Pioneer, and the Defiance.

The Good Intent Line was organized by an ardent temperance man, General N. P. Talmadge. He ran his coaches as a "temperance" line, requiring all his agents and drivers to take the pledge, and urging his travelers, by placards in his offices, to abstain from alcoholic drink. The general often traveled his line, making temperance speeches along the way. At busy places he had a quartet of drivers to attract business by singing the song of the Good Intent Line:

> *Our horses are true and coaches fine,*
> *No upsets or runaways,*
> *Nor drunken drivers to swear or curse;*
> *We take cold water all our days.*
> *For our agents and drivers*
> *Are fully bent*

To go for cold water
On line Good Intent;
So, go it, my hearties—
Cold water for me.

Whether or not it was the abstemious drivers who brought the trade, the Good Intent carried a good share of the business. General Talmadge supplied his line with fine horseflesh and new rolling stock, and he kept on schedule.

In general, the stage drivers were jovial, jaunty and weatherbeaten. Many were widely known for story-telling or for fine singing voices with which they entertained their passengers. All were wonderfully wary and skillful horsemen. They were a kind of loose fraternity of men, meeting frequently, exchanging bugle blasts as they passed on the way, sharing fortunes of the road. Among Ohio drivers were the Smith brothers from Guernsey County—they could almost staff a stage line by themselves. There were "Nat Smith, Sam Smith, Jim Smith, Bate Smith, Joe Smith, Quil Smith, Bill Smith, and more of the Smith family." They all sounded their horns and went flying past the carts and carryalls and wagons on the road to Columbus. Other widely known drivers were Sam and Jake Crouse, Sam and Tom Kirk, Andy Caster, Wash Crawford, Henry Hight and Ross Briggs. Paris Eaches was a driver with a clear baritone voice and a fondness for the ballad, "When I Left Alabama," which he sang for hours at a time to the beat of the horses' hoofs and generally to the satisfaction of his passengers. The drivers were very popular with travelers, and they were idols of the children in every town and village on the National Road.

One dissenting voice was that of Charles Dickens, who had little good to say about any aspect of interior America. Traveling the stageroads of Ohio and Indiana, he found the inns dull and silent, the tea and coffee bad, the water worse and brandy not obtainable at the frequent "temperance" hotels. At one time he expressed a kind of enthusiasm at seeing a speeding mail coach with twelve passengers inside and a rocking chair and dining table on top. But he repeatedly complained that the drivers were taciturn and sullen, that the coaches were dirty and the drivers seemed always chewing, spitting, and blowing their noses with their fingers. With evident relish he reported finding on an Ohio River steamboat a fellow passenger with his head bound up for a wound received when a stagecoach had overturned.

But in general, the traveling public found the stage drivers cheerful and hearty, kind to their horses and attentive to passengers, and highest admiration was given them for the skill with which they got their coaches past bogs and mudholes and through herds of cattle, pigs and sheep. In Indiana, the National Road carried a heavy traffic before it was finished with plank surface, and both nerve and skill were demanded of drivers who raced their coaches over a rutted earth in which lurked vicious roots and boulders. Near Blue River bears came out of the woods to wallow in mudholes in the highway. In those years a driver had to keep a sharp eye on the road and a firm hand on the reins.

There were famous taverns where the coaches made overnight stops along the pike. Despite Dickens' complaints, travelers generally praised the hospitality of the landlord and the cheerful atmosphere of the inns. Some of them were known the length of the National Road—the American House at Columbus, Billy Werden's Tavern at Springfield, Ohio, the Starr Tavern at Richmond, Indiana, the Palmer House at Indianapolis and the Prairie House at Terre Haute. The old Neil House at Columbus, once a popular coaching inn and headquarters of Neil, Moore and Company's line, is now replaced by the modern hotel of that name, but twenty miles west of Columbus, at the crossroads of Lafayette, there still stands on U. S. 40 the Red Brick Tavern, which was a noted inn of stagecoach days.

Apparently great enthusiasm prevailed for billiards in the roadside inns. Establishments that lacked all other luxuries were equipped with billiard tables for their patrons' amusement after supper. Without exception, tavern larders were well stocked and after a long day on the road, travelers found the food plentiful and satisfying. They ate "family style," at a long table with dishes passing from hand to hand. So there was some advantage to the traveler whose landlord assured him of "a good position in the first rush for a chance at the head of the table."

Often a blacksmith shop was located near the inn. While refreshing themselves in the taproom travelers could hear the anvil clanging and they would know that the four-horse team of blacks or grays or chestnuts would be sharply shod when the driver's horn sounded departure.

For a few months, in 1836-7, a daily Pony Express Line traveled the pike. It was established by Postmaster General Amos Kendall for carrying urgent and valuable mails. Like the later Pony Express of the western plains and mountains, it was a relay of riders making five-mile dashes with mail bags attached to their saddles. When the rider raced into a relay station, his new mount was ready. With quick, sure hands the saddle was transferred, wet and warm, from a heavily breathing horse to a fresh, impatient one. Straps were pulled tight, the rider leaped astride, and the clatter of hoofs faded on the road. It seemed a breathless speed in the days before the mail trains. But its cost so far outran its revenue that the Pony Express was soon abandoned.

The pony express rider was the only traveler who could pass the tollgates without stopping. All the rest—farmers, wagoners, peddlers, drovers, coachmen—pulled up at the tollgates. Weight of wagon-loads was estimated and herds of cattle, hogs and sheep were counted before they could pass through. Tolls were charged in proportion to the wear caused to the road—a coach and four-horse team paid 20 cents, wagons paid 10 to 30 cents, a horse and rider were charged a nickel, cows could pass the gate for 1 cent each, hogs 5 for a cent. At first, tollgates barred the road every twenty miles. Later the intervals were shortened to ten miles, with a tollman's cottage beside each barrier. In Ohio, the peak year of 1839 brought a toll revenue on the National Road of $62,000. It was used to keep the road in repair.

Freight and passenger traffic was a two-way trade, but one traffic moved west only and never came back. Thousands of immigrants traveled the pike, some on foot, some on horseback, some in carts and gigs and towcloth-hooded wagons. A few of them put up for the night at inns, but many had no money for that comfort. They pulled up at evening on the wide shoulder of the road, made their campfire and picketed their animals in the grass. At a few places there were immigrant houses, affording cooking and sleeping quarters for persons who brought their own food and would spread their blankets on the floor. In the course of a single season, a medley of many tongues sounded in those rooms—German and Irish, Swedish and Italian, thin Yankee speech and soft Virginian. Whatever the language, the words of westward-faring people were much the same—good land, good crops, water, wood and meadow within the border stakes, a log house at first but eventually a brick one.

The tide of travel quickly rose and then even more quickly it ebbed away. By 1850, the locomotive whistle was as familiar as the coachman's horn, and more important. Early railroads in the middle states ran north and south, like the canals, but soon those tracks were crossed with new and longer-reaching lines, ready to carry the east-west flow of trade. As the racing engine and the rumbling cars took life from the rivers and canals, so they took the traffic from the pike. By 1860, the importance of the National Road had ended. What was left was memory of the motley traffic of the urgent years and the old milestones with the rank grass growing up around them. Then there was a looking back—as Mark Twain looked back at *Old Times on the Mississippi,* at the years when its tide of life ran high. One of the ardent, artless books about America is Thomas B. Searight's *The Old Pike.* It is a loving, lavish, not always accurate record, which calls the roll of all the old wagoners, stage drivers, tavern keepers and even the loafers along the way. It sees the National Road as a course of history and a bond of union, linking the seaboard with the Mississippi in the years of the nation's youth.

Searight wrote the road's epitaph, but in the twentieth century
it came to life again. As U. S. 40, the old National Road is now a
part of the most important motor route across the continent. Big
red trucks, swift blue busses, glinting motor cars, repeat the life it
had when the road was new. Its location, a century ago, served
the opening of empty areas. Now it serves one of the most populous and productive regions in the world. Beneath it a pipeline carries oil from the Illinois fields to eastern refineries and above it, in
the blue Mid-Western sky, silver planes fly the transcontinental air
route. Its milestones now are the flashing airway beacons at their
ten-mile intervals. In the prairie night, with a green star and a red
star on wingtips, an airliner soars above the long straight road that
once sounded with the pounding of horses' hoofs and the rumble
of iron-shod wheels.

But memory is not entirely gone. Now there are twelve memorial
monuments along the 700-mile route between the Potomac and
the Mississippi. The best known and most expressive is the "Ma-
donna of the Trail," which stands before the old Illinois state house
in the time-worn town of Vandalia. Beside the hurrying modern
traffic of U. S. 40, it shows a pioneer woman, with a child clinging
to her skirts and an infant in her arms, facing the West and the
future.

XX

Engine, Engine, Number Nine

AN AWKWARD PROBLEM for the early railroads was to get the locomotive to the track. A canal boat or a river barge could be built at the water's edge, but locomotives were built in eastern foundries hundreds of miles from the first little segments of railroad beyond the mountains. Western railroads began with "stub" lines making a short haul from a lake or river port. But first, there was the matter of transporting rolling stock to the waiting rails. Even the dwarf locomotives of a century ago could not be freighted in a Conestoga wagon, and they could not deliver themselves— though that was tried in Illinois when an engine was mounted on broad wooden wheels and run across country till it struck a bog and stayed there. Just one way remained—the western locomotives all arrived at the railheads on a vessel's deck. Twenty years later they had put the steamboats out of business.

The first locomotive in the West was "No. 80," which puffed a cloud of smoke and pulled the original one-car train on the pioneer railroad from Toledo. "No. 80" arrived at the Toledo docks on the deck of a Lake Erie schooner. When the first railroad entered Chicago in 1848 (it came from the west), the famous locomotive "Pioneer" arrived in the Chicago River lashed to a schooner's foredeck. Nine years later the storied old "Sebastopol," the first locomotive on the iron-bearing shores of Lake Superior, was landed at Marquette from the brig "Columbia." It happened again and again, at all the early railheads. Sometimes a locomotive's headlamp lighted the way over tossing water for a ship to gain the harbor entrance and find her berth.

The first railroad beyond the Alleghenies was the Erie and Kalamazoo. In 1836, it was completed from Toledo to the market town of Adrian, in Michigan Territory, a distance of thirty-three miles.

Its first cars were drawn by horsepower on oak rails. But soon the wooden rails were capped with a strip of strapiron and, in 1837, steam locomotion was provided. In that year, when Michigan achieved statehood, old "No. 80" was brought from Philadelphia, by way of the Hudson River, the Erie Canal and Lake Erie, to serve the first railroad west of Schenectady and one of the earliest in the United States. It attained a speed of twenty miles an hour and was considered so dangerous that an act of Ohio law gave city councils the right to regulate the speed of trains within city limits to a minimum of four miles an hour.

The West was ardently concerned with transportation—its development can best be told in terms of river, lake, canal, highway and railroad commerce. So it is not surprising that the railroad won believers in the level inland country when its usefulness was still doubted in the seaboard states. The bold innovation of the Erie and Kalamazoo in a region that had not yet attained statehood stimulated railroad building at other points from Lake Erie and Lake Michigan. In 1836, one year after its incorporation, the village of Milwaukee sought rail connection with the Mississippi. Despite financial panic, a railroad survey was begun in 1837. Twenty-four railroads were chartered in Ohio before 1840, with a route projected in every portion of the state. It is easier to plot a railroad on paper than to lay the track and get the trains in motion, and of the twenty-four chartered roads only one was actually constructed. But others were projected and some were realized. Soon Ohio was the leading railroad state in the country.

Sandusky, on Lake Erie, eyed the pioneer railroad out of Toledo with understandable jealousy, as Toledo already had a canal leading inland and Sandusky had only the rutted wagonroads of Erie and Huron counties. Soon Sandusky business men proposed a railroad all the way from Lake Erie to the Ohio River. While "No. 80" and its companion, "Adrian No. 1," were still novel sights, puffing into Toledo with their single open cars, work began on the Sandusky lowlands. Surveyors laid out the right of way, grading crews built up the roadbeds and tracks were laid from Sandusky to Bellevue, a distance of sixteen miles. This was the first segment of the road projected to Springfield, Ohio, and was called the Mad River and Lake Erie Line. It was a major railroad project at that time, and "Mad River" bonds were talked about in Eastern business and financial circles. Ralph Waldo Emerson was one of its first investors. The initial run from Sandusky to Bellevue was made in 1839. The sixteen miles were covered in forty minutes, with cheering crowds at every crossroad.

The plan to link Lake Erie and the Ohio by rail required ten years to materialize. In 1842, a line was laid north from Cincinnati for fifteen miles, and a local service began on the Little Miami Railroad. The road was extended to Xenia, in 1845, and to Springfield, in 1848. In the same year the line from Sandusky triumphantly reached Springfield; then there was an unbroken rail route between the lake and the river. But as it turned out this road, like all the north-south railroads, lost money. The first bold railroadmen were not bold enough. They thought of railways as adjuncts to waterborne commerce and built their lines to connect water routes. When, a decade later, iron rails paralleled the lake shores and the rivers, in line with the dominant east-west commerce, the railroads grew rich and powerful.

In the 1840s another lake-to-river railroad was projected from Cleveland to Columbus and Cincinnati, a route which today carries some of the heaviest railroad tonnage in the world. In 1851, the northern half of the line was completed and a cannon boomed as the first train pulled out of Columbus for Cleveland. After its steady growth from lake and canal traffic, Cleveland was acutely conscious of the value of transportation routes. In 1851, with a population of 17,000, it had a railroad leading to the south and another, the Cleveland, Painesville and Ashtabula, operating eastward along the Erie shore. This was the beginning of a feverish period of railroad building. In 1850, Ohio had 300 miles of railroad in 1857, it had 3,000 miles, considerably more than any other state in the nation. Then the panic of 1857 put an end to construction and no new tracks were laid till after the Civil War. But already there were rails enough to paralyze the traffic on the canals and to imperil the passenger traffic on the lakes and the river. In 1870 began another period of expansion. By 1880, there were 6,000 miles of railroad within the state.

Michigan had grandiose railroad projects even before it achieved statehood. The graceful grain schooners and the stubby steamboats delivered goods and people on the waterfront at Detroit, and there was need of transport leading directly west. Canals were out of the question, as the principal rivers ran north and south, so railroad lines were drawn across the maps of empty country. In the 1830s, when the iron horse was still an unproved wonder, three parallel lines were projected across Michigan. One of these was pushed from Detroit to Kalamazoo in 1837. It passed into private hands and as the Michigan Central it was extended toward Chicago. This vigorous company saw the railroad as a competitor to water transport in handling east-west traffic.

The lake trade between Buffalo and Chicago was growing rapidly, and a logical cut-off from the loop up Lake Huron and down Lake Michigan was to run a railroad straight from Detroit to Chicago. Not content to lure traffic from the lake steamers, the Michigan Central went into the shipping business to feed its rail facilities. In 1848, it began a service on its own steamships from Buffalo to the western end of Lake Erie, where goods and passengers were transferred to west-bound trains. In 1849, they launched the two largest ships on the lakes, the *Atlantic* and the *Mayflower;* each accommodated six hundred passengers on a high-speed schedule of eighteen hours between Buffalo and Detroit. But these fine vessels had short lives.

On a foggy summer night in 1852, the palatial *Atlantic* with seven pennants on her staffs, was rammed by the steamer *Ogdensburg*. She carried half her five hundred passengers to the bottom of Lake Erie. Two years later another Lake Erie fog took the life of her sister ship. In the autumn of 1854, the *Mayflower* piled up on the fog-wrapped shores of Point Pelee Island, at the western end of the lake.

Despite their marine disasters, the Michigan Central men pushed their rails across Michigan and around the oval end of the lake. They were running a construction race with the Michigan Southern, from Toledo. Both roads were built to Chicago by swearing foremen and sweating crews. The last sections were graded and the last rails laid in almost a dead heat. But the Michigan Central won the race. While the final rails went down and the spikes were driven in, a panting engine waited to make the dash. So, on a fine spring day in 1852, the first train from the east, with its whistle shrilling, steamed into Chicago. A day later the first train arrived over the Michigan Southern.

These were not stub lines but important links in a long-range transportation system. As railroads came from the East—from Buffalo to Toledo by the Michigan Southern, and from Buffalo to Windsor, across river from Detroit, on the Great Western—an all-rail connection was completed between Chicago and New York. By 1855, passenger traffic on the lakes had passed its peak. Now it was by railroad that merchants and army men, tradesmen and speculators, westward-moving Yankees and European immigrants arrived in the states that border the Mississippi.

Trunk lines were in the north, between Chicago, Detroit and the Lake Erie cities, but railroads were also transforming the Ohio Valley. The old river town of Madison, Indiana, was larger than Indianapolis, until the Hoosier capital became "the Railroad City." In 1847, the first train ran over the Madison Line and it promptly put Indianapolis ahead of all the river and canal towns in Indiana. When other railroads radiated from Indianapolis to Chicago, St. Louis, Cincinnati and Detroit, the Indiana capital became the commercial as well as the political center of the state. For half a century Cincinnati had been the "Queen City" of the West. Until the Civil War, it was the largest city west of Philadelphia. From two hundred miles up the Valley, farmers floated their produce to the Cincinnati levee, and they returned home wide-eyed with the wonders of the city.

In November, 1836, Rotheus Hayward of Waterford, Ohio, on

the Muskingum, arrived at Cincinnati with a flatboat cargo of wheat, cheese and cider. When he had sold his goods he climbed the steep slant of Broadway to see the storied city. He was not disappointed. The great public market, he wrote, "was truly wonderful, the Market House being lined with all sorts of meats & the streets being strung on both sides with waggons loaded with fruits, vegetables, etc., of all kinds & sorts & 'tis said no Market in the world can equal Cincinnati for abundance and variety of its articles." A few years later a well informed British traveler, J. S. Buckingham, remarked that Cincinnati had more architectural beauty than any city of the same age on the surface of the globe.

Certainly no western city could match Cincinnati's great porkpacking plants, its brass and iron foundries, its spacious hotels—when the stately Burnet House was completed, in 1851, it was seriously described as "probably the best hotel, in its interior and domestic arrangements of any in the world." All these superlatives were the result of Cincinnati's commanding position on the Ohio. But when the railroads webbed the Mid West, it lost its advantage. In the 1850s canal trade dwindled and steamboats stood idle at the landings. After the Civil War, the Queen City was overshadowed by cities that had been only a huddle of huts or an army garrison a generation before. Long freight trains rumbled across the midlands, and cities along the forty-second parallel—Cleveland, Detroit, Chicago—were the new wonders of the West.

To the old Illinois state house at Vandalia, in 1837, went the famous "Long Nine"—nine Whig legislators all over six feet in height and averaging 200 pounds. They were big men—one of them was lean, long-striding young Abe Lincoln—and they had big plans for the development of the still-frontier state of Illinois. That year the Illinois Legislature appropriated twelve million dollars for the improvement of transportation. Prairie people could look a long distance. They had never traveled on a railroad or even seen a locomotive puffing woodsmoke at the sky, but they crisscrossed their state with projected railroad lines. Under the leadership of the Long Nine, the Legislature authorized, in 1837, when there was not fifty miles of completed railroad west of the Alleghenies, the building of 1,340 miles of railroad in Illinois. The plan called for a north and south line connecting two cities of the future (which never grew)—Cairo and Galena—and four east-west lines crossing the state at fifty-mile intervals. The first two of these were to be called the Northern Cross and the Southern Cross. Under the transportation program towns that did not get a railroad were to have a steamboat, through improvement of rivers and canals, and every remaining village in the state was to be provided with an improved highway. This was a typically western program, based on the sanguine reasoning that transportation routes would increase the value of land, the state would sell large tracts at a profit, foreign capital would be attracted to Illinois investments and could be taxed to pay interest on the debt—and so roads, railroads and canals would pay for their own construction.

Hardly was the ink dry on this Legislative act when the nation was swept by the cold wind of financial panic. One short spur of railroad was actually laid across the prairie. The other thirteen hundred miles remained on paper. In 1839, the state capital was removed to Springfield, another accomplishment of the Long Nine. In Vandalia they still tell how Abe Lincoln jumped out of a second-story window in the old state house to break a quorum that would have retained the capital at Vandalia twenty years longer.

Springfield was near the center of the state, in the rich corn country, and closer by seventy miles to the new commercial vigor of northern Illinois. Of the Long Nine's visionary program, the only railroad built by the state was a twenty-four-mile line from Meredosia, on the Illinois River, to Jacksonville. Under private enterprise this road was extended east to Springfield. It was called the Northern Cross Line and over it passed the first train in Illinois, drawn by a locomotive named "Rogers," in 1838. Though the road eventually became a part of the Chicago, Burlington and Quincy system, its first operation was a failure. Farmers protested that their cows were frightened dry by the "Rogers'" shrill whistle. To combat that menace, they stole the strapiron from the rails to make sled runners and wagon tires. At last "Rogers" was taken from the rails and run across country as a steam wagon. Its career ended in a bog.

Better fortunes awaited railroads in the north, where Chicago on the lake and Galena near the Mississippi sent a growing traffic onto the old Galena trail and the Chicago-Galena stage road. In the 1830s Galena, on the Fever River—a corruption of the French name *Fèbre,* for the wild bean vines that softened its steep banks— near its confluence with the Mississippi, was an older and busier town than Chicago and it had bright prospects of becoming the metropolis of the West. Its lead-veined valley had attracted thousands of miners, who pitted the fields and hillsides with their shallow shafts so that Galena had become the first center of settlement north of St. Louis. When a railroad was first projected, what is now West Chicago was called Galena Junction, in deference to the important town a hundred and fifty miles away. In January, 1836, the Galena and Chicago Union Railroad received its charter. The next year surveyors were busy laying out the right of way and marking the elevations of the roadbed. Then the panic came. For ten years nothing but a row of surveyors' stakes marked the empty prairie. That was the condition of the Galena and Chicago Union when two restless young men, William B. Ogden and John Young Scammon, took it over.

Eventually Ogden was to run a railroad all the epic way to the Pacific and to leave his name on the map of Utah. His first aim was to build ten miles of track into the Chicago prairies. With John Scammon he traveled the staked-out route in a democrat wagon, holding meetings at every village, knocking at farmhouse doors, selling railroad stock to persons who would eventually watch his trains go by. In the summer of 1838, surveyors were again marking out construction lines. By November, ten miles of track were ready. Then, in the last rough voyage of the season, the brig *Buffalo* arrived in the Chicago River with a deckload consisting of a stubby, high-stacked ten-ton locomotive and six small open freight cars. Ogden named the locomotive "Pioneer."

In those simple and sootless days, Chicagoans objected to a rail-road because it would scare cattle and soot the family wash. But after deliberation, the city officials gave permission for a route of temporary rails by which the "Pioneer" and its six boxcars could be launched onto the western run. Over the ten-mile road, with Chicago's first families seated on wooden benches in the open cars, it made its inaugural passage. For the return trip, Ogden had a line of farmers waiting to shovel grain into an empty car, so he brought both freight and passengers back to Chicago. This was the beginning of the 9,000-mile system of the Chicago and North-western Railway and the forerunner of the long grain and cattle trains that would stream into Chicago. The old "Pioneer," eating up cordwood in its firebox, clattered for years over the strapiron rails. Now it is on display, like a retired racehorse, in the Museum of Science and Industry in Chicago. Meanwhile, Ogden pushed his tracks on west to Elgin, and eventually to Galena. The pound of hoofs diminished on the Chicago-Galena road and travelers on the old Sucker Trail, from St. Louis to Wiota, Wisconsin, stared at the trains clattering across their highway. It was the old watching the new. William Ogden had persuaded those Illinois farmers to put their money in a good thing. By 1850, the Galena and Chicago Union was paying dividends of 20 per cent.

But Chicago was not yet a railroad city and railroad men were outnumbered by believers in improved highways and wagon traffic. Plank roads laid on the prairie, they declared, were cheaper, safer and more dependable than railroads, and at a rate of ten miles an hour, without stops to take on fuel wood for the locomotive, a wagon would rival the speed of a train. Further, wagons could be brought into every street of every town, to the door of every fac-tory, grain elevator, lumberyard and warehouse. So the highway men talked of a system of three hundred miles of plank road, radi-ating in six directions from Chicago. While the first trains chuffed in from Elgin, the road builders were scraping off a roadbed and laying a pavement of planks.

The Southwestern Plank Road pointed out over the grasslands

for sixteen level miles. Then came the Northwestern Plank Road with a branch running to the Des Plaines River. The Western Plank Road led to the western limit of Dupage County, and the Elgin and Genoa Plank Road boldly paralleled the railroad for a haul of twenty-eight miles. The Southern and Blue Island Plank Road reached out south of Chicago and the Lake Shore Plank Road was laid on the beaches of Lake Michigan. This roadbuilding went on into the early 1850s, while the railroads were bringing a growing commerce from east and west. The roads carried a lively traffic in farm produce, grain and livestock, but time quickly put its mark on them. The planks warped in sun and rain. Under heavy loads they snapped in two. Soon these were rough and broken roads, impassable for loaded wagons. Not until years later, when they were surfaced with modern paving, were the stubs of the old planking pulled out of the mud.

In 1850, the Federal Congress began granting tracts of land to railroad builders. This kind of subsidy made possible large-scale projects, and the dream of Stephen A. Douglas, of a railroad running the entire length of Illinois, could now be realized. Lured by a grant of 2,500,000 prairie acres, Robert Rantoul brought a group of Eastern capitalists to Chicago and organized the Illinois Central Railroad. This was railroading on a new scale—not a squad of men laying iron-capped rails on a dirt roadbed, but vast construction crews building up a ballasted bed to carry heavy trains on long-distance traffic. Thousands of iron rails, shipped from England by way of the Great Lakes and the Mississippi River, were unloaded on the wharves of Chicago and Cairo, terminals of the road. An army of laborers speaking German, Irish and Scandinavian went to work on the long right of way. By 1855 a hundred thousand men had pitched their camps on the prairie. Behind them the rails stretched taut to the horizon. That line of march was marked at intervals by newly platted towns, streets staked out in the blowing grass, sites of depots, grain elevators, business blocks, churches, schools and residences.

Robert Rantoul left his name on one of these unborn settlements.

It was still a dirt-road town sixty years later when my brothers and I flew our kites on the Rantoul prairie, sending them almost out of sight in the tall blue April sky. A few springs later the air-age found Rantoul. In 1917, the Army Air Corps built Chanute Field on those broad prairies. Now the big army bombers soar where our kites once hung in the wind.

In 1856, the Illinois Central was the longest railroad in America, with trains racing 366 miles between Chicago and the tip of the Illinois arrowhead at Cairo. It opened up thousands of prairie townships to cultivation and settlement. But Rantoul and his associates wanted something more. They wanted the lake front at Chicago, and they were shrewd and powerful enough to get it. During the middle 1850s a succession of acts of the Chicago City Council gave the railroad a right of way 300 feet wide, between Twelfth and Randolph streets on the lake front. With its branch lines, the Illinois Central now had 700 miles of track, all tributary to Chicago. Of the lake front, the special glory of Chicago, it made a switching yard. For fifty years it threw a cloud of soot, smoke and cinders over Michigan Avenue. Finally, in the twentieth century, the lines were electrified and the tracks lowered between cement ramparts. Now the clean lake air sweeps Michigan Avenue and the façade of the city, from Roosevelt Road to the river, stands clear against the sky.

In 1857, while the new railroad towns were dotting the map of Illinois, the Milwaukee and Mississippi Line reached across southern Wisconsin to Prairie du Chien. A year later, trains were operating out of La Crosse on the La Crosse and Milwaukee road. The Illinois Central had already reached the Mississippi at Dunlieth, just west of Galena. With railheads on the river, the railroad companies went into the steamboat business to feed their trains with traffic from the Mississippi. A rate war resulted, with the old-line steamboatmen resisting the inroads of the railway men. In 1860, after four years of mounting rivalry, the combined railway and steamer fare from Chicago to St. Paul dropped to fifty cents. Twelve years later, passengers could choose between two all-rail routes from Chicago to the Twin Cities, and the steamboats were left to rot at the landings.

By that time Chicago had become the greatest railroad center of the world, with a dozen systems bringing in grain, livestock and thousands of eager immigrants and settlers, and carrying away its pork, beef, lumber, leather and farm machinery. In those years a transcontinental traffic was just beginning. Men who remembered the crude little "Pioneer" pulling its string of open cars would live to see the mile-long freights bringing coal and grain, refrigerated California fruit and bawling Kansas cattle, and the vari-colored Limiteds—the "Century," "Golden Arrow," "Shenandoah," "Flamingo," "Portland Rose," "Challenger," "Chief"—arriving in the cavernous trainsheds from the three sea-rims of America.

In 1850, a hundred thousand cords of wood went up in smoke from the stacks of railroad engines. Ten years later, locomotives were burning coal and no longer was wood ricked up in fueling yards along the track. The new locomotives had a splendor of brass bells and balls and a jutting forepiece that in England was called a plough but in America became the "cow-catcher." They had names like today's streamliner. They were called "North Wind," "West Wind," "Golden Eagle," "Stag Hound," "Arab," "Antelope," "Whirlwind," "Samson," "Starlight," "Moonlight," "Reindeer." As the engines grew larger, stronger and faster, freight cars grew bigger and passenger coaches more commodious. It was a Chicago man who made the boldest innovations.

George M. Pullman came to Chicago from New York State in the spring of 1858. He found a hectic, clamorous city, for at that moment every business street in Chicago was being raised above the old level of the sand marshes and thousands of buildings were being hoisted flush with the newly elevated streets. That was a year of welter and commotion—as so many of Chicago's years have been —with its turbulent life going on amid the prodigious labor of raising a city out of a swamp.

One of the last buildings to remain on the old level was the Tremont House, a big, four-story, solid brick hotel. No contractor was bold enough to try lifting it out of the mud. Seeing that job waiting for him, George Pullman stood happy in the midst of Chicago's tumult. He had begun his career by moving houses out of the way of the Erie Canal. Now he went to the owners of the Tremont House, offering to raise their building without an hour's interruption of business and without cracking a pane of glass. With twelve hundred men, he concluded that job in seven weeks. Then George Pullman went out on other construction jobs in newly building western towns. While riding in the three-decked bunks of early sleeping cars, with an iron stove at one end of the car and a candle bracket shedding a dim, uncertain light, he thought of something that was to bring a new era in railroad travel.

In Chicago, he persuaded the officials of the Chicago and Alton Route to let him have two old daycoaches to experiment with. He fitted the cars with rows of upper and lower berths which folded into cushioned seats for day time travel. He provided them with washrooms and dressing rooms, and gave every berth its own illumination. Here was a new kind of traveler's comfort, but his cars were too expensive for the railroads to build. George Pullman charged that fiasco to experience and went to the Colorado gold mines. But the idea of a sleeping car followed him. Lying in the hard bunks of miners' cabins, he pictured a car of comfort, convenience and character, soothing weary travelers to sleep as the wheels clicked off the miles in darkness. Back in Chicago, with a miner's grubstake to use for capital, he built a "palace" car, frescoed, carpeted and upholstered, with sections of roomy seats that unfolded into soft, commodious beds. His model, like the first Chicago locomotive, he called the "Pioneer."

But again the railroadmen found his car too expensive. They also found it too high to pass under existing bridges and too wide to clear station platforms. The "Pioneer" in all its luxury lay idle on a Chicago siding. But at the end of the sorrowful month of April, 1865, the Lincoln funeral train arrived in Chicago after its solemn twelve-day journey from the East, and in Chicago Mrs. Lincoln collapsed from exhaustion. At that trying moment, with mingled shrewdness and generosity, George Pullman offered his palace car to take the President's widow home to Springfield. In a mood of anxiousness and sympathy, the railroad officials called out crews on every section of track. Station platforms were torn up and bridges cleared of underbraces to let the car pass through. The "Pioneer" carried Mrs. Lincoln to Springfield, and every newspaper in America described its comfort and dignity.

Now the railroads were ready to try Pullman cars. Each trial brought a demand for more. George Pullman enlarged his shops and turned out dining, parlor and sleeping cars. He couldn't keep up with the orders. He built new plants at Chicago, St. Louis, Detroit, Elmira and Wilmington, and Pullman cars were a part of the American railroad.

WHEREVER THE railroad went, it brought the future. It changed Chicago's destiny and it changed the destiny of thousands of other places great and small. Its presence built cities where there had been an empty crossroad, and its absence doomed settlements that had sprung up with expectant life. Countless towns were passed by when the shining rails were laid. For them the future was a slow decay. From Ohio to Wisconsin, by-passed villages were left without life, or with only the life of a generation waiting there to die. When they died the sun peeled the paint from their houses —the doors hung loose and sunset flared blankly in their windows. Orchards grew up to fennel and goldenrod, gardens went back to wild mustard, and around the rotting doorsteps rank grass tasseled.

At the same time, just over the horizon, a long whistle wavered and a train slowed into a busy town with an elevator shouldering the sky and cattle bawling from the stock pens and people streaming across the station platform as the engine panted past. The West was a land of trade and transport, of things and men in movement. By 1900, Illinois alone had twelve thousand miles of railroad and the dream of the Long Nine seemed trivial in retrospect. Then there was a web of railroads over the middle states with a windswept lakeshore city at its center, and in all the schoolyards children repeated a rhyme that no one could have made sense of a hundred years ago——

> *Engine, Engine, Number Nine,*
> *Running on Chicago Line.*

Part IV

FOUR-THOUSAND-MILE SHORELINE

XXI

Ohio Harbors

WHEN THE NORTHWEST Territory was created, the United States had a new shoreline bordering four of the Great Lakes—longer than the Atlantic or Pacific coastlines of the country. Since then it has become as important in the national life as the ocean seaboards themselves. It is a shoreline that runs in all directions—from Buffalo west to Toledo, north to Mackinac, south to Chicago, north to Manistique, east to De Tour, then north and west again, with many bays and promontories, to Lake Superior's ultimate arrowhead at Duluth. Its four thousand miles present every kind of shore, from the shifting dunes of Lake Michigan to the granite cliffs of Superior, from the quiet beaches of Ohio to the rock-ribbed northern capes.

Geology made it a various coastline, and history has added a further variety—of orchards blooming beside Lake Michigan and cornfields tasseling along Lake Erie, of fishing villages on the northern coves and cities lifting above the lake fronts of Ohio and Illinois. It includes many strains of American settlement—pure New England towns like Painesville and Mentor on Lake Erie; Dutch settlements around Holland, Michigan; German towns and cities on the Wisconsin shore; Swedish and Finnish communities like Sven's Bluff on Green Bay and Finland on the wild north shore of Lake Superior, and Indian villages on a dozen northern coves and islands. When I boarded my first freighter on the red-stained docks of Ashtabula, the mate stared at my school sweater and spat over the chain rail. "Well," he said, "you stay with us a season and you'll learn more than they ever put in your geography books."

American travelers in Europe are urged to sail down the Rhine, with history passing like a panorama, or down the Danube, or through the linked lakes of Sweden by the storied Göta Canal. As far as I know, European travelers in America are never urged to tour the Great Lakes, but there is no better way of seeing the heartland of America. To make the journey is to see the present in all its variety, to be reminded at many places of the American past, and often to feel a strong sense of the future. St. Ignace and Mackinac, with the white cloud of gulls over their beaches, have not changed essentially since the Indians came across the radiant water in canoes piled with beaver skins. Gary and River Rouge wear a dark cloud of smoke, and in the night their blast furnaces glare where Indian campfires gleamed on the shore. The four lakes begin and end in cities, but on the long, intricate shores between them are almost every aspect of American life and landscape.

A port is best approached by water. London, Copenhagen, Stockholm, Naples—by ship you see their outlines growing; you have a sweeping impression which grows into sharpness and detail; with space and light around you draw near and are encircled by their life. It is that way with Buffalo, Cleveland, Toledo, Detroit, Chicago, Milwaukee, Duluth—all inland cities with a sea beside them.

From the narrowing point of Lake Erie, Buffalo rises beyond the enormous walls of its grain elevators. It spreads north along the lake and east along the historic route of the canal, and down by the harbor front it lifts upward in solid masses and tapering towers. Inside the breakwater, the overnight boats from Cleveland and Detroit nose to their berths, past the long freighters just down from Superior with 15,000 tons of iron ore. Canal barges nudge through the basin, between oil tankers, towboats and dredging scows. Over the harbor come short little tugboat blasts and the roar of departing freighters. At night, a fresh wind fans the basin. Long, dark freighters slip out between the winking harbor piers and lighted liners carry radiance with them. Beyond the breakwater, the engine pulse grows deeper and the curling water rushes past the ship's bow. It is a long way from tidewater, but behind you the lights are blinking from the harbor entrance, under your feet the deck is lifting, and a sea-fresh wind is on your face. You think then of a restless snatch of Kipling:

> *And out at sea, behold the dock lights die,*
> *And meet my mate, the wind that tramps. the world.*

Here it is an inland wind, but it blows sea-keen over 1,000 miles of water.

There are two lanes of traffic along the Erie shore. Both have been traveled from the early life of the Northwest. One is a water lane, followed by freighters, tankers, excursion boats, within sight of the level Ohio shoreline and the hovering smoke of its cities. The other is U. S. 20, sometimes skirting the sandy beaches and the pale wide water, sometimes curving inland between the farms and orchards of a fertile shore. It carries a never ceasing motor traffic, of goods and people, on one of the busiest crosscountry routes of the nation.

The shore of Lake Erie is the straightest and most featureless of all the lakes. From Buffalo to Cleveland, for two hundred miles, it is laid off on the map as though drawn with a ruler. Not till you reach its western end, at Cedar Point and Sandusky, is there a natural harbor. But there are river mouths, larger now than nature made them, with deep channels leading from the lake. Breakwaters make a harbor entrance and long docks line the inlets. Here the land and water routes come together, the highway threading the cities and the shipping lanes branching in from open water. On Lake Erie every fissure in the long straight shore became a shipping port.

Conneaut had not a river, but only a creek. It was a lonely place, ragged in foxgrass, with no sound but the slurred note of blackbirds flying among the reeds, when the first surveying party of the Connecticut Land Company stopped there a century and a half ago. That was the beginning of history for the empty Erie shore. For the Connecticut Land Company owned three million acres extending for 120 miles along the shoreline west of Pennsylvania's

boundary. In 1796, General Moses Cleaveland brought fifty surveyors to make a blueprint of the lifeless country. They were the
Mayflower party of the Western Reserve—all the beginnings go
back to them. At the mouth of Conneaut Creek they made a camp
and then moved on, leaving the place unmarked except by a circle
of charred embers. But within five years a settlement began there
and soon the Lake Erie schooners found the sheltered inlet. So a
trade began, in barreled fish and flour. Today, mile-long cement
docks berth the 600-foot ore ships, and humped up on the creek
bank are black hills of Pennsylvania coal and red ranges of iron
ore from the yawning pits of Minnesota. Conneaut has become the
second iron-ore port in America, with a traffic that dwarfs the
trade of many famous seaports of the world.

Ashtabula—accented like Cincinnati—is one of the native Wyandot words that maintained themselves despite the import of Connecticut names throughout the Western Reserve. For a brief time
it had another name. When the surveyors camped at the river
mouth, Moses Cleaveland broke out two casks of wine and asked
his men to celebrate the christening of Mary Esther River, named
for his daughter back in a quiet village in Connecticut. But the
party moved on, and the old, uncouth name remained. It meant
"place of many fish," and the winding gorge of the Ashtabula
River was still a fishing ground for the Indians when the surveyors tramped west along the shore. Now there are fishing boats
putt-putting around the breakwater, but Ashtabula is famous for
its coal and ore trade. With two railheads bringing acres of coal-
cars to the switching yards and electric scoops emptying the cavernous holds of freighters, it is a place where tugboats churn under
the bows of long, deep-laden ships.

Ashtabula Harbor, clustered on hilly ground between the curving river and the straight lakeshore, is one of the most marine
settlements on the lakes. Its stores are filled with seamen's goods
—boots, burlap, dungarees, lanterns, lanyards and marlin spikes.
On its corners loiter fishermen, deckhands, coal passers, and marine
firemen. The smoke of commerce blows over its steep streets and

deep whistles sound night and day. Ashtabula began as a New England settlement, but it filled up with Germans, Swedes and Finns.

The level shore, with its deep and fertile land once overlaid by Lake Erie's waters, has become a famous nursery and vineyard region. Thousands of acres around the graceful town of Painesville are bright with many-colored flowers, and other thousands of acres are ranked with vineyards which flourish in the lake-tempered air. In the farmyards, century-old elms arch above the dignified Western Reserve houses with their recessed entries and their strong corner timbers outlining the clapboard walls.

Moses Cleaveland and his men did not linger here, but other Connecticut Yankees followed them early in the last century and planted the lakeshore towns. Now the region has a serene and smiling beauty that even tourists racing over U. S. 20 remember as one of the precious aspects of America.

This part of the Erie shore pays respect to an ancient Greek of Alexandria. The town of Euclid was settled in in 1798 and named in a mathematical mood by the surveyors in Cleaveland's expedition. Later the geometer's name was given to the road which connected Euclid and the neighboring village of Cleaveland. Now Euclid is a busy metropolitan suburb and Euclid Avenue is one of the famous streets of America, with a variety of memories behind it. Once it was a game trace trampled by files of buffalo; the Indians used it as a part of the Lake Trail, and in the eighteenth century, traders found it ready for their pack-horse traffic from Fort Pitt to Detroit. With the settlement of the Reserve, it was gashed with wagon wheels and rutted with travel. As commerce grew, the dirt roadbed was surfaced with planking, and over it heavy movers' wagons rumbled steadily to the West. Finally, it became a paved highway and as part of U. S. 20 it carries transcontinental motorists on the old historic way. In the plush nineties Euclid Avenue was framed by the estates of Rockefeller, Huntington, Hanna and other industrialists of the Gilded Age. For thirty years the landscaped grounds and ornate mansions

made it one of the stately avenues of America. Now the Rockefeller mansion is replaced by a filling station and Euclid Avenue
is a turbulent city street with a few once-splendid residences serving as business schools, boarding houses and neon-lighted night
clubs.

Cuyahoga might have been the name of Cleveland, but this time
the Indian name clung to the river only. It means "crooked river,"
and no river anywhere makes more tortuous bends and turns than
those around which the long lake ships grope with their cargoes
for Cleveland's mills. The river lies in a broad gorge, eighty feet
below the level of the wide-spreading city. High-level bridges stride
across the basin where the river writhes amid a tangle of railroad
tracks, unloading docks, millyards, power plants, oil tanks and
elevators. This is the pounding heart of Cleveland, hazed in smoke
and shrill with industry. It would be a strange spectacle to its
founder.

Moses Cleaveland owned two shares in the Ohio Company,
which had made the Marietta settlement, and he was one of thirty-
six founders of the Connecticut Land Company. He was a thick-
set, muscular man, so dark that the Indians mistook him for one
of themselves and his men nicknamed him "Paqua" for a Wyandot
chief. He had humor, resourcefulness, magnetism, and he believed
whole-heartedly in the West. When he laid out streets in the
Cuyahoga woods, at the exact midway point in the Western Reserve shoreline, he was confident that a town would grow there
as large as his native Connecticut village of Old Windham. That
was in 1796. By 1800, the community had a population of seven
persons, and when Cleaveland died, back in Connecticut, in 1806,
there were not yet fifty persons on the Cuyahoga. But the prophecy was on its way to fulfillment, and the town reached a population of 1,000 by 1830.

At that time Cleaveland became Cleveland, when a newspaper
publisher shortened the name to fit it into his masthead, and the
city entered a new era. The sudden rush of commerce on the lake
and the opening of the Ohio Canal brought a flood of life that

continued until Cleveland was the sixth city of America, with a million persons living around the public square which the Connecticut party had marked out as a village grazing ground.

West of Cleveland, U. S. 20 dips inland while U. S. 6 skirts the lakeshore. In summer, the lake road is a busy highway between green fields and flashing water. Generally, this is a quiet shore, lapping at summer camps and bathing beaches, but under a west wind the shallow lake turns violent and long gray combers pound against the land.

Lorain is a steel town with an annual lilac festival. It is a place of great energy and surprising composure. At the mouth of Black River, the Lorain Light, flashing white six times a minute, guides the long ore carriers into the harbor. In May, the wind brings a fragrance of lilacs, but at the red-stained docks that subtle scent is lost in the acrid air of the steel plant. For more than a century some of the finest of lake vessels have been launched into the Black River, for shipbuilding was Lorain's first big industry. If all the Lorain-built craft could be assembled, they would make an absorbing spectacle—winged sloops and schooners, paddle-box steamers, wooden and iron cargo ships and, at last, the great 600-foot steel freighters that bring the ore to Lorain's smoking mills.

On a summer day, in 1924, the Lorain sky grew suddenly darker than any drift of smoke. The air was menacingly still and heavy. Lake Erie lay sullen, leaden-colored, without a ripple anywhere. Then the tornado struck with deafening violence. A few minutes later the sky was bright and the air was still again, with the menace lifted—and ten thousand people were homeless. Lorain was a devastated city, with boats flung up on the harbor shore, the river strewn with wreckage and every street a tangle of destruction. But the harbor was still there.

That night the Lorain Light flashed its strong white signal across the heaving lake and freighters steamed in to the disheveled docks. Lorain was rebuilt, better than before, with miles of lilac—the flower of the French province of Lorraine—along its bright new streets. Now Lorain has a radio telephone station which serves

hundreds of vessels on the lakes, so that a person in the middle
of Lake Huron or Superior may speak to anyone, anywhere.

It is a pleasure coast from Lorain through Vermilion and Huron
and on out to the tip of Cedar Point where, on summer nights,
the colored lanterns twinkle along the boardwalk and ballroom
music drifts on the lake wind. Once this was a wheat-shipping
region. In 1839, the citizens of the inland village of Milan deepened the channel of the Huron River and opened a shipping
basin in the Milan meadows. Then lake vessels put in to the mile-
long Milan landing, and from all the northwestern counties of
Ohio farmers brought heaped loads of wheat to the twin rows of
Milan warehouses. Hundreds of wagons arrived every day, and
scores of schooners crept out to Lake Erie and steered eastward
with Ohio grain. For twenty years the village of Milan was one
of the great wheat ports of the world. But after the mid-century,
Ohio wheatlands were turned to dairying and truck farming, and
the railroads put an end to Milan's dwindling commerce. Now it
is a quiet riverside town through which motor traffic streams toward the colored lights of Cedar Point.

Sandusky has the most commodious harbor on Lake Erie—a
long bay almost enclosed by the converging capes of Cedar Point
and Marblehead. White excursion boats churn across to the Point
and among them steam the big dark freighters, coming in empty
with their long decks slanting upward, going out loaded to the
water-line with coal. Last year 14,000,000 tons of coal were loaded
at the Pennsylvania Railroad docks into ships bound up the lakes.
Day and night the big gondolas tip, one every seventy seconds,
into the yawning holds. Thunder rumbles and black haze rises—
for acres the bright bay carries a film of coaldust. When the coal
docks break a loading record, all the whistles around the harbor
sound the town's excitement, and even in Sandusky people forget
that this waterfront was once the largest freshwater fishing market
in the world. Fishing boats still scurry out to the long lanes of nets
beyond Marblehead and Catawba Island, but the herring are gone
from the water and the famous whitefish are depleted. Only the

old men remember the long line of boats waiting to unload their catch at the busy piers.

Out in the lake, beyond the narrows that shelter Sandusky Bay, lie the twenty various Lake Erie Islands. The French who discovered them, in the seventeenth century, called them the Isles of the Apostles, as they had named a similar group of islands at the western end of Lake Superior. But the name did not remain on Lake Erie, and now the separate island names—Kelley's, Starve, Mouse, Gibraltar, Ballast (where Oliver Hazard Perry loaded stone ballast for his frigates), Rattlesnake, Hen and Chickens— have no religious bearing. Fourteen of the twenty islands are American, though the largest, Pelee Island, famed for its fishing waters, belongs to Canada.

The islands remained unsettled long after Perry made one of them famous when he sailed out of Put in Bay to a brilliant victory over the British fleet on a September day in 1813. Kelly's Island took its name from two brothers who settled there in 1833 and began the vineyard culture for which the island became widely known. But its limestone strata suggested another enterprise, and the island quarries have been worked for nearly a hundred years. From June to September, summer residents throng its rocky shores. Excursion boats call daily in the harbor and tourists stream over pleasant paths to Inscription Rock, with its prehistoric hieroglyphs and to the fluted Glacial Grooves carved in limestone by the glacier long ago. Kelly's Island, with the quiet wash of the lake around it, is a good place to feel the long, slow, patient flow of time.

North, South and Middle Bass Islands recall the famous fishing in these waters. The Bass Islands were once planted to wheat, except for their wide wastes of swamp. Then a Spanish merchant tried to make sheep ranches of them. But grapes were the most profitable product of the gravelly soil and tempered air, and the islands became patterned with vineyards. Wine cellars were opened in the limestone strata and German wine-makers settled there and produced the popular Lake Erie wines. At the same time, fishermen were busy off the shores and sportsmen were boasting that there was no better fishing in the world than in channels of the Wine Islands. Half a century ago, Middle Bass Island was one of the foremost summer resorts of America. Four presidents—Hayes, Harrison, Cleveland and Taft—summered there and added to the fishing lore in the clubhouses. Another celebrated visitor was Jay Cooke of Philadelphia, who bought Gibraltar Island and built a towered villa from which he could look across to the Sandusky shores, where he had played with Indians in his boyhood, when transcontinental railroads and vast financial projects were in the undreamed future.

In the twentieth century bass have diminished in the waters, grand hotels have burned down, and daily trippers picnic where capitalists and statesmen once lived in luxury. For a few days each summer, Put in Bay is a gala scene, when the harbor is white with tall sloops and racing yachts that gather for the regatta of the Inter-Lake Yacht Association. When that event is over, the harbor is very quiet, with the cottages drowsing in the sun and the little *Mystic Isle* trailing a web of smoke toward Port Clinton on the mainland. Ten years ago, in the time of peace, a little-known newspaperman named Ernie Pyle looked around the islands and was reluctant to leave. He wrote one of his full-flavored American sketches about Middle Bass Island with its shady bluffs, its sunny beaches and the cool dim quiet of its wineries.

In winter, the islands are left to the farmers and the fishermen. The west wind blows, snow mounds up on the sandy beaches and Lake Erie is a gray plain of ice to the horizon. Sitting around their fires, the islanders have the past to think about—not the Hotel Victory, once the largest summer hotel in America where a thousand persons gathered in the main lobby for nightly concerts, and capitalists driving over the wooded roads in gleaming carriages, but the deeper and simpler past of Doctor Girty, and the sons of John Brown who raided Harper's Ferry, and old Ben Napier, the squatter of Put in Bay. Doctor Girty bore a dreadful name. He was, in fact, a descendant of the villainous Simon. But he was beloved from Kelly's Island to the remote West Sister eighty years ago. For a generation he was the only doctor on the islands, and he made his rounds, summer and winter, in skiff and sailboat or plodding over the windswept ice. On the Bass Islands, Girty is still a name for courage and kindness, for gentleness and a healing hand.

The Brown brothers, John, Owen, and Jason, came to the islands to escape the notoriety that followed them after their father's capture and execution. Owen Brown, tall, gentle and bearded like a prophet, lived in a hut like a hermit on the south shore of Put in Bay, eating fish and Indian meal, studying shellfish and swamp grasses. It was strange to think that he had ridden on midnight raids in Kansas, shooting the slavers in their nightclothes against the kitchen wall, or that from a window in the arsenal at Harper's Ferry he had mowed men down in the cobbled streets. It was strange that he had fled like a fox through the wild mountains of Pennsylvania, with a price of $25,000 on his head. On the islands, he collected butterflies and went berry-picking with children on the wind-blown meadows.

Another man who lived alone was Ben Napier, first white resident of the Islands. He came to fish. The fishing was good. After a season, he built a cedar cabin and decided to stay. When the Connecticut owners came to look at their island property, Ben refused to move. The natives, silently watching the invasion of the summer people, could understand a man like that.

Old Ben seems a far-off figure, but there is one memory earlier still—of a young commodore who anchored his fleet in Put in Bay, when Inscription Rock and the Indian mounds were the only sign of man in all the islands. Now a lofty granite shaft soars above the harbor where Perry sailed out to win control of Lake Erie and hasten the end of the War of 1812. Few of the natives have been curious about the view from that high balcony. But the summer people swarm around it. From its airy height the shores of Ohio, Michigan and Canada appear, with scores of freighters plodding on their courses with a smudge of smoke behind them. A telescope brings the towers of Cleveland and Toledo into view.

Toledo was a place of seventy scattered houses in 1835. Even then it was recognized as a strategic point, controlling the commerce of the Maumee River and Lake Erie. It became the object of heated rivalry between Ohio and Michigan, and the "Toledo War" flared up with armed militiamen disputing possession of the straggling town. The dispute had resulted from a geographical error. Early map-makers had drawn the southern tip of Lake Michigan ten miles farther north than its actual extent. This error entered into the fixing of Ohio's northwestern boundary. Later, when Michigan Territory was created in 1805, its southern boundary was designated as a line drawn east to Lake Erie from the southern tip of Lake Michigan. This gave Michigan a strip of land nearly ten miles wide across northwestern Ohio. So Michigan claimed Toledo and the mouth of the Maumee.

Both states sent surveying crews to establish lines in harmony with their claims. With western settlement growing and statehood for Michigan imminent, the question became vital in the spring of 1835. The twenty-one-year-old governor of Michigan, Stevens T. Mason, sent militia to occupy the strip. Governor Robert Lucas of Ohio dispatched 1,000 Ohio troops to the Maumee. Then Washington became concerned and two agents of President Andrew Jackson hurried over Lake Erie on the steamer *Detroit*. While fist fights and shooting frays went on in the muddy April streets, the presidential agents urged a truce until the Federal Congress could take action. But the Michigan troops, angered at legal maneuvering by the Ohio officials, marched through the area with fingers on their triggers. By good fortune, no armed Ohio men appeared in their way and casualties were limited to two work horses and some hogs. When they entered Toledo and hauled down the Ohio banner, the air was tense over all the western shores of Lake Erie.

But in Washington, Congress was moving toward a solution. The Legislators voted to support Ohio's claim to the disputed strip and to recompense Michigan with an area of 9,000 square miles beyond the Straits of Mackinac. At that time the Upper

Peninsula was wild, forbidding, unexplored land and Michigan accepted it without a syllable of enthusiasm. With Toledo an acknowledged part of Ohio, Michigan was admitted into the Union in 1836, and a geological party set out to survey the upper wilderness. Toledo became a great commercial city, the largest coal-shipping port in the world, with miles of railroad yards, loading docks and acres of furnaces, factories and refineries bordering the Maumee mouth. But Michigan had got a bargain. In the timbered hills and ridges, even under the swamps and lakes of the Upper Peninsula, were vast deposits of iron ore and out on the long cape of Keeweenaw were mile-deep veins of copper. The Northwest was vaster and richer than its disputatious people could understand. In the end, both Ohio and Michigan were satisfied.

XXII

North to Mackinac

WHEN LA SALLE sailed his *Griffin* through the Detroit River, his men found the smiling green shores "one of the fairest prospects in the world." It was a land full of promise— the woods were rife with game, the waters teemed with fish, the fertile earth awaited men to lay out gardens and orchards. Now it is a land of another promise, with vast industrial plants lining the shores of the shortest and busiest river in the world. Though founded two and a half centuries ago, Detroit still has the feeling of a frontier town. You are impressed with its energy, the restlessness of its people, the preponderance of young men, the violence of its economic ups and downs.

In the early 1800s it was still a settlement that faced the river, each little strip farm having a water frontage and every cottage looking at the bright current by which all trade and travel moved. Now Detroit has spread inland for many miles and the river is walled with warehouses, elevators, oil tanks and power plants. Docks are heaped with stockpiles of iron, limestone, coal, sulphur. Between the low green shores of Canada and the smoking stacks of Ecorse and Wyandotte pass oil barges, excursion boats, sand-suckers, package freighters and the long, low ore carriers. Though Detroit has become a name for travel on wheels, the river brings it the vital goods of industry, as it brought the beaver skins which were the unit of value in the early town.

The river is best seen from Belle Isle Park, a leafy pleasure ground of a thousand acres. Belle Isle was once infested by rattle snakes, so that the Indians shunned it. French settlers pastured hogs on the island to rid it of snakes, and it remained "Hog Island" for a hundred years. Now, on a summer Sunday, it

thronged with people. Around the picnic tables under the trees
you may hear the many languages—Polish, Ukrainian, Bulgarian,
Italian, Russian, Syrian, Greek—of Detroit's polyglot life. Around
Belle Isle the river and its commerce flow. The park has lagoons,
sunken gardens and artificial lakes, along with a zoo, two famous
fountains and the only marble lighthouse in the world. But its
most absorbing sight is the commerce always passing in the river.
At first, the lake freighters look ungainly, with their long flat
lines and the dwarfed deckhouses at bow and stern. But there
is a growing pleasure in the symmetry of the tiered pilothouse
balancing the stern cabin with its raked stack and leaning spar.
And the long, clear, open deck, twice as long as a football field,
slightly curved and tilted, makes it a clean, uncluttered ship. These
vessels, unlike any others in the world, have evolved from a century's experience in the carrying of bulk cargo. Their honest, un-
adorned, functional structure appeals to the eye and to the mind.

Though a vast commercial tonnage crosses Lake St. Clair, the
radiant waters have a holiday look, with white sails leaning in
the wind and speedboats skimming. Every prospect pleases on
Lake St. Clair, but it is best to come down the lake at sunset
with Detroit's towers growing in a golden haze and the shore
lights flashing in the dusk. Few cities have so splendid an approach. At the lake's northern end, shallow channels fan into the
St. Clair River. Here are the St. Clair Flats, a kind of little Venice
whose low-lying islands are crowded with trim summer houses.
Among the islands weave narrow canals framed in little docks
and colored awnings and bright green plots of grass. Summer
residents have made a festive place where once there was a duck-
hunter's swampland.

The St. Clair River is a narrow channel through which varied
commerce passes. People wave from their verandas and men aboard
a steamer call ashore as the ship moves by. Along this intimate
shore people feel like mariners, though they may never set foot
on a vessel's deck. They know every houseflag fluttering from a
steamer's masthead and the banded stacks of all the shipping lines.

One St. Clair cottager has kept a record of all the vessels big enough to have a name, that pass in a single season. She has 604 names, of freighters, tankers, tugboats, yachts, excursion boats and barges, and the list is still growing. The river ends at Port Huron, with Sarnia opposite on the Canadian shore. Lumbering was a big industry on these riverbanks seventy years ago. Log rafts and schooner loads of sawed lumber went down the river and across Lake St. Clair to build the spreading city of Detroit. In those days tugboats towed strings of white-sailed schooners against the current. At Port Huron, the schooners loosed their towlines and scattered like gulls over the northern water. Now the long freighters plod under the high span of the Blue Water international bridge. They pass the lightship rocking above a reef and diminish over the blue levels of Lake Huron.

The "thumb" of Michigan presents a long straight shoreline ending at Pointe aux Barques, where sharp rocks cleave the breaking water like the bows of ships. On that coast a few fishing and resort villages lie between blue water and wide fields of wheat and corn. At Pointe aux Barques the lake opens deeply into Saginaw Bay.

The upper part of the Michigan mitten is drained by four rivers that once were famous logging streams—Saginaw, Au Sable, Thunder Bay and Cheboygan rivers. Lumbering is a dramatic industry and it leaves a tradition long after the forest is gone. Now Bay City, at the mouth of the Saginaw, is an orderly and busy town without a grain of sawdust anywhere. Fifty years ago it was a place of sawdust streets and boardwalks pitted with the calked boots of lumberjacks. For miles the river was walled in palisades of drying lumber, and the scream of the mills guided schooner captains through the fog of Saginaw Bay. Masts of lumber schooners made a thick and leafless forest in the harbor, and tugboats brought endless acres of pine logs to the hungry mills.

North of Saginaw Bay every lake port has the same memory— of men who went into the woods, of log drives plunging down the rivers, of sawblades whining and yellow sawdust creeping like a stain through the settlement, of lumber ships putting out to Lake Huron with a yellow deckload lashed beneath white sails. The great years lasted from the Civil War to 1890. Then the boom was over. At one town after another, foremen saw the last logs go through the mills. Then they tied the whistle cord—the long whistle shrilled and faded as the boiler spent its steam. Men moved out and mills weathered in the sun. No more white-winged ships flew in from Lake Huron. Behind the silent town lay a waste— stumpland and brush slashings. Fire blackened the country and the shore was silent as when the land-looker had first made his way into the twilit pineries.

Today, Oscoda is a quiet village of six hundred persons. In 1890, it had ten times that number. Like so many lumber towns it was burned to the ground and the sawdust smoldered for weeks after the settlement became a waste of ashes. Now its people live by fishing, picking berries and entertaining summer visitors. Sometimes they look up from the burned blueberry meadows to the Lumberman's Memorial on a height above the Au Sable River. The memorial shows three bronze figures—a riverman thrusting his peavy into a rough-barked pine log, a timber cruiser studying his map and a woodsman striding along with his ax and crosscut. The ax was the beginning of it all.

With his instinct for the essential symbols of America, Walt Whitman wrote a poem about the ax——

Weapon shapely, naked, wan—

A cunning instrument, the poised, lean handle carrying the wedged blade lightly——

Wooded flesh and metal bone—

Hickory and steel combined to make a weapon that has changed the continent. Thud, thud, thud—along the Ohio, in the knobs of Indiana, by the rivers of Michigan, on the long lakeshores. Thud, thud, thud! The sound advanced across the whole Northwest, from Pittsburgh to St. Louis, from Marietta to St. Paul. For fifty years it was a prophetic sound, like marching footsteps, of men in a new country. In that sound the future of America was beating like a pulse.

The axe leaps!
The solid forest gives fluid utterances;
They tumble forth, they rise and form,
Hut, tent, landing, survey,
Flail, plow, pick, crowbar, spade,
Shingle, rail, prop, wainscot, jamb, lath, panel, gable,
Citadel, ceiling, saloon, academy, organ, exhibition house, library,
Cornice trellis, pilaster, balcony, window, turret porch,

The shapes arise!
Shapes of the using of axes—

Whitman had been a carpenter and he saw the shapes that the ax brought out of clear-grained lumber. He was also a poet, and he saw more than that.

The main shapes arise!
Shapes of Democracy total, result of centuries!

Beneath that too was the broadax.

Now the North has empires of wasteland where the forest cannot come back for scores of years. But a thousand lumber schooners whitened the lake lanes sixty years ago, so farms and towns and cities grew where nothing had ever been before.

North of Saginaw lies much desolation, but the people living there have a surprising pride in their country. They live in an area without cities—a severe and primitive country—and they have closer identity with their land than have any other people of the Middle-West. People on the northern coasts, from Thunder Bay to the tip of Lake Superior, are possessed by their country in a way that would elude the understanding of the pleasant vacation colonies on the populous lower shores.

Alpena, on the inlet of Thunder Bay, was one of the roaring lumber towns, sixty years ago. But unlike the others it did not dwindle. Its mills went silent, one by one, and the timber on Thunder Bay River was finally exhausted—even the "weed trees," good only for pulpwood, were stripped from the inland counties. At the opening of the twentieth century, mills were idle and lake fleets passed on the horizon. Alpena harbor had no life except its untidy little fishing boats. It looked like the familiar end of a sawmill town. But then a curious Alpena grocer found limestone on the flat Huron shore. He brought some home and melted it down in a cookstove in the backroom of his store. It made a fine white Portland cement. That was the beginning of a new era for Thunder Bay. Now the big, gray-dusted freighters lie at the loading docks under the huge cement works, and Alpena ships have a greater tonnage than the vanished schooners carried. In the northward-stretching pine barrens live Polish and Norwegian settlers who cleared the cut-over land and have stayed to farm reluctant acres. Rogers City is bordered by yawning limestone quarries—from the nearby port of Calcite it is shipped down the lakes for flux in steel-making. Nature seemingly designed the lakes for the age of steel, with iron ranges ringing Lake Superior, deep coal beds in the Ohio Valley and limestone halfway between the two, on the edge of Lake Huron.

Cheboygan is now a tourist town, with a busy commercial fishing fleet. In the harbor some old wooden ships lie rotting at the warped old wharves—vessels that once carried the lumber from Cheboygan's noisy mills. Now all the mills are gone, but across the State Street Bridge there stands a mountain of sawdust, 1,000 feet long and 100 feet high—all that is left of the pine and hemlock, the birch and maple forests that darkened the northern counties of lower Michigan. Across from Cheboygan are the birch-barred shores of Bois Blanc (Bob-Lo) Island. The mainland is a lonely curving shore of sand and second-growth timber.

At the tip of the peninsula is Mackinaw City, one of the historic sites of America. Three hundred years ago French explorers

rounded the point on their way to the unknown western waters.
Two hundred years ago the Indians brought their peltry here to
trade for blankets, traps and knives—on a dreadful summer day
they massacred the British garrison while Alexander Henry stared
from his cottage window. Now a few Indians lounge along the
street, but the village is busy with another traffic. All the travel
to the Upper Peninsula passes through Mackinaw City and onto
the white Straits ferries which ply across the wide blue strait to
St. Ignace. Out in the straits lies graceful Mackinac Island with
its white hotels and cottages against the green hood of its forest.
Ferry boats steam to the island where Indian boys, descended from
the braves who massacred the British, drive you in pony carts
over forest-framed roads and along the rocky beaches.

There have been three Fort Michilimackinacs—the first at St.
Ignace, the second at Mackinaw City, the third on a handsome
height above the village of Mackinac Island. This final fort is
well preserved—neater by far than it ever was in the years of its
garrison—and stored with many reminders of the past. Among its
souvenirs are the records of Dr. William Beaumont. So you recall
that this lonely island is a kind of shrine, not only to lovers of
the fur trade and Indian lore but even to the medical profession.
There occurred at Fort Mackinac one of the great discoveries in
the long, laborious history of medicine.

William Beaumont began his career as apprentice to a doctor
in the remote village of St. Albans, Vermont, far from hospitals,
medical academies, and societies for the advancement of science.
He became famous in the even more remote village of Mackinac
Island. Having served as an army surgeon in the War of 1812,
he remained in military service and was sent for a tour of duty
as surgeon at Fort Mackinac in the far Northwest. Life was un-
exciting there, with sick call in the morning, a brief round of his
tiny sick bay, and an occasional knife cut or powder burn to treat.
The rest was lounging in the parade ground, talking with officers,
watching the sailing ships lean through the straits and speculating
on when again the astonishing little *Walk-in-the-Water*, the first

steamship on the lakes, would find her way over the blue distances of Huron and lie smoking at the Mackinac dock. It seemed far away from the world—so far that nothing could happen there that the world would ever notice.

Below the fort, where the village rambled along the shore, stood the retail store of the American Fur Company. Here the trappers smoked and lounged and pondered over the trade goods their next season's catch might buy. They exchanged gossip about the Indians, whittled countless toothpicks with their long-bladed knives and cleaned their guns over and over. To that place, on a bland June day in 1822, Dr. Beaumont was called by a breathless man who had raced up the steep Fort trail. At the store, the surgeon found a young half-breed trader, Alexis St. Martin, stretched out with a gaping wound in his stomach, from the accidental discharge of a gun. The side wall of his stomach was blown away and he was already weak from loss of blood.

Dr. Beaumont gave him twenty minutes to live. But the hardy young woodsman lived all night, and was stronger in the morning. Then Dr. Beaumont took the nineteen-year-old trapper to his cottage at the Fort and cared for him there. Weeks became months, months lengthened into years, and still the wound did not close. Dr. Beaumont could look directly into his patient's stomach. Gradually he realized the startling opportunity before him. He began his experiments in digestion—suspending food by a thread into the open stomach and watching the organ's action, collecting gastric juice and comparing digestion inside and outside the body. In time, a flap grew over the stomach opening, but it did not close together. Dr. Beaumont lifted the flap and went on with his observations. But after three years the young trader grew restless and ran away. He took up the arduous life of the woods trails and canoe routes, even with that opening in his stomach, and Beaumont lost all touch with him.

Four years later the two met again, at Prairie du Chien, the old fur post at the mouth of the Wisconsin River. To Beaumont's joy he found the trader's stomach still open. This time he drew up a contract with St. Martin, agreeing to pay him for submitting to medical experiments. St. Martin stayed with him at Prairie du Chien and accompanied the doctor when he was transferred to Plattsburg. Meanwhile, Beaumont was meticulously keeping his observations, determining the movements of the stomach during digestion, studying the effect of temperature, sleep and anger on the flow of gastric juice, describing the results of starvation and of overcharging the stomach with food. At last, in 1833, he published his "Experiments and observations in the gastric juice, and the physiology of digestion." It became one of the great documents in medical literature. Dr. Beaumont died in St. Louis after a fall on the ice, in 1853. St. Martin lived on for twenty years longer, with the lid on his stomach, and became the father of twenty children.

Now Mackinac Island, with its white houses against the green forest, its wave-washed rocky shores and its widows and spinsters keeping summer boarders, has the sense of another age. Its streets sound with the *clop-clop* of horses' hoofs and the jingle of bicycle bells, and people watch the water from their porches. There has never been an automobile on the island, though it is a familiar sight to see a big freighter passing with solid ranks of cars, like a long parking-lot, upon its deck. In winter, when teams haul bobsleds across the frozen Straits, it is a village of Indians and fishermen, of retired lighthouse-keepers and lakemen. No place on all the 4,000-mile shoreline has a deeper sense of the past.

From Mackinaw City, on the mainland, you look east, north and west at water. Here freighters coming down Lake Michigan whistle their identification, in a code of long and short blasts, and at the lighthouse their passing is recorded. From the days when the ice goes out in April till the Straits are sealed in December, there is always a mellow voice drifting along that shore.

Across the freighters' paths steam the Straits ferries. They keep a year-round schedule, with powerful ice-breakers smashing a channel in the windrowed ice of mid-winter, for they are the vital link of Upper Michigan with the lower peninsula. Now there is a growing demand for a Straits bridge to unite the two with a solid highway. It is an impressive project, for the Straits are six miles wide and they reach a depth of 240 feet. In time it will be realized, and the upper country will seem less remote than it has always been. But until then it is right to see the blue Straits opening where Nicolet passed into Lake Michigan, which he took for the Pacific, three hundred years ago, and to make the water crossing as every Indian and trader, every soldier and fisherman, every hunter and hay fever victim bound for the north country has done.

XXIII

The Long Looped Lake

T HE NORTHWEST gave its people large ideas. The free winds and broad lands of the waiting country loosed their minds from the tight, tidy patterns of life in New England and the Old World. They built the longest canals, the longest highways, the longest railroads. They plowed the largest fields and laid out cities with no discernible limit. They built ocean-going brigs on the headwaters of the Ohio, and on the Great Lakes they launched the finest and fastest steamships in the world.

But one of their large ideas was never realized. It was too large even for the Wolverines and Hoosiers, the Suckers and Badgers, who lived in the four states bordering the longest of the lakes. Seventy years ago there was airy, avid talk of draining all the water from Lake Michigan. Land was still wide and empty around the lakeshores, but much of it was in forest, or was stumpland after the forest had been leveled. And people who see a vast acreage can imagine a vaster country. "He wants all the land he can see for himself, and all he can't see for his son John." There were no fences in the country they came to.

But not satisfied with that, some men pictured the bottom of Lake Michigan as a huge basin of rich fields, with straight highways connecting busy cities. They saw long, dark furrows of earth, instead of the blue water that quickly closed over the track of ships. Though they talked in all seriousness, it was pure delusion. Knowing that the low-lying divide could be opened so that lake water would flow to the Mississippi—as was later done, reversing the flow of the Chicago River—they imagined that all of Lake Michigan could be drained away. But the lake is nearly 1,000 feet deep at its extreme sounding, with much of its bottom below sea

334

level. And if they had drained it they would not have found a
bowl of level land. A mid-lake depth between Port Washington
and Muskegon is 144 feet; another, between Kewaunee and Frankfort, is 924 feet. The lake bottom would have presented more ridges
and valleys, more sidehills to plow and steeper grades to haul a
wheat wagon over than appear in any of the lake counties of Wisconsin and Michigan.

This was a farmer's dream and a mistaken one. More valuable
than farming land were the 15,000,000 acres of blue water that
linked Muskegon, Milwaukee and Chicago to each other, and to
ocean outlets by the St. Lawrence and the Erie Canal.

Lake Michigan is as long as from New York to Montreal and
it spans the same latitudes. It has two climates, with solid ice over
the northern waters in the long winter of that country and living
water the year round at its temperate southern end. When bathers
throng the summer beaches at Chicago, the lake is numbing cold
at Manistique and Escanaba. Its shores have the variety of all the
other lakes combined- dune and cliff, orchard and pinery, fishing
inlet and industrial harbor. At one end, moonlight whitens the
dreaming shores of Mackinac. At the other end the skies are lurid
from the blast furnaces of Gary. There is the artists' colony at
Saugatuck, in the unearthly dune country, and there is a community of Icelandic fishermen on Washington Island at the entrance to Green Bay.

Names that fringe the lake convey its variety. There are Indian
names that seem as old as the naked cliffs and the wave-lashed
ledges—Kewadin, for the northwest wind; Escanaba, land of the
red buck; Menominee, wild rice country. Also old and deeply
rooted are the French names—Pointe La Barbe (Beard Point),
where the voyageurs stopped to shave before going in to the posts
and taverns of St. Ignace; Seul Choix (Only Choice), guarding
a cove that offered the only shelter during sudden storms; Epou-
fette (Place of Rest), where Marquette first camped on his journey
down the lonely and arduous Lake Michigan shore. Much later
came British names—Gladstone, Brampton, Kipling (there is also

a separate Rudyard). They represent years of railroad building, when promoters tried to make their properties attractive to British investors four thousand miles away.

All around the lake are names brought by the immigrants who planted Old World seeds in virgin country—Holland, Oostburg, Norway, Germantown, Denmark, Brussels. Other places mark the enterprise of American industrialists—Mears, named for a lumberman who built his own vessels and manned his own mills; Ludington, for another lumberman, whose name replaced Marquette's on the Michigan shore (every August a High Mass is sung on a bluff above the Ludington dunes where Father Marquette died three centuries ago); Gary, the city that was built in a single twentieth-century season, named for a president of the United States Steel Corporation. So the varied names span the long tradition of the lake.

Now there are gulls flying over the fishing boats at St. Ignace, and other gulls hover above the light cribs at Chicago. Sometimes they follow a freighter the full length of the lake. Along their flight has unfolded so much of American life that our history would be incomplete without it. Somewhere in its depths, Lake Michigan hides the wreck of La Salle's *Griffin*. Its waters have carried heavy-oared bateaux of the fur traders, tall schooners laden with lumber and grain, and long, low freighters of the age of steel. At the time of Black Hawk's War a fleet of paddle-box transports hurried down to Chicago with troops to drive the Indians across the Mississippi; now the vast excursion liner *Seeandbee* prowls the lake as a flattop, made over into an aircraft carrier for training naval fliers.

Lake Michigan's shores are still marked by blackened circles of stone where the Indians crouched at council fires. Its inlets show the old rotting rollways from which lumberjacks sent the winter cut of logs crashing into spring water. North Manitou Island is owned by a syndicate of Chicago business men who fish in its waters and hunt in its forest—a city the tribes could never have conceived has reached out to possess a remote island that the Indians gave their most venerable name. Steelmen from Gary and South Chicago have summer homes on Little Traverse Bay, where a remnant of Indians live as they did five hundred years ago. So the layers intermingle.

The first layer is the Indians who still belong to the upper shores on both sides of the lake. At Cross Village and Preshabestown, at Nahma and on Beaver Island, they carry on a life little changed by the age of steel. They are still men of the woods, uncurious about the modern world, rooted in the primitive. They meet civilization a reluctant quarter of the way by guiding fishermen and hunters, tinkering with an outboard motor, smoothing a canoe paddle and making birch-bark boxes for the tourists at Charlevoix and Petoskey. In the height of the summer season, no more self-conscious than a white man who goes to his desk or stands behind a counter to earn his living, they perform the Sun Dance, the War Dance, the Buffalo Dance, the Deer Dance, and count the proceeds when the crowd has gone. They know the meaning of the white man's money. They drink beer and cola in the taverns, they play the slot machines and some of them line up at the post-office window to file an income tax return. But when the summer people disappear, they take up their old life again, concerned with the color of the sky at evening and the track of animals in the snow.

The north shores are still primitive, by reason of climate and soil and remoteness from centers of civilization. So the Indian signs are still a natural aspect of the country. In the center of Frankfort, just north of the busy Main Street, is the Crooked Tree, its trunk bent over and pointing, that marked an Indian trail long before summer visitors from Ohio and Indiana found the way to Frankfort's curving bowl of hills. At Torch Lake, Indians once speared fish by the light of smoking rushes. At Kewadin, travelers stare at an Indian copper kettle, centuries old, capacious enough to boil a whole bear. The ridge above South Haven shows hundreds of circles of burned and broken stones—once that high ground was populous with Indian camps and at night, from the lake's darkness, their fires twinkled like a fallen constellation. Around old fire pits visitors still pick up fragments of flint, chert and pipe-stone—this was one of the implement-making centers of the western tribes.

Across the lake on Washington Island, Iceland fishermen dry their nets on the site of Indian fireplaces, and the ground around their cottages shows the earth foundations of log houses in which the tribes endured the long siege of winter. At Nahma, on Little Bay de Noc, a community of Chippewa, Ottawa and Potawatomi families live in a reservation town. The men work in the one remaining sawmill on that shore and the women weave grass baskets for the tourist trade. In summer, they stare uncuriously at motorists in slacks and halters and colored bathing suits. In winter, the white, still land becomes theirs again. They are used to cold and silence and crouching at a smoky fire. Unlike all the other western people they have no instinct for change. They go on in the old way—enough food, a little clothing, a meager shelter. Something in them remains native, deep-rooted and resistant, like the rocky outcrop that the Anglo-Saxons called a tor.

If the long-looped lake had borne no Indian name, it would have become Pine Lake—it was surrounded by the richest domain of pine forest in the world. Pine was the first lure of the lumber-men. Here were billions of tall-standing pines, ready to go through the mills for every kind of building purposes—timbers, joists, clap-boards, sash, doors and furniture. Millions of persons needed houses, barns, tables, chests and chairs; scores of counties needed plank roads across their marshes. Here was the timber to house and pave and furnish a new country.

The whole coast of Lake Michigan north of Grand Haven and Milwaukee remembers the logging era. First, the timber cruiser came with a pack on his shoulders and a notebook in the pocket of his hunting shirt. He went into the woods by winter, when rivers were frozen and swamps were hard. He made his way into country no white man had ever seen before. He counted his paces, calculated distance, noted landmarks and mapped the timber. When he came out, he carried the key to the logging of whole counties of dim, mysterious land where rivers ran in perpetual twilight and wind roared like a tidal ocean in the trees.

Next season came the foreman with a crew of axmen and carpenters. In a chosen place they cleared an acre of woods, using the logs to build a bunkhouse, a stable and an office. Then, as the ice was forming on the rivers, the lumberjacks arrived. At first, they were gangs of Maine men, French-Canadians and Bluenose Nova Scotians. They had logged off the forests of Maine and New Brunswick and in the process had evolved a system and a lore which was to move west across the continent. Later came Irishmen, Norwegians, Swedes and Finns. The crew of men was organized like a small army, each unit with its own job in which the men developed enormous skill and confidence. In the woods their hands hardened and their beards grew black. They were cut off all winter from the world, like men on a long voyage. Their tasks were prodigious and unvarying. First, the sawyers took their places, two on a team, at the base of a lofty pine. They rocked from the hips and the see-saw clang of the crosscut was like a great beast slowly panting in the winter forest. Then came the cry, "Timber-r-r!" and the giant tree crashed down.

Swampers went along the prostrate trunk, slashing off the branches with quick sure strokes of their axes. A second team of sawyers reduced the pillared trunk to stocky sawlogs. Meanwhile, road monkeys were busy on the skidways they had cleared to river or lake. They kept them iced and grooved like a toboggan slide, with hay spread on the slopes to slow the load from running away. Behind the big shaggy-coated horses came teamsters on their bobsleds. The logs made a steep pyramid on the sled and from its peak the driver's voice rang out. The horses' nostrils smoked in the frosty air and the load moved over the icy road to the rollways. There the logs remained, drifted with snow and locked in ice, until the warm bright days of spring. At that season the jacks shed their heavy mackinaws and ax-shortened their pants so they would not trip in the delicate business of riding logs in a racing current. They became rivermen, herding the logs down to the sawmill towns on the lake shore.

Now the uproar in the woods was over. But a new uproar began at the mill towns—donkey engines puffing, log chains clanking, buzzsaws and bandsaws screaming night and day. Charlevoix, East Jordan, Ludington, Manistee, Muskegon, Grand Haven, and all the towns on the west shore from Green Bay to St. Ignace were covered everywhere with sawdust and they lived for a generation to the fierce cry of the saws. People burned slabs in their stoves. They walked on plank sidewalks. Their streets were paved with wooden blocks. In wooden shipyards they built wooden schooners to carry cargoes of sawed lumber.

To the mill towns came the lumber buyers from Toledo, Cleveland, Buffalo, Oswego, Milwaukee, Chicago. During the 1870s and '80s Muskegon shipped annually enough lumber to build a city of a hundred thousand persons. Chicago alone had a fleet of five hundred lumber vessels endlessly bringing north woods lumber to the miles of lumberyards that lined the Chicago River. Some of the mill towns produced many kinds of finished lumber. The once hectic village of East Jordan had planing mills, shingle mills, hoop plants, cabinet factories. In the space of four city blocks along the waterfront, a log floated down the Jordan River went through the entire process from pine trunk to a finished piece of furniture.

The peak of Lake Michigan lumbering came in the early 1890s when there were a hundred thousand men in the woods and every river carried a scum of sawdust onto the blue waters of the lake. Those years saw many disasters in the mill towns and on the shipping lanes. After a storm, the beaches were strewn with yellow lumber and vessels put into refuge ports with tattered sails and deckloads like spilled toothpicks, while haggard sailors waved wearily from the rail.

For thirty years fire was a hazard to the woods towns. The most dreadful season was the autumn of 1871, after a dry and ominous summer that had left the forest tinder-dry and rivers stagnant in their beds. On the eighth of October, while flames were raging through the heart of Chicago, the town of Holland burned furiously and the town of Manistee was engulfed by a racing forest fire. At the same time, fire swept for forty miles along Green Bay, leaving the towns of Peshtigo and Menominee in ashes and hundreds of persons dead. Afterward, people remembered like a terrible dream how vessels burned in the harbors and Lake Michigan gave back the glare of destruction.

By the early twentieth century, lumbering on Lake Michigan neared its end. A few mills went on operating, but the sound of the saw was a lonely scream along a quiet shore. Now there are some landmarks left. In the woods you may come across the old ruined buildings and the grass-grown compound of a logging camp, with porcupines waddling around the ruined stables. At lake towns you may see an old sawmill, with muskrats burrowing beneath the landing. At a few places on the shore, you may find the timber cribs of old rollways where the sawlogs thundered down to the water. Scattered over the north country are wistful memorials of a hearty age—annual lumberjack festivals in the old woods towns, county museums of logging tools and lumber companies' records, spontaneous little collections of newspaper clippings and yellowed photographs made by persons who feel a kind of grandeur in the past and want to keep it as a dimension of their land.

Early Michigan settlements were said to be made up of Yankee, Hoosier, New Yorker, Yahoo, Buckskin, Buckeye, Chegoe, Sucker. These were hearty names for Americans from the bordering areas who came to Michigan in its first years of statehood. But soon Lake Michigan shores were settled by Germans, Dutch, Swedes, Belgians, Norwegians, Poles, Bohemians. They brought a third layer of tradition to the region. Lumberjacks didn't settle. They moved on, as the forest was felled, to Lake Superior's shores, to the tributaries of the Mississippi, to the far north wilderness of Minnesota and the Canadian border. But the immigrant families came over the lakes with a vision of land to till and towns to settle and a permanent life to plant in new country. They had come a long distance and they intended to stay.

The Great Lakes form a kind of Mediterranean Sea of the New World, opening two thousand miles inland from the Gulf of the St. Lawrence. That luring waterway attracted Europeans in the greatest numbers, and the lakes area filled up with the greatest variety of immigrant peoples. The upper lakes states were suddenly opened to settlement in the very years when political and economic pressures in Europe sent millions to America. They passed over Lake Erie, stared at the growing city of Detroit, sailed up the long coast of Lake Huron and around the forest shores of the North.

Most of them came to Lake Michigan and there founded their colonies. Germans settled whole districts of Chicago and Milwaukee and established towns all the way north to Green Bay. The Norwegians walked from Milwaukee to Lake Muskego, in southern Wisconsin, and began their first strong colony in America. Swedes hiked thirty miles west of Milwaukee and made their first settlement at Pine Lake. Dutch came in a stream of sturdy, freedom-loving, religious protestants to form the towns of Holland, Vreeland and Vriesland, on the Michigan shore, and Oostburg across the lake, in Wisconsin. At Oostburg there stands a tablet commemorating the death of 127 Holland pilgrims when the steamer *Phoenix* burned to the water's edge in sight of the shores they had come so far to settle.

From Flemish fields came the Belgians, who founded the town of Brussels on Green Bay. Their first industry was cutting cordwood for lake steamers. Then they turned their cleared land into fruitful farms and orchards. Gill's Rock, at the tip of Door Peninsula, was a Scandinavian settlement, lonely and wave-lashed like the fishing hamlets on the Lofoten Islands off the Norway coast. Right at their door was Porte des Morts, hazardous entrance to Green Bay where, in the single year of 1871, with the perils of fog and storm and the smoke of forest fires, a hundred vessels came to grief. Ephraim, now a resort village on Green Bay, began as a

Norwegian Socialist community, supported by fishing and the shipping of cedar telegraph poles to Chicago.

In all the immigrant communities, life had a dual quality. It was as though the people lived two lives. Around them lay the spacious new country, the hard work of pioneering, summer's heat and winter's cold, the feeling of the future. And there were other scenes and seasons in the memory—a steep Norway town and beyond it the darkness of forest, the roar of waterfalls and the high green' pastures where cattle grazed in radiant northern summer; a busy Belgian market place with carts rattling on cobblestones and old women carrying big wicker baskets full of live geese hissing; a Danish waterfront with silvered fish spilling out of wooden tubs and bright red crayfish crawling in their crates and women in wet burlap aprons skinning eels like peeling off a stocking; a concert in a Bohemian garden, with families eating bread and cheese under linden trees, while yellow leaves sifted down; a Dutch canal where slow boats moved under the city's bridges and between sunny tulip fields; Midsummer Eve in a Swedish village with the costumed people dancing around the Maypole, while the old fiddler sawed at his strings.

But gradually memories faded. They grew dim and distant, and people talked about the first arduous years in Michigan or Wisconsin, when men fought storm and wolves and forest fires, or made long journeys through the lonely country. By that time they were living on cleared land and in busy towns—they had an American memory. In Holland and Manitowac and Manistee people spoke languages from four thousand miles away, but their thoughts were American. They still cooked Old World dishes and sang Old World songs and at church they heard the sermon in the old tongue. But there was a new restlessness in their eyes, a new ring in their voices. They had new possessions—not only deeds of entry filed in the courthouse, but of the mind and heart. They had a new equality and participation. Wisconsin was settled by thirty different nationalities. Its population had diverse memories, but a common aspiration. The diversity helped to make its people tolerant—it kept them from quickly settling into a fixed society. They became cooperative, flexible, capable of new ideas, hospitable to change. They became American.

Of the four states which touch Lake Michigan, Indiana is least conscious of its lake frontage. Michigan City, at the terminus of Indiana's old Michigan Road, was once a greater port than Chicago, and Gary is one of the vital ports of today. But these realizations rarely enter the mind of down-state Hoosiers. Indiana seems the most inland of the lakes states and it has retained an identity unique among them. That identity has made the term "Hoosier" as meaningful as "Yankee," and as familiar.

Without distinctive landscape or tradition, the Hoosiers have created symbols. The Wabash is less romantic in history, scenery and surroundings than the Illinois, which means nothing to most Illinoisans; the rustic charm of Brown County can be matched by the Scioto counties of Ohio, which few Ohioans know; Turkey Run, Clifty Falls and Spring Mill are pretty places, which have a meaning for Indiana that seems strange in Wisconsin or Michigan. Frontier ebullience led to Indiana place-names like Greencastle, Montezuma, Paoli, Hindustan, but the Hoosiers overlaid these exotic names with their impervious provincialism. They called Terre Haute "Tare Holt." For a century they have had an unshakable satisfaction in things that are their own. "Hoosier" means contentment, memory, local satisfactions. It means hollyhocks in the dooryard and Tom Marshall talking in the Senate about a good five-cent cigar, and James Whitcomb Riley writing about the frost on the pumpkin. It means "folks." That is an inland consciousness which has not developed in the other lakes states.

Indiana was filled by people from across the Ohio River—Kentuckians, Virginians, Carolinians. It has the smallest proportion of foreign-born residents in all the middle states. So it developed sentiment, tradition and a grass-roots conservatism. Wisconsin, with the greatest proportion of foreign-born, became restless, radical, aggressive. It is less than fifty miles on the lakeshore from Indiana to Wisconsin, but the two states seem a thousand miles apart. The difference between a Marshall and a La Follette, between Paul Dresser and Frank Lloyd Wright, between George Ade and Hamlin Garland is in part the difference between a homogeneous and a heterogeneous society. The mingled racial strains, the clash of temperaments and traditions have given the country about Lake Michigan its political ferment and intellectual restlessness.

Indian villages dwindled and all but disappeared, lumber towns sprang into a hectic life and almost as quickly declined to a trade in summer visitors, immigrant settlements grew into permanent American communities. But Chicago did not assume its shape. It kept changing, evolving, bursting into new violence, expanding into new space and height and power.

The Potawatomis—a small tribe at the southern end of Lake Michigan—gave an uncouth name to a sluggish river. Now the two thousand remaining Potawatomis (they never numbered many more) are scattered from Oklahoma to Canada and their claim to Lake Michigan's swamps and prairies is forgotten. But one word of their language is known around the world—the name for a garlic weed that grew beside the stagnant river. They pronounced it in a way that was difficult for English tongues, and it has been spelled in a variety of ways. On early maps, in Jesuit manuscripts, in Indian treaties and military records it appears as She-kag-ong, Eschikakau, Jigagong, Chekagawa, Chekakau, Checaugau, Chicka-goua, Chickagau, Chickagwa, Chicagau, Chicagoe—and occasionally in the simpler form, Chicago.

The city that grew up by the sluggish river was entirely a product of human energy. Other cities began in wilderness, but Chicago began in emptiness. Nature didn't plan for a city here. There was nothing to build with, except wild grasses that marsh-birds used to line their nests. There was nothing to build on but a sinking swamp. There was no natural harbor—for years vessels anchored in the open lake because the river entrance was blocked by a shifting sandbar. Indians never tried to build a village on this unlikely site, though they used the portage across the Chicagau marshes. So the makeshift, drafty hut where Marquette spent a winter's illness, in 1674-5, was the first building in Chicago. Then for 130 years—a generation longer than it has been a city—the place was merely a portage and Chicago a name for hauling heavy canoes through swampgrass, for toiling kneedeep in prairie mud, for fighting clouds of gnats and mosquitoes, for wading ice-scummed marshes, for camping on a desolate shore.

In 1803, Captain John Whistler, whose grandson's most famous painting was to be delivered ninety years later on Michigan Avenue in an armored car, arrived on that forsaken spot to take military possession. He found four cabins on the north bank of the brackish river. Three were occupied by French traders with impassive Indian wives. The fourth had been abandoned by a San Domingo Negro and it stood vacant until John Kinzie arrived to trade axes, knives and kettles for beaver pelts and shaved deerskins.

Even after Fort Dearborn was erected, there was nothing to promise a city. There was no crossroads here. No travelers came across the empty prairie or down the long miles of the vacant lake. Fort Dearborn meant isolation and boredom. It meant losing touch with the events of the world in such busy places as Cincinnati, St. Louis and Detroit. It meant a waste of sand, a web of gulls, and blackbirds swaying on the reeds. It meant Indians begging beans and whisky, and the poor festivity of a fiddle plaintive in John Kinzie's cabin while snow drifted on the prairie and the lake tossed on the shore. Finally, in the calamitous summer of 1812, it meant sudden death from painted Potawatomis and blackened ashes where the fort had stood.

For four years the only sign of habitation was the bones of the massacred bleaching on the shore. Then the fort was rebuilt, with a huddle of huts around it. But the fur trade declined and Chicago's days seemed ended. Still, geography had made this a portage, and there was a prophetic restlessness with the wind always blowing. This country was huge, rich, empty, waiting to produce corn, wheat and cattle, all the way to the Rockies. A strong light shone over that empty shore so that sometimes idle troops looking over wide water and wide land felt like men on the verge of history.

In 1830, the river mouth was surveyed as the terminus of a canal to link Lake Michigan and the Illinois River. Two years later Black Hawk's Indians were driven forever across the Mississippi. In 1833 twenty thousand persons arrived at Chicago on lake vessels from Buffalo. They milled through mud streets and fanned out over open country. They brought life to a silent land. Now Chicago's great expectations began. The prairie wind cleared men's minds of old doubts and defeats and brought them a sense of boundless future. Carl Sandburg still felt it a century later:

I tell you the past is a bucket of ashes,
I tell you yesterday is a wind gone down, a sun dropped in the
  west,
There is nothing in the world, only an ocean of tomorrows,
  only a sky of tomorrows.

In 1840, with just five thousand persons in the newly incorporated town, a merchant in an unpainted frame store on Lake Street declared that Chicago would become the greatest commercial city of the world. Four years later the editor of the first city directory, as though he had just taken a fresh look all around, wrote soberly that he could see no limit to the city's growth. It would go on and on. It would change and evolve and develop. It would never rest.

Change is so essential to Chicago that any impression of the city involves two impressions. There are always two pictures. There is the old wooden bridge over the river on Michigan Avenue and the massive new bascule, carrying two lanes of traffic, jack-knifing when a big ship roars in the channel. There is the old Union Station—the great red-brick beehive with its swarming life—and the vast new Union Station with its lofty rotunda hushed and lighted like a church and eddying with endless currents of people. There are the old mudflats beyond Michigan Avenue, as though a tide had gone out forever, and the splendid avenues, gardens and terraces of Grant Park. Once the Blackstone Hotel towered alone on the lakefront with a ring of lights around its roof like a liner's lights seen from a tender. Now there is the solid rampart of the city's facade.

There are old market stalls of Water Street and the clean new curve and sweep of Wacker Drive. It must always have been that way—the changing city, new features evolving before the old had faded from the mind—back to the fire when the whole prodigious thing began anew, back to the raising of the ground level when the entire Loop was lifted twelve feet above the swamp, back to the burning of Fort Dearborn by the Potawatomis. It goes on changing into the future.

So Chicago is not only the youngest of the world's great cities but it has been the least continuous of them. You look in vain for anything as old as a man's full lifetime. Gurdon Hubbard, burned and bearded from weeks on the prairie trails, first saw Fort Dearborn a mile off as he climbed a swamp oak tree. In his last years he was shaved at the brilliant Palmer House, where the barber shop was floored with silver dollars. Now that hotel is replaced by a new one and an airway beacon on the tip of a building near the site of Fort Dearborn is visible to fliers over Buffalo and Pittsburgh. John H. Kinzie was nine years old when the Potawatomis massacred the garrison and danced around scalped bodies on the shore. He lived to see Kinzie Avenue grow into a great street, where the Indians formerly had worn a path in the sand.

Long John Wentworth, first of Chicago's hectic mayors, presided over a far-spreading city and recalled a wolf drive when men on ponies rounded up sixty prairie wolves and drove them down the frozen Chicago River to the lake. Cyrus Hall McCormick came to raw, frame-built Chicago from a hill farm in the Blue Ridge Mountains, in 1847, with a faded carpet bag and a dream

of a harvesting machine. He died in a mansion modeled on the
Paris Opera House.

Men who knew Chicago in 1840 would not have recognized it
in 1860. Men who knew it in 1860 could not have found anything
familiar in the newly built city of 1880. People who saw the city
of one World's Fair in 1893 stared in disbelief at the city of another World's Fair forty years later, when for twenty-five miles
along the lakeshore there unfolded Chicago's parks, drives, mansions, hotels, playgrounds, museums and amphitheaters in the most
magificent waterfront ever created by man.

From the earliest years, the winding Onion River fed the city.
With its sandbar dredged away and the channel deepened, it was
open to the full tides of commerce on Lake Michigan. Quickly
Chicago became the leading grain market in the world. Within a
few years, it grew to be the greatest lumber market, with more
shipping arrivals than the first five American seaports combined.
Railroads brought western cattle to its enormous stockyards and
Chicago was known as the largest meat-packing center and the
foremost leather market. Population multiplied four, five, six times
in a decade. Railways fanned in from six directions and Chicago
became the world's greatest railroad center.

All this time men were making a city where nature hadn't
planned for one. The original ground level was so low that the
streets oozed swamp water. Miles of plank paving were laid, but
planks soon rotted in the mud. Sand and cobblestones were tried—
they sank out of sight. So, in a few years of toil and confusion,
the city's streets were raised and thousands of buildings were lifted
to the new level. By engineering projects fifty miles back in the
prairie, the Onion River was made to flow backward, toward the
Gulf of Mexico, and Chicago's waste no longer polluted the lakeshore. Miles of trestles were built along Lake Michigan to carry
trains into the city. Hundreds of wharves made a solid landing
on both sides of the river. When these labors were accomplished,
Chicago burned to the ground.

It burned furiously. That Chicago was a wooden city, with

thirteen miles of wooden docks along the river and its branches, twenty-four wooden bridges, seventeen huge wooden elevators, miles of lumberyards, mills, factories, and hundreds of wooden ships jamming the river to make a bridge of flame. A high October wind fanned the flames and a searing blast burst over Lake Michigan. Heat of the fire was felt a hundred miles away. In the lurid night people at Des Plaines, twenty miles distant, could read by the light of its glare. It burned for twenty-seven terrible hours. Then Chicago was a smoking ruin and the river crept ash-strewn between its blackened wharves.

But it was as feverishly rebuilt. Tents and barracks rose among the still-smoking ruins. A hundred thousand workmen cleared away the rubble. Thousands of carts and wagons carried it to a vast dumping ground before Michigan Avenue—in that desolate season men began the construction of a lakefront park.

In five years scars of fire had vanished. In ten years Chicago was a center of vast industries and enormous trade. In twenty years it was a city of a million people, ready to celebrate the discovery of America with the most lavish exposition ever held. That, too, was done in Chicago's way—starting with a bid of ten million dollars, which took the breath out of the New York delegation. When Congress chose Chicago as the Exposition City, a desolate waste of shore lay at Jackson Park, where domes and towers were planned. In January, 1891, in a freezing wind, a score of architects, painters and sculptors tramped snow-streaked dunes, scrub-oak ridges and frozen swamps. The eastern men said it couldn't be done in two years. But Chicago went ahead. Before the ground had thawed, a vast camp rose along the shore—barracks, messhalls, offices, studios. Thousands of men milled over the waste of sand—steel workers, carpenters, stone masons, painters, sculptors, architects. At night, around the campfires, men revived memories of the academies in Paris, London and Rome. "The greatest gathering of artists since the fifteenth century," Saint-Gaudens said. They worked in mud, rain and snow, through heat and cold, amid a forest of derricks and cranes, among smoking engines and hissing boilers.

The dream began to take form. Gleaming buildings rose out of the mud. Swamps became lagoons, arched with bridges, reflecting white colonnades, marble gateways, domes of exhibition halls. There were courts and terraces and esplanades. There was a Wooded Island, with full-grown trees and fifty thousand rose bushes ringed about its shore. Above plashing fountains rose a gleaming Statue of Liberty. At the formal opening, on the first of May, 1893, half a million persons marveled at the White City, the stately Court of Honor and the Grand Basin. Soon Chicago was talked about on five continents.

For a season excursion trains carried multitudes of people along the lakeshore, and the big excursion steamer *Christopher Columbus* conveyed other multitudes to the vast and splendid circus at Jackson Park. Throughout the city there was gaiety, splendor, music—and that winter, with the panic of 1893, ragged files of persons shivered outside soup kitchens. Chicago has always been a city of extremes.

But a new era was beginning. Now the goddess Ceres stands on the lofty Board of Trade Building, pouring grain from her horn of plenty, and in that building half the grain in the world is bought and sold. Though Greek temples lined the lagoons at Jackson Park, Chicago was a prairie city. In the railroad yards stood miles of cattle cars, and miles of grain cars, and to its twenty-six terminals came the green, maroon and yellow trains from every quarter of America. It had become the crossroads of the nation.

One of the city's most persistent scenes was the vanished old Union Station—smoky, smelly and noisy, with the rumble and hiss in the trainsheds and the din of drays on the cobblestones outside. The waiting room smelled of coffee, tobacco, banana peel and train smoke. Up from the murky track level streamed immigrants without a word of English, dressed in capes and shawls and homespun jackets. Between trains they crowded around a tin trunk, eating crusty bread and sausages which a mustached man with a big pocket knife cut off in discs like a dollar. They spoke quick, uneasy syllables in some distant language—German, Italian, Russian, Greek, Swedish, or Lithuanian, occasionally interlaced with a familiar word like Omaha, Burlington, or Cedar Rapids. They added to the smoky room a tang of garlic and dried herring.

They made it strange and exciting. Past them strode cigar-chewing salesmen—glad to be in the big town again after the long circuit through Iowa and Kansas—and sunburned youths from cornfield counties of Illinois, mule farms of Missouri, wheat stubble of Nebraska. It was a faintly German building, that great red pile with the smoking trains behind a fence of iron, but it was all American. Over it hung the feeling of the prairies. It was vast and strange and noisy, but sometimes it made you think of little towns under the shadow of a loading elevator, with cornfields at the end of every street.

Outside waited the city. Just across Canal Street stood a solid wall of employment agencies, each littered with notices of men wanted in the Kansas harvest fields, in Wisconsin logging camps, on river dredges and railroad section gangs and construction crews. Beyond was the polyglot life of Halsted Street with its Mexicans, Italians, Greeks and Gypsies (for years half of Chicago's population was foreign-born), the raucous life of Water Street markets, the stately life of Michigan Avenue beside the mudflats that would one day be a terraced park between the upward-reaching city and the far-spreading lake.

In those years, a horse-drawn Parmelee coach transferred travelers between stations—a long coach with two benches facing and a huge baggage rack on its roof. It had a sharp, ammoniac smell, like no smell left in the world. The horses pounded on the paving stones, the coach lurched and swayed. A glimpse of black water showed under dark brick walls. Then the vehicle plunged across town, with huge bright buildings reeling by and the noisiest streets in history ringing. Through the din came the nervous shrill of a police whistle and the *clang, clang, clang* of trolley cars. There were sound and color and the gusty wind blowing. Behind all that sharpness of sensation lay an entity beyond sensation—the mass and immensity of Chicago. The coach swayed under the calamitous roar of the elevated on Van Buren Street and drew up in a sooty twilight at another station. Even in an hour between trains, thirty years ago, Chicago left an impression that would never fade.

Though it is a young city, it has had a spell for many people. Sometimes it seems restless and stormy, sometimes wistful and mysterious. Though nothing in it is a century old, it can make writers like Carl Sandburg, Sherwood Anderson and Ben Hecht think old, sad, plaintive thoughts—of moonlight in a deserted brickyard, of an old man lying awake at midnight while the steamers whistle from the river, of patterned rooftops like dungeons and cathedrals, of electric signs that make Chinese writing in the river and "L" trains reflecting under bridges like a ghostly waterfall.

Perhaps it is the combination of multitude and solitude, of uproar and silence, that haunts the imagination. Only in Chicago can you stand on a seawall and see a tiered city lifting while you feel the spell of space. There is the lake, vast, dim and troubled, with a lighthouse winking from a windswept reef. Across Grant Park is the tremendous front wall of the city, the blazing lights, the nervous neon colors. There tossing water, oldest sound in the world, mingles with the other roar, deep, prolonged and haunting, of the city.

In the triumphant summer of 1893, while millions marveled at the White City in Jackson Park, on the newly laid-out Midway, in the newly established University of Chicago, the American Historical Society held its first meeting. To the assembled scholars a young man from Wisconsin, Frederick Jackson Turner, read a paper destined to become famous in the literature of American history. It was entitled "The Significance of the Frontier in American History." He began with the census of 1890, pointing out that for the first time in the four centuries since its discovery, there was no longer a clearly marked frontier line in America. The continent had been crossed—every portion of it had been entered and in some measure occupied. The vanished frontier, he said, had

been the most significant part of American experience and had
exerted the greatest influence on American character. The frontier
environment mastered men, reshaped them, made them original
again. At the point of the frontier custom breaks, restraints drop
off, and there emerge new experiences, new activities, new institutions. Now, he said, that long adventure was passed. The end of
an era had come in America—and the beginning of another.

In the new era change goes on, as dynamically as in the past.
The city of 1,000,000 in 1893 has grown to 3,500,000 fifty years later.
And Chicago still breathes the air of the future. The St. Lawrence
Seaway will open the Mid-West to the markets of the world. Liners
from Europe, Africa, the Mediterranean, South America will leave
Chicago's docks. Other liners will fly from Chicago's airports
straight over the polar North to London, Moscow, Shanghai and
Bombay. Grain and cattle will still stream in from the prairies,
coal from Kentucky will meet iron from Minnesota in Chicago's
mills. In the new era the winding Checagau River will be bordered
by the greatest city in the world.

XXIV

A Coast of Wilderness

BEYOND THE Straits of Mackinac lies a big, dark, lonely country which few Americans can think of without emotion. It cast a spell over Henry Wadsworth Longfellow, even though he came no nearer to it than a translation of Chippewa legends in his Cambridge study. Through him it has touched successive generations of American schoolchildren, leaving them with a lifelong picture of the dark forest and the shining water in an America that still has room for solitude and silence.

The first way into it, when the forest stretched unbroken from Lake Michigan to Lake Superior, was by the St. Marys River, and that is still the best way. Actually the St. Marys is not a river but an intricate and beautiful strait which links Lake Huron with Lake Superior. Its shores and islands are a domain of deer, bear, moose—and a few persons. The region was more populous in Indian times, when three thousand Ottawas and Chippewas camped by seasons at De Tour, than today. A few hundred persons live beside the St. Marys, but many thousands pass through it in the traffic which keeps a sound of whistles booming where the beaver slide into the water and leaves a line of steamer smoke across the northern sky. Lake seamen lean on the rail to watch the wilderness move past. Excursionists on the sleek, white liners stare from their deckchairs at the twilit shores. Hunters enter the country with respect and carry its feeling back to the clamor of Chicago and Detroit. Now De Tour is a village of 600 weathered persons. Drummond Island, with 87,000 acres, has forty inland lakes and one village of 150 fishermen and woodsmen. St. Joseph Island has 00,000 acres and barely more than a 100 residents. On Neebish and

Sugar islands a few Finnish farmers tend their cattle, and scattered Indians live in dark huts in the woods. The greatest shipping commerce in the world moves through a land as wild as when its only traffic was the Indian canoe.

Sault Sainte Marie is a town as old as Boston, but it still is primitive. Its streets end in a darkness of spruce and hemlock or in an emptiness of water. In winter, it is locked in white silence. Even in summer, with the cold water hurrying by and ships always passing, it seems a remote place. Yet the canal around the St. Marys Rapids is a key to America's industrial life and to the security of the world—during the somber early 1940s fifty-one barrage balloons hung over it, a ring of troops guarded the vast excavation of the new MacArthur lock, and its airplane spotter system extended from Hudson Bay to Tennessee. The Soo is a border town with a cosmopolitan population—French Canadian, Scandinavian, English, Scotch, German and Chippewa. A sense of history clings to the wooded canal front with its memorials going back to the rule of France and the commerce of the voyageurs.

When I was a deckhand, swinging over the side of a freighter on a rope and tackle to handle the mooring lines, I used to wonder about the town screened in the fringe of trees that line the locks. At night, when the lights were twinkling along Portage Street, it seemed a secure and quiet village, with the forest around it and the water flowing by. But in daylight, with a tall Egyptian obelisk, a Japanese torii archway, and various kiosks and markers spaced about the canal grounds, it has an exotic look. Once I asked the mate about those structures. He thought perhaps the obelisk might be a Chippewa burial stone dug up from the canal bed. About the torii, with its inclined uprights and curved crosspieces, he wouldn't even guess. A few years later, when I saw hundreds of torii along the Inland Sea of Japan, I understood the gateway beside the canal locks at the Soo. The fanatical Japanese people are a fanciful people also. They have a belief that fine weather and fair fortune will follow any vessel that passes before the sacred arch. So that gateway was a fitting gift at the fiftieth anniversary of the opening of the canal, and it is a pleasant symbol to face the greatest stream of marine traffic in the world.

Silence closes over the locks and over the town in December. Deep snow and the stark winter keep the river ice-locked until April. Then a plume of smoke blows over the St. Marys channel and a deep voice sounds from the head of Sugar Island. For eight months, night and day, the Soo lives to the sound of whistles calling. When fog or forest fire shroud the channel, whole fleets assemble and deep, disturbing voices fill the dim air with a sense of greatness. When the fog lifts, long ships file ponderously into line. The procession moves again, spaced out, down the St. Marys channels and out on Whitefish Bay.

Around Whitefish Bay the last big forest was logged off ten years ago. Till the middle 1930s the shore was spaced with lumber towns. Whine of whirling saws, crunch of logs in the bullpond, slap of boards on decks of barges, cries of scalers and tally men—all sounded on what is now a silent shore. Superior is the only lake not girdled by a highway. A road runs along its noble northern shore, but on all its broken southern coast highways border the lake only for brief segments. Now U. S. 28 runs inland from the Soo, touching the shore at Munising, Marquette and L'Anse at the foot of the Keweenaw cape. It is an excellent highway, through wild, desolate and brooding country, but it slights a shoreline which the far-ranging Henry Rowe Schoolcraft said surpassed in grandeur anything he had ever seen. He traveled it many times, on foot and in a Chippewa canoe, and even after it was a familiar journey he said, "We held our breath in passing that coast." Though he knew it with the thoroughness of a geologist's survey and an ethnologist's study of native legend, its appeal never faded—"the eye is never done looking and admiring."

In a later day Michigan's governor, Chase Osborn, a Northwoods man at heart and a resident of the St. Marys shore, walked around the entire lake, and paddled its circuit in a canoe. As the northwest wind swept down, he exulted in the knowledge that it had never been breathed by man. Beyond Whitefish Point are the Grand Sable Banks, radiant ranges of sand which rise two hundred feet above the lake and extend for miles inland. At Grand Marais that shifting shore gives way to a coast of carved and colored sandstone. Here are the Pictured Rocks, with lofty headlands, caverns big enough to berth a ship in, grottoes and towers shaped by centuries of wind and water. Indians lived in awe of this shoreline. When explorers described it, back in the bustling compounds of Quebec and Montreal, they spoke as though they had been to an unreal country. Now a highway is projected along this coast, over the lofty dunes and above the sculptured walls.

Meanwhile, U. S. 28 swings inland through logged-off land. The road is screened by fringes of birch and maple forest, maintained for beauty and utility—in winter that screen of timber catches drifting snow and keeps the highway open. Between the highway and the lake lies a great, dim cedar swamp, drained by the wild and beautiful Tahquamenon. This is the "dark and golden river" in *Hiawatha,* on whose shores the grandson of old Nokomis built his bark canoe. It is also the land where another far-traveled American name sprang from. A generation ago Robert Dollar left his name on the lifeless logging camp of Dollarville and went to the Pacific coast and the shipping business. Now his ships with the dollar sign on their smokestacks call at seaports around the world.

Munising is a harbor town in a bowl of hills facing Grand Island and the cold blue bay. Here stood the wigwam of Nokomis and here Hiawatha learned the legends of the pictured shores and the lore of woods and water. It is a coast of contrast——

> *Dark behind it rose the forest,*
> *Rose the black and gloomy forest,*
>
> *   *   *   *   *   *
>
> *Bright before it beat the water,*
> *Beat the clear and sunny water,*
> *Beat the shining big sea water.*

You see dark glens, colored fields of fireweed and Indian paint-brush, muffled banks of fog and the unearthly brilliance of Northern Lights.

Beyond Munising, the land humps up into old worn timbered ridges, and here the iron range begins. Marquette was first called Iron Bay—for ninety years ore cars loaded with brown and purple hematite have come rocking down the hills from Negaunee and Ishpeming. Marquette was the earliest iron-shipping port on Lake Superior. Its first cargoes were portaged around the Soo Rapids before the canal was opened. In the Negaunee hills, a dozen miles away, are old rust-colored pits and quarries, softened now by scrub cedar and deerbrush. In the woods, ruins remain of the old charcoal furnaces where the first Lake Superior ore was burned. Now the mines are deep shafts, with galleries far underground, and shafthouses loom up like pyramids above the red-stained towns.

But memory is deep-rooted in a remote and arduous region. Over the Marquette range, the old lore is still living—of Surveyor William Burt, who first found outcrop iron; of the Chippewa Chief Majji Gessick, who knew the way to the hill of heavy stone but feared to go near it; of Philo Everett, who came to prospect copper but by chance located the first iron mine on Lake Superior; of Robert J. Graveraet, who tramped on snowshoes from Marquette to Saginaw, three hundred miles, and went on by stage and train to Worcester, Massachusetts, to raise capital to develop iron mines that nobody believed in; of Peter White, who came to the North as a gangling boy of fifteen, shipped the first Marquette ore to Lake Erie and lived to be a legend on the range and a power in the steel industry.

There were other giants in the land—iron, lumber and shipping men. And there were the men whose names didn't matter but whose hands swung the picks and the axes, who sent metal and timber out of the hills. They were a motley lot—gnomish little Cornishmen, big, soft-spoken Swedes, fiery Irishmen, hearty Germans, voluble Italians, worn and weathered Finns. The Cornishmen lived half their lives in the bowels of the earth and came up smiling, ready for a wrestling match, a song-fest, and a meat and vegetable "pasty." The Italians and the Germans worked in the deep shafts, sometimes resenting the authority of an Irish mine captain. Even the Finns went underground, though their first instinct was for the woods and the water. They were a tough-fibered people, who could find their way like foxes through the forest and could travel in snowstorms that sent Indians to shelter.

A hard country is by necessity a heroic country, compelling men to believe in themselves. Instinctively, these people like their land. They like its violent boom-town past and its empty ghost towns of today. They like its loneliness and austerity and the demands it makes upon them. Their stories deal with danger and defiance— the Indian woman on Isle Royale watched her white husband go mad and die of hunger while she lived by gnawing the bark of trees; to bring a few Christmas letters and some out-of-date newspapers the old-time mail drivers mushed their dogteams all the way to Green Bay and back again, through country without as much as a footprint in the snow for a hundred miles; the blinded miner took the lamed miner on his shoulders, after their dynamite had gone off, and so both reached the settlement thirty miles away. The land still offers hardship and peril. Hunters get lost in the woods, fishermen are marooned on floating floes of ice. But its people would not trade it for any country less severe.

Beyond Marquette, the wild Huron Mountains line the shore. Inland, the highway passes through declining iron towns and into the timber country. Here, in a nearly incredible contrast to the old decaying sawmill towns, is the new village of Alberta. You pass through miles of dense and tangled forest and come suddenly upon broad sunlight and an arc of brightly painted cottages. Across a smooth green park is a flower-bordered log pond, with a saw mill, white as a wedding cake, reflected in the water. This is one of Henry Ford's luxuries. For his timber crews he built a model town, with a church, a school and a fire department. He provided electric lights and interior plumbing for its twenty families, and every safety precaution in the mill. Old logging hands stare at the place and tramp on to their shacks in the woods. The men who live in Alberta found a few virgin pines back in the swamp, prime timber among the second growth, and they saved those logs for Henry Ford's first visit. When they ran them through the mill the scream of the saw was wild and fierce over the little landscaped log pond and the arc of painted cottages.

Beyond L'Anse, the long rugged Keweenaw peninsula begins. This is the copper country. Seen from a freighter on the lake, it is a lonely, lifeless land—but it has a quiet life now, after a turbulent and exciting life for nearly eighty years. The highway passes through the twin cities, Hancock and Houghton, pitching up steeply on either side of the Portage Canal, which cuts the cape in two. Beyond is a region of abandoned mining camps, ruined shaft houses and lifeless valleys of brush and scrub forest. There are old locations, quiet where once there was the clamor of the copper rush—Calumet, Larium, Phoenix, Copper Harbor. Here were the famous mines—Quincy, Ahmeek, Tamarack, Mohawk, and Calumet and Hecla, known in financial circles of Boston, London and Paris, which produced fortunes for people who could not pronounce "Keweenaw" or locate it on a map, and which drew to the lonely cape men of thirty-five nationalities.

It began one hundred years ago, when slender young Douglass Houghton, first state geologist of Michigan, paddled his canoe along the lifeless shores and struck inland, with his specimen sack, from every cove and bay. He found copper and he lost his life. In the dusk of an October day, in 1845, he was heading his small craft around a rocky tongue of land, with the lights of Eagle River gleaming in the harbor. But a wind squall struck and a curtain of snow dimmed the harbor lights. The next spring Douglass Houghton's body was found cast up on the rocky coast. Now Eagle River is a village of eighty persons, with the old mine buildings converted into summer cottages. At its edge stands a modest monument, made of specimens of copper and iron ores—"In Memoriam, Douglass Houghton, The Father of U. S. Copper Mining." He was thirty-four when he died.

Men flocked into the country Houghton's reports described. They came by water—in heavy-oared bateaux, in mackinaw boats with a tanbark sail, in vessels that had been hauled by land around the loud rapids at the Soo. For a generation there was no road to Keweenaw—the copper range was as dependent on water as a mid-ocean island. In copper camps the big event was the coming of a vessel over the blank, bright horizon of Superior. During the long winter, there was no event at all—only the rumble and shudder of dynamite in the earth, endless thudding of stampmills, and the men coming up out of cold, dark galleries into the cold, white land. From November to April camps were as lost as Crusoe from the world.

Then came the great event—the arrival of the first ship of the new season. For weeks the men had watched the blank waste of ice for signs of its breaking up. For other weeks they watched the waters slowly open, as the drift ice dwindled and floated away. Then a lookout took his place at the highest point above the town of Hancock, on the top gable of the shafthouse of the Quincy mine. He stared eastward like a man at a topmast searching for rescue. When at last he saw the feather of smoke, he rubbed his eyes and stared again. It was too dark for cloud—it was moving, growing. He cupped his voice and shouted to the workers below him.

With that cry, the engineer tied down his whistle. All out the cape, men were waiting for that signal. It was relayed from minehead to minehead, from camp to camp, and the shrill chorus grew in a screaming, off-key welcome to a toy ship on the horizon. A cannon boomed from the Houghton bluff. That sound crept down the deepest shafts, along dim galleries far underground, and men and mules stopped in their tracks. When the vessel was still far out on the water, the landing was black with laughing, shouting, waving men, guessing which ship it was they were welcoming, laying bets while it was still too far away to tell.

They were all small ships on Lake Superior, before the Soo Canal was opened in 1855. They had been hauled on rollers through snowy streets of Sault Sainte Marie, a tiny fleet to launch into the vast waters of Superior—the erratic, exiled little *Ocean* that had to change her name because of misfortunes on the lower lakes, the top-heavy, swaying little *Merchant,* the plodding *Independence* built for sail and converted half-heartedly to steam, the fussy, broad-beamed *Julia Palmer* that waddled over the water. But whichever ship it was that came over the horizon in the waiting weeks of spring, it looked like a liner and a lady to the castaways on the Keweenaw shore.

In the second quarter of the twentieth century, the last veins of highgrade copper ore ran out and life ebbed from the old locations. Copper Harbor, once the chief port of the peninsula, with mine shafts honeycombing the hills above the town, declined to a population of sixteen persons. In 1930, 85 per cent of Keweenaw's population was on relief. Then the tough-fibered copper miners were left in a country that had no use for their strength and skill. Some moved away, others went to work for the W.P.A. A few toiled on in the deep shafts, heaping a low-grade ore into the battered tramcars that had trundled pure copper through the long galleries. Once the stampmills dumped vast tonnages of dross into the lake. Now a moderately profitable operation is the salvage of copper from the sands that in hectic years were thrown away.

But the new life of the copper country is not in the mines. It is in the summer resorts growing up on the sites of old locations. The modern highway climbs spectacularly up Brockway Mountain in a grandeur that the Middle-West is not supposed to possess. From that windswept ridge, 700 feet above Lake Superior, the cape curves out grandly to its point in the vast blue northern sea. The highway comes down, through woodland and along a broken shore, to Copper Harbor. The old port has a brisk life in the summer months, and though the long ore freighters pass hull-down on the horizon, the little *Isle Royale Queen,* steaming with tourists to the wilderness of Isle Royale, smokes across the harbor like the *Ocean* or the *Merchant* of ninety years ago.

On the tip of the cape, log buildings of Fort Wilkins still stand,

as they did when the fort was established in 1844 to protect prospectors from the Indians. It was as remote then as any place in
America. Even in 1870, when the garrison was withdrawn and
the post abandoned, it was a remote place. The government offered
it for sale, but there were no bidders. For a decade it served as a
home for disabled soldiers of the Civil War—they must have felt
forgotten in that distant barracks with the waves of Lake Superior
pounding all around them. Now it is a state park, alive with
summer visitors, and the old stockade is carved with the names
of tourists. Here ends U. S. 41, a highway that begins at the palm-
girt sands and tiled hotel terraces of Miami, Florida. Though the
multitudes have not yet discovered it, the northern terminus of
that long and varied highway is a more absorbing place than the
boardwalks of Miami Beach.

Copper made fortunes all the way down the Keweenaw peninsula to Ontanogan where, in the Ontanogan River, there stood a
pure copper boulder, weighing a ton, which the Indians sold repeatedly to explorers and prospectors. At last a Detroit man got it
loaded into a boat and carried it away. Now it is on exhibit in the
Smithsonian Institution in Washington. There were rumors of
silver in the Ontanogan district two centuries ago. Alexander
Henry led a primitive expedition to find the place from which
came the pure silver nuggets that occasional Chippewa hunters
carried with them. Henry found no trace of silver but was led
away by another rumor. Out in the emptiness of western Lake
Superior he landed on an island reported to bear gold. He found
it overrun by caribou, but he was more excited by its yellow sands.
In a burst of anticipation, he named it Isle of Golden Sands, but
there was no gold in them. Now it goes by the name of Caribou
Island. That ended Alexander Henry's search for metal treasure,
although the rumor of silver was revived again a century after his
search on the Ontanogan shore. Hundreds of men scrambled
through the rough hills—and found nothing. They left a camp
called Silver City, now a fishing hamlet between the wild Porcupine Mountains and the windy shore.

Beyond the Porcupine Mountains, the coast opens into broad, blue Chequamegon Bay. Here, at an ancient Chippewa village, was established the first French mission in the Northwest. For two hundred years it remained a lonely trading post. But soon after the Civil War, iron was found in the Gogebic Range and a railroad was built from Ashland to the mines. Then Ashland boomed with trade in timber and iron. Now it sends millions of tons of Gogebic ore down the lakes and, though its timber is gone, Ashland harbor still carries great rafts of pulpwood, towed across from Canada and bound for Wisconsin's paper mills.

Beyond Red Cliff Point lie the Apostles, a score of cliff-walled, forested islands inhabited by a few Indians and fishermen, by summer visitors and by deer, beaver, otter, wolves and bear. On the horizon move the long freighters in their up- and down-bound channels. But the islands have been little changed since the Chippewas were the rulers of that country. Some of the Apostles have never had human habitation.

The Wisconsin shore leading to the head of Lake Superior is a low-lying, cut-over forest land, farmed by hardy Scandinavians. But it is not a tamed country. Second-growth forest makes a wilderness around plowed fields, and highway warnings indicate where deer cross the cement road on their way to water. The village store becomes a "trading post," and Indian curios are on sale in roadside taverns and filling stations. This seems to be a jumping-off place, at the edge of settlement, until you see the ships trailing their long drifts of smoke across the skyline.

At the tip of the lake, where the freighters file in and out in a dramatic procession, are the twin cities of Superior and Duluth. Superior lies on level land south of the curving St. Louis River. Duluth climbs, tier on tier, up the steep northern hillside. A century ago this was the loneliest place in America. Now it is a setting of other superlatives—the greatest grain elevators, the longest ore docks, the greatest coal terminals, the most prodigious iron traffic anywhere.

When the first Lake Erie steamboat churned out of Buffalo, in

1818, the city of Duluth was unconceived and inconceivable. It is somewhat incredible even now. You approach through two hundred miles of dark woods and desolate stumplands, or across a vast lake rimmed in wilderness—and there, dramatically, is Duluth. By day, it is a city spread for miles along its rugged slope of rock. By night, it is a swimming sea of lights, tilted for miles against the northern sky. Deep voices of commerce roar in its harbor, the cold blue water washes its shore, the wind roars in the forest at its edges. Up the long hill every steep street tugs at the eye and the imagination. Over that 800-foot ridge lie the desolate muskeg country, the yawning pit mines of the Mesabi, rock-rimmed lakes and endless woods.

Duluth receives the iron ore from the giant lodes of the Mesabi, sending it down to the shore that Moses Cleaveland surveyed and to the steel mills on the Ohio, where the flatboat *Mayflower* passed, a century and a half ago. The civilization that began at Marietta is here, with a wilderness around it.

Time has brought many changes to the land that once was the Northwest, but it is still a new country, restless, vigorous, not yet settled into permanence. From the lake's darkness the lights of Duluth tremble in the wind as the first campfires flickered on the Muskingum shore.

Acknowledgments

BIBLIOGRAPHY of the region once called the Northwest, now a central area of the United States, is so extensive that there is hardly any end to it. In many of the chapters of this book I am indebted to other writers, from Justin Winsor, Francis Parkman and Theodore Roosevelt to the anonymous compilers of the various State Guides produced by the Federal Writers' Project, and to contributors to the historical collections and the quarterly magazines of history published by the historical societies of the several states.

For aid in finding information relating to various aspects of the subject, I am indebted to Mr. E. W. King of the Miami University Library, to staff members of the Marietta College Library, the Ohio State Library and the Ohio State Museum.

For the kind loan of manuscript and published material, I am indebted to Mr. Oscar Chase Hayward of Winnetka, Illinois, Dr. Stephen Riggs Williams of Oxford, Ohio, and the late George A. Marr of Cleveland.

For revealing points of view and illuminating information, I am indebted to William A. Titus of Fond du Lac, Wisconsin, George N. Secord of Pine Bluff Arsenal, Arkansas, Maurice A. Blaney of Vancouver, British Columbia, Ernst M. Ruder of Oxford, Ohio, and Mrs. J. F. Johnston of Grand Haven, Michigan.

INDEX